Pursuits of Happiness

Pursuits of Happiness

THE SOCIAL DEVELOPMENT OF EARLY MODERN BRITISH COLONIES AND THE FORMATION OF AMERICAN CULTURE

JACK P. GREENE

THE UNIVERSITY OF NORTH CAROLINA PRESS

CHAPEL HILL & LONDON

© 1988 The University of North Carolina Press

All rights reserved

Manufactured in the United States of America

The paper in this book meets the guidelines for permanence

and durability of the Committee on Production Guidelines for

Book Longevity of the Council on Library Resources.

99   98   10   9   8   7

Library of Congress Cataloging-in-Publication Data
Greene, Jack P.
Pursuits of happiness: the social development of early modern
British colonies and the formation of American culture / by Jack P. Greene.
p. cm.
Includes bibliographical references and index.
ISBN 0-8078-1804-6 (alk. paper).   ISBN 0-8078-4227-3 (pbk: alk. paper)
1. Great Britain—Colonies—America—Social conditions. 2. United
States—Social conditions—To 1865. 3. United States—Civilization—
To 1783. 4. Great Britain—Colonies—Social conditions.
I. Title.
HN50.G74   1988   88-5908
306'.0973—dc19   CIP

For the members of the

continuing Research Seminar on the

Sociology of Early Modern British Colonization

at The Johns Hopkins University,

1966–1988

CONTENTS

TABLES & FIGURES

TABLES

FIGURES

PREFACE

Building on the literature of the new social history produced over the past two decades, this book has four complementary goals. First, and most important, it seeks to use that literature as a basis for evaluating the central assumptions that have informed the analysis of colonial British American history over the past two generations, assumptions that, to one degree or another, have emphasized the preeminence or normative character of the experience of the orthodox puritan colonies of New England in the process of early modern British colonial social development and the formation of American culture. Second, through a close evaluation of the experiences of the settler societies in each of the major regions of settlement in the early modern British Empire—Ireland, the Chesapeake, New England, the Atlantic island colonies of Bermuda and the Bahamas, the West Indian colonies, the Middle Colonies, and the Lower South—and a comparison between those experiences and the social history of metropolitan England or, after 1707, Britain, the volume attempts in Chapters 1 through 7 to formulate a model of colonial social development that may be more broadly applicable than the declension model around which much British colonial history has been organized. Third, it seeks in Chapter 8 to delineate the process by which a general American culture began to emerge out of these several regional cultures during the century after 1660 and to outline the most important elements in that emerging culture. Finally, around these themes, the book attempts to provide a synthesis of existing literature on the social development of the settler societies of the early modern British Empire.

On several occasions while I was composing this volume, I impishly told colleagues whose research interests focused upon New England that its subject was the irrelevance of New England in the formation of American culture. But I was wholly taken by surprise recently when one colleague told me that he had heard that my intentions were to try "to push the New Englanders completely aside as anachronistic and irrelevant" and to depict "the Chesapeake as the only significant social and cultural model for American development." Those are emphatically not my goals. The book is meant neither to deny all relevance to

New England in the process of early American sociocultural development nor to argue either that the experience of every region except New England was like that of the Chesapeake or that American culture derived exclusively out of Chesapeake culture.

On the contrary, I regard this book as an attack on the reductionist, and often either unconscious or unstated, assumptions that have supported precisely those kinds of arguments in reference to the alleged centrality of New England or the Middle Colonies in colonial British American history. My intention throughout has been to call attention to the considerable diversity within the early modern British-American social world and to depict the emergence of American cultural patterns during the century beginning about 1660 as the product not of the influence of any one predominant region but of a powerful social convergence among all four of the broad cultural regions—the Chesapeake, New England, the Middle Colonies, and the Lower South—that beginning in 1776 would constitute the United States.

At the same time, I have attempted to develop an analytical or interpretive framework within which these distinctive regional experiences can be both related to one another and comprehended as part of a generalized process of social formation that may help to provide some larger coherence to colonial studies. This effort scarcely represents a new impulse in colonial historiography. For more than a half century, many scholars have written the history of colonial British America in terms of the gemeinschaft-gesellschaft model developed by late nineteenth- and early twentieth-century social scientists and more recently elaborated by proponents of modernization theory.[1]

Depicting early modern historical development as a transition from traditional to modern social forms and modes of behavior, the declension model continues to carry considerable explanatory utility in reference to the early experiences of the orthodox puritan colonies of Massachusetts Bay and Connecticut, where it has the sanction of much explicit contemporary testimony. As several recent students of colonial New England have suggested, however, it fails to subsume much of the complex religious and social history even of those colonies, and, as I try to demonstrate in the pages that follow, it seems to have no applicability whatever to the experiences of the other regions of colonial British America.

As an alternative, I have proposed what I call a developmental model, which looks at historical change in new societies as a movement from the simple to the complex. Constructed on the basis of the regional portraits outlined in Chapters 1 through 7, this model seeks to provide an abstract rendering of a process that, at least in colonial *British* America, was first manifest in the oldest settled region, the Chesapeake, but was also evident in every other region, including even, in several important respects, New England. This model, which may very well be applicable not just to the experience of the British colonies but also to those of most of the new colonial societies created during the early modern era, is fully elaborated in the last section of Chapter 7. Readers who wish to examine it more closely before they get into the body of the book should perhaps read that section first.

In arguing for the utility of a developmental, as opposed to a declension, model for the interpretation of colonial British American social development, I have inevitably emphasized the atypicality of the experience of orthodox puritan New England and the normative character of that of the Chesapeake and thereby challenged those who have assumed that the history of that development can be told within a framework derived from the New England experience. To suggest that New England's experience was in significant respects different from those of the other principal regions of the early modern British world is not by any means to imply that it was irrelevant or can be ignored. Similarly, to argue that New England's influence in shaping American culture during the colonial era has been exaggerated is not in any sense to contend that it was without substantial importance.

Three additional points of clarification about my intentions perhaps need to be made here. First, the focus of the book is upon social development, and it considers religious, political, and even economic developments only insofar as they have social dimensions. Second, my concern throughout has been with the settler societies created by European and African immigrants and their descendants. Thus, despite much superb recent work on the subject, I have made no effort to treat the aboriginal cultures with which those societies interacted. Third, I have throughout tried to avoid the sort of anachronism that derives out of what Marc Bloch referred to as the "idol of origins."[2] For instance, I have not assumed that because the Chesapeake and the Lower South allegedly were hostile to innovation and economically static in the nineteenth century they were that way from the beginning, that because New England and the Middle Colonies eliminated slavery in the generations following the American Revolution they were always hostile to slavery, or that because the West Indian and Atlantic island colonies did not join in the American Revolution they must always have been on a divergent social course from the rest of colonial British America. Rather, I have endeavored to look at each region in terms not of what it became but of the range of possibilities that were open to it as those possibilities and the potentialities inherent in them shifted over time and might have been perceived by contemporaries.

The origins of this volume go back at least to the early 1970s and to my own attempt to make some sense out of the explosion of literature on the social history of the early modern British Empire. Some of my early thoughts appeared in the mid-1970s in two review essays.[3] But I did not begin to think about doing a book on this subject until 1979, when John Loos of the Department of History at Louisiana State University invited me to give the Walter Lynwood Fleming Lectures in Southern History during the spring of 1981. Initially conceived in 1979–80 while I held a fellowship from the National Endowment for the Humanities at the Center for Advanced Study in the Behavorial Sciences at Stanford, the manuscript was long in composition, my work on it having been repeatedly interrupted by other obligations during the five years since I gave the original lectures. Indeed, most of the chapters were not put in final form until the academic year 1985–86 while I was, successively, a member of the Institute for Advanced Study in Princeton and an Overseas Fellow at Churchill College, Cambridge. The last bits of the manuscript were finished during the fall and winter of 1986–87 while I was a Fulbright lecturer and Professeur Invité at the Centre d'Études Nord-Américaines at the École des Hautes Études en Science Sociale in Paris. A few last-minute revisions were made in the summer of 1987 while I was a Fellow at the National Humanities Center in Research Triangle Park, North Carolina. I am grateful to all these institutions and to The Johns Hopkins University for providing resources and help with this project.

Many people have helped me put this book together. Most important are the many authors, mostly much younger than myself, whose numerous works are cited in the footnotes. I profited considerably from discussions of Chapter 2 in seminars at the Philadelphia Center for Early American Studies in the fall of 1981; the American history seminars at Corpus Christi College, Cambridge, and St. Catherine's College, Oxford, during the spring of 1986; and the doctoral seminar of the Centre de Recherches d'Histoire Nord-Américaine at the Université de Paris I during the fall of 1986. With a few minor omissions, the chapters served as the core for the seminar I conducted on the social history of colonial British America at the Centre d'Études Nord-Américaine between November 1986 and January 1987. The members of that seminar, including especially Professor Jean Heffer and Dr. Jean Chase, offered many useful suggestions, as did the twenty-five participants in two summer seminars on this subject I offered for the National Endowment for the Humanities at Johns Hopkins in 1982 and 1985.

Nicholas P. Canny, Richard S. Dunn, Richard P. Gildrie, and Don Higginbotham each read the entire manuscript, and Warren M. Billings, Patricia U. Bonomi, Edward M. Cook, Barry Gaspar, Rhys Isaac, Francis James, Philip Morgan, Jean Russo, Alan Tully, Richard Sheridan, William A. Speck, James P. Walsh, Robert Weir, and Michael Zuckerman all read at least one of the chapters. I am extraordinarily grateful to each one of them for taking time out of their busy schedules to offer criticisms and suggestions for improving the manuscript as well as for pointing out several errors and provoking me to reconsider various points in my analysis. That the book is not better than it is cannot be in any way attributed to them.

Most of all, however, I have learned from discussions of the manuscript and the literature on which it is based with the many members of my continuing Research Seminar in the Sociology of Early Modern British Colonization at Johns Hopkins. Both past and present members of that seminar have provided me with a lively critical forum for the development of my ideas. Indeed, it is probably accurate to say that had they been less lively and less critical this volume would have been finished a lot sooner. It is to them that it is dedicated. Sue N. Greene was extremely supportive. Several of my research assistants— Marc Harris, Joyce Chaplin, Mary Gwaltney Vaz, Trevor Burnard, Li Xiaoxiong, and Stephen A. Young—helped me gather material. Trevor Burnard, Grant Mabie, Steven A. Young, Kurt Nagel, Rina Palumbo, and Elizabeth Paynter aided in preparing the manuscript for the press. Jacqueline Megan Greene did the index. I am grateful to each of them.

Jack P. Greene
Research Triangle Park, North Carolina
September 1, 1987

Pursuits of Happiness

PROLOGUE

For a nation that announced its creation with the declaration that "all men are created equal" and whose birth was hailed by British and European philosophers as the "most important step in the progressive course of human improvement" since the introduction of Christianity,[1] the American South, with its hordes of black chattel slaves, was bound to become an embarrassment—perhaps for southerners quite as much as for other Americans. For its first seventy-five years, the predominance of southerners in the political counsels of the new nation helped to disguise the extent to which, during the generations following the American Revolution, the southern states rapidly became not just a *distinctive* but, at least on the issue of its inhabitants' continuing commitment to chattel slavery, a *deviant* section of American society.

As cultural and political leaders in both areas developed and articulated an enhanced sense of the differences between North and South after 1820, more and more northerners became militantly critical of the southern mode of life, and southerners became increasingly defensive, a new posture that left little place for the overt self-criticism that had been so conspicuously present among the revolutionary generation in the southern states. In the process, a rising chorus of spokespeople for both regions emphatically agreed that, however many similarities they shared, southern society had diverged sharply from that of the North.[2]

Perhaps no fact of America's cultural development was any more obvious to contemporaries during the years from 1820 to 1860. Like the rest of the most advanced centers of the "civilized" western world, the states of the North seemed to be becoming more and more *modern*—urban, industrial, and free. Northerners appeared to be rushing headlong into a world of change and progress, an impersonal and highly materialistic world oriented toward the future and characterized by technological, institutional, cultural, and economic innovation. Far from being oriented toward the future, the southern states, by contrast, seemed to be moving in exactly the opposite direction. Totally counter to the central thrust of "progressive human improvement," they appeared to be becoming ever more *traditional*—rural, agricultural, and slave. Indeed, southerners appeared to be deliberately—even happily—retreating into the past, self-consciously endeavoring to re-create in a peculiar American context an idealized version of the sharply stratified patronage societies that had characterized early modern Europe and, southerners liked to emphasize, many of the great civilizations of antiquity.

With no positive cultural models available to them from the "progressive" contemporary world, southerners had thus found them in their distant European heritage. Their conspicuous wealth and masses of black slaves, many southerners asserted, indignantly and with mounting vigor in response to ever sharper condemnation from the North and Europe, provided the basis for a genteel and affectively warm society that in its fierce devotion to individual liberty, taste for the finer elements of life, and potential for cultural achievement was both palpably redolent of ancient Athens and obviously preferable to the selfish money-grubbing society of the northern states. To run counter to the main currents of western European and northern American development, then, militant southern apologists protested, with a stridency that betrayed a manifest lack of conviction, was a sign not of moral inferiority and social backwardness but of an admirable and heroic commitment to the recovery and exemplification of many of the greatest achievements of humankind.[3]

However desperate and contrived such claims may have seemed, even to many of the southerners who made them, they were rendered at least temporarily moot by the outcome of the Civil War. Once that bloody event had destroyed the anomalous system of racial slavery, some people confidently expected that the South would quickly be incorporated into the mainstream of American life. But the old cultural patterns were too deeply engraved upon the southern landscape to be easily erased. The "stains" of slavery remained even after the institution itself had been destroyed. If, after 1865, the South was finally moving in the same direction as the rest of the country, it was doing so at a vastly slower pace. The South continued to lag well behind the North in economic, urban, and cultural development, remaining an exception to the dominant American pattern as represented most fully by the bustling urban centers in the Northeast and Midwest.

Combined with the bitterness of the until quite recently untypically American experience of military defeat and political subjugation, the growing disparity in wealth, power, and development between North and South produced among white southerners a mixture of resentment and envy toward northerners similar to that their own black neighbors had felt for them—before and after slavery. Among northerners, it merely intensified those feelings of cultural superiority and condescension that had been so sharply articulated in the decades before the Civil War. Until well after World War II, the South seemed destined to remain forever on the peripheries of American society, its inhabitants, if they wished to pursue the *American* dream of happiness, forced either to move to one of the cultural or economic centers of American life or to content themselves with a pale southern reflection of that dream.[4]

Throughout this process of sectional differentiation and, for the South, cultural debasement, there seemed to be little need to ask whether the South had contributed in any important way to the shape and content of that dream. Cultural power followed economic and political power. Beginning in the mid-1870s, three generations of professional scholars and analysts, trained in the new graduate universities that were very heavily concentrated in the states to the north of the Potomac River, followed a path marked out for them by the amateur New England historian George Bancroft. Certainly the most influential mid-nineteenth-century interpreter of the American past, Bancroft wrote the story of what America was and how it had become that way very largely in terms of the experience of the North and northerners, and more particularly of New England and New Englanders. Although they were critical of Bancroft's overt whiggery and his tendency to employ the Divine Hand of Providence to explain complex historical developments, the new professional historians for the most part accepted without question his implicit belief that the main line of American political and cultural development ran not from Jamestown but from Plymouth to the present with the history of the South and southerners serving mostly as a negative example of what America had to overcome before it could finally realize its true self.

No less than other arbiters of American culture, American historians seem to have found it difficult to come to terms with its slave origins. As long as they could continue to believe that New England, the region of colonial British America in which black slavery was least well entrenched, was indeed the most direct and important source of later American sociocultural patterns, historians could continue to perpetuate the comforting illusion that slavery, that blatant anomaly in republican and egalitarian America, had never been central to American culture but had always been only a marginal institution confined to the cultural peripheries of the colonial British American world.

Perhaps as a measure of their own acceptance of this view of the role of slavery and the South in American development, even southern historians showed remarkably little disposition to challenge it, except in some of its details. As if to emphasize the separate and peculiar character of the southern past, in fact, they even organized in the early 1930s their own, specifically southern, historical association, the first and certainly the most influential such regional professional historical association in the United States. Thenceforth, the history of the South became a special—and, of course, a separate and unequal—subject in the history curricula first of southern and then of northern universities.

Not even the intensification of professional interest represented by this increased attention to the history of the South resulted in a comprehensive reconstruction of that history, however. For historians of the South, it appears to an outsider, have been obsessed with only a few major themes: the character and institutions of the Old South at the pinnacle—or nadir—of its development between 1830 and 1860; the South's gallant but unsuccessful defense of its way of life during the Civil War and, for the South, the humiliating aftermath of that war; the intermittent and difficult efforts thereafter to build a New South in the image of the North; and the continuing burden of the region's past upon its present. In the process, they have devoted all too little attention to the origins of the South in the colonial and early national periods.[5]

If historians of the South have rarely interested themselves in the history of the region before it became self-consciously "southern" in the decades after 1820, students of colonial history have been almost as neglectful. Until relatively recently, they have devoted far more attention to the northern colonies, specifically to New England. Sanctioned by an increasingly powerful tradition of historical study, this concentration upon New England has been facilitated by a rich and easily accessible cache of literary sources left behind by its dominant puritan settlers. Along with the neglect of the history of the southern colonies by historians of the South, this heavy emphasis upon New England by colonial historians has contributed to add weight to the symbiotic, if rarely explicitly articulated, assumptions that in British-American colonial development during the seventeenth and eighteenth centuries the southern colonies were deviant and the New England colonies normative. Not surprisingly, the emergence of an American culture during the colonial and revolutionary eras has been depicted as having been to an astonishing degree simply an extension of New England culture, the American Self deriving directly and almost exclusively out of the puritan Self and American moral sensibilities out of the puritan ethic.[6]

Until quite recently, however, we have not had the detailed work necessary to assess the validity of this line of argument. Before the resurgence of interest in colonial British-American history over the past three decades, we simply did not know enough about any of the colonies, including New England, to be able either to assess the precise and relative roles of any group of colonies in the formation of an American culture or to analyze the extent to which, as the work of so many early American cultural historians seems implicitly to have assumed, the southern colonies may or may not have already been a distinctive cultural unit that stood outside the mainstream of American development. Although relatively few historians have been interested in such questions, they are of evident importance in the history of southern *and* American culture. To the degree that the South was indeed a deviant section, we ought to know if it was always that way and, if not, what made it that way and when—questions that can scarcely be satisfactorily answered without going back to the very beginnings of British-American settlement at Jamestown in 1607.

Based upon a close reading of the large number of impressive recent studies of many aspects of the demographic, economic, social, and cultural history of Britain's American colonies during the seventeenth and eighteenth centuries, this volume represents an attempt to suggest some preliminary answers to these questions. It argues that, far from having been a peripheral, much less a deviant, area, the southern colonies and states were before 1800 in the mainstream of British-American development. Indeed, perhaps as much as any of the several distinctive regional entities that emerged in colonial British America during the early modern era, they epitomized what was arguably the most important element in the emerging British-American culture: the conception of America as a place in which free people could pursue their own individual happinesses in safety and with a fair prospect that they might be successful in their several quests.

Chapter One

TWO MODELS OF ENGLISH COLONIZATION, 1600–1660

During the first six decades of the seventeenth century, an astonishing number of English people and smaller numbers of Welsh and Scots poured out of their native island in a massive movement west and south into and across the Atlantic. Without parallel in earlier English history or indeed even in the exodus of Portuguese and Spaniards to the East and to America over the previous century, this migration began slowly. No more than 25,000 to 30,000 people left during the first three decades of the century. Over the next thirty years, however, it reached substantial proportions, averaging as many as 6,500 to 8,000 people annually. Although surviving data are far too fragmentary to permit precise estimates of total emigration, probably no fewer than 240,000 and perhaps as many as 295,000 people left Britain before 1660.

This surging tide of humanity went primarily to five destinations. Beginning in 1603 and continuing for over forty years, 70,000 to 100,000 English and Scots joined a smaller group of Elizabethan emigrants to the "New English" plantations in Ireland. Four years later, in 1607, a small contingent of adventurers established the first permanent English American settlement in the new colony of Virginia. Along with its neighboring Chesapeake colony, Maryland, founded in 1634, Virginia was the destination of roughly 50,000 settlers by 1660, by far the greatest number of them arriving after the mid-1630s. Another, much more modest migration, consisting perhaps of 3,000 to 4,000 people, went to the western Atlantic island of Bermuda starting in 1612. Beginning with a small migration to Plymouth in 1620 and continuing with a huge influx into Massachusetts Bay between 1629 and the early 1640s, an additional 20,000 to 25,000 went to New England, many of them spilling over into the new colonies of Connecticut, Rhode Island, and New Haven after the mid-1630s. Also in the 1620s, several small islands in the eastern Caribbean, including principally Barbados and the Leeward Islands of St. Kitts, Nevis, Antigua, and Montserrat, became the destination for another, far larger migration of perhaps as many as 110,000 to 135,000.[1]

By the 1640s and 1650s, England thus had five substantial areas of overseas settlements—the Irish plantations of Ulster and Munster; the Chesapeake colonies of Virginia and Maryland; Bermuda; the New England colonies of Plymouth, Massachusetts Bay, Connecticut, Rhode Island, and New Haven; and the West Indian colonies of Barbados and the Leeward Islands. The predominantly English people who went to these areas all intended to one degree or another for the new societies they were creating to be fundamentally and recognizably English. Yet the new research into the cultural dynamics and socioeconomic and demographic configurations of the two major centers of English settlement on the North American continent has made it clearer than ever before that during these early years of settlement the Chesapeake colonies of Virginia and Maryland differed profoundly from the principal New England colonies of Massachusetts Bay and Connecticut. Indeed, it would be difficult to imagine how any two fragments from the same metropolitan culture could have been any more different. About the only characteristics they had in common were their ethnic homogeneity, their ruralness, their primitive material conditions, their remoteness from England, and, after their first few years, an abundant local food supply. In virtually every other respect, they seem to have been diametric opposites.

VIRGINIA, as England's oldest American colony, occupied the crucial place in the transformation of the English conception of colonization during the first quarter of the seventeenth century. Largely as a consequence of that "acquisitive and predatory drive for commodities and for the profits to be made on the rich products of the outer world" that characterized European overseas expansion during the sixteenth and early seventeenth centuries, Virginia's orientation was almost wholly commercial from the beginning.[2] Yet, like the Elizabethans who had earlier formed projects for plantations in Ireland and America, the first organizers of the Virginia Company and many of the first adventurers to Virginia were still thinking primarily in terms of the Spanish experience in America. Hoping to secure a foothold in America before Spain and other rival European nations had occupied it all, they aspired, like the great Spanish *conquistadores*, to make some bold conquest that would bring them instant riches and fame and the nation wealth and power equivalent to that achieved by the Iberians over the previous century. Failing that, they thought of establishing commercial outposts, or factories such as those set up by the East India, Levant, and Muscovy companies in their respective spheres of influence during the last half of the sixteenth century, which would develop a lucrative trade with the natives. Even as it rapidly became clear that Virginia could succeed only if it could develop products that would be salable in European markets, those involved initially patterned their thinking on the English experience in Ireland, where such products were produced on units managed by the English but worked largely by native labor.[3]

An understanding of the ways participants in the Virginia enterprise initially conceived of the undertaking helps to explain many puzzling aspects of the colony's early history. Accustomed to thinking of colonies as commercial agricultural settlements, as Virginia quickly became, later generations of historians have had difficulty comprehending why the Virginia Company sent military adventurers rather than farmers in its initial thrust into the Chesapeake, why these adventurers did not work harder to try to feed themselves, and why the company and its leaders in the colony found it necessary to govern for so long through a severe military regimen. But when it is recognized that conquest, not agriculture, was the primary object of the Virginia outpost during its first years, that the initial adventurers expected to get food not by dint of their own labor but, like their Elizabethan counterparts in Ireland and elsewhere, from the local population, and that all earlier trading company factories established in the midst of potentially hostile and numerically superior populations had been operated as military and commercial organizations rather than as agricultural societies, the history of Virginia during its early years becomes much more comprehensible.[4]

If the first English people came to Virginia looking for conquests or trade to make them wealthy and if they organized themselves so as to exploit the fruits of their hoped-for discoveries, they soon realized that neither conquest nor trade was likely to yield returns sufficient to sustain the colony, and the rapid development of tobacco as a viable

commercial crop quickly transformed Virginia into the sort of commercial agricultural settlement that comes to mind when one thinks of
early modern British colonies. Within a decade after its initial settlement in 1607, Virginia was organized for the production of a single
agricultural staple—tobacco—for the metropolitan market. The high
profits yielded by tobacco turned the colony into a boom settlement in
which the reckless and single-minded pursuit of individual gain became the central animating impulse and the chief social determinant.
In quest of wealth that would provide them with the civilized comforts
they had left behind in England, men greedily took great risks. They
dispersed themselves over the landscape with scant regard for the sensibilities of its Indian occupants. And they vigorously competed with
one another for labor, the one commodity that provided the key to
success in an economy that revolved around production of so labor-
intensive a crop as tobacco.[5]

From these early decades, then, the labor requirements of producing
tobacco were a primary force in shaping Chesapeake society. Aware
that they had neither the coercive nor the persuasive resources necessary to reduce the local native populations to the hard labor involved
in tobacco production, Virginia Company leaders moved quickly to
solve their problem by guaranteeing prospective immigrants land and
freedom in return for a specified period of labor as servants.[6] For the
next century, such servants constituted far and away the largest single
source of European immigrants to the Chesapeake, probably 80 to 90
percent of the roughly 130,000 to 150,000 Europeans who migrated to
the area before 1700. Almost wholly people who had not yet acquired
much stake in society in England, these servant immigrants were
drawn throughout the century from a broad cross section of English
society, including, in roughly equal proportions, unskilled laborers and
youths, agricultural workers, and tradesmen. They came mostly from
areas within a forty-mile radius of three main ports of embarkation:
London, Bristol, and Liverpool. Most important for the character of
emerging Chesapeake society, they were predominantly young (aged
fifteen to twenty-four with twenty to twenty-one the most frequent
age) and male (ranging over time from six to two and one-half males
for every female).[7]

These people came to the Chesapeake with hopes for a better life
or at least one in which their sustenance was less problematic than
it had been in England, and Virginia Company leaders fully intended

that their hopes should not be disappointed. Once they had committed themselves to establishing an agricultural colony, company
leaders sought to create a "stable, diversified society, where men would
make reasonable profits and live ordinary, reasonable lives" in a context of traditional English political, religious, and cultural institutions.[8] From the foundation of the colony, of course, the company, as
Perry Miller has shown, had conceived of Virginia as considerably
more than a purely economic venture. Along with its investors, back-
ers, and the people it sent out to America, the company thought of the
colony as part of a Divinely ordered plan in which English Protestants
chosen by God would carry out the redemptive mission of reclaiming
Virginia and its heathen inhabitants for His true church. The "conscious and powerful intention" of both promoters and adventurers,
Miller has correctly argued, was "to merge the [colony's] society with
the purposes of God."[9] In the boom conditions that obtained between
1615 and 1625, however, such concerns, which had never been at the
forefront of the Virginia enterprise, were thoroughly overridden by
the race for tobacco profits. The company's broader social and religious goals, including its design of fixing Virginia firmly within a
"religious framework," were very largely frustrated by the behavior of
its settlers in Virginia, including even that of its own officers.

Indeed, the society that took shape in Virginia during these deter-
minative formative years was a drastically simplified and considerably
distorted version of contemporary English society. With no permanent
commitment to the colony, property owners in Virginia showed little
concern for the public weal of the colony and routinely sacrificed the
corporate welfare to their own individual ends. Company officials led
the way by expropriating so many of the resources the company sent to
Virginia that, despite continuing heavy outlays, the company was on
the verge of economic ruin by the time of its dissolution in 1624.
Extremely reluctant to devote time or energy to any endeavor that did
not contribute directly to their immediate tobacco profits, the free
settlers often failed to produce enough food to feed themselves and
their servants, whom they exploited ruthlessly and treated more as
disposable commodities than as fellow human beings.[10]

By failing to grow enough food, overworking their servants, and
unwittingly settling in areas with contaminated water, they also contributed to an astonishingly high mortality rate that took as much as
30 percent of the total European population in some years and was

probably even higher among fresh immigrants. At the same time that they made their powerful Indian neighbors anxious by steadily encroaching upon their lands, they neglected to take adequate precautions against Indian attack and paid dearly for their laxity when Indians killed 347 people—more than a quarter of the total number of English settlers—in a surprise massacre on March 22, 1622. Of the some 7,200 people who came to Virginia during the eighteen years of company supervision, only slightly more than 1,200 remained in 1624. Though there was obviously some leakage to the Indians and some reemigration to England or other Anglo-American outposts, most of this startling population loss was the product of a grim mortality. By the mid-1620s, a few immigrants had managed to accumulate substantial fortunes and to monopolize a highly disproportionate share of the colony's wealth. But their success had been purchased at an enormous cost in human life, and they had presided over the establishment of a society in which life for most of its inhabitants was little better than the hard, nasty, brutish, and short existence later attributed to the state of nature by the philosopher Thomas Hobbes.[11]

By the time Charles I made Virginia England's first royal colony in 1625, Chesapeake society had developed a set of social and demographic characteristics that would prove remarkably durable. Oriented primarily toward the production of tobacco for European markets and deeply materialistic, Virginia was a highly exploitive, labor-intensive, and sharply differentiated society in which a few of the people who survived the high mortality had become rich and the vast majority worked in harsh conditions as servants, hoping to live long enough to work out their terms and become independent, landowning producers. With few people having any long-term commitment to the colony, religion and other traditional institutions were weak, a sense of community tenuous, and cultural amenities almost nonexistent. The population was mostly young, male, immigrant, outside the bounds of conventional family discipline, and incapable of reproducing itself. Men outnumbered women by three to one; three-fourths of the people were under thirty years of age, with nearly half falling into the age group between twenty and twenty-nine; more than nine out of ten were European born. Although the colony contained a small core of nuclear families, they formed no more than the earliest beginnings of a settled family structure. Created mostly after their members had arrived in the colony, families were predominantly childless; about two-thirds of the roughly 45 percent of couples that did have children had only one. High mortality resulted in more than half of Virginia's few children living in broken families in which one or both parents were dead. Along with the absence of a clear correspondence between wealth and the traditional attributes of leadership as they were understood by Englishmen at home, the fragility of life—and fortune—in the colony meant that social and political authority was weak, impermanent, and open to challenge and that the potential for social discord was high.[12]

During the thirty-five years following the demise of the Virginia Company, however, conditions in this still contingent and rudimentary settlement on the Chesapeake improved substantially for its new English inhabitants. With the fall of tobacco prices beginning in the mid-1620s, the initial boom gradually dissipated. As profits fell, socioeconomic life in the Chesapeake may have lost some of its harsh competitive edge and become somewhat less intensely exploitive. Yet although prices continued to fall and the tobacco market went through recurrent cycles of prosperity and depression, growing productivity and lowered shipping and distribution costs combined to produce a long-term period of growth that lasted until 1680. A response to a steady rise in European demand for tobacco, this rapid expansion brought increasing wealth to the Chesapeake. Estimated annual income for the area as a whole increased from less than £10,000 sterling in 1630 to over £70,000 by 1670.[13]

Wealth, in turn, encouraged considerable immigration. More and more after the mid-1630s, younger sons of substantial gentry and urban families, some with wives and children, migrated to the Chesapeake to seek their fortunes and their independence in the production and marketing of tobacco.[14] But the vast majority of immigrants continued to be servants, who, whenever (as in the late 1630s and throughout the 1650s) the tobacco market was bullish and demand for labor correspondingly high, came at the astonishing rate of 1,500 to 1,900 per year.[15] Directed to the Chesapeake by servant factors hoping to profit from buoyant labor and tobacco markets, these thousands of servant immigrants were enticed by the prospects of themselves achieving land, servants, independence, and perhaps even affluence at the conclusion of their terms.

Before 1660, those servants who survived, especially those fortunate enough to acquire wives and families, were seldom disappointed in their hopes. With land cheap and fixed capital costs for tools and equipment low, any person who could command modest amounts of labor additional to his own from either family members or servants could produce tobacco successfully. At least until the end of the 1650s, Chesapeake society, as Russell Menard has shown for Maryland, "was open enough to allow a man who started at the bottom without special advantages to acquire a substantial estate and a responsible [social and political] position": "any healthy man" who "worked hard, practiced thrift, avoided expensive lawsuits, and did not suffer from plain bad luck, could become a landowner in a short time."[16] For those free immigrants from higher social statuses in England who brought with them even modest amounts of capital with which to acquire servants, prospects were even brighter. They could confidently expect to do well economically, hold public office, and, in general, as one scholar has phrased it, "step a notch upward in the social scale."[17]

By 1660, these favorable economic conditions had drawn enough people into the Chesapeake to raise the total Euro-American population to around twenty-five thousand, an astonishing increase from the twelve hundred souls left by the Virginia Company in 1624.[18] Some of this increase was the result of lower mortality and a higher birthrate. As Carville Earle has suggested, Jamestown and many other early Chesapeake settlements were located in a "deadly estuarine zone" in which the annual summer invasion of saltwater contaminated the drinking supply with salt, sediment, and fecal material containing pathogens of typhoid and dysentery that floated back and forth past the settlements with the summer tide. This condition, Earle estimates, produced sufficient incidence of typhoid, dysentery, and salt poisoning to account for roughly two-thirds of the high mortality under the Virginia Company. Subsequent redistribution of population to higher land and to freshwater zones after 1624 cut mortality rates by as much as 50 percent.[19] Similarly, losses at the hands of the Indians diminished sharply. Following the 1622 massacre, colonists systematically subjugated Indian villages in the immediate vicinity of their own settlements, killing or destroying resisters, and carefully separated themselves from the rest of their Indian neighbors. Despite a second uprising in 1644 that took the lives of about five hundred whites, this policy was at least partly responsible for a higher survival rate among Euro-Virginians after 1630.[20] At the same time, a slowly improving ratio of women to men may have accounted for a modest rise in the birthrate.[21]

Notwithstanding these favorable developments, far and away the most significant source of population growth in the Chesapeake between 1624 and 1660 was continuing immigration. If mortality was falling dramatically, it nevertheless was still "comparable . . . to that of severe epidemic years in England." Malaria and periodic epidemics continued to take a high toll. Life expectancy for adult males remained somewhat lower than for people who stayed in England.[22] Similarly, despite apparently higher survival rates for women in the Chesapeake, the continuing disproportion of males to females among servant immigrants meant that many men could not expect to form families and prevented the achievement of the more balanced sex ratio necessary for the population to sustain itself, much less to yield strong natural growth.[23]

Indeed, as several recent studies have shown, persistently high mortality had a profound impact upon patterns of life among those people who had been able to form families. In one Maryland county half of all marriages were broken by death within seven years; in a Virginia county a quarter of all children had lost one or both parents by age five, one-half of them by age thirteen, and three-quarters by age twenty-one. Parental death was such an integral part of the fabric of life that it was the norm for most children. Because men died earlier than women, women were "accorded an unusually influential role in managing the estate and bringing up children," and the omnipresence of death impelled parents to set their sons up independently as soon as they reached maturity. Indeed, with so many children left so early without natural parents in the Chesapeake, parental control and sexual mores were unusually weak, and prudent parents must have sought to encourage autonomy and adaptability, not dependence and inflexibility, in their offspring.[24]

At the same time that it produced an exceptional emphasis upon autonomy and independence, however, the continuing fragility of life in the Chesapeake was one of the several elements contributing to a growing sense of community. As scholars have traditionally emphasized, the harsh, competitive, and highly individualistic and materialistic impulses manifested during the first tobacco boom continued to be strongly evident in succeeding decades. But recent research has made clear that such impulses were significantly mitigated by several developments after 1630. First, the cooling off of the economy also slackened the pace of economic differentiation and thereby helped to blunt the intense competitiveness that had characterized social relations during the boom years. Of course, some men with superior resources continued to acquire more wealth than others. But wealth actually seems to have been more equitably distributed through the 1640s and 1650s than it had been earlier. Although a few large producers had substantial holdings, most settlers had only small ones. Large and small holders alike still concentrated on producing tobacco for export. But they paid far more attention than earlier to domestic husbandry, including livestock raising, food production, and horticulture. Chesapeake society appeared to be slowly undergoing a transformation into a settled pasture-farming area that, despite its continuing emphasis on tobacco, was becoming more and more similar to many areas of rural England. The changing character of agriculture after 1630 thus helped to give the Chesapeake a more settled English appearance.[25]

So also did the steady growth of population. People continued to disperse in nonnuclear settlements over the richest tobacco lands close to navigable streams. By 1660, however, population increases had resulted in the development of many areas of concentrated settlement, which were already well into the process of forming densely interconnecting societal networks based on kin, neighborhood, and economic ties. These networks in turn fostered the emergence of a shared sense of mutual interdependence and locally felt community. The Chesapeake, in short, was slowly being transformed into a "mosaic of close-knit neighborhoods" in which residents depended upon one another for association and assistance. In particular, the frequency of parental death operated as a powerful cohesive force among neighbors by accentuating the importance of extended kinship and quasi-kinship connections for rearing orphaned children.[26]

As the Chesapeake area gradually took on a less contingent character, its white inhabitants made a concerted effort to recreate the institutional structures that had given social coherence and a sense of security to the world they had left behind in England. "Little by little," Warren M. Billings has remarked, these materialistic people "came to understand that a well-ordered society was a regulated community that kept its members at peace with one another and out of harm's way." Intensity of religious conviction was never sufficient to constitute a primary shaping influence in this early Chesapeake society, and religious opinions were every bit as diverse as they were in old England. Nevertheless, leaders in both Virginia and Maryland had moved to institute the established church during the early years of settlement, and they subsequently proceeded to mark out new parishes "at a remarkably regular and prolific pace" and to endow them with most of the same broad social responsibilities performed by English parishes, including especially poor relief.[27]

By creating county courts in the mid-1630s, they similarly gave vent to a growing desire for security of their liberties and property through the establishment of a legal and judicial order in the metropolitan tradition. The chief agencies for the articulation of local needs, these courts came to serve both as effective devices for implementing a uniform system of justice and as a visible institutional location for the embodiment and exertion of legitimate authority. With broad jurisdiction extending to virtually all aspects of life at the local level, the county courts in both Virginia and Maryland became the primary centers of power, more important in most respects than institutions at the provincial level, including even the representative lawmaking assemblies, the first of which convened in Virginia in 1619.

Along with the gradual thickening of social networks, courts and parishes made a substantial contribution toward the achievement of a more stable and coherent social and political order. To be sure, the courts also became the principal arenas of conflict for ambitious men who competed vigorously, sometimes violently, for power, advantage, and preeminence. Through this alternating process of conflict and cooperation, however, they laid the foundations for a ruling elite that could eventually perform functions, enjoy status, and exert influence similar to those of the county gentry in England. Just as provincial leaders in both Virginia and Maryland proved on several occasions that they could quickly unite against any metropolitan efforts to lessen their socioeconomic and political autonomy, so also did rivals within county magistracies often present a common front against the provincial government whenever local interests were at stake.[28]

Between 1625 and 1660, the Chesapeake slowly became more heavily settled. Its demographic patterns were yet peculiar by metropolitan standards. Its Euro-American population, which made up more than 95 percent of the non-Indian people living in the area, was younger and more male; it had a high proportion of single-person male households, especially in areas of newest settlement; numbers of families and children were limited by a shortage of women; mortality rates were high. Though these demographic characteristics were far less pronounced than they had been thirty or even ten years earlier, their continuance as well as the persistence of a strongly materialistic and individualistic orientation among settlers meant that the Chesapeake settlements still fell considerably short of the traditional ideals of an anglicized society.

Nevertheless, as it had slowly become more settled and socially more elaborate and less inimical to human life, the Chesapeake had also become far less fragile and had acquired an air of permanence that had been missing a mere thirty-five years earlier. These developments inspired its more sanguine leaders with visions of even more impressive achievements in the foreseeable future. Such people now actively sought to establish urban centers, develop more compact settlements, and diversify the economy to make it less susceptible to sudden fluctuations in the international tobacco trade. Through these and other similar changes, including a continuing improvement in demographic circumstances, Chesapeake leaders in the early 1660s looked forward to the eventual transformation of England's most ancient transatlantic dominion into a more fully anglicized society.[29]

I F the early history of the Chesapeake colonies was a story of a long search for sustenance, stability, and definition, England's New England colonies underwent no such uncertain travail. The first permanent New England colony at Plymouth was settled in 1620, thirteen years after the founding of Jamestown. With a significant proportion of families among the earliest immigrants, a considerably less malignant disease environment, better relations with a far less numerous native population, and, after the first winter, no severe food shortages such as beset Virginia during its early years, Plymouth had been able from very early on to establish a more settled society organized around the nuclear family and producing enough children to permit modest population growth. Population numbered no more than four hundred people after a decade and did not reach two thousand before 1660. This slow increase was the result not, as in the Chesapeake, of high mortality, which in Plymouth was somewhat lower even than in England, but of low rates of immigration.

Through mixed agriculture and some fur trading with Indians along the Maine coast, the Plymouth colonists were able both to sustain themselves and to produce a surplus sufficient to pay off their substantial debts to the English merchants who had underwritten their venture. In contrast to the Chesapeake colonies, however, they never discovered a source of wealth that either made Plymouth attractive to immigrants or produced a strong demand for labor, much less the resources necessary to purchase that labor. Throughout the seventeenth century, standards of living were moderate, the pace of social differentiation and wealth concentration was slow, and men's economic ambitions necessarily remained comparatively modest.

Plymouth differed from Virginia and Maryland not only in its relative inability to generate much wealth but also in the deeply and persistently religious orientation of its separatist puritan leaders. Like the Chesapeake colonies, however, Plymouth was characterized by a significant degree of religious pluralism from the beginning, and neither the strength nor perhaps the internal logic of the separatist persuasion of the dominant group proved powerful enough either to prevent population dispersion or to foster the development of a strong sense of community. Not much less than the Chesapeake colonies, then, Plymouth was marked by geographic mobility, a high degree of individualistic behavior, and relatively weak ties of community.[30]

If Plymouth differed from the Chesapeake colonies in its slow pace of economic and demographic growth and the more deeply religious orientation of its dominant leaders and settlers, the puritan settlements begun with the founding of the new colony of Massachusetts Bay in 1629 presented an even more striking contrast. For one thing, Massachusetts was initially peopled largely by a short, sudden, and carefully organized burst of immigration. Between twenty and twenty-five thousand Englishmen poured into the colony and adjacent areas in just twelve short years between 1630 and 1642. For another, most of these immigrants, as many as 70 percent, came not as unmarried, young, and unfree servants but as members of established families, independent farmers and artisans with some accumulated resources. "Unlike the simultaneous outpouring of Englishmen to other New World colonies," then, this "Great Migration to New England . . . was a voluntary exodus of families and included relatively few indentured servants." Virtually from the beginning, therefore, the age structure and sex ratio in New England resembled those of established societies all over western Europe far more closely than was the case with any other new societies established by the English in America during the early modern era. Unlike the Chesapeake colonies, which could never have sustained themselves without a constant flow of new arrivals from England, New England was the destination of relatively few new immigrants following the outbreak of the English Civil War in 1642. Indeed, there was a substantial counterflow of disillusioned settlers back to England during the 1640s and 1650s, involving as much as 10 percent of the population of some towns. Nor does it appear that immigration from England to New England ever again became substantial at any later time during the colonial period.[31]

Nevertheless, New England's population grew rapidly from the large base of initial immigrants. Largely free of serious epidemics, New England experienced much lower mortality rates than either England or any of its colonies. Recent studies have shown that infant mortality was low—of an average of 8.3 children born to a group of sample families in Andover, 7.2 survived to age twenty-one—and those who lived to that age could anticipate long and healthy lives: 71.8 for men and 70.8 for women among the first generation of settlers and 64.2 for men and 61.6 for women among the second. Combined with relatively young ages at first marriages for women (19.0 for the first generation and 22.3 for the second) and a correspondingly high number of births per marriage, this low rate of mortality sent population surging upward. Within a generation, population had doubled. By 1660, New England as a whole contained between fifty-five and sixty thousand inhabitants of European descent, more than twice the number in the Chesapeake colonies, which had been in existence for a full generation longer. In vivid contrast to the Chesapeake, moreover, most of these people were native born, New England becoming the first region of Anglo-American settlement to develop a predominantly creole population.[32]

Simultaneously New England's new inhabitants were fanning out all over eastern and southern New England. Local Indians provided much less resistance than in the Chesapeake. They were not nearly so numerous nor so powerful as those who occupied eastern Virginia and Maryland, and the New Englanders pursued a more conciliatory and paternalistic, albeit no less culturally arrogant, policy toward them. Except for the brief war with the Pequots in 1637 during which the New Englanders virtually exterminated one of the most powerful tribes in the region, white-Indian relations were comparatively harmonious. Within just three decades, New Englanders had established settlements all along the coast from southern Maine to western Long Island Sound as well as in the rich Connecticut Valley and on Long Island itself. By the early 1640s, New England consisted of five separate colonies: Plymouth, Massachusetts Bay, Connecticut, New Haven, and Rhode Island.[33]

The great migration to New England between 1630 and 1642 had an even deeper religious coloring than had the earlier and smaller immigration to Plymouth. Indeed, as a collectivity, New England immigrants, in Perry Miller's words, were "primarily occupied with religious ideas," and the depth and extent of this religious impulse provided yet another striking contrast with the palpably more secular settlements that had taken shape around Chesapeake Bay. Participants in the great migration were far from being all of one mind with regard to theology, church government, and other religious questions, and the congregational church polity preferred by most of them was conducive to the accommodation of a wide diversity of religious opinion. Nevertheless, an overwhelming majority of New England settlers were dedicated puritans. "Adherence to Puritan principles" was "the common thread that stitched individual emigrants together into a larger movement," and puritanism "remained the dominant force of New England culture" throughout the seventeenth century.

Unlike their predecessors at Plymouth, they came to America not simply to find a refuge from the religious impositions of the early Stuarts. Rather, they were moved by the vision of establishing a redemptive community of God's chosen people in the New World. They saw themselves as a special group joined in a binding covenant with God and sent by Him into the wilderness "as instruments of a sacred historical design." Their "peculiar mission" was to establish the true Christian commonwealth that would thenceforth serve as a model for the rest of the Christian world. In the societies they created, the church and the clergy necessarily had unusually powerful roles, the relationship between clerical and secular leaders was both intimate and mutually supportive, and full civil rights, including the franchise, were in many communities limited to church members.[34]

The millennial vision of the New England puritan colonists had a powerful social as well as religious dimension. They came to America not only because they were unable to realize their religious aspirations in old England. They were also driven by a profound disquiet over the state of contemporary English society. In towns and rural areas alike, new social and economic forces seemed to be producing a disturbing and ever-widening gap between inherited prescriptions of social order and actual circumstances of life, and the crown and its agents were

more and more intruding into many aspects of local affairs—civil as
well as religious. To an important degree, the great migration to New
England was an "essentially defensive, conservative, even reactionary"
response to these developments, betraying a profound fear of social
chaos and a deep yearning for order and control. Hence its members
were determined not only to achieve perfection in the church but also
to create a society that, in contrast to the seemingly increasingly anarchic and beleaguered world they were leaving behind, would conform
as closely as possible to traditional English conceptions of the ideal,
well-ordered commonwealth.[35]

This determination was, moreover, powerfully reinforced by the puritans' fear of the American wilderness. The great plenty of land was
certainly an important element in drawing them to the New World. In
contrast to the settlers of the other English colonies in America, however, they seem to have displayed fewer paradisiacal fantasies of a life of
ease assisted by the natural abundance of a new Eden in America.
Rather, nature, symbolized by the untamed wilderness and its wild and
savage Indian inhabitants, seemed to the puritans to be corrupt and
out of control. Like unredeemed man himself, it had to be subdued
and subjected to good order.[36]

In their grand design of building the ideal, traditional, ordered English world in the untamed American wilderness, the puritan settlers
of New England organized their new societies around a series of
tightly constructed and relatively independent settled permanent communities in which the inhabitants formally covenanted with each other
to found unified social organisms. There was considerable diversity in
the form of these communities. A few, like Andover, seem to have
been classical nucleated villages in which the inhabitants lived around
the meetinghouse, itself an omnipresent symbol of the commonality of
their lives and social goals, and went forth each working morning to
fields arranged according to the traditional open field system that still
prevailed in several areas of England. But most, like Sudbury, quickly
broke up into dispersed rural settlements with the inhabitants living
on individual farms. The way any group of settlers organized themselves on the land seems to have been determined to a significant
degree by their own prior experience in England.[37]

But everywhere, at least in the three "orthodox colonies" of Massachusetts Bay, Connecticut, and New Haven, the purpose of their settlements was the same. Although they were by no means disinterested

in achieving sustenance and prosperity, they put enormous emphasis upon establishing well-ordered communities knit together by Christian love and composed only of like-minded people with a common religious ideology and a strong sense of communal responsibility. Insofar as possible, they intended to maintain order, hierarchy, and subordination; to subordinate individual interests to the public good; to shun all public disputes; to maintain tight control over economic life, including especially the unruly forces of the market; to subject the moral and social conduct of themselves and their neighbors to the closest possible social discipline; and systematically to exclude the contentious and the deviant from their midst.[38]

These tightly constructed and communally oriented villages were only one means of achieving order and harmony in puritan New England. Strong extended and highly patriarchal families also helped to preserve social control and guarantee a relatively high degree of peace throughout the first generation of settlement. The process of migration from England evidently limited the degree to which families among the first settlers were likely to be extended in structure. But a combination of abundant land, large families, great longevity among parents, a proclivity for children to remain in the communities of their nativity, and long delays in the transmission of land to the second generation contributed to the rapid development of families that were extended in structure, patriarchal in character, and deeply rooted in their local communities. A majority of households remained nuclear into the second generation in the sense that sons usually lived apart from their parents after they were married. As Philip Greven has found for Andover, however, the proximity of residences laid the basis for elaborate kinship networks that continued to expand for generations. In Andover, the most salient characteristic of the family during the first generation of settlement was the enormous strength of parental authority, with fathers retaining control of land to ensure that their children would continue dutiful and dependent. In this regard, as in so many others, the society of puritan New England provided a stark contrast to the improvisational family and household arrangements and the emphasis on autonomy and adaptability in child rearing dictated by high parental mortality in the Chesapeake colonies.[39]

Both to reinforce the role of the family and to promote religious and social cohesion, puritan magistrates tried to create an educational system that was extraordinarily elaborate for a new colonial society. Established within a decade after the first settlement of Massachusetts, Harvard College, conceived of as the functional equivalent of Emmanuel College, Cambridge, and Trinity College, Dublin, was intended to provide puritan America with its own supply of orthodox ministers who, as Hugh Kearney has pointed out, could be relied upon to mitigate "the dangers of unlicensed, uncontrolled theological debate, which carried within it the seeds of social disturbance." Similarly, the magistrates passed laws in the 1640s requiring towns to establish schools for the explicit purpose of instilling the young with the correct religious and social principles as they were being gradually worked out in the communities of the saints. Far from being an agency for modernization, education in New England thus seems at least during the earliest generations to have been more a vehicle for achieving religious uniformity and social control through inculcation and reinforcement of the traditional values and social order the puritans were trying to build into the foundations of their new American societies.[40]

Presiding over the puritan colonial experiments in Massachusetts, Connecticut, and New Haven and imparting vigor and authority to government as well as to churches, communities, families, and educational institutions was a numerous and highly visible group of established secular and clerical leaders. To a far greater extent than any other English colonists in America, the puritans brought their leaders with them to New England. Political and religious authority and social status survived the Atlantic crossing and the process of reimplantation in the New World without serious disruption. Unlike the hothouse elites that sprang up among the winners in the race for tobacco profits in the early Chesapeake, New England leaders at both the local and provincial levels were to a significant degree during the first decades people who had brought all the traditional attributes of sociopolitical authority with them to the New World.

As Stephen Foster has pointed out, the political societies of the New England colonies were based not on the "customary engines of social coercion of early modern Europe," not on "a hereditary monarch, a titled nobility, a church hierarchy, and a landlord class," but on "a radical voluntarism" deriving from the logic of the social covenants that served as the foundations for colonies and communities alike. Because all freemen, initially defined as church members who had assumed full civil rights, were theoretically parties to those covenants and because the proportion of freemen ran as high as 60 to 70 percent of the adult male population in most towns, the potential for political participation was—by English standards—extraordinarily high. Nor were the broad body of freemen hesitant to take an active political role whenever they perceived that their privileges or interests were not being adequately protected. Most of the time, however, they willingly deferred to the magistrates, who assumed the dominant role in establishing political institutions, allocating land, making laws, dispensing justice, and reinforcing the position of the clergy and churches.

The astonishing deference of the relatively extensive constituencies of New England to their magisterial elites was without parallel in the other new English societies in America during their initial decades and constituted vivid testimony to the depth of New Englanders' devotion to the traditional ideal of an organic social hierarchy and their acceptance of the authority of their magistrates. At least during the first generation of settlement, that authority was even further reinforced by a high degree of cooperation among lay and clerical leaders, all of whom agreed that their primary responsibilities were to implement and maintain a stable "political society which would have as its primary emphasis the protection of the rights of the churches" and to nourish the strong corporate impulse that had animated and characterized the puritan colonies from their first establishment.[41]

A comparatively slow pace of economic development also helped the puritans to achieve their socioreligious goals in New England. Many immigrants, including even some of the clergy, certainly had economic as well as religious and social reasons for coming to New England, and, although the economy of the region seems to have been reasonably prosperous and even to have enjoyed considerable growth over much of the seventeenth century, neither the soil nor the climate was conducive to the development of staple agriculture. Very early, fish, timber, furs, and shipping brought some people more than ordinary returns, and in seaboard towns a substantial proportion of the population engaged in fishing. But most settlers had no alternative source of income than cereal agriculture and animal husbandry, which yielded only modest profits. Hence, except in the emergent port centers of Boston and Salem, the wealth structure of the New England colonies, at least down to 1660, remained far more equitable than in the colonies of the Chesapeake. Nor, except perhaps in the fishing industry, did New Englanders have either the need, the incentive, or the resources to recruit a large force of unfree laborers. The labor of family members and perhaps a few servants who resided in the nuclear family households was all that was either necessary or profitable for most economic enterprises in the region. In all these respects, New England again seemed to be wholly dissimilar from the colonies along the Chesapeake.[42]

Along with the strong cohesive force exerted by the church, village, family, schools, and visible and authoritative leadership structures that characterized the New England villages, the absence of exceptional economic opportunities inhibited the urge to scatter that was so powerful among the settlers in the Chesapeake. The initial colonists moved fairly often during the first two decades of settlement, and people who either had tenuous ties to the community or lived in the economically most active areas tended to be highly mobile. But those with close economic, family, political, and religious involvement seem to have developed a deep emotional attachment to their communities, which in turn seems to have fostered a persistence and spatial immobility that may have been greater even than in most established village populations in England.[43]

These same conditions also helped to produce several decades of "relative social peace." Notwithstanding the well-known theological controversies between Bay Colony magistrates and religious rebels such as Roger Williams and Anne Hutchinson, the challenges presented by the arrival of the Quakers in the mid-1650s, and the presence of considerable controversy in the churches and contention in the courts, major social discord was rare and conflict restrained throughout most of the seventeenth century. As Timothy Breen and Stephen Foster have aptly observed in regard to Massachusetts, the harmony of New England society placed it in contrast not only to the Chesapeake but to virtually the whole of the contemporary civilized world and constituted perhaps the single "most startling accomplishment" of the orthodox puritan colonies of Massachusetts, Connecticut, and New Haven.[44]

BETWEEN 1607 and 1660, the English emigration to America thus had produced on the eastern coastline of continental North America two simplified expressions of contemporary English society. But they were extremely different from each other. Chesapeake society was highly materialistic, infinitely more secular, competitive, exploitive, and very heavily devoted to commercial agricultural production for an export market. Its high demand for labor and high mortality rates combined to produce a population that was disproportionately male, young, single, immigrant, and mobile. The process of family formation was slow. Social institutions were weak, authority was tenuous, and individualism was strong. With only a slowly developing sense of community, the Chesapeake exhibited a marked proclivity toward public discord.

If, in many of these respects, the Chesapeake was "the most dynamic and innovative society on the Atlantic seaboard" during the early seventeenth century, the puritan colonies of New England were the most self-consciously and successfully traditional. With low mortality, rapid population growth, a benign disease environment, and a far more fully and rapidly articulated Old World–style society, the intensely religious colonies of Massachusetts, Connecticut, and New Haven, moved by powerful millennial and communal impulses, exhibited rapid community and family development. With strong patriarchal families, elaborate kinship networks, and visible and authoritative leaders, localities quickly developed vigorous social institutions, including many schools, and deeply rooted populations. Mostly involved in cereal agriculture and with no generalized source of great economic profit, the puritan colonies displayed a relatively egalitarian wealth structure and an extraordinarily low incidence of social discord and contention. It is hardly possible to conceive how any two settlements composed almost entirely of Englishmen could have been much more different.[45]

Chapter Two

RECONSIDERATIONS

The detailed characterization, in the first chapter, of the new Anglo-American societies established in the Chesapeake and New England during the first six decades of the seventeenth century is a necessary foundation for the evaluation of four assumptions about the relative character and significance of the two areas in Anglo-American colonial development. These assumptions are not only deeply embedded in American historiographical traditions; they also continue to occupy a central place even in the "new" colonial history. The first of these assumptions is that New England was a far more exact replica of old English society than the Chesapeake. The second is that the New England, rather than the Chesapeake, experience was normative in Anglo-American colonial development. The third, an analog of the second, is that a framework or model derived from the New England experience is appropriate for analyzing the whole of the Anglo-American colonial experience. The fourth, to refer the reader back to the Prologue, is that the main outlines of later American society as it developed from the early eighteenth century were derived very largely from New England rather than the Chesapeake, that the puritan tradition evolved directly into and constituted the core of the American tradition. By acknowledging the temporal precedence of the Chesapeake colonies, historians have further underlined the greater significance of New England. If the Chesapeake colonies have had to be granted pride of precedence, the New England colonies, historians have widely assumed, deserved to be assigned what is infinitely more important, pride of influence. This chapter will examine the plausibility of the first two of these assumptions. Chapters 3 through 7 will further examine the second and evaluate the third. Chapter 8 will consider the fourth.

T H E assumption that of all of England's early modern American colonies New England was most successful in the effort to recreate English society in the New World has long been and continues to be fundamental to American colonial historiography. A few quotations will suffice to make the point. "The only nearly complete transfer of English society to the New World," Carl Bridenbaugh, one of the most respected senior social historians, wrote recently in giving explicit formulation to this assumption, "was to be found in New England." Throughout the colonial period, Bridenbaugh observed, New England remained "more purely English" than any of the other colonies. Nor have many younger historians disagreed. Most recent students of colonial New England, both of its intellectual and social history, have assumed without question the truth of this conventional wisdom. Thus the various authors of the many recent studies of New England communities have virtually all emphasized the great extent to which those communities exemplified the "retention of Old World forms." "No other colonies," Timothy Breen has insisted, were able "to replicate so fully the traditional life they left behind in the Old World." Within just two short decades, argued Breen, the New England "countryside appeared remarkably like . . . traditional English society." The puritans, echoed John M. Murrin, "came closer than any other overseas enterprise to reproducing the Old World in the New." By contrast, the Chesapeake colonies, settled by "an unusual group of Jacobeans," who, in Breen's words, "in no way . . . represent[ed] a random sample of seventeenth-century English society or a cross section of English values," have generally been depicted as a serious distortion of English society.[1]

On the surface at least, there would seem to be little reason to challenge these judgments. With their agricultural household economies, their social organizations based on a well-developed system of families and rapidly extending kinship networks, their well-articulated matrix of social institutions presided over by leaders with all the characteristics of traditional authority, the relatively compact, settled, cohesive, small-scale rural settlements of New England, many with a group of households and a meetinghouse at the center of an area of cultivated land, doubtless did appear more like their counterparts in rural England than did the acquisitive, competitive society of the Chesapeake with its straggling tobacco plantations; broken or undeveloped families; preponderance of young, volatile male workers; new leaders with uncertain claims to legitimacy; and primitive social institutions.

But there are many difficulties with this casual and general depiction of New England villages as close approximations of early modern English rural communities. Recent scholarship has raised serious doubts about the degree to which the traditional portrait of English village life to which New England communities supposedly conformed is actually true. The thrust of this scholarship is strongly toward a reconception of English village life as altogether less "traditional"—less peasant, static, closed, cohesive, corporate, and settled—than has previously been supposed.

The new picture of early modern England that has been emerging over the past quarter-century is one of a society that was undergoing rapid social change and was by the last half of the sixteenth century far more complex, fluid, and "modern" than has long been supposed. As Keith Wrightson has noted, "The myth of the relatively isolated, self-contained and static rural community . . . is at best a half-truth." Many, if not most, parishes seem not to have been "composed of self-sufficient, small, farming households" organized into a domestic agricultural economy in which extended family groups or "even the smaller household of parents and children" operated "as communal units of production and consumption." Rather, parishes were dominated by large landowners—some resident, some not—who held as much as two-thirds of the land. Social relationships between owners and the people who worked for them on these estates were doubtless often paternal. Paternalistic behavior, Wrightson has remarked, "gave stability to a society which . . . embraced gross inequalities and which was, in the final analysis, based upon the individualistic pursuit of self-interest." But agricultural estates were also "rational enterprise[s], run . . . for economic profit." Organized for large-scale production of specialized commodities for the county, new urban, or foreign markets, they employed large numbers of tenants and hired laborers.

Operating on a much smaller scale, copyholders or leaseholders usually occupied the remainder of the land in a parish. But even for these small producers the unit of production was not the nuclear, much less the extended, family of the traditional portrait but the husband and wife and hired laborers, not including their own children, who were typically apprenticed to other families as soon as they became net producers in their early teens. Many other householders and laborers were engaged in nonagricultural activity including food processing, crafts, and the cloth industry. The incidence of servanthood and hired labor in all households and enterprises, whether agricultural or not, was high. Altogether, at least half of the population of a given parish usually consisted of dependents who were employed by others.[2]

The old image of the rural English "village filled with small yeoman families" is thus now being rapidly supplanted by a picture of a community "dominated by a few large landowners, with a multitude of small producers, agricultural and otherwise," as well as large numbers of dependents, virtually all of whom, like it or not, were heavily "involved in a capitalist and cash marketing system." Stimulated by an expanding population that doubled during the course of the sixteenth and seventeenth centuries, by increasing rural industrialization based on a strong foreign demand for English cloth, and by a rising commercialization of agriculture in response to a growing urban and rural food market, commercial activity, including active land, labor, and commodity markets, was widespread, and the market was central to, if not preeminent in, the lives of most Englishmen, at least in the south and west, from which most immigrants to the colonies were drawn. "In rural as well as urban England," Carole Shammas has observed, "a large number of people . . . depended primarily on wages for their livelihood and purchased the bulk of their diet on the market."

"Far from being peasant subsistence farmers concerned only to provide for their families' needs from their own holdings," small yeomen and husbandmen, to a great extent, had "already become commercial farmers," "in many respects individualistic economic agents," who "took a thoroughly rational and calculating attitude towards profit" and, as Mildred Campbell long ago pointed out, were "determined to take advantage of every [economic] opportunity, whatever its origin for increasing profit." Thus, although "England retained pockets of simple subsistence farming," virtually none of the gentry and "very few small farmers were isolated from the market, and for most," Wrightson has stressed, "market opportunities were the first factor to consider in their husbandry."

In this "fiercely competitive climate," property concentration and the economic inequality and social polarization that accompanied it were proceeding at a rapid pace, poverty was increasing, and labor had long been treated as a commodity to be bought and sold as economic need dictated. Both opportunity and risk were considerable, and there was "a quickened pace of both upward and downward social mobility." Unrestrained by a rigid hierarchy of status, the successful could move up the social scale almost as suddenly as the unsuccessful could slide down it. Although "the most fundamental structural characteristic of [early modern] English society was its high degree of stratification and all-pervasive system of social inequality," the "line dividing gentlemen from the rest of society was a permeable membrane." Because "birth, a genteel life-style, and activity in places of authority were [all] secondary criteria" to "the acquisition and retention of landed wealth" in "the establishment and maintenance of gentility," there was necessarily "a constant flux, involving shifts within the gentry and even more a steady turnover of families on the lower edges of gentility." Not just commercial agriculture, urban industry, and trade but the professions as well served as possible channels for upward social mobility.[3]

If people moved rapidly up and down the economic scale, they also moved laterally from place to place. "Far from being a bounded community which contained people from birth to death" and from one generation to the next, the typical early modern English parish, as Alan Macfarlane has observed, "was a geographical area through which very large numbers of people flowed, staying a few years or a lifetime, but not settling with their families for generations." Some people moved only short distances to a nearby village or parish. But others participated in a much more dramatic movement of population from the country into urban areas, with London the destination of thousands, or from areas of conventional and established agriculture in the south and east into the more remote pasture-farming and forest lands of the north and west.

To a considerable degree, as James Horn has noted, emigration to America was simply an extension of these established patterns of wholesale population shift within England: many, if not most, emigrants apparently decided to leave the country after failing to find opportunity in London or one of the other growing urban centers. Not surprisingly, those with the smallest stake in society—laborers, servants, and the young—were the most mobile. Usually pushed along "by the pressure of economic deprivation," they were "subsistence" migrants. But the "more substantial members" of rural society—gentry, freeholders, copyholders—were not always deeply attached to their properties, selling their old and buying new ones as it suited their advantage or convenience. Such "betterment" migrants were often pulled along by the attraction of "better opportunities elsewhere, land to buy, a good farm to lease, trade opportunities." Many people doubt-less had strong attachments to home and locality. But these attach-ments rarely extended over many generations, as the rural population manifested far less of that deep rootedness and commitment to place usually associated with traditional agricultural societies.[4]

Because of the typically flow-through population and rapid social changes, English communities, contrary to the conventional view, were of necessity neither closed nor very cohesive. They were com-posed not of strong ancient patriarchal families embedded in a tangled and secure web of extended kinship networks and long-standing neigh-borhood associations. Rather, most people, even the most settled, lived in conjugal families in which patriarchy could have been little more than a folk ideal. "Kinship ties beyond those of the nuclear family were of limited significance" because the practice of impartible inheritance sharply limited the range and depth of extended family and co-resident kinship connections. Although parents made a consider-able "material and emotional investment in their children," they ex-pected "very little" in return, and parental control was typically weak. The "myth of parental despotism in the selection of marriage partners" and in "control of their children's choice of occupations," Wrightson argues, is "insubstantial." Governed by "an implicit acceptance of the ultimate autonomy and individuality of the child," the "whole sys-tem of child-rearing," he concludes, "was directed towards (and well adapted to) the 'putting forth' of children . . . into a highly individual-istic and competitive social environment in which they would have to stand on their own feet." To that end, children were routinely appren-ticed away from home, sometimes at distances of fifty to a hundred miles.[5]

In this "relatively fluid society in which individuals and independent nuclear families were little cushioned by kinship ties and obligations," Wrightson has observed, neighborliness and friendship doubtless "op-erated both to promote harmonious and co-operative relationships among groups of largely unrelated householders and to overcome per-sonal and family isolation." But it is a mistake to assume that "pre-dominant patterns of relationships . . . functioned to produce a local society that was a comfortable idyll of order and harmony." Rather, he contends, "such equilibrium as local society possessed was the product of a constant dynamism in its social relations and the impetus for this dynamic came, as often as not, from conflict." Apparently rooted in a pronounced tendency toward self-assertiveness and a jealous regard for individual rights and possessions that was expressed in rampant litigation, conflict among residents of local communities was ubiquitous, "an essential feature of the constant process of readjustment of social relationships at the local level."

Nor were social institutions either very strong or very coercive. Government was less an instrument for moral discipline, which seems, in any case, to have been relatively slack and permissive, than a simple device for the protection of life and property and the maintenance of orderly relations in an impermanent and fluctuating world. Similarly, the parish church, except where it had been radicalized by puritan divines, was usually a flexible institution with a relatively loose system of religious discipline that could accommodate people who were notoriously pluralistic in their religious opinions. Efforts by civil and religious authorities to "tighten social discipline" at the local level during the century after 1560 mostly "achieved only limited success, in which the rulers of the parish enjoyed only severely qualified authority, and in which social relationships were characterized not by control and deference but by dissociation and mutual wariness." The loose and transitory character of English life was vividly underlined, moreover, by persistently high mortality, which, along with low fertility, prevented genuinely dramatic population growth.[6]

No wonder that in this mobile, fluid, rapidly changing society a highly competitive, individualistic, and acquisitive "modern" mentality flourished without serious check from those ideas of moral economy and suspicions of the market usually associated with traditional peasant societies. "However one defined 'Community,'" Alan Macfarlane has noted in reference to two closely studied villages, "there was relatively little of it . . . as far back as the sixteenth century." "Beneath the rhetoric of contemporary ideals of commonwealth," Wrightson notes, "was concealed the cold reality of a harsh, competitive, contract society" that "was already deeply permeated by the ethos of agrarian and commercial capitalism" and "a cultural emphasis on the interests of the individual nuclear family which was a powerful enough incentive to override traditional social obligations where there was gain to be made."

As their bold and eager entry into foreign trade and colonizing ventures between 1550 and 1650 so dramatically underlined, Englishmen were neither lacking in entrepreneurial impulses nor resistant to economic innovation. On the contrary, over and over again they showed themselves willing to take high risks, adept in shaping situations to their own advantage, and eager to exploit the economic opportunities they were creating. Such people—at the county and local as well as at the national levels—obviously gave a much higher priority to the individual acquisition of wealth and improvement of social and material status than to the maintenance of traditional obligations and established hierarchies of rank and power.[7]

In the process, such people helped to endow English social and economic life with a vigor that was unparalleled in Europe. "Compared with the other countries of Europe," Charles Wilson has written, English society "possessed [a] unique dynamism" that, right down to the community level, made it much more individualistic and much less intradependent, corporate-oriented, cohesive, provincial, and skeptical of change than has earlier been supposed. The dynamic character of English life was, moreover, no doubt enhanced by rapid urbanization, technological innovations in agriculture and trade, and improved literacy associated with the "educational revolution"—all developments that were powerfully in evidence during the very decades of the initial movement of English people out to the new overseas possessions in Ireland and America.[8]

This is not to suggest, of course, that the old picture of English society was not descriptive of at least some portion of the British Isles. If it obtained anywhere, however, it was most likely, as Hugh Kearney has observed, to have been confined largely "to the Celtic-speaking areas of Ireland, the Scottish Highlands, and Wales or to the remoter areas of England" and, as Wrightson has noted, was both "an utterly untypical product of very special conditions and . . . increasingly regarded at the time as anachronistic." As Kearney points out, these areas were precisely those from which emigration did not take place. More recently, Alan Macfarlane has questioned the extent to which even these areas may have conformed to the old picture.[9]

However that question is decided, it should be obvious to the reader by now that, if this new picture of English society as a dynamic, mobile, loose, open, individualistic, competitive, conflicted, acquisitive, highly stratified, and market-based society undergoing rapid economic and social change is correct, between 1630 and 1660 the Chesapeake colonies represented a much closer approximation of old England than did the puritan colonies of Connecticut and Massachusetts Bay. With its skewed sex and age ratios, its consequent slow rate of family formation, its scattered pattern of rural settlements, and its primitive cultural development, early Chesapeake society might superficially appear to be, at best, a very imperfect and highly simplified recreation of old England.

But in its most basic social features and attitudes, Chesapeake society was fundamentally similar to all but the least dynamic parts of metropolitan society. In its permissiveness, lack of social cohesion, weak social institutions, slowly developing community spirit, religious pluralism, secular orientation, competitiveness, acquisitiveness, high levels of property concentration, rapidly circulating elite, reliance upon dependent servant labor, treatment of labor as a disposable commodity, mobility, strong orientation toward large-scale production for the market, and dispersal of population onto the most fertile and best situated lands for the production of tobacco profits, Chesapeake society reflected, and only in a few instances to an exaggerated degree, characteristics that were deeply and undeniably English. Even its high death rate deviated less from the metropolitan mean than did the low mortality of New England.

Far from being the only successful recreation of English society among the early colonies on the North American mainland, New England thus deviated as sharply from the mainstream of English development as it did from that of the Chesapeake. Indeed, it must be argued that New England not only deviated from the mainstream but represented a sharp reaction to, even a rejection of, it. More than two decades ago, Michael Walzer argued persuasively that puritanism was to an important extent a "peculiarly intense" response to the rapid change and unsettledness in early modern English socioeconomic life and to the rising disorder and worldliness thought to have been its consequences. As Michael McGiffert has shown, dismay over the social and moral state of English society was by no means limited to puritan clergymen. Yet they and their followers among the laity seem to have been animated by a particularly "acute fear of disorder and 'wickedness,'" and they devised a socioreligious system calculated to enable them to cope with their own overwhelming insecurity in the face of such developments. This system required both "constant warfare" on the part of individuals against their own natural inclinations toward wickedness and the implementation of a social system that would enable men, through willful activity, to settle the unsettledness around them, to exert control over a chaotic world.

The world puritans hoped to substitute for the one in which they lived used suspicion and mutual surveillance to achieve a tight social regimen and to suppress individual deviance and sin, to exert tight control over the unruly forces of the market, diminish acquisitiveness and the covetousness or frivolous indulgence it engendered, locate every person in an appropriate calling, urge diligence and a careful use of time upon individuals, submerge the rampant assertion of self in a concern for the next world rather than this, and achieve a degree of communal unity virtually unknown in the fluctuating world of early modern England. This world, Hugh Kearney has remarked, was "an idealized version of the gentry-cum-yeoman society" which the puritans thought they had seen disappearing in England.[10]

Although it is still an open question whether such a society still or ever had actually existed in England, the puritans there were of course unsuccessful in their efforts to establish it in the home islands. Able to begin anew with no old society to destroy and few external controls, the puritans who fled the disorienting and changing world of old England for Massachusetts Bay, Connecticut, and New Haven were far more successful. On the blank slate of America, they were able, as they had fully intended from the beginning, to translate their ideas into reality, at least for a generation and except in larger commercial centers such as Boston and Salem, which early became prosperous mercantile entrepots with relatively large, concentrated, heterogeneous populations, differentiated societies, considerable contact with the outside world, higher mortality, and less stability and unity.[11]

Elsewhere in the rural settlements that dotted the countryside of all three colonies, however, the puritans established a society that, however much it may have resembled rural England in its patterns of settlement, legal practices, and agricultural modes, contrasted markedly with the world they had left behind. Its virtually unique patterns of high fertility and low mortality, the deep rootedness of its population, the strong patriarchal character of its reticulating family structure, its egalitarian social structure, its excessive preoccupation with establishing and maintaining a pure—and exclusive—church, its unswerving resolve to achieve communal unity and a solidary social order, its suspicion of commerce and acquisitivensss—in all of these ways and more, New England puritans tried to create a world that was a far cry from the one they had left behind or even perhaps from an older tangible world they had actually lost. Rather, it was an idealized world derived from their own discontents with emerging socioeconomic trends, altogether more traditional than the world of most of contemporary England and certainly of its most dynamic elements. As Mark Kishlansky has noted, the puritans' "careful attempts in America to recreate English village life, seen spatially and agriculturally," were strongly tempered by "their desire to avoid the most recent transformations of that life." In so many respects militantly antimodern, the world established by the New England puritans was intended not to replicate but to move in precisely the opposite direction of the world they had abandoned in old England.[12]

I F, despite its demographic peculiarities and primitive rural simplicity, Chesapeake society was more expressive of the dominant features and impulses of contemporary English life than was the regressive world of orthodox puritan New England, the possibility remains that the second convention of colonial American historiography may yet be true: that the New England experience may have been more typical of that of other English colonies than was the Chesapeake's. Even a cursory look at the histories of both the colonies established during the early seventeenth century and those founded later, however, reveals that, at least insofar as it has been applied to the earliest generations of settlement, this supposition is as implausible as the assumption that of all the earliest English colonies New England most fully and accurately reproduced the society of old England.

England's oldest colonizing ventures in Ireland were in many respects profoundly different from those in the New World. First, Ireland was both much closer to England and had already been the scene of repeated English penetration long before intensive colonization had begun during the first years of the seventeenth century. Second, it contained a much larger, more densely settled, Christian, and, from a European point of view, considerably more culturally advanced native population of at least one and a half million people by the early seventeenth century, a population, moreover, that had considerable admixtures of English blood. Third, proximity made possible and the size of the native population demanded the employment of a large permanent English military force. Indeed, Ireland was the only early modern English colony in which a sizable military presence persisted beyond the first few years of settlement.[13]

Despite differences, however, a few of the English settlements in Ireland seem more closely to have resembled those in New England than did those in any other colonies. Initially, the colonizers of Ireland had hoped that all English settlements would be tightly knit, nucleated communities segregated from the native Irish population and presided over by representatives of good English elite families. But this hope was realized, and then just partially, only in a few areas of Ulster. Although, as Raymond Gillespie has noted, there was "no Irish parallel of the church or town covenants which became an integral part of early New England life" and although "New England settlements had a degree of cohesion which the Irish settlements never attained," an influx of Scottish Presbyterian ministers in the 1620s seems to have facilitated the coalescence of existing Scottish immigrants into a series of largely self-contained covenanting communities of small farmers and artisans. Exhibiting "a spirit of co-operation . . . which must have been nearly unique in Ireland," these communities tended to try to keep the Irish natives at a distance and, like the New England puritans, were deeply religious and perhaps even somewhat suspicious of market forces, intent upon maintaining "traditional" communal values and patterns of familial and social relations, and determined to use the church and education as means not to transform but to reinforce the assumptions and practices of the traditional world of folk memory.[14]

Elsewhere in Anglo-Ireland, however, in the plantations in Leix and Offaly, in Munster, and in most areas of Ulster, the plans of the colonizers, like those of the early Virginia Company, were largely frustrated by the character, orientation, and behavior of the initial settlers as well as by existing conditions. All segments of the metropolitan populations of England and Scotland seem to have been represented among the immigrants. Many of the plantation "undertakers," those to whom the English crown granted large tracts in exchange for undertaking to people them with English and Scottish planters, were from established gentry families. Along with some discharged army officers and immigrating landless younger sons of gentry, commercial, or professional families, these people provided, as had similar people in the Chesapeake, some semblance of continuity of authority from metropolis to colony, and a few of them were eventually elevated to the Irish peerage. Some substantial leaseholders, cottagers, artisans, and even a few ministers also participated in the immigration. But most immigrants were from the least affluent and most mobile sections of the metropolitan population, from precisely the same groups as went to the Chesapeake. Few except those in need of employment, Nicholas Canny has remarked, could be enticed to the colony.[15]

From the beginning, then, the central animating impulses governing England's Irish plantations were not religious or even military but, as in the Chesapeake, economic. Even in Ulster, M. Perceval-Maxwell has observed, few immigrants "initially . . . seem to have possessed strong religious convictions," and religion was not "a significant motive" for venturing to Ireland. Rather, virtually all immigrants—undertakers and undertenants alike— "possessed a common economic motive." "For all groups, from landless men and impoverished gentry to major landowners anxious to acquire further estates," Michael MacCarthy-Morrogh has written, "the prospect of land . . . was a strong force in producing settlers." Primarily, Englishmen and Scotsmen went to or stayed in Ireland "hoping for an increase in wealth and status." They intended, in short, to exploit Irish natural resources for their own economic and social advancement and, if they had them, for their families, clients, or followers. Munster gradually developed a lively trade with England in timber, iron, fish, cattle, and wool and with the American plantations in foodstuffs and livestock; Ulster ultimately was the site of a growing linen manufactury. Yet none of the Irish plantations discovered a staple such as tobacco or sugar that would yield vast and immediate profits.

Nonetheless, the concern for economic returns was central, and the leading undertakers vigorously competed with one another for land and labor. They engrossed larger estates than they could possibly settle and then, wherever possible, engaged, as did Chesapeake leaders with their servants, in sometimes ruthless exploitation of their tenants. Although scarcity of tenants soon forced landlords to offer generous leases, certainly in the early days they exacted the highest possible rents in return for inadequate housing and lease terms that left tenants with as few rights as possible. "Malice, disputation and bitterness," Perceval-Maxwell has noted in the case of Ulster, frequently "followed from the grasping competition of [these] ambitious men" and from disagreements over how best to conquer, settle, and administer the new plantations. In this conflicted society, immigrants usually established themselves, as had their counterparts in the Chesapeake, not in the close habitations initially envisioned by the projectors but in dispersed towns and agricultural settlements as it suited their personal advantage. Food supplies were often inadequate, housing was crude, and those undertakers who could afford to remained in or returned to England and operated their plantations as absentees.

Typically, these people came not as families, as had the immigrants to New England, but as single men and women. As in the Chesapeake, the sex ratio was heavily skewed in favor of males, a situation that was exacerbated by the decision of large numbers of disbanded soldiers to settle in Ireland. Often knowing little agriculture, incapable of much self-discipline, antagonistic to established authority, and not overly religious, these people, like the early Chesapeake colonists, had to be governed initially by a military mode and subjected to strong labor discipline. The heavy preponderance of single males led to considerable intermarriage with the native Irish, and the failure of Ireland to attract sufficient English and Scottish people to meet the labor demands on Irish plantations led to a far greater reliance on native Irish labor than had been originally intended. Indeed, the ready availability of such labor meant that the Irish adventurers ultimately had to invest a considerably smaller share of their resources to import labor than did their counterparts in the Chesapeake and other colonies in America.

Although these early settlers in Ireland, like those in the Chesapeake, were able to establish little more than a thin, weak veneer of English legal and religious institutions, they had the same overwhelming confidence exhibited by the Chesapeake colonists in the immunity of their own supposedly superior civility to that of the natives and a corollary contempt for native military capacity. Along with the dispersion of settlement and the amalgamation of English and native populations, these attitudes resulted in a weak English military establishment. Instead of the close-knit, nucleated, segregated, tightly controlled, and well-defended settlements prescribed by the original goals of English colonization in Ireland, the English settlers had produced a conflicted, loose, dispersed, poorly integrated, and militarily weak society much like that being established contemporaneously in the Chesapeake. The strong economic orientation and high mortality deriving from a lethal (for the English) disease environment in Ireland further underlined the similarities between these two early English plantations and their dissimilarity from the later settlements in New England.[16]

If the English settlements in the Chesapeake and Ireland in their early decades displayed a similar inability to achieve the social order prescribed by their founders, so also did those in the other English colonies founded during the first half of the seventeenth century—

with the notable exception of New England. Of the colonies outside New England, Bermuda was perhaps the most puritan. Though the puritans never enjoyed a religious monopoly in the island, they were the predominant sect through the middle decades of the seventeenth century. Like the New England colonies, albeit to a much smaller extent, Bermuda attracted several prominent puritan divines who played a conspicuous role in shaping the island's society and government. With their secular supporters, they introduced a church polity that closely resembled that of New England, attempted to establish an effective school, and sought to secure enforcement of a strict moral and social discipline. An unusually healthy environment and the small size of the island also meant that population density and closeness of neighborhood probably exceeded even that found in New England.[17]

From the first days of the colony under the Virginia and Bermuda companies, however, the primary orientation of the settlers had been toward the acquisition of profits from agricultural production for external markets. To this end, the settlers quickly dispersed themselves over the island, albeit in a more orderly and systematic way than had the settlers in the Chesapeake. Within a decade they had taken up all available land. For labor, they imported indentured servants, as did their Chesapeake counterparts, although in much smaller numbers, and almost all of these servants had to leave the colony at the end of their terms to find land in places where it was more abundant. This overflow population served as a source of colonists for many mainland and West Indian colonies. In 1616, Bermuda became the first English colony to import blacks as laborers. For most of the first six decades in the seventeenth century, Bermudians, like the Chesapeake settlers, employed their land and labor in producing tobacco, which found a ready outlet in England. But tobacco never brought such enormous profits to or so thoroughly shaped the social life of Bermuda. By the 1640s its inhabitants were seeking to supplement their tobacco economy by raising livestock and foodstuffs and providing lumber for the sugar colonies in the West Indies.[18]

If Bermuda was not a place where people could grow very rich, it was not for want of effort on the part of the colonists. Bermudians, as Virginia Bernhard has noted, were every bit "as anxious as Virginians to make a profit." Whether Bermuda suffered from the same distortion of sex ratios and family development as had the tobacco colonies on the mainland is unknown. There has not yet been any systematic research into the colony's early social and demographic history. In all likelihood, however, favorable health conditions prevented such distortions from persisting beyond a generation and a half, at most.[19]

Despite its puritan cast and its failure to develop an economy vigorous enough to cause men to neglect most other concerns in the pursuit of wealth, Bermuda seems never to have exhibited the zealously religious, cohesive, and solidary social order that obtained in orthodox puritan New England. Social institutions, including even the church, schools, and the law, never achieved the vigor they did in New England during the seventeenth century, urban development was limited to one simple village, and the religious pluralism of the population was a source of recurrent social and political conflict.[20]

Farther south in the Caribbean, Barbados, which became both a base and a prototype for the colonies settled at about the same time in the smaller Leeward Islands of Antigua, Montserrat, Nevis, and St. Kitts, could, given its limited size, scarcely have been any more similar to the Chesapeake. For ten years after its initial settlement in 1627, Barbados, like Bermuda, concentrated very largely on tobacco culture, though it also began producing considerable quantities of cotton and indigo during the late 1630s. From the beginning, Barbados was much more successful as a producer of staples for the English market than Bermuda. As Robert Carlyle Batie has emphasized, its early settlers "made extraordinary profits from tobacco" with the result that "the first decades of [English] Caribee colonization were boom times." This early success both drew large numbers of immigrants to the Caribbean and set off a feverish rush for land that, within a decade, had resulted in the occupation of virtually all of the arable land in Barbados and the Leeward Islands.[21]

As in the Chesapeake, the society was organized entirely for profit. A few members of gentry and commercial families came to make their fortunes, but most emigrants were single, male, dependent indentured servants imported to labor in the cultivation and processing of tobacco, cotton, and indigo. Every bit as competitive, exploitive, and materialistic as the Chesapeake colonies, the West Indian colonies experienced a rapid concentration of wealth, as the society polarized into small groups of proprietors making up less than 10 percent of the population and a mass of dependent indentured or mobile free laborers. Paying but scant attention to religious or other social and cultural institutions, the inhabitants of Barbados and the Leeward Islands were notorious for their riotous and abandoned style of life. High mortality among new emigrants, dysentery, and occasional epidemics combined with the imbalance of women in the population all helped slow the process of family development.[22]

Most of these early tendencies were further enhanced by the gradual substitution of sugar for cultivation of minor staples beginning in Barbados in the mid-1640s and gradually extending to the Leeward Islands in subsequent decades. This capital- and labor-intensive crop led to the further concentration of property in the hands of those few people who could command the capital to purchase the labor and equipment necessary to produce sugar competitively. At the same time they were amassing larger and larger estates for themselves, these plantation owners were replacing white servants and free white laborers with African slaves, who seem to have been both a more economical and a more reliable source of labor. Like their counterparts in the Chesapeake, West Indian sugar planters had, from the beginning of settlement, shown no reluctance to treat white servant labor as a disposable commodity, and the wholesale importation of African slaves into Barbados and the Leeward Islands was both a logical extension of that impulse and the first large-scale use of slavery and non-European labor in any of the English colonies.

By the early 1650s, as a result of the sugar revolution, Barbados had achieved a population density greater than that of any comparable area in the English-speaking world except London. But the introduction of black slaves into Barbados contributed to a significant decline in white population, as many whites migrated to other colonies where there were greater opportunities to acquire land or returned to England. From a high of about 30,000 in 1650, the number of whites fell to about 20,000 in 1680 and 15,500 in 1700. Despite the loss of white settlers, Barbados, in 1670, was certainly, as Richard S. Dunn has written, "the richest, most highly developed, most populous, and most congested English colony in America, with a thriving sugar industry and 50,000 inhabitants, including 30,000 Negroes."

As the population of Barbados and its neighboring colonies in the Leeward Islands became more black and the concentration on sugar production became ever more intensive, profits soared and the possessing classes accumulated phenomenal wealth. By 1660, the wealth of Barbados, the earliest and best developed of the island colonies, not only exceeded that of any other contemporary English overseas possession but made it "the most prosperous 17th century insular colony on the globe." But the rapid rise of a wealthy and conspicuous elite did not immediately give either much cohesion or stability to these English West Indian societies. Indeed, many of those few wealthy proprietors who could afford it fled the tropical sugar factories they had established for the more settled and healthier world of England. If in its concentration upon a single staple, its single-minded concern with gain, and its use of African slave labor, Barbados by 1660 was beginning to diverge sharply from the Chesapeake, it nevertheless presented an even sharper contrast with the stable settlements of Massachusetts and Connecticut. It represented merely an intensely exaggerated version of the same impulses and socioeconomic configurations that characterized the older Chesapeake settlements.[23]

But the English colonies in Ireland, Bermuda, and the West Indies were not the only ones that adhered far more closely to the Chesapeake than to the New England puritan model of colonization. In New England itself, Rhode Island, contiguous to and contemporaneous with both Massachusetts and Connecticut and also settled almost wholly by religious dissenters, appears to have deviated markedly from the dominant model of an orthodox New England puritan colony. Like most New Englanders, most Rhode Islanders lived in small, undifferentiated agricultural settlements with little opportunity to acquire even modest wealth. Nevertheless, without an all-encompassing religious and social vision of the kind that restrained individualism and gave coherence, cohesion, and a larger sense of purpose to life in the other puritan colonies and with a wide range of religious opinions among them, Rhode Islanders lived in a world that except for the longer life expectancy of its inhabitants and its mature state of family development was every bit as unsettled as that of the Chesapeake. Indeed, perhaps nowhere in Anglophone America during the seventeenth century were religious struggles any more acrimonious.[24]

Thus, if in 1660, one arranged all of the early seventeenth-century English colonies along a hypothetical continuum between two poles from the most centrifugal to the most centripetal, the most unsettled to the most settled, Barbados and the other West Indian colonies would have to be placed at the centrifugal pole and orthodox New England at the centripetal pole. But the Chesapeake colonies, the Irish plantations, Bermuda, and Rhode Island—in that order—would all be considerably closer to the centrifugal pole than to the centripetal one, albeit Rhode Island probably belongs very near the middle.

As was the case with these first English colonies, the first-generation societies of at least seven of the eight English colonies founded in America between 1650 and 1700 were far more similar to the loose, expansive, conflicted, and materialistic world of the Chesapeake than to the contained and ordered ambience of orthodox puritan New England. The single exception was New Hampshire, which for almost fifty years before its incorporation as a separate colony in 1679 was a series of communities under the political and social jurisdiction of Massachusetts. In its commitment to the construction of a society of tightly knit communities, its relatively greater disorderliness, and its casual toleration of a greater variety of religious beliefs, New Hampshire differed considerably from both Massachusetts and Connecticut during their early histories. Nevertheless, it came the closest of all the new colonies to replicating the orthodox New England model.[25]

At the other extreme, Jamaica, conquered from the Spanish in 1656 and first settled by disbanded soldiers and excess population from England's older Caribbean colonies, was a near approximation of Barbados. Because it was many times larger and did not for many decades have access to such a plentiful supply of slaves, Jamaica was much slower to concentrate exclusively on sugar production. Following the example of the Spaniards, all of whom had fled the colony within three or four years after the English conquest, leaving large stocks of cattle behind, many of Jamaica's new proprietors raised cattle and other livestock for food consumption in Jamaica and elsewhere in the Caribbean. Others produced less labor-intensive minor staples such as cocoa, indigo, and provisions. Not until the beginning of the eighteenth century did Jamaica export as much sugar as tiny Barbados.

Thus although Jamaica quickly rivaled Barbados in riches, during the early decades of English occupation a large proportion of its wealth came from the activities of its freebooting buccaneers, who used its strategic position in the central Caribbean to tap the vast treasure of the Hispanic-American empire. Through a combination of trade and raids, they made their Jamaican base at Port Royal the richest spot in English America. Despite these dissimilarities from the older West Indian settlements, however, Jamaica—with its tropical climate, high mortality, stunted family development, concentration on staple production for foreign markets, highly exploitive African slave labor system, stratified social structure, engrossment of land by large holders, rapid circulation of elites, small and transient white population, lack of supportive social institutions, and strong materialistic cast—was more like Barbados and the Leeward Islands than like any of the other English colonies established during the second half of the seventeenth century.[26]

The six other English colonies established during the last half of the seventeenth century were all on the continent of North America and fell into two new and distinctive nodes of settlement. The first was sandwiched in between New England and the Chesapeake on lands wrested from the Dutch in 1664 and consisted of the four colonies of New York, New Jersey, Delaware, and Pennsylvania. The second, stretching south from Virginia to the Spanish settlements in Florida, was the new colony of Carolina, started in the mid-1660s and by the end of the century divided into the two colonies of South Carolina and North Carolina.

The northern group, often referred to as the Middle Colonies, dif fered from every other group of early modern English colonies. Like early New England, Pennsylvania, started in 1681 and the last of the Middle Colonies to be established, was a holy experiment. Like the puritan leaders of Massachusetts, its founder, Quaker William Penn, intended it to be an agrarian utopia of stable communities, dominated by Quakers and free from all the political, social, and religious impurities that offended Penn and other Quakers in England. Also like New England, Pennsylvania was begun with a massive migration of families that brought eight thousand people to the colony in just five years. Although about a third of these immigrants were servants, most, like the early puritan settlers, were independent yeoman and artisan families. They included significant numbers of people of prominence and wealth whom Penn originally hoped to invest with the prescriptive political authority appropriate for such visible leaders. A large portion settled on small farms and in villages and engaged in domestic agriculture in the manner of New England. They also appear to have enjoyed the same low mortality and high fertility that contributed to the astonishing natural increase of population in early New England. With no immediate source of quick and large profits that would lead to substantial concentrations of wealth, Pennsylvania, like New England, was

far less differentiated and far more egalitarian than the societies of the
Chesapeake or the Caribbean.[27]

In marked contrast to the puritan settlers, however, early Pennsylvanians, like Penn himself, arrived with powerful economic goals. They
fully intended to establish not only a well-ordered but a prosperous
society that would provide wide scope for the economic ambitions
of its members. In combination with the powerful antiauthoritarian
strain within Quakerism and chronic friction among sects, groups, and
individuals, this strong material urge quickly eroded whatever communal aspirations the settlers had brought with them and prevented
Pennsylvanians from ever achieving a close-knit, well-ordered, stable,
community-oriented society on the New England model. Despite the
vast numbers of non-Quakers drawn to the colony as a result of Penn's
vigorous promotions, Quaker leaders retained predominance in public
life. For nearly fifty years, however, they were unable to achieve a high
degree of cohesion among themselves, and the resulting political environment was conflicted and unstable. With this rapid breakdown of
the communal goals of the founders, Pennsylvania resembled the other
new English colonies in the middle region between the Chesapeake
and New England.[28]

Substantial numbers of Dutch or Scandinavian, primarily Swedish,
settlers had come to Delaware, New Jersey, and New York before the
English expelled Dutch authorities in 1664. New York, in particular,
had a large population of roughly nine thousand inhabitants, the vast
majority of whom were Dutch, strung out in villages and farms between small urban settlements around Manhattan and the fur-trading
post at Albany on the upper Hudson River.[29] In Jamaica, England's
other colony conquered in the seventeenth century, the Spanish settlers had all fled into the Blue Mountains with their slaves and eventually drifted off to other Spanish settlements around the Caribbean. But
in New York, virtually all of the former inhabitants from the Nether-
lands remained following the English conquest, making New York and
to a much lesser extent New Jersey and Delaware the only seventeenth-century colonies other than the Irish plantations in which the
English had to deal with a substantial, firmly established, settled alien
population.[30]

These alien populations gave these colonies a diversity that was
largely missing in the relatively ethnically homogeneous colonies established earlier in the Chesapeake, New England, Bermuda, and even

the West Indies, and this ethnic pluralism was soon increased by the influx of large numbers of Welsh, Scots, Irish, and Germans into all the Middle Colonies, especially Pennsylvania. People of English descent probably never constituted much more than half of the population in any of the Middle Colonies at any point in their history. Religious and linguistic variety were a direct outgrowth of this ethnic heterogeneity. New York and eastern New Jersey contained a mixture of Dutch Reformed, Congregationalists, Anglicans, French Huguenots, Presbyterians, and Jews, and western New Jersey, Pennsylvania, and Delaware included Quakers, Anglicans, Huguenots, Swedish and German Lutherans, Presbyterians, Baptists, and a variety of reformed German sects.[31]

Ethnic, religious, and linguistic diversity were only part of the cultural pluralism of the Middle Colonies. Like all of England's American colonies, their settlements were primarily rural and agricultural. To a greater extent than the earlier colonies, however, these settlements were oriented around the rapidly growing port towns of New York and Philadelphia, which served as transshipment points for the grains, foodstuffs, furs, and other products of their respective hinterlands, New York's extending into western Connecticut and eastern New Jersey and Philadelphia's into western New Jersey and much of Delaware. These urban centers gave the Middle Colonies considerably greater social diversity than could be found in either the Chesapeake or rural New England.[32]

So also did the variegated patterns of rural settlement. The vast majority of English, Dutch, and French settlers in New York and East Jersey and of the English, Scottish, Swedish, and German settlers in West Jersey, Pennsylvania, and Delaware made their homes, as had the Chesapeake colonists, on moderate-sized, dispersed, irregularly shaped, and isolated farmsteads or in small crossroads communities. Long Island and substantial parts of eastern New Jersey were settled by New Englanders, who established a somewhat looser variant of the village communities they had left behind. In all four colonies, but especially in New York and eastern New Jersey, some powerful and successful individuals engrossed large tracts of land which they tried to exploit by using tenants.[33]

Although economic opportunity was less than in the Chesapeake, it was considerably greater than in most of New England and more than sufficient to push the entire region toward the material orientation already noted in the case of Pennsylvania. Furs acquired from the Indians, lumber products, livestock, and grain products grown on rich agricultural lands provided early and continuing items of profit, and throughout the Middle Colonies the inhabitants demonstrated that profoundly acquisitive and accumulating spirit that was such a conspicuous feature of virtually all early modern English colonial societies and, indeed, of England itself. As Michael Kammen has suggested, New York may well have been the most "pervasively materialistic" of all the English mainland colonies. Already becoming powerfully evident by the early decades of the eighteenth century, the results of this burgeoning materialism and the concomitant active pursuit of individual gain were the same as those earlier manifested in the Chesapeake, Ireland, and the West Indies: growing economic differentiation, a high degree of social stratification, marked concentrations of political power, and an eagerness to resort to and exploit bound labor—white servants or African slaves—whenever it was profitable and the resources necessary to do so were available.

Largely a collection of individuals organized into nuclear families, the residents of the Middle Colonies, with the exception of those in the puritan communities on Long Island and in East Jersey, displayed no strong commitment to the communal mode that typified early New England. They were characterized by little civic consciousness, slight concern for achieving social cohesion, high levels of individual competitiveness and public contention, and probably eventually, as befitted societies composed of such diverse parts, a pragmatic, accommodative, and tolerant approach to one another.[34] No less than in Ireland and the English West Indian colonies, though perhaps somewhat more than in Rhode Island or Bermuda, the social configurations and orientations of these new Middle Colonies were much closer to those of the mid-seventeenth-century Chesapeake than to New England.

So were the new settlements in the Lower South. Indeed, the northernmost portion of that region was actually an extension of the Chesapeake,[35] and the southern part, radiating out from Charleston north into the Cape Fear River valley in southern North Carolina and south to the Savannah River, rapidly came to look less like the early Chesapeake and more like Barbados, the source of almost half of the whites and more than half of the blacks among the original colonists. With significant numbers of French Huguenots, Scots, and New Englanders, as well as English and Caribbean settlers, South Carolina, like almost all of the late seventeenth-century colonies, was ethnically and religiously far more diverse than either the Chesapeake or the West Indies. Similarly, its demographic development does not seem to have suffered as severely as did both of those groups of colonies from a markedly unequal sex ratio.[36]

In almost every other respect, however, the Carolinas were very much like those earlier plantation societies. They had a malignant disease environment and a strong commercial orientation. The only English mainland colony that began its existence with a preference for African slave labor and a significant number of African slaves among its original settlers, South Carolina early displayed that powerful materialistic and exploitive mentality that had found such a ready field for action in the Chesapeake and the West Indies. For a generation, it functioned effectively as its Caribbean proponents had initially intended, as an adjunct to the West Indian economy. It developed a vigorous grazing industry that in size rivaled that of Jamaica, and, in return for sugar products and black slaves, it sent large quantities of beef, pork, corn, lumber, naval stores, and Indian slaves to Barbados, the Leeward Islands, and Jamaica.

Even in its earliest days, however, the Carolina economy was never wholly dependent on this trade with the West Indies. Provisioning privateers and pirates and, even more important, trading with the large number of Indians residing in the southeastern part of the North American continent for great quantities of deerskins for export to England were also lucrative activities. No less than early Englishmen in the Chesapeake and the West Indies, however, early inhabitants of the Lower South were avid in their search for a profitable agricultural staple. Early experiments with tobacco and indigo were reasonably successful, but it was not until the successful cultivation of rice in the 1690s that Carolina's planters found a staple that was sufficiently profitable to provide the basis for its rapid transition to a staple economy with a high demand for labor and a large force of bound laborers on the West Indian model.

The cultivation of rice laid the foundation for South Carolina's enormous wealth in the mid-eighteenth century and both financed and stimulated its rapid conversion to an almost wholly African slave labor force in the manner of the sugar colonies. Already by 1710 in South Carolina there were more blacks than whites; in 1720 blacks outnumbered whites by almost two to one. In some rural localities, the black-white ratio was as high as five to one, a figure rapidly approaching those found in the rural parishes of the West Indies. With a weak sense of community, inchoate social institutions, and a high degree of individual competitiveness and social contentiousness, this emerging plantation society during its first half-century closely replicated the earlier experiences of the Chesapeake and West Indian colonies.[37]

ESTABLISHMENT of these new American colonies during the last half of the seventeenth century added greatly to the cultural diversity of the English overseas dominions. In addition to Ireland, there were by 1700 six distinctive cultural regions in colonial Anglo-America[38]— the Chesapeake; Bermuda and the similar colony of the Bahamas, permanently established in 1718;[39] New England, including Nova Scotia after it was acquired from the French in 1713;[40] the West Indian colonies; the Middle Colonies; and the Lower South, which included Georgia after its founding in 1732.[41] Within each of these cultural regions, moreover, there was significant local diversity, which, for instance, distinguished Rhode Island from Massachusetts and Connecticut, Barbados from Jamaica, and New York from Pennsylvania.

Notwithstanding these important regional and local divergences, there was also a single broad fault line that, at least during their early histories, divided these colonies into two sharply different categories. First, there was puritan New England, by which I refer principally to Massachusetts, Connecticut, New Haven, and some of the early New Hampshire towns. With their strong religious orientation, communal impulses, perfectionist aspirations, sense of chosenness, belief in social and religious exclusivity and uniformity, suspicion of the modern market world, and modest economic opportunity, these contained and closely knit settlements constituted what Richard S. Dunn has correctly characterized as "a highly distinctive society." They represented a deep commitment to an effort to recover a stable, harmonious, Christian, and traditional world which, if it had ever existed, was rapidly disappearing from England. Only such an intense commitment, along with the absence of strong and immediate environmental pressures to relinquish it, could, as John M. Murrin has observed, have overcome the powerful impulses, "obvious in all the secular colonial experiments of the period, to scatter through the wilderness in search of something better."[42]

During the early decades of settlement, in every one of the English colonies outside New England except possibly for some communities in Ulster and to a large extent even in Rhode Island and New Hampshire, settlement patterns, sociocultural configurations, and individual priorities were shaped by the economic opportunities that the colonists found, created, and manipulated in their new environments and by the ambitions and aspirations they thereby unleashed. Invariably, the societies they created tended to be individualistic, without much cohesion, permissive, secular, exploitive, differentiated, conflicted, even contingent. To one degree or another, they all represented a logical, if still also a greatly simplified, extension—and not in any sense a rejection—of the dynamic, fluctuating, and increasingly "modern" world the settlers had known in England and upon which they mostly remained heavily dependent for capital, markets, finished goods, and manpower.

Insofar as all of these settlements were in these and other ways similar to each other and dissimilar from orthodox New England, they represented variations of a colonial model first established in the very earliest southern settlements in the Chesapeake. Just as the Chesapeake was in most important respects more like old England than was New England, so the experiences during their early years of all the rest of England's overseas possessions were more like those of the early Chesapeake than like those of New England. Rather than being "unlike those formed by English migrants in other parts of the world," as Timothy H. Breen has suggested, Chesapeake society before 1660 exhibited impulses and social and cultural configurations that were broadly representative of those in the first generations of settlement all over the early modern English colonial world—with the notable exception of the orthodox New England colonies. Far from being normative, then, as colonial historiography has too often assumed, the societies of orthodox New England, at least in their earliest decades, were, in Nicholas Canny's words, "totally exceptional by [British] colonial standards" and represented a deviant strain in English colonial history of which there were no other comparable examples except perhaps for a few villages in Ulster.[43]

To test further the assumption that the New England experience was normative in Anglo-American colonial development as well as to evaluate the corollary assumption that a model derived from the New

England experience is appropriate for analyzing the entire early modern Anglo-American colonial experience will require a detailed comparative examination of the development of the several regions of colonial Anglo-America in the period after the founding generations. This task will be undertaken in the next five chapters. Chapters 3 and 4 will examine, respectively, the two regions initially discussed in Chapter 1, New England and the Chesapeake. Chapter 5 will treat Britain and Ireland, Chapter 6 the Middle Colonies and the Lower South, and Chapter 7 the Atlantic and West Indian islands.

Chapter Three

A DECLENSION MODEL:
NEW ENGLAND, 1660–1760

For at least thirty years and considerably longer in many areas, power-ful cultural restraints (both social and religious), a relatively stingy physical environment, and comparative isolation combined to keep Massachusetts and Connecticut from following the other English American colonies into an enthusiastic acceptance of social atomism and the behavioral mandates of initiative and autonomy. Increasingly after 1660, however, and in a few places even before, other conditions emerged to push these puritan societies inexorably in that direction. To contemporary puritan settlers, the coherent social and cultural or-der they had so carefully fabricated during the first generation of set-tlement seemed to be falling apart, and they interpreted this develop-ment, in all of its many manifestations, as evidence of social and moral declension, a pervasive and steady turning away from the original goals of the founders by their descendants.

The explanatory structure they articulated to make this development comprehensible to themselves still provides the basic framework for the declension model that modern historians have conventionally em-ployed to characterize the process of historical change in colonial New England. Indeed, in their efforts to find a coherent pattern in the seemingly fragmented histories of the many entities of colonial British America, historians have extended this model well beyond the bound-aries of New England history, applying it not only to the colonies as a whole but even to all of American society in the postrevolutionary era. This model, which posits a largely linear process of change from gemeinschaft to gesellschaft, from community to individualism, from traditional to modern, has come under sharp attack in recent years. As the discussion that follows will show, however, it still carries considerable plausibility when applied to some aspects of the history of the orthodox New England colonies between 1660 and the American Revolution.

AMONG the most important of the conditions pushing the orthodox New England colonies into social patterns that at once suggested declension to contemporary inhabitants and were more congruent with those of other English American colonies was their rapid demographic growth. Immigration continued low, in all probability amounting to no more than ten to twelve thousand new settlers for the last half of the seventeenth century and never averaging more than a few hundred per year before the American Revolution. Yet population grew rapidly in response to highly favorable conditions of life. With an abundant food supply, a relatively equal sex ratio, a low population density, and a low incidence of epidemic diseases, New England settlers, especially in the rural areas that were the homes of all but 5 to 10 percent of them, enjoyed low mortality, a high percentage of married women, and a vigorous birthrate that, for most of the seventeenth century, produced completed families averaging in excess of seven children. Notwithstanding considerably less favorable conditions in seaport towns such as Boston and Salem, the number of people of European descent in Massachusetts, Connecticut, Plymouth, Rhode Island, and New Hampshire soared from just over thirty thousand in 1660 to over ninety thousand by 1700.

During the eighteenth century, the rate of population growth slowed significantly in New England. One case study has shown that for the quarter of a century beginning in 1690, the age of marriage rose and the number of children per completed family fell by nearly 40 percent to 4.6 before rising again to around 7 in subsequent decades. At the same time, mortality increased, partly as a result of periodic epidemics that were probably a function of higher population density and closer ties with the outside world. Declining life expectancy seems by midcentury to have brought mortality figures closer to both those long characteristic of Britain and those recently achieved in the Chesapeake. Despite these developments and although New England's proportion of total colonial population fell steadily from about 60 percent in 1640 to less than 40 percent in 1700 and only 25 percent in 1780, natural population growth remained vigorous, averaging between 26 and 28 percent per decade through the first seventy years of the eighteenth century. The total population, surpassing 115,000 by 1710 and 215,000 by 1730, had reached nearly 450,000 by 1760.[1]

The effects of this burgeoning population were profound. Intensifying an already powerful demand for land, it supplied the energy for the rapid expansion of settlement. Although King Philip's War in the mid-1670s and the first set of intercolonial wars between 1689 and 1713 operated as a temporary brake on expansion, by the early eighteenth century New Englanders had occupied a broad band extending fifty to seventy miles inland and from New York north to southern Maine. Driving out the Indians or shunting them off to marginal areas, settlers were rapidly replacing the forests with a European-style landscape of farm buildings, fields, orchards, pastures, and fences. By 1700, the four New England colonies of Massachusetts, Connecticut, Rhode Island, and New Hampshire contained about 120 towns. This expansive process accelerated after 1713. More than a hundred new towns were founded during the next fifty years, and the area of settlement both became far more compact in areas of older occupation and spread over all of southern New England and north and east into New Hampshire, Maine, and Nova Scotia.[2]

Already by the 1660s within the oldest settlements, population growth had led to the dispersal of people out from the early clusters of settlement. In the few places that had been initially settled as nucleated villages, this process sometimes resulted in the physical and social disintegration of the original village centers. Instead of settling together, people tended more and more to establish their families on individual farmsteads and some moved so far away from the original meetinghouses that they found it desirable to form new semi-independent and sometimes antagonistic settlements. Contrary to the designs of the original puritan leaders, this movement helped to destroy the prescriptive unity of the towns and perhaps to weaken the bonds of neighborhood and the authority of political and social institutions.

Despite this dispersion, second- and even third-generation settlers may have been more rooted and less mobile than those of the first generation. When they moved, they did not usually leave the political jurisdictions in which they had been born and often stayed within fifteen to thirty miles of their birthplaces. By the third and fourth generations, however, land in the older agricultural communities was usually all taken up, and young people found that they either had to enter nonfarming occupations or move to new towns to the north,

west, or east. Outmigration from old communities and the founding
of new towns proliferated after 1715, as New Englanders became increasingly more mobile. Although a significant proportion of long-
distance migrants consisted of middle-aged people who moved with
their children only after the death of their parents to what they hoped
would be better lands, many others were young, unmarried adults
who, by the 1730s and 1740s, displayed little resistance to moving away
from their homes and families. This willingness of young adults to
migrate seems to have weakened parental authority and pushed children more and more toward the imperatives of autonomy and independence that had been so powerfully manifest everywhere else in the
English American world throughout the seventeenth century.[3]

Even before population growth had helped to accelerate the general
processes of dispersion and mobility, the intense spiritual energies
and utopian impulses that had been so central to the founding generation of puritan colonists began to attenuate. Relative to population
growth, church membership seems to have declined from about 1650
until 1675. Although absolute numbers remained fairly steady and there
was even a revival of spiritual interest and church membership during
the last quarter of the seventeenth century among the third generation,
the clergy throughout these years decried the decay in godliness and
the growth in worldliness among the laity. In response, many ministers sought to broaden church membership beyond merely the visible
saints. Though it was never adopted by all congregations, the half-
way covenant of 1662 permitted baptized but unconverted children of
church members to be "halfway" members and to have their children
baptized. By the 1680s and 1690s, a few clergymen, such as Solomon
Stoddard of Northampton, advocated even further liberalization of
membership requirements. Discovering "that a pure membership was
a flimsy foundation on which to construct an ecclesiastical system, and
that the restraining influence of the church on the entire community
was more important than the preservation of a [pure] congregation of
saints," the churches opted to sacrifice purity for community.[4]

Problems involving church membership were compounded by dissension within and among churches. By the 1660s, the search for a
single orthodox and uniform way in theology and church government to which the emigrants had been committed had already been revealed to be a chimera. The autonomy of individual congregations
rendered any attempt to achieve regional religious uniformity impossi-

ble, and disagreements among the godly over baptism and other sacraments, predestination, and the proper form of church government revealed deep fissures and contradictions within the puritan movement. Whether or not, as Paul Lucas has argued, these disputes "made dissension a way of life" in New England during the last half of the seventeenth century, they certainly unleashed "a continuing struggle for control of church government." By seriously eroding "the community's power to suppress dissent," they eventually forced colony and community leaders into a grudging acceptance of it.[5]

Nor did ministers of the second and third generations enjoy the stature and immediate influence of those of the first. Although it is certainly an exaggeration to speak of the "collapse of clerical authority," strife among the clergy, disputes between the clergy and the laity, and what David Hall has called the "diminished charisma" of the ministers who replaced the first occupants of the pulpits of New England combined to undermine clerical authority. Although it may be true that "the clergy's involvement with the mental images of the laity was as intense as ever after 1660" and that "the ministry remained the most important calling in New England," the clergy no longer exerted such a profound influence in defining life in the puritan colonies, and many congregations even revealed a growing reluctance to support their ministers in the style to which their predecessors had been accustomed. By the early decades of the eighteenth century, it was a general lament among ministers that they "did not enjoy the prestige, influence, and social status" of their seventeenth-century predecessors.[6]

All these developments stimulated the clergy to articulate a broadly diffused sense of religious decline. Increasingly after 1660, declension became the omnipresent theme in sermons, and the jeremiad, which publicly reviewed the "shortcomings of society" and called on the people to renounce their sins and return to the primitive religious and social purity of the emigrants, became the standard form of sermon on all "the great occasions of communal life, when the body politic met in solemn conclave to consider the state of society." Few modern historians accept these contemporary laments at face value. They recognize that New England was not declining but only changing, undergoing a series of intellectual and institutional adaptations to reflect the changing needs of the churches and society. As increasingly through the middle decades of the century, hope fell victim to experience and the "ideal of community" dimmed before the "shortcomings of community life," the original New England way, in Stephen Foster's words, dissolved "into unrelated, often irreconcilable parts." In the process, as Perry Miller noted nearly a half-century ago, it became "something other than it had started out to be, in spite of the fact that many . . . still desired with all their hearts that it remain unchanged."[7]

If the jeremiads of the late seventeenth century cannot be read as literal indications of New England's declension, they certainly revealed a widespread discontent with contemporary religious and social behavior that gripped the laity as well as the clergy. By the 1660s, few colonists still had any very vivid sense of the urgency of the original mission that had brought their parents and grandparents to New England. As the "formulations of the first two decades" lost "their near monopoly position as the fulcrum for their members' imaginative lives," New Englanders seemed—to themselves—to be irresistibly carried "away from the original dedication to holiness and the will of God." The crown's assumption of control over New England in 1684 effectively shattered "any lingering sense among the colonists that they formed a special, divinely chosen community."

By that action, the crown at once destroyed the old government that had theoretically "bound the whole community in Covenant with God," rendered impossible any further efforts to enforce a religious orthodoxy by requiring toleration of all Protestant religions, and "left the third generation of settlers with no clear definition of the status" to which their grandparents and even parents had aspired "as the chosen children of God." Subsequently, the founders' prophetic vision of establishing God's city upon a hill became little more than "a pious memory, faithfully recorded by Cotton Mather [and other clergymen] but [largely] exotic to the religious life of the province" as a whole. During the first six decades of the eighteenth century, the idea of New England's special place in God's plan for humankind increasingly lost force and was gradually merged with the more general conception of the entire Anglo-American Protestant world as the bulwark against popery.[8]

Especially during the late seventeenth century, this declining sense of mission, this pervasive feeling of having fallen away from the faith of the fathers, may have contributed to alter still other aspects of the religious landscape of New England. By stirring "severe feelings of inadequacy and insecurity," it may have been largely responsible for driving people more and more "into the terrible wilderness of their own inner selves" and into an excessive preoccupation with the internal strife of the local communities in which they lived. Certainly, the ancient corporate religious impulse was no longer sufficiently strong to provide a vehicle through which communities could join together to contain the astonishing contention and aggression that were vividly manifest in the rise in criminal prosecutions for deviance and in the various witchcraft episodes, especially the one at Salem in 1692–93.[9]

Although, as Perry Miller has emphasized, New England religious culture remained vital and adaptable throughout the years from 1670 to 1730, it lost its former preeminence in community life. Despite some occasional local revivals, the spiritual life of New England seemed to the clergy throughout the first three or four decades of the eighteenth century to have become ever more "shamelessly secular." The continuing diminution of religious concern seemed to be indicated by further declines both in the proportion of the population who were full and active church members and in the authority and status of the clergy and by the persistence of religious discord in many communities. For the first time, moreover, the Anglican church began to make significant inroads among the formerly almost wholly Congregational population. By the 1720s, some prominent ministers had defected to the Anglicans, who by 1770 had seventy-four congregations in New England and counted as many as twenty-five thousand adherents drawn from all segments of the population.[10]

Even more subversive of the old New England way was the moderate acceleration and changing character of the economy during the last half of the seventeenth century. Economic goals had never been absent from the puritan settlements. Despite some religious scruples against excessive profiteering, the colonists had been responsive to economic opportunities from the beginning. If, throughout the seventeenth century, most of them were involved in agriculture, they were successful in producing not only enough food to feed their families but a surplus to exchange for tools and other finished goods that they were unable to produce efficiently themselves and that had to be imported from England or some other major processing center. This surplus, at first primarily grains but increasingly composed of meat, dairy, and orchard products, both sustained a growing non- or semiagricultural population in the coastal seaports that developed to handle the exchange and acted as a stimulus for overseas trade.

In contrast to the early Chesapeake, agricultural produce was not the principal item of trade. By the late 1630s and early 1640s, Boston, Salem, and Charlestown were also developing a vigorous trade in furs, fish, and timber products, including planks, barrel staves, shingles, oars, naval stores, and masts. The fur supply dwindled rapidly by midcentury, and by the mid-1670s the fur trade had declined to insignificance. But the fish and lumber industries expanded to meet the demands of new markets in the West Indies, the Wine Islands, and the Iberian peninsula. Fishing provided far and away the most important export item and employed large numbers of people throughout the colonial period, perhaps never less than 10 percent of the population. By the early eighteenth century in Salem fishing exceeded the value of timber exports, "the second most valuable export," by twelve to one. Because most fish exported had to be processed and packed in barrels, significant local processing industries grew up that provided a livelihood for substantial numbers either in the localities of production or at the points of export. A growing shipbuilding industry emerged along the coast to produce the vessels that carried these products across the seas.[11]

Never a purely subsistence society, the New England colonies were thus from early in their histories and increasingly during the seventeenth century heavily involved in trade. By 1660, it was clear that, to an important extent, the emerging economy of New England, as Terry Anderson has observed, would "be centered around" its "shipping sector and that many institutions" would have "to be developed or changed to meet the needs of a commercial society." The merchants who presided over this process of commercialization became leading agents of change. Aggressively seeking out new markets in North America, the West Indies, England, and Europe, they first acquired and then supplied the capital and managerial expertise needed to link the producers and consumers of the interior towns of New England to the larger world economy, and, when the resource base of the region proved insufficient to support continuous long-term economic growth, they increasingly began to supply "shipping services to major parts of the Atlantic world." By the second and third decades of the eighteenth century, they had thereby "created a well-integrated commercial economy based on the carrying trade."[12]

Nor were the economic activities of this rising commercial elite limited to trade. Especially after King Philip's War in the mid-1670s, they were among the heaviest land speculators and developers, many of them acquiring thousands of acres which they hoped eventually to sell for a profit to people eager to move to new lands. In the rich Connecticut River valley, the Pynchon family, as Stephen Innes has shown, turned Springfield into a company town by engrossing a large proportion of the land and exerting a near monopoly on the region's trade. Owning the only store and all the town's gristmills and sawmills and employing a significant proportion of the adult male population as workmen in their various agricultural, processing, and trading enterprises, the Pynchons presided over a process of progressive social and economic stratification in which by 1680 at least one-half of the adult males in Springfield lived as tenants, renters, and dependents in a socioeconomic system that contrasted sharply with the egalitarian villages envisioned by the first settlers.[13]

As an ever-enlarging circle of towns became involved in producing foodstuffs and other items for export during the last half of the seventeenth century, the hinterlands of both the larger ports and commercialized towns such as Springfield seem to have enjoyed substantial economic growth, to have developed diverse occupational structures, and to have experienced substantial economic stratification. Some experts have suggested that economic growth may have averaged as high as 6 percent per annum in some of the more dynamic areas. At least in Connecticut, Jackson Turner Main has shown, opportunity to acquire wealth actually seems to have declined for several decades after 1660 before it began to rise again in 1690. But for New England as a whole during the second half of the century, it has been estimated that this commercially and demographically driven economic growth contributed between 1650 and 1710 to a substantial rise in per capita real income at an annual rate of about 1.6 percent and to a 295 percent increase in real aggregate economic output. Over the same period, these same areas supported a growing number of artisans and craftsmen, many of whom continued to engage in farming, and exhibited growing concentrations of wealth in the hands of its richest inhabitants. In Salem, for instance, the amount of inventoried wealth owned by the most affluent 10 percent of the population rose from 21 percent before 1661 to 62 percent thereafter.[14]

A far cry from the closed, cohesive, and contained villages originally envisioned by puritan leaders, Boston, Salem, and other ports and commercial towns thus became prosperous mercantile centers with relatively large, concentrated, heterogeneous populations, many new economic opportunities in nonfarm occupations, significant concentrations of wealth in the hands of their leading merchants, marked social and economic distinctions, considerable contact with the outside world, and a rising spirit of enterprise that gradually spread outward to the surrounding countryside. The growing intensity of economic activity and the emerging complexity of social patterns in these dynamic areas of New England operated to undermine the communal unity, corporate and religious orientation, and social goals of the first settlers. In these dynamic areas, the old religious-based corporatism began to give way to the atomistic pursuit of wealth and self-interest.[15]

As Bernard Bailyn has written, the ethos of the mercantile groups that dominated these commercial centers "represented the spirit of a new age. Its guiding principles were not social stability, order, and the discipline of the senses, but mobility, growth, and the enjoyment of life." Among this strategic segment of the population, the desire to "succeed in trade" and emulate the lives of their London trading associates was far "stronger than any counterforce the clergy could exert." Increasingly after 1670, successful merchants and farmers constituted a new economically based elite, which exerted an influence greatly disproportionate to their numbers in the public life of Massachusetts and to a lesser extent in Connecticut, New Hampshire, and Rhode Island. Certainly at the provincial and, in many areas, also at the local levels of government, wealth and property, rather than piety, became the basis for political leadership and participation. Moreover, as rival groups among the elite vigorously competed with one another within the political arena for profits, land, and influence, the old consensual politics gave way to division, conflict, and discord.[16]

Accompanying this contention and discord in public life was a rising volume of litigation, most of it concerning economic issues involving property and debt. Denounced by many contemporaries in the orthodox puritan colonies of Massachusetts and Connecticut as an indication of creeping *"Rhode Islandism,"* this acrimony and divisiveness revealed the long-term ineffectiveness of religious and social communalism as devices to preserve social harmony in communities undergoing substantial demographic and economic growth and social diversification. "The force of ideological commitment alone," Stephen Foster has noted, "could [not] maintain a system of political and social subordination for which the traditional material and institutional bases were lacking."

As David T. Konig has emphasized, however, the founders of New England had never expected to achieve their social vision without viable legal institutions, which they carefully incorporated into the governmental structure during the 1630s. As the force of that original vision continued to attenuate in the face of economic growth and the "intensified resentments of compact town life," Konig shows in his analysis of patterns of litigation in Essex County, Massachusetts, individuals increasingly found it useful "to turn to the outside authority of extratown institutions like the courts" to resolve their differences, and such legal institutions, he persuasively insists, "were to large degree responsible" for Essex County's remaining a "remarkably stable society" throughout the seventeenth century. If, in their passage from "communalism to litigation," the residents of Essex County had become contentious and disunited, they were still fundamentally a "well-ordered people," and, so far from being an indication of social disruption, increasing litigation, Konig contends, was "an agent of orderly social change and economic growth."[17]

Existing largely on the margins of—if by no means entirely cut off from—this increasingly bustling economic and social world, much of rural New England was relatively untouched by these social and economic developments during the seventeenth and early eighteenth centuries. Many inland towns, described by Edward M. Cook as "small, self-contained farming villages," remained comparatively isolated, economically underdeveloped, socially egalitarian, and religiously homogeneous. Certainly during the seventeenth century, all but a few Connecticut towns seem to have belonged to this category: in Jackson Turner Main's words, they were "not very flourishing, predominantly agricultural and middle class, with few large property holders." In these "peaceable kingdoms," traditional institutions of community, family, and church continued to display a vitality that was considerably less evident either in the bustling market centers and seaport towns of New England or in the other Anglo-American colonies, and the corporate impulse probably remained strong.[18]

WITH the further acceleration of the economy as a result of rapid internal population growth and the increasing integration of the New England economy into that of the larger Atlantic area during the early decades of the eighteenth century and especially after 1720, however, more and more of New England was drawn out of a relatively isolated existence and pushed toward greater social differentiation, geographical and economic mobility, and individualism. The vast majority of New Englanders continued to live on farms. Recent scholarship has, however, effectively challenged the ancient myth that these farms were self-sufficient and independent units of production on which yeoman families, concerned with little more than their own security, produced all that was required to meet their needs without the help of additional labor.

As Bettye Hobbs Pruitt has shown in the case of the agricultural society of mid-eighteenth-century Massachusetts, "interdependence rather than self-sufficiency" best describes that society. Although local communities were often self-sufficient, at least in foodstuffs and other primary services, most individual units were not. Only those few farms with relatively large amounts of both labor and land under cultivation did not have to involve themselves in local networks of exchange in which they traded products, labor, and skills simply to meet the subsistence requirements of their families. In this situation, Pruitt emphasizes, "production for home consumption and production for sale or exchange were complementary . . . objectives."[19]

If virtually all New England agricultural communities were thus "not atomistic but integrated" into a series of "local networks of exchange involving all sorts of goods and services," they were also increasingly "linked either directly or through . . . dealings with others" to the larger provincial and Atlantic worlds. New England's rapid demographic growth not only generated dozens of additional rural settlements but also produced significant urbanization. New England had only two major cities: Boston, which, despite a decline in its population and relative importance as a commercial entrepot after 1740, continued to be the region's primary urban center, and Newport, which developed impressively after 1710. As the second largest city in New England, Newport had more than two-thirds as many people as Boston by 1775.

After 1715 and increasingly during the boom years of the 1740s and 1750s, however, a large number of towns, many of which had been little more than hamlets through most of the seventeenth century, developed into important secondary commercial centers. These included seaports—Portsmouth in New Hampshire; Salem, Marblehead, and Gloucester in Massachusetts; Providence in Rhode Island; and New Haven, New London, and Norwich in Connecticut—and inland commercial and administrative centers—Worcester and Springfield in Massachusetts and Hartford and Middletown in Connecticut. Perhaps another two to three dozen places were urbanized by 1770.[20]

To a significant extent, this urbanization was a function not merely of growing population but also of a steady expansion of external trade. Although New England's exports were relatively unimpressive compared to those of all the other regions of colonial British America, they were nonetheless substantial and underwent "an enormous expansion" during the century from 1660 to 1760. Not including the coastal trade, which may have accounted for as much as 40 percent of the value of its total trade, New England annually exported products worth almost £440,000 by 1770. Fish accounted for around 35 percent of the whole; livestock, beef, and pork for 20 percent; wood products, 15 percent; whale products, 14 percent; potash and grain products, 5 percent each; rum, 4 percent; and a variety of other items for the remaining 2 percent. Far and away the largest proportion of this trade—63 percent—went to the West Indies. Britain and Ireland with 19 percent and southern Europe with 15 percent were second and third, and Africa with only 3 to 4 percent was a distant fourth.[21]

Though the growing populations that inhabited New England's increasing number of urban places produced some of their own food and necessities, they all required significant supplements of both food and timber products. Together with the demand for those products for export to the West Indies and elsewhere, these requirements produced a lively commercial exchange between town and country, which were more and more linked together by a proliferating network of roads, bridges, and ferries. This exchange in turn helped to raise levels of agricultural production and to stimulate timber industries in the countryside, first in the immediate vicinities of the towns and then in areas farther away. By the mid-eighteenth century, as Pruitt has remarked, few New England "communities existed wholly beyond the reach of [these] market forces" and most were inextricably tied into, and deeply affected by, not just the local regional markets with which they had long been associated but also "the larger provincial and Atlantic economies of which they were a part."[22]

Compared with their counterparts in the Chesapeake and elsewhere in colonial British America, eighteenth-century New England farmers were, perhaps, "not highly commercialized." Yet the commercialization of agriculture and the expansion of the fishing, timber, and whaling industries in response to growing internal and external demand had a significant impact on the social landscape of the region. That impact can be seen clearly in the development of regional specialization. Of course, fishing and whaling had always been confined to the coast, the former concentrated in the area north of Boston and the latter in the coastal and island area along the southeastern coast of Massachusetts.

During the seventeenth century, most other products had been diffused throughout the region. As time went on, however, the timber industry came to center in New Hampshire and Maine, grain production tended to concentrate in the breadbasket areas of the Connecticut River valley and in Middlesex and eastern Worcester County in Massachusetts, grazing and livestock production in hilly and rocky regions and along the southern coast of New England, and dairying in areas near urban centers. The Narragansett region of Rhode Island was particularly noted for its large estates, which concentrated on raising stock, especially horses, and dairy farming.[23]

Although a few farmers in eighteenth-century New England—the Narragansett planters and the owners of the larger farms in the rich Connecticut River valley and along the southern coast of New England—seem to have "crossed a line where commercial production brought sufficient returns to warrant a preponderant investment" in large landed estates and market crops, the principal beneficiary of the growing commercialization of New England seems to have been the expanding service sector of society. To an important extent the result of the population's strenuous and purposeful efforts to wrest economic returns from disadvantageous circumstances as well as an indication of the growing economic and social diversity of the region, this development led to an increasingly complex occupational structure that provided new opportunities for young men who did not inherit land or did not want to stay on the farm. Most numerous of these service occupations were the artisans and craftsmen ranging, in status and wealth, from shoemakers, tailors, and weavers at the bottom through coopers, carpenters, and joiners in the middle up to millers and tanners at the top. The last two often operated comparatively large-scale enterprises. Representatives of all these occupations could be found in rural as well as urban areas. But some more specialized artisans—shipwrights, distillers, silversmiths, printers, and rope and iron manufacturers—rarely resided outside the larger towns. Out of this proliferating body of skilled artisans derived the well-known New

England penchant for mechanical ingenuity that during the closing decades of the eighteenth century would make such a powerful contribution to the beginnings of industrial change in the new American republic.[24]

Two other groups, merchants and professionals, also expanded in numbers, wealth, and influence in the increasingly diverse society of eighteenth-century New England. The mercantile group, consisting of large overseas traders, shipowners, ship captains, shopkeepers, and peddlers, was increasingly complex and prosperous. The large overseas merchants who organized and presided over the region's commerce with the outside world and, as in the case of Rhode Island slave traders, provided freight and shipping services for other areas of the Atlantic commercial world were usually the richest people in the region. Professionals—ministers, doctors, and lawyers—were far fewer in number. But the last two became more numerous during the eighteenth century, and lawyers were more and more often among the wealthiest and most influential inhabitants. Together with some prominent officeholders, the wealthier lawyers, overseas merchants, and inland traders played an entrepreneurial role in New England's economic development and profited disproportionately from it. Often among the investors in industrial enterprises such as shipbuilding, distilling, and iron production, they were also frequently involved as land speculators in the development of new towns on the eastern, northern, and western frontiers.[25]

The acceleration and growing complexity of the economy during the eighteenth century also helped to produce and reinforce a more typically British social structure. The comparative economic equality that had characterized much of early New England had never obtained in Boston, where from the late seventeenth century onward the concentration of wealth remained relatively high and relatively stable over time, with the wealthiest 30 percent of property holders possessing around 85 percent of the town's private wealth. By contrast, during the eighteenth century, rural areas experienced a slow but steady growth in the concentration of property until by the 1760s and 1770s the richest 30 percent owned between 65 and 75 percent of the total wealth. In urban areas, this trend toward the consolidation of wealth was even more pronounced, with towns like Portsmouth, Salem, Newport, Providence, New Haven, and Hartford already moving powerfully toward Boston levels by the early decades of the century.

Although in comparison with most of the rest of the British American world, the wealthiest men in late colonial New England enjoyed only "moderate rather than large fortunes," had fewer servants and slaves, lived less genteelly, and had to share political office with men "entirely lacking in family connections and large estates," some individuals, especially in the towns, managed to accumulate impressive wealth. In New Hampshire, for instance, only two estates probated before 1740 were valued at more than £3,000 in New Hampshire old tenor currency, but twenty-one people who went through probate between 1741 and 1760 and twenty-seven between 1761 and 1770 had estates that exceeded that amount. Indeed, the wealthiest decedents after 1740 greatly exceeded that figure. The estate of Ebenezer Smith, who died in 1764, was valued at just over £90,000, that of John Gilman in 1751 at nearly £48,000, and that of Nicholas Gilman in 1749 at just under £34,000. Three other decedents had estates valued at over £20,000 and twelve others at over £10,000.[26]

If few New Englanders enjoyed such impressive wealth, those who did aspired, as did the Chesapeake gentry, to recreate the genteel culture of contemporary Britain. To that end, they built larger and more commodious houses and filled them with English and Continental furnishings and other fashionable consumer items, made charitable bequests, filled their towns with impressive public buildings, created a host of urban voluntary associations, and otherwise sought to reproduce the urban amenities of British provincial cities. The elite of Newport, where the old puritan sanctions against conspicuous consumption were less powerful, could carry this process farther than its counterparts in either Boston or smaller cities in the orthodox puritan colonies of Massachusetts and Connecticut. Everywhere, however, elite behavior in New England was calculated to reinforce the traditional prescriptive association among wealth, social status, and political authority.[27]

To an increasing extent during the eighteenth century, New England's wealthy inhabitants also monopolized public office. To be sure, patterns of officeholding in many small agricultural towns remained relatively egalitarian throughout the century. But towns with more developed economic structures showed a powerful tendency toward oligarchy, with a handful of wealthy and prominent families, often as few as one to three, dominating both appointed and elective offices. In most towns, these family political dynasties were based on long association with the town's history. But in the few towns in which a coherent and continuous elite had been slow to develop—Marblehead provides one example and, perhaps, Portsmouth, New Hampshire, another—a significant number of relative newcomers could be found among the eighteenth-century elite. In large towns like Boston and Newport, the structure of local elites was too complex, too open, and too broadly based and economic power was too often independent of political power to permit such heavy concentrations of political power in a few families. Whatever the local variations, however, most commercially oriented towns displayed a strong correlation between wealth and officeholding. The growing number of Anglicans who held political office in communities where they were numerous testifed to the diminishing importance of Congregational church membership in New England public life.[28]

Increasing concentrations of wealth and the solidification of an economic and familial elite were also accompanied by the spread of both slavery and poverty. Slavery was a direct function of growing wealth. From early in the settlement of New England, there had been a few Indian and black slaves. As late as 1690, however, there were fewer than a thousand blacks—about 1 percent of the total population—in the entire region. Over the next three decades, they increased slowly if steadily to over six thousand, or about 3 percent of the total population. Though their numbers continued to increase to over fifteen thousand by the early 1770s and though slavery was still an expanding institution in all the New England colonies on the eve of the American Revolution, the proportion of blacks in the population remained steady at around 3 percent for the rest of the colonial period.

But these aggregate figures mask much greater concentrations of slaves in the more commercialized areas, particularly in the port towns, where they served as domestics, artisans, watermen, dock workers, and emblems of conspicuous consumption for urban elites. Although Jackson Turner Main is certainly right to point out that there were few incentives to develop a plantation-style agriculture with a large servile labor force in most parts of New England and although most rural slaves were distributed in small numbers of one or two among farm families for whom they performed agricultural or household labor, they were present in more substantial numbers on many of the commercial plantations in the Narragansett country of Rhode Island, where some estates employed as many as twenty slaves as stockmen and in the dairy industry. Indeed, as Louis Masur has emphasized, "slavery flourished in eighteenth-century Rhode Island." Slaves made up as much as 18 percent of the population of Newport in 1755, and as many as 30 percent of white households in several Rhode Island towns in 1774 "contained slaves or blacks bonded in some manner." For the colony as a whole, 14 percent of households owned slaves. Without dispute, these figures represent "a substantial commitment to the institution." If New England as a whole was not heavily dependent on slave labor, as were colonies farther south, it certainly condoned slavery, and it contained a few areas that had concentrations of slaves roughly comparable to those in the Chesapeake during the early period of its transition to a slave plantation system after 1680.[29]

If the increasing social stratification of New England during the eighteenth century provided some families with the wherewithal to live a genteel life and to own slaves, it does not seem to have resulted in a manifest proletarianization of the population. To be sure, as Charles Grant, Kenneth Lockridge, and several other historians have observed, by the third and fourth generations in most towns vigorous demographic growth rendered existing land resources inadequate to enable many families to provide a viable farm for each of their male offspring. As a result, there was a sharp increase in the number of young adult males with minimal property. By the mid-eighteenth century, as many as a third of the adult males in most communities were landless laborers. As Jackson Turner Main has shown in the case of Connecticut, however, this situation was very largely a function of age. Typically, laborers were young men who were either waiting to inherit land from their fathers or preparing themselves to enter a craft, profession, or trade, and those who found inadequate opportunity within their own communities simply joined the stream of immigrants to new settlements or to urban areas.

Whichever of these choices they made, Main has found, laboring was, for the vast majority of whites, only "a temporary line of work." If more and more young men began adult life with few assets, almost all of them could expect to obtain property "as they passed through the life cycle," and the "great majority of Connecticut's people fared as well in 1774 as in 1700 or 1670." "By contrast with most pre-industrial societies," Main concludes, "virtually all of the married men and their families . . . did not simply escape poverty but enjoyed real plenty."

Main's findings have been reinforced by work on the changing diet of colonial New England by Sarah F. McMahon, who has found that changes in land use and improvements in food production and preservation over the course of the colonial period meant that the region produced enough food so that few families could fail to enjoy a "comfortable subsistence."[30]

Yet this is not to suggest that eighteenth-century New England knew no poverty. Poor relief had been a feature of New England life from the beginning, and it increased visibly during the eighteenth century as population growth, personal misfortune, the typically high loss of males in a seafaring economy, and other factors arising out of the increasingly complex character of New England society produced, in both city and country, an expanding class of both transient poor in search of employment and impoverished people unable to care for themselves. The towns dealt with this problem either by "warning out" nonresidents or by providing public relief for residents. But the costs of placing poor people in families or caring for them in almshouses became so high in major urban centers that several of them— Newport in the 1720s, Boston in the late 1730s, Providence and other towns in the 1750s and 1760s—built workhouses in an effort to make the able-bodied poor pay for themselves.

The extent of poverty in New England is easy to exaggerate. A close examination of the ranks of the poor reveals that they contained a small number of adult male heads of households. The vast majority seem to have fallen into one of two principal categories: first, young unemployed single men and women who, if Main's findings for Connecticut can be extended to the rest of New England, presumably eventually found employment and rose out of the ranks of the poor, and, second, members of traditionally dependent groups—widows, the aged, the sick, the disabled, and orphans, only the last of which could usually be expected ever to escape their dependence upon the community for support. Yet, though transiency and poverty were increasing all over New England in the eighteenth century, they were still far below levels exhibited in contemporary British or European cities. With never more than 5 to 7 percent of a given locality's population receiving poor relief—and in most rural areas much lower a percentage—New Englanders, as David Flaherty has observed, "had only limited experience with poverty in comparison with their fellow coun-

try men in Great Britain," where as "much as one-third of the . . .
population may not have been able to feed and clothe themselves
adequately."[31]

Along with the continuing internalization of puritan religious constraints and a "high standard of law enforcement," students of legal
records have cited this relative lack of poverty as at least part of the
explanation for a low incidence of serious crime in New England.
Roger Thompson found in his study of sexual misbehavior in Middlesex County, Massachusetts, that throughout the last half of the seventeenth century "New Englanders in general . . . were markedly
more law-abiding" than English people in the home islands. Although
crimes involving fornication, "by far the largest part of the criminal
business" of local sessions courts, were being progressively and "effectively decriminalized" during the eighteenth century, the "rate of
prosecution for crimes of violence, sexual offenses, and miscellaneous
crimes," David Flaherty found in the case of Massachusetts, was far
higher than in England. But a much lower incidence of crimes against
property, traditionally associated with poverty, meant that the per
capita crime rate in Massachusetts was 43 percent lower than that in
Essex County, England, and far below that in London.[32]

But a low crime rate did not betoken inactivity on the part of the
courts. At least in Massachusetts, civil litigation increased dramatically
throughout the eighteenth century. Though inhabitants of some more
isolated communities continued to eschew the courts and to try to
resolve differences through the church or the town government, litigation rose steadily and at a much faster rate in rural areas than in towns,
and there was a marked increase in the number of cases involving
disputes across town boundaries. An indication of the penetration of
the commercial economy into the countryside, the growing interdependence between urban and rural areas, and the further attenuation
of the consensual communalism of the founders, these developments,
together with low crime rates and high prosecution rates for criminal
offenses, provide powerful testimony to both the public acceptance
and the efficacy of the courts as "instruments of social control."[33]

Increasing civil litigation may have been linked to a general "wither-
ing of traditional parental and community control." The first generation of rural New Englanders founded remarkably stable and closely
integrated communities around a base of strong patriarchal families.

The second generation put down even deeper roots and developed a series of complex and overlapping extended kinship networks within the community. By the third generation, however, which came to maturity in the early eighteenth century, and certainly by the fourth generation, which reached adulthood beginning in the 1730s and 1740s, the pressure of population growth, the decreasing availability of land, the opening up of new towns, and the emergence of many new opportunities for young men outside agriculture in an increasingly varied occupational structure all contributed to a significant diminution of patriarchal authority and loosening of family ties.

As evidence of these changes, historians have noted a rising proportion of impartible inheritances, a tendency to convey land to sons at earlier ages, a steady increase in the outmigration of sons, a sharp drop in the age of marriage among both men and women, a major rise in daughters marrying out of the birth order, a diminution of parental control in marriage and a corresponding rise in the importance of romantic love in mate selection, a surge in premarital pregnancy, a shift away from parent-naming and Bible-naming, the provision of more space—and hence more privacy—for individual members of households, and perhaps even a rise in the number of female offenders in the courts. Along with an apparent improvement in the status of women as suggested by "their more frequent petitions for divorce and their greater success in obtaining it," all of these developments have been interpreted as indications that the circumstances of eighteenth-century New England life were forcing fathers and husbands to redefine their roles, changing the character of the family, and helping to accelerate a powerful process of individuation among children and young adults.

The effects of these changes on the basic character of New England life were profound. No longer "patriarchs grandly presiding over an ancestral estate and minutely controlling the lives of their sons and heirs," fathers now tended to act as "benefactors responsible for the future well-being and prosperity of their offspring." At the same time, the tendency for parents to find fulfillment "in the success of their children" has been alleged to have produced a "new and different type of family life . . . characterized by solicitude and sentimentality towards children and by more intimate, personal, and equal relationships" among members. Finally, this new "organization of family life contributed to the emergence of a liberated individual, a person who was exempt from all except voluntary ties to the family of his birth and free to achieve his own goals."[34]

By further undermining the coercive power of the old socioreligious regime that the founders of the orthodox puritan colonies had set out to implement and thereby opening up New England society, increasing population growth and the changing character of religious, economic, social, and familial life provided, as Richard L. Bushman has argued, the necessary preconditions for nothing less than a behavioral revolution that stretched over and had a transforming effect on all but the least dynamic areas of the region. Far from merely playing a passive role, people became active agents in this process. Increasingly ignoring traditional ideological and social restraints, they turned energies formerly devoted to religious and community endeavors to their own private pursuits of personal and individual happiness.

By encouraging a considerable amount of autonomous and aggressively competitive behavior, this behavioral revolution also provided identity models and standards of personal conduct for the society at large that stood at marked variance with the original values of the leaders of the founding generation. No longer was the moral and psychological necessity of obedience to the authority of the community and its traditional leaders—magistrates, pastors, and fathers—automatically assumed. Rather, contemporary models of behavior emphasized the authority of self rather than of the community; individual economic achievement and success rather than ascriptive criteria for political leadership and social status; the fulfillment, privacy, and comfort of the individual rather than self-denial in favor of the common good; and the "capacity of the individual to direct his own existence rather than . . . an unquestioning response to public morality." With this behavioral revolution, the pursuit of wealth and gentility became as important as the pursuit of salvation and even more important than the pursuit of consensus and community.[35]

If all of these developments combined to push New England in the direction of greater individualism, personal autonomy, and social fluidity, the revolution in behavior they exemplified was by no means universal. Nor did it produce a social environment that could be exclusively characterized in terms of "fluid, unstable social relations [that were] conducive [only] to individual mobility and a competitive ethos." Not just rural areas like those described by Michael Zuckerman and Christopher Jedrey but also urban communities continued, throughout the colonial period, to show remarkable stability in family life and to exhibit many other powerful residues of their puritan cultural inheritance. "Rather than being at odds with the ideals of Puritanism or the ends of communitarianism," Christine Heyrman argues in her study of eighteenth-century Salem and Marblehead, "commercial capitalism coexisted with and was molded by the cultural patterns of the past." As Heyrman shows, New England communities could become more populous, stratified, complex, diverse, and mobile without lapsing into social disorder. In Salem and Marblehead, at least, civic consciousness, deference to leaders and institutions, church membership, "traditional patterns of association," and, perhaps, family authority remained strong. The abiding power of these traditional elements of the old puritan social order, Heyrman plausibly contends, testifies to both the resilience of that order and the enduring authority of inherited beliefs and values.[36]

Certainly, the revolution in behavior suggested by the growing evidence of increasing individuation had not yet been accompanied by a revolution in values. In their quest for land and wealth, men might challenge traditional leaders and established institutions. But they could not challenge so easily the old system of values that deplored both self-oriented behavior and resistance to authority. Notwithstanding the continuing strength of so many aspects of the old social order, the increasingly palpable divergence between the values attached to that order and individual behavior produced a gnawing guilt that was evident in persistent demands, especially from the clergy, for a return to the traditional imperatives of community and obedience to authority. The fear that excessively atomistic behavior would lead to social chaos and loss of control and the belief that man could not tolerate freedom without strong societal restraints were still too deeply embedded in cultural consciousness and too easily activated to permit the development of an alternative morality that would more accurately reflect the new modes of behavior.

Although the old millennial impulses of the founders had been severely attenuated by the latter decades of the seventeenth century, they had been "replaced by a conservative determination to perpetuate the symbols and institutions of the colonial founders." Cotton Mather and others engaged in what Robert Pope has referred to as "an oppressive filiopietism that transformed the founding generations into paragons of social virtue, wisdom, and saintliness," who were constantly held up as a model for later generations and as a contrast that provided a framework for the interpretation of American puritan history as a process of steady declension. The guilt felt by later generations over this declension and the disjuncture between the values of the founders and their own behavior made men, as several scholars have suggested, peculiarly susceptible to the atavistic appeals of the midcentury Great Awakening, the first large-scale religious revival in American history.[37]

Though the Great Awakening helped those men most deeply affected by it to cleanse themselves of guilt by throwing off their worldly ambitions, it did not result in a return to the old communal mode and the old values. Instead, as Bushman and other scholars have shown, it intensified religious divisions. Although some communities managed to contain those divisions within the existing church, many others split into rival congregations, thereby shattering all hope of religious unity. Such developments and the bitter enmity they engendered further undermined the authority of the church and the clergy and made it clear that "revivalism, the ministry's favorite panacea [for the restoration of the old puritan social order], could no longer be counted on to preserve [communal] order and harmony." Because they inevitably spilled over into politics and brought into the open personal and factional animosities that had previously operated beneath the surface of public life, the religious disputes generated by the Awakening also helped to transform politics by legitimizing factionalism and contention in the public realm and thereby weakening the traditional deference accorded magistrates.

The egoistical impulses and frank pursuit of self-interest set free by the Awakening seemed to New England leaders of all persuasions to portend only social and political chaos. Many of them demanded a return to the old social order and decried attempts by a few "worldly individuals" to develop a new conception of the social order that, by giving "self-interest . . . a free rein" and making "the satisfaction of human desires the main end of government," would once again bring values and behavior into harmony. At best, however, such people were fighting a delaying action. Already by the mid-eighteenth century, the expansive impulses in New England economic and religious life had sufficiently "relaxed the restraints of men's feelings and actions" and sapped the authority of traditional social institutions that they had significantly altered the nature of social life and the character of the inhabitants. That the spread of autonomous behavior did not immediately lead to social chaos did, however, enable New Englanders to live with the behavioral revolution even when they could not bring themselves to endorse it.[38]

DESPITE the enduring vitality of so many aspects of the original puritan social order, New England changed dramatically between 1660 and 1760. Far more populous and more densely settled and stretching over a far larger area, it had a much more complex economy. Less reliant on family agriculture and more heavily involved in trade, it had developed several important urban areas that were closely linked by an already well-articulated transportation and marketing network with the countryside, many parts of which were engaged in more specialized and market-oriented agriculture and small-scale processing and natural resource manufacturing. Except perhaps in some isolated rural areas, its society was considerably more differentiated with greater extremes between the richest and poorest inhabitants and a more complex occupational structure. That society was also far less cohesive and solidary as the social agencies of church, community, and family had all become much less coercive and the individuation process had become considerably more powerful.

In the words of Perry Miller, this "progression of the communities from primitive simplicity to complexity and diversity . . . irresistibly" carried New England "away from the original dedication to holiness and the will of God." In the process, not only, as Miller suggested, did religion become less central to the lives of its people but also the strength of the corporate impulse that had been so powerfully manifest during the first and even second generations of settlement was sapped and the old puritan social order greatly loosened. As New England society became both more complex and looser, it also lost many of the distinctive features it had exhibited during the seventeenth century. Although it may be an exaggeration to say, as have John J. McCusker and Russell R. Menard, that by the late colonial period the region's well-integrated agricultural and commercial society "resembled nothing so much as old England itself," through the long process of social change over the previous hundred years it had certainly become by the middle decades of the eighteenth century far more demonstrably English than it had been during the decades immediately after its establishment.[39]

To the extent that these changes can be seen, as so many clerical leaders at the time saw them, as an attenuation of the original puritan social order and can be represented as a decline from the radically traditional world envisioned and, to a remarkable degree, actually achieved, by the founding generations of orthodox puritans, the declension model still provides a plausible framework for describing the social history of colonial New England. As has been suggested above, however, the process of social change in New England during the century after 1660 also involved considerable demographic and economic growth as well as social elaboration, stratification, and consolidation, and such trends can be at best only partially and inaccurately comprehended within a declension model. Whether such a model works even that well for other regions of the early modern British world is the subject of the next four chapters.

Chapter Four

A DEVELOPMENTAL MODEL:
THE CHESAPEAKE, 1660–1760

If, in the century after 1660, the societies of the orthodox puritan colonies seemed to many of their leading figures to be coming apart, those of the Chesapeake colonies appeared to be coming together. Far from conforming to the declension model derived from the experience of New England, they were moving in precisely the opposite direction, becoming more settled, cohesive, and coherent. This pronounced deviation from the pattern of New England makes it obvious that an alternative explanatory framework is necessary to describe the process of historical change in the Chesapeake colonies. A developmental model seems best to suit their experiences between 1660 and 1760. In this model the simplified and inchoate social structures that were so evident in the first two generations of settlement in the Chesapeake slowly gave way through a process of social elaboration during the century after 1660 to a more complex society that more closely resembled that of the metropolitan society of Great Britain. This chapter describes how this model worked in the Chesapeake.

WELL into the last half of the seventeenth century, the Chesapeake continued to be characterized by an excess of men over women, late age of marriage, a high death rate, a rough economic equality among free people, considerable political strife and disunity, and weak social institutions. Those characteristics gave the area an improvisational character that made its claims to an identity as a settled English society seem less than fully persuasive to contemporaries. Nevertheless, Timothy Breen's contention that the Chesapeake colonies "never succeeded in forming a coherent society" during the seventeenth century is certainly a grave overstatement. By the 1660s, the Chesapeake was far less fragile and much more coherent than Breen's statement suggests. During the last quarter of the century, moreover, the Chesapeake lost much of its contingent character as it entered the initial stages of a profound social transformation.[1]

Manifest in virtually all areas of Chesapeake life, this transformation was especially evident in the changing demography of the region. English immigration, still predominantly male, continued strong, more than half of the total number of people who came to the Chesapeake during the seventeenth century arriving between 1660 and 1700. Yet after 1680, as population grew more dense and opportunity for new settlers to acquire land in older settled areas declined, as tobacco prices settled into a long-term depression that persisted for three decades, and as the new post-1650 colonies of Jamaica, the Carolinas, Pennsylvania, New Jersey, and New York became more attractive to prospective settlers, immigration fell from around twenty thousand in the 1660s and 1670s to about sixteen thousand in the 1690s. Simultaneously, improved life expectancy, a more equal sex ratio, and earlier marriages among creoles raised the birthrate, net reproduction nearly equaling deaths by the 1670s and exceeding them by the 1690s. In combination, these developments contributed by the end of the century to a total white population of nearly ninety thousand, a majority of whom were native-born. These same developments also led to a more settled and typically European nuclear family structure, more extended kinship networks, and considerably more compact settlements in all but the most newly occupied areas.[2]

Equally important in the late seventeenth-century transformation of Chesapeake society was the slow displacement of white servitude by black slavery as the predominant form of labor after 1675. Chesapeake tobacco planters did not immediately adopt an almost exclusively slave labor force as had Barbadian sugar planters a generation earlier. As late as 1700, blacks still constituted fewer than one in ten people living in the English-controlled sections of the Chesapeake. By 1690, they predominated in the labor force, but for the next few decades, servitude and slavery seem to have existed side by side. Larger producers moved quickly toward adopting a heavily slave labor system, but most small planters continued to use servants. Nevertheless, by 1710 Chesapeake tobacco culture was "irrevocably wedded to slave labor." White servants continued to be imported throughout the colonial period by small planters to provide general labor and by larger planters to handle skilled and supervisory tasks. But the number of black slaves rose dramatically to meet the labor needs of an expanding tobacco culture. By 1720, they made up a quarter of the population. By 1740, this figure had risen to nearly 30 percent. By 1760, it had climbed to almost 40 percent, where it remained for the rest of the eighteenth century.

The reasons why the Chesapeake abandoned servitude for slavery between 1680 and 1720 are complex. Doubtless, as Russell Menard has emphasized, a short-term decline in the supply of servants and a corresponding increase in the supply of slaves was of crucial importance initially. Once slavery was established, its economic advantages rapidly became obvious to white planters. To be sure, slaves initially cost more than servants, which is probably the most important reason why small planters lagged behind large ones in moving from servitude to slavery. But this early cost differential gradually lessened as the price of servants rose during the early decades of the eighteenth century. Slaves did not leave at the end of a short set term; they cost less to maintain; they may have been more skilled at agricultural labor than many white servants; and, as tobacco growers increasingly came to appreciate, within a few decades they added to their masters' wealth through their offspring.[3]

As Edmund S. Morgan and Timothy Breen have pointed out, the transition to slavery carried with it important social as well as economic benefits. After 1660, at the expiration of their indentures, white freedmen were faced with diminishing prospects for acquiring land and achieving upward mobility in the Chesapeake and became restless and discontented. Some of them participated in a servant uprising in 1663. Others apparently provided ready recruits during Bacon's Rebellion in 1675–76, the largest and most violent political revolt in any of England's American colonies during the seventeenth century; the tobacco cutting riots of 1683; and, to a considerably lesser extent, the Protestant Rebellion against proprietors in Maryland in 1688. Though it scarcely seems to have been deliberate policy, the substitution of slavery for servitude, along with the opening up of new areas of settlement in the Chesapeake and elsewhere, was instrumental in resolving the continuous social threat posed by the proliferation of young white free men. By the 1690s, as Breen has emphasized, fear of servant or lower-class white revolt, which had been prevalent in the Chesapeake during the previous forty years, had been replaced by fear of slave rebellion. Along with the racism that accompanied it, slavery and the fears it produced thus gradually created profound pressures toward white solidarity that led to a variety of elite concessions to the lower orders, a diminution of lower-class hostility toward the rich, and a common identity that linked whites of all social classes.[4]

Since their introduction into the Chesapeake in 1619, blacks had been relegated to a lower status than whites. For the next half century, their numbers had been few, and, despite white prejudice, the line between them and white servants was often blurred, blacks and whites were not rigorously segregated, and the benefits of white society were not automatically closed to them on grounds of race. At least a few blacks found their way to freedom, acquired land and property, and enjoyed civil rights roughly comparable to those of free whites. But their position deteriorated rapidly after 1670 as their numbers grew. As slaveowners systematically reduced their slaves to the status of a permanent labor force, the Chesapeake became a caste society organized along racial lines in which all white people, regardless of wealth or status, occupied a superior position to all blacks, even the very few blacks who subsequently managed to escape slavery.[5]

In addition to growing population density, family and neighborhood development, and the transition to slavery, the contemporaneous rise of a native elite contributed to make the Chesapeake a more settled and coherent society. At least into the 1690s, patterns of political and social life were comparable to those that characterized the family. Low life expectancy and the small proportion of immigrants with much political experience inevitably meant that officeholding at all levels was distinguished by considerable discontinuity, lack of sustained and qualified leadership, and failure to develop a governing elite capable of perpetuating itself from one generation to another. As a result, a "continuing progression of relatively young men, almost exclusively first-generation settlers," presided over public affairs in the Chesapeake. If the "prolonged ascendancy of immigrants" constituted a "striking feature" of its political life, the fragmented character of this elite was of comparable importance. With little sense of political unity, elites in the counties were riven by factionalism, and those at the provincial level were brittle and prone to being split asunder, as Bacon's Rebellion in Virginia and the Protestant Rebellion in Maryland so powerfully revealed. With such fragmentation, the seventeenth-century Chesapeake elite was incapable not only of achieving long-term social order but also of either establishing the legitimacy of its own claims to authority or generating any "positive symbols" or "historical myths strong enough to overcome individual differences."

The emergence of a creole majority among the Chesapeake elite after 1690 was one of the first changes in this situation. The earlier, discontinuous immigrant elite had been primarily interested in making fortunes and returning to England as quickly as material circumstances would permit. Stung by metropolitan condescension and anxious about the Chesapeake's almost wholly unsavory reputation in England, members of the new creole elite self-consciously set about trying to make the area more recognizably English and threw themselves into its "improvement" with a public spiritedness and a sense of community and corporate responsibility that had been rare among earlier generations. They established the new planned and more self-consciously authoritative and elegant capital cities of Annapolis and Williamsburg, sought to stimulate further urban development, founded the College of William and Mary in Williamsburg, actively cultivated a richer public life, and attempted to make existing political and religious institutions more vigorous and more responsive. Robert Beverley, a member of Virginia's new creole elite, even wrote his *History of Virginia*, which provided that colony "with a sense of permanence and legitimacy . . . it had never before possessed."[6]

By these and other actions Chesapeake creoles manifested their commitment to the places of their nativity and finally provided some of the most essential foundations for both the development of "a recognizable, hereditary provincial elite" during the first half of the eighteenth century and the achievement of that proud sense of place and preeminence displayed by Virginians during the late colonial and revolutionary years. Beginning in the 1720s, a substantial expansion and diversification of the economy that continued for nearly fifty years combined with the earlier emergence of a native-born majority and the transition to a slave system to make Chesapeake society far less fragile and far more cohesive than it had been during its first century.

This expansion can be seen most clearly in the tobacco trade. After a long period of stagnation during the first quarter of the eighteenth century, tobacco exports to Britain, stimulated by low prices and an expanding reexport trade to the Continent and financed by the credit sustained by that trade, rose by more than 250 percent in total volume between 1725 and 1775. From an annual average of just under 30 million pounds in the 1720s, tobacco exports increased to over 100,000 million pounds during the early 1770s.[7]

More and more after 1730, however, labor resources in the Chesapeake were being channeled into grain production to meet an unprecedented demand for food among the growing populations of Europe and the West Indies, and tobacco profits were being supplemented by those from grain exports. Well before the end of the seventeenth century, the Chesapeake colonies had achieved self-sufficiency in foodstuffs and were exporting small quantities of corn and wheat. By the late 1730s, Virginia alone was annually producing a sufficient surplus to enable it to export 122,433 bushels of corn and 35,428 bushels of wheat with a combined value of £11,500. Over the next three decades, grain exports increased dramatically, corn exports rising 4.6 times to 566,672 bushels and wheat 11 times to 403,328 bushels.

These quantities constituted a significant proportion of grain exports for the whole of the British-American colonies: Virginia exported between 3.5 and 4 times as much corn and at least a fifth as much wheat as did the "grain colonies" of Pennsylvania, New Jersey, and New York. By the early 1770s, the combined annual average value of Virginia's grain exports, including nearly 3,000 tons of bread and flour, was over £130,000. This sum, which does not include figures for Maryland (which probably produced even more grain per capita than Virginia), was almost equal to a third of the average annual value of all Chesapeake tobacco exports. Accounting for roughly a quarter of the total value of agricultural exports, grain production was certainly the most dynamic element in the Chesapeake economy between 1735 and 1775. In all probability, it made the difference between a slowly growing or even a stagnating and a vigorously expanding economy.[8]

Rising grain exports were by no means the only index of economic development and diversification in the Chesapeake colonies during the late colonial period. By the late 1760s, Virginia was exporting nearly 3,000 tons of flour and bread annually, an indication of the initiation of a strong milling industry that would eventually center in the northern Chesapeake and make Baltimore the leading flour market in the United States by the end of the century. Even earlier, between 1716 and 1733, the Chesapeake colonies had begun to produce significant amounts of pig iron. By the 1730s, they were exporting nearly 2,200 tons per year to Britain, more than thirteen times as much as the Middle Colonies of Pennsylvania and New York combined. By the early 1750s, the Middle Colonies were beginning to close the gap but still exported only about a fifth of an annual Chesapeake average in excess of 2,500 tons. Nor were these export figures more than a fraction of total production, as much as three-fourths of which was probably consumed in a growing domestic market. In addition to flour, bread, and iron, shipbuilding also emerged as an important industry in response to the stimulus of the burgeoning coastwise trade in grains. Along with some naval stores and beef and pork deriving from southern Virginia and North Carolina and vended through Norfolk, the expansion of tobacco, grain, iron, and ship production kept per capita export values for the Chesapeake colonies well above those for other areas of British North America throughout the middle decades of the eighteenth century. In the early 1770s, those values exceeded those for the "colonies of the lower south by 16 per cent; the middle colonies by 64 per cent; and the New England colonies by 112 per cent."[9]

The Chesapeake's long-term economic expansion and diversification in turn helped sustain and was also the product of a dramatic rise in population. Although the proportion of the total population of British North America living in the Chesapeake declined slowly during the eighteenth century from a high of 36 percent in 1710, it hovered around a third through the 1730s and 1740s and still exceeded 30 percent as late as 1770. Reduced mortality, improved life expectancy, and more rapid family formation in older settled areas combined, especially after 1720, with steady immigration from the Middle Colonies into newly opened lands in the Piedmont and tramontane areas to swell the number of people. From around 90,000 in 1700, white population jumped to almost 160,000 in 1730, around 225,000 in 1750, and nearly 400,000 in 1770.

The number of blacks also increased very rapidly. From just over 30,000 in 1710, it rose to almost 50,000 in 1730, just under 145,000 in 1750, and about 250,000 in 1770. By the 1740s, a significant proportion of this growth in the black population was the result of natural increase, as the Chesapeake became the first major American slave society to experience a net natural increase in its slave population. But imports, very largely directly from Africa, also continued high. Stimulated by a rising demand for additional labor to man the expanding staple economy and financed by profits and credit deriving from proliferating exports, slave imports fluctuated considerably from one year to the next and exceeded more than a few hundred in only five years between 1752 and 1770. But for most years from 1732 to 1752, they averaged in excess of two thousand per annum, probably exceeded three thousand in at least five years, and may have reached as high as forty-five hundred in 1736.[10]

Economic and demographic expansion joined with the lure of cheap land to extend the area of settlement in the Chesapeake to the Allegheny Mountains and beyond by the early 1770s. People from eastern Virginia moved up the James, Rappahannock, and Potomac river valleys into the Piedmont after 1713 and into the southside, the region south and west of the James River, in the late 1720s. By the close of the 1730s, they were pushing across the Blue Ridge Mountains into the Shenandoah Valley, where they mixed with a flood of immigrants pouring south from the Middle Colonies. Between 1721 and 1776, forty-two new counties, thirty-six in Virginia and six in Maryland, were formed, nine in the 1720s and 1730s, twenty in the 1740s and 1750s, and thirteen between 1760 and 1776. A few were subdivisions of older counties in the east. But over 90 percent were in the newly settled areas in the west.

By bringing vast areas not particularly well suited for traditional tobacco culture under occupation and drawing thousands of new people from different ethnic and religious groups into the Chesapeake, this enormous expansion further contributed to the economic and cultural diversification of Chesapeake society. At the same time, it provided opportunities not only for newcomers but for the surplus population of the older counties, including a growing class of geographically mobile landless people, to pursue the traditional goals of Chesapeake residents: the acquisition of land and independence and the establishment of families. For those few families whose dominant economic and political position gave them access to public lands, it offered significant new opportunities to acquire wealth through land speculation and development. Beginning especially after 1713 in both Virginia and Maryland, well-connected families acquired huge grants for hundreds of thousands of acres in undeveloped areas in the west and south. Although they retained some of these acres for their offspring, they intended most for rent or sale.[11]

Nor was the development of the Chesapeake during the eighteenth century merely extensive. With economic diversification came regional specialization. Tobacco continued to predominate in the center of the region, in the broad area stretching from the James River north across the lower western shore of Maryland and west across the Piedmont to the Blue Ridge. But peripheral areas in the new western settlements and in the inferior tobacco-growing zones south of the James River, on the Eastern Shore, and in the northernmost counties of Maryland more and more concentrated on grain and other food production.[12]

Partly also as a function of the rising importance of grain and partly as a result of growing population density, the social landscape of the Chesapeake changed remarkably in a variety of ways between 1700 and 1775. Though the vast majority of people continued to live on dispersed farms and plantations, settlements gradually became far less scattered and the size of households considerably larger. Although the landless continued to be highly mobile, the landowning population after 1720 became far more rooted, kinship networks much deeper and more extensive, and feelings of community and identification with neighborhood and locality presumably much more pronounced.[13]

No longer confined to areas adjacent to navigable streams, settlements and localities were knit together by an ever more intricate overland transportation network of roads, bridges, and ferries over which a growing number of horses, apparently always the predominant form of transportation in the Chesapeake, pulled an increasing number of carts, wagons, and other vehicles engaged in what by the 1750s was becoming an active interregional commercial exchange. At the same time, the proportion of the population engaged in the service sector of the economy expanded substantially, perhaps reaching as high as 15 percent in many older settled areas by the middle of the eighteenth century. Of particular significance were three separate groups: artisans, including carpenters, builders, coopers, tailors, blacksmiths, and leatherworkers, who provided vital economic services to the production of tobacco, grain, and other foodstuffs; merchants and innkeepers, whose stores and ordinaries served as links in an increasingly complex internal economic system and, along with courthouses and churches, as focal points for social exchange; and lawyers, whose technical expertise was necessary for the successful operation of a legal system that had become more and more sophisticated as it tried to cope with a rising volume of litigation over land, debts, and many other commercial transactions.[14]

Although people involved in these service occupations mostly combined them with agricultural pursuits and continued to live in the countryside or in small hamlets, more and more of them could be found in urban settlements following the acceleration of the pace of urban development after 1720. Except for the political capitals of Annapolis and Williamsburg, both established around the turn of the century, most of the new towns initially were small communities along the coast and in the Piedmont whose primary function was to serve as nodes for the collection of tobacco by the new factors of Scottish and English outport mercantile houses who successfully inserted themselves into the tobacco trade during the half century beginning around 1725.

Much more impressive as urban settlements, if still modest compared to Philadelphia, Boston, Newport, and New York, were the series of towns developed on the peripheries of the tobacco region to service the wheat and food economies: Chestertown and Norfolk in the 1720s and 1730s, Frederick and Winchester in the 1740s and 1750s, and Baltimore, Alexandria, Fredericksburg, Richmond, and Petersburg in the 1760s and 1770s. Whereas the tobacco towns had typically contained only a few merchants and craftsmen, these newer towns had much larger populations, performed a fuller range of urban services, and served as centers for an expanding network of villages, communities, and crossroads junctions that now punctuated a landscape that as late as 1710 had been almost entirely rural.[15]

Despite growing occupational diversity and urbanization, the overwhelming majority—80 to 90 percent—of the free population continued to be engaged primarily in agricultural production. Like that of the seventeenth century, eighteenth-century Chesapeake agriculture continued to be dominated by small producers operating on family units with a handful of extra laborers. In the oldest settled areas, between a fifth and a third of all landholders possessed one hundred acres or less, and another one- to two-fifths owned between one hundred and two hundred acres. At the same time, the ranks of small producers were swelled in many areas by a rising number of tenants, most of whom had one hundred acres or less. In one Maryland parish, the number of small tenants increased from around 30 percent of all householders during the early decades of the eighteenth century to around 50 percent in the 1770s.

Moreover, although the number of householders increased dramatically during the century between 1670 and 1770, householders and landholders together usually constituted no more than half of the free adult male population in such areas. Notwithstanding the continuing numerical predominance of servants, laborers, tenants, and small land-holders, the number of middling producers with landholdings of from two hundred to a thousand acres increased substantially over the same period to between a fifth and a third of all landholders by the eve of the American Revolution. At the same time, a larger and larger pro-portion of householders acquired slaves, mostly in small numbers, until by the 1760s over 50 percent of heads of households in many more prosperous localities had slaves.[16]

Along with rising export figures, the growing number of house-holds supported by the economy and the downward diffusion of slav-ery into the social structure provides still further indication of the Chesapeake's growing wealth in the eighteenth century. This develop-ment is even more vividly underlined by a rising volume of imports from Britain and the increased buying power those purchases repre-sented. Between 1730 and 1775, the value of British imports, almost entirely composed of finished products, grew at an average decennial rate of around 35 percent from an average of slightly under £200,000 per annum during the 1720s to nearly £885,000 during the early 1770s, from just under £1 per capita during the 1730s to £1.36 in the 1750s and £1.53 in the early 1770s.

That the Chesapeake's rising wealth was not limited to the more substantial inhabitants is indicated by evidence of improving standards of living at every level of free society. Life was becoming less austere at the bottom, more comfortable in the middle, and reasonably genteel at the top. Through the first three-quarters of the eighteenth century, the mean value of estates at their owners' deaths rose steadily, the number of estates with assets sufficient to cover debts grew from about 25 percent in the 1690s to over 85 percent in the 1750s, and those valued at under £50 declined from almost 60 percent at the beginning of the century to about 35 percent by the time of the American Revolution.

This increased prosperity was reflected in significant capital im-provements in cleared lands, fencing, orchards, livestock, farm build-ings, and family housing and in a wider and more valuable range of material possessions at all levels of free society. Luxuries in the sev-enteenth century—forks, spices, ceramics, and other "items of com-fort and convenience"—had by the late 1750s become commonplace throughout the eastern Chesapeake in "middling as well as wealthy households and increasingly, too, at the bottom." Nor does there ap-pear to have been much poverty among the free population. Though many people continued to live a relatively crude existence and some families, especially tenants in eastern Maryland, may have been falling into living conditions below those of earlier generations, the presence of land and opportunity in the new settlements in the west and south helped to draw off surplus population and prevent the rise of a significant class of permanent laboring poor among the free segment of society, and poverty, as measured by poor relief, was very largely confined to a "handful of permanently destitute individuals" consisting primarily of the sick, disabled, widowed, and orphaned.[17]

NOTWITHSTANDING this general diffusion of wealth, Chesapeake society was becoming more and more sharply differentiated during the eighteenth century. Already during the last four decades of the seventeenth century, inequality was increasing dramatically in older settled areas. By 1700 in such areas the top 10 percent of landowners, who probably never constituted more than 5 percent of the total free adult population, had monopolized from half to two-thirds of the land, and those with little money or influence who hoped to acquire more than modest estates had to move to newer areas. With the transition to slavery, the larger landowners acquired even further advantages over their poorer neighbors. Only they or men with money derived from trade, public office, the law, or inheritance commanded the resources necessary to purchase the large numbers of slaves who contributed so heavily to the growth, largely after 1710, of the many great fortunes and families that dominated the Chesapeake through the middle decades of the eighteenth century.

Even if one includes not only the largest estates—those with several thousand acres of land and at least forty to fifty slaves—but also the merely substantial estates—those with at least a thousand acres and five to ten slaves—this emergent elite constituted only a small fraction of the landowning population—from 2 to 5 percent in most counties. Nevertheless, members of this group controlled close to 50 percent of the total wealth and exerted a disproportionate influence on Chesapeake life. During the first four decades of the eighteenth century, they transformed the spatial and social landscape by establishing the large slave-powered plantations, those diversified and, in a few cases, perhaps even almost self-sufficient communities that quickly became the "principal symbol of Chesapeake society."[18]

During the half century beginning around 1720, the great families who presided over these plantations—the second and third generations of the creole elite that had begun to emerge between 1680 and 1720—consolidated their economic, social, and political position by intermarrying across local political boundaries. In the process, they established a far-ranging and complex network of provincewide, to some extent even regionwide, interrelated, highly visible, and prestigious elite families. As they amassed more and more wealth, they pursued a lifestyle appropriate to an English rural gentry. They built grand new brick houses commanding the countryside and broad rivers and inlets of the Chesapeake; they employed more of their slaves in domestic service; they filled their houses with luxury possessions, including imported carpets, silver plate, books, and other items that would help to confirm their own self-conceptions and to identify them to others as people of status and wealth. They provided their sons, sometimes in Britain, with the formal classical educations appropriate for gentlemen of English descent.

Though they by no means neglected their private material interests, they gradually learned to sublimate the drive toward personal aggrandizement and the impulse toward anarchic individualism that had been so powerfully evident among their seventeenth-century ancestors. They proudly retained that militant devotion to personal independence and the sanctity of individual property that was thought to be the hallmark of true Britons, but they also consciously cultivated countervailing traditional British upper-class political and social values, including politeness, liberality, sociability, and stewardship. Setting themselves up as exemplars of public spiritedness and authority and eagerly grasping the social and political obligations appropriate to their status, they assumed an almost total hegemony over civil and religious institutions at both the local and provincial levels and thereby endowed those institutions with enormously more energy and authority than they had ever enjoyed during the region's first century of existence.

To symbolize that authority, they built new, classically proportioned brick public buildings in the provincial capitals in Williamsburg and Annapolis and courthouses and churches at central places in the localities. Further to "traditionalize" their societies, they sought to bring Chesapeake legal, inheritance, and religious practices into closer conformity with those in Britain and thereby eliminated many of the "creolisms" that had formerly made those practices both more simple and more flexible than those of metropolitan culture. As sources of capital, services, and counsel for their less affluent neighbors, they became the centers of local networks of dependence in much the same way, if probably not to anywhere near the same degree, as had the landed elite in Britain. With their great wealth, their affluent and more refined lifestyles, their provincewide connections and cosmopolitan outlook, their growing family charisma, and their social and political authority, members of the Chesapeake elite thus came through the middle decades of the eighteenth century to be ever more sharply distinguished from people of less wealth.[19]

As the elite became increasingly more tightly interconnected and as political and religious institutions acquired more vigor, the Chesapeake also became less conflicted, better integrated, and more cohesive. Intraelite competition, which in the seventeenth century had contributed to a high degree of public divisiveness, had by the 1730s been largely confined to much less disruptive and highly structured cultural channels, including horseracing, gambling, dancing, social display, and political debate. With no serious vertical or horizontal social fissures within the free white population, the lower and middling ranks became ever more depoliticized and deferential toward this relatively cohesive, responsive, even paternal elite, and an astonishing degree of public harmony prevailed, especially in Virginia, where leaders took great pride in their society's political tranquillity, in the liberality and community-mindedness—the patriotism—of its wealthiest and most prominent inhabitants, and in the almost total absence of factionalism and party strife.[20]

In the private world of the family, quite as much as in the public world of politics and religion, the Chesapeake became far more settled—and far more like metropolitan Britain—during the eighteenth century. Despite improving demographic conditions, the genealogical depth of families remained shallow and the range of kinship connections relatively narrow during the early decades of the century. As in the previous century, this shallowness encouraged a broad conception of the family. Households tended to be open and associations with non-kin both intimate and extensive. With continuing increases in life expectancy through the middle decades of the century, however, the Chesapeake family became more susceptible to traditional definition. Parents began to live longer, typically into their mid-fifties, and to have an average of four to five children who survived into adulthood. Grandparenthood, relatively rare in the previous century, became widespread and kinship networks much more extensive and intensive.

These developments may have turned Chesapeake families inward and made them more private, child-centered, nurturant, and affectionate and thereby brought them into close conformity with trends that were evident throughout the contemporary North Atlantic world. Much more important, they seem to have altered power relationships within the family. Just as an enlarging pool of older men lent strength to political and religious institutions at the local and provincial levels, so longer-lived fathers helped to bolster paternal authority within families. In the seventeenth century, higher survival rates for women had turned the Chesapeake into what one scholar has termed a "widowarchy" in which women, despite their disproportionately small numbers, enjoyed a role in family and economic life far more extensive than was usual among their counterparts in England. As disparities in survival rates among women and men dropped in the eighteenth century, however, husbands and fathers sought to transform the family into the well-ordered patriarchal units that had long been the ideal, if not necessarily always the norm, in metropolitan Britain. In consequence of these efforts, women found themselves more and more restricted to a domestic and ornamental role, and the Chesapeake, like Britain, became an even more male-dominated society.

Yet if Chesapeake fathers liked to think of themselves as patriarchs who presided firmly over deferential wives and children, the patriarchy they actually succeeded in establishing seems to have been a highly permissive one. They may have preached obedience to parents and encouraged passivity in daughters, but few of them, recent studies suggest, appear to have tried to use their control over family land and other resources to establish a tight family discipline. Indeed, to enable their sons to function effectively in the fluid and competitive world of the Chesapeake, parents seem rather to have tried to inculcate in their offspring not obedience and deference but independence, self-assertiveness, self-confidence, and a reliance upon self-control. Not restraint but indulgence seems to have characterized parents' relations with their children, who enjoyed wide latitude in their behavior and were subjected to a minimum of parental interference in their lives.[21]

Relations between masters and slaves seem to have been similarly permissive. Slavery in the Chesapeake was by no means a benevolent institution. As in the rest of the British-American slave world from the Caribbean north to New England, slaves had only minimal rights in law; they were subject to harsh punishments and hard labor discipline; families and friends were always subject to separation through sales, mortgage foreclosures, or bequests; many had cruel masters; and some, especially newly enslaved Africans, found it extremely difficult to adjust to conditions of enslavement. Particularly in comparison with the lethal disease environment and harsh labor regimes found in the intensive sugar-producing colonies, however, Chesapeake slavery seems to have been both somewhat milder and "remarkably flexible and unstructured." Material and health conditions were sufficiently favorable to permit vigorous natural increase within six decades after the beginning of massive importations in the 1680s.

At the same time, the desirability of a contented work force combined with the increasingly predominant self-conception of masters not merely as estate managers but as patriarchs whose paternal obligations extended to all of their dependents, including slaves, gave Chesapeake slavery an increasingly "familial, domestic character." Slaves who became domestic servants, agricultural managers, or skilled craftsmen were drawn to the center of the master's family; most could count on their masters to respect their private property and customary rights; and all except those on smaller production units had a substantial "measure of self-determination in their family life, in their religions, and in the ways they celebrated or mourned."

Indeed, as importations slowed, the sex ratio became more equal, and a greater proportion of slaves tended to be congregated on larger and more dispersed plantations through the middle decades of the eighteenth century, more and more slaves were able to achieve a settled social life. Permitted wide autonomy in shaping their lives within their own quarters, they gradually forged a common culture out of their many diverse heritages and perhaps also began to develop a more coherent and stable family life. At least on larger units of production, slaves, like Chesapeake whites, often now "lived in families," increasingly in "two-parent and extended households" in the midst of proliferating kinship networks that included grandparents, uncles, aunts, and cousins.

With few supervisory personnel and weak coercive resources, masters were unable to exert very tight control over their slaves. As a result, slaves enjoyed considerable freedom of movement and association within neighborhoods and created complex "cross-plantation social networks." If slaves still continued to resent and resist their enslavement, that resistance was "usually [only] sporadic and solitary." Although fears of slave uprising were never far below a conscious level and could be easily activated, the white population displayed "a general complacency" about slavery, and the Chesapeake was a relatively "secure 'slave society.'"[22]

If most Chesapeake families were relaxed in their treatment of children and slaves, they also seem to have exercised little discipline over themselves. With growing wealth, the single-minded pursuit of gain that had animated earlier generations appears to have given way to a liberal sociability and a notorious self-indulgence. Increasingly after 1730, both residents and visitors to the Chesapeake decried the exorbitant rise of improvidence, extravagance, luxury, and ostentation among the elite and a growing addiction to pleasure, especially gambling, with a corresponding disregard for the traditional values of industry, thrift, sobriety, and private morality at every level of white society. By the 1760s in Virginia, though not yet in Maryland, members of the elite worried about the rising indebtedness among a seemingly growing number of spendthrifts among them.[23]

This "relaxed private morality" was apparently accompanied by the absence of a sustained concern for the enforcement of public morality. One study has shown that in contrast to the situation in England, Richmond County, Virginia, during the 1720s and 1730s was the scene of a significant effort to punish people for failure to attend church and for such moral offenses as adultery, bastardy, fornication, swearing, and drunkenness. But this effort seems to have given way beginning in the 1740s to a much more permissive atmosphere represented by a rising tolerance for the frailties of individuals, including unmarried lovers, drunks, and other obvious violators of stated social norms.[24]

This permissiveness was both reflected in and reinforced by the religious establishments of the Chesapeake. During the first half of the eighteenth century, the Anglican church became more entrenched. Despite the presence of a substantial number of Catholics in Maryland and pockets of Quakers and other dissenters both there and in Virginia, both societies were overwhelmingly Anglican. With its emphasis on inclusivity of all free people, formal liturgy, and a learned clergy, the established church functioned more and more like its metropolitan model. Retaining the latitudinarian orientation it had exhibited throughout most of the seventeenth century, it could accommodate a wide variety of religious beliefs and did not insist on a strict religious life. As a consequence, the tone of Chesapeake society remained, as it had been from the beginning, highly secular.

That the Anglican church was much less deeply rooted than it appeared rapidly became evident during the 1740s and 1750s, when a strong evangelical movement, spearheaded first by Presbyterians and then by Baptists, successfully challenged its hegemony. By the 1760s, conflict, sectarianism, and diversity had supplanted the harmony and unity that had seemed to be so secure during the previous half-century, and evangelicals and antievangelicals were locked in a fierce competition for the religious allegiances of the inhabitants. Just as the evangelical movement drew much of its appeal from the failure of the established church to satisfy a deep yearning, especially among the middle and lower orders, for a more intense spiritual life, so opposition to that movement proceeded from a powerful revulsion against the tight religiosity and strict moral discipline advocated by the new sects and reaffirmed a strong cultural preference for the more relaxed and moderate mode of life that had come to prevail in the Chesapeake during its first century and a half.

By the late 1740s and 1750s, Anglicans had anticipated the evangelicals' "mounting sense of social disorder" and open anxiety about proliferating corruption in Chesapeake society. But the vast majority in this slave society seems to have been compulsively unyielding only in regard to the exertion and maintenance of that love of liberty and personal independence and autonomy that were thought by contemporaries all over the British-American world to be the defining characteristics of free British men and therefore absolutely essential to the credibility of all claims to a British identity.[25]

As the Chesapeake moved away from the chronic competitive disarray and inchoateness of the seventeenth century to a more relaxed, settled, and traditional hierarchical stability between 1690 and 1740 and then to a more diverse socioeconomic and religious order after 1750, it emphatically did not exhibit a climate that was "uncongenial to the capitalist spirit." The "market mentality" so powerfully exhibited by its early seventeenth-century inhabitants by no means dissipated but coexisted—easily—with rising aspirations for the establishment of a traditional patriarchy. In no sense a "legally sanctioned," much less a "feudal," aristocracy, members of the rising Chesapeake elite did not abandon their plantations to become leisured rentiers. Rather, they continued, in the tradition of their ancestors and like most of the smaller landholders surrounding them, to devote themselves to the active and energetic pursuit of profit through the production of tobacco for an international commercial market.

As their growing interest in western lands as a source of income, the rapidity with which they sought to take advantage of new economic opportunities in grain and iron production beginning in the 1720s and 1730s, and their avid pursuit of internal public improvements in water transportation in the 1760s and 1770s so powerfully attest, however, they were by no means insensitive to the shifting potentialities of the market. Rather, like so many of their counterparts in contemporary Britain, they were constantly on the lookout for and eager to take advantage of new market possibilities to add to their wealth and to support their increasingly polite and expensive lifestyles.

No less than 150 years earlier, the dream that had originally drawn people to the Chesapeake, the dream of a better material life through their own individual pursuits of happiness, still animated their successors. The counterpointing of hedonism and virtue, acquisitiveness and social responsibility, activity and indolence, independence and slavery, large plantations and small farms, was the logical result of that dream as it had gradually assumed concrete shape on the shores and in the hinterlands of the Chesapeake Bay.[26]

IN both its inner dynamics and its organization, the increasingly hierarchical society of the eighteenth-century Chesapeake probably came closer than that of any other contemporary British-American cultural region to replicating what Harold J. Perkin has referred to as the "old society" of rural England, as that society had gradually cohered and assumed definable shape between 1650 and 1750. Like the English countryside, the Chesapeake was dominated by a small enterprising elite that, in imitation of the English country gentry, made every effort to unite "in itself the political, economic and social power of the community."

This increasingly authoritative group presided over a society that was becoming both more settled and more cohesive. As in England, there was a large population of middling and small planters and farmers, a growing number of tenants, a "numerous class of geographically mobile poor whites," and a large rural proletariat. Denser settlement; more roads, bridges, and ferries; a growing number of artisans, traders, attorneys, and others in occupations that were not strictly agricultural; the appearance of several moderate-sized towns; the mixture of family and commercial farming in an increasingly diversified economy; and, after 1750, the movement toward religious pluralism all combined, as Paul Clemons has remarked, to make the Chesapeake "world very much like the farming regions of England."

This is not to suggest, of course, that the developing correspondence between the Chesapeake and rural England was in any sense complete. With far more black slaves than white servants and laborers, Chesapeake society had a system of racial caste that was without precedent in Britain, albeit the distinction between slavery and servitude had not yet been so pointedly defined as it would be after 1760 and English servants and laborers seem to have been exploited just as callously and as thoroughly as Chesapeake slaves. With far fewer tenants, with an apparently considerably higher proportion of independent property owners of middling rank, and with weaker and less extensive vertical links between patrons and clients, the Chesapeake seems to have had less poverty, less social inequality, less subordination, and less dependency among its free population than was characteristic of rural Britain, yet the authority of its upper-class leaders was probably less secure and almost certainly based more on property and less on patronage than was the case with the British country gentry.

With far fewer bustling county towns or such a highly specialized occupational structure and with the notable conflation and simplification of conventional metropolitan status systems, Chesapeake society obviously lacked the complexity and subtleties of definition of British rural society and was probably still considerably more open, even in older settled areas. With its lack of voluntary associations and schools, the institutional infrastructure of the Chesapeake was undoubtedly much less well developed. If eighteenth-century Virginians and Marylanders had not yet managed to anglicize their societies completely, however, they had by the 1740s and 1750s created a social landscape that, far from being "radically different" or "far removed from" that of England, both looked remarkably English and was more demonstrably so than it had ever been before.[27]

Chapter Five

EXEMPLAR AND VARIATION:

BRITAIN AND IRELAND, 1660–1760

Over the century between 1660 and 1760, the oldest British continental colonies, those in New England and in the Chesapeake, had thus been moving in opposite directions. Both regions were becoming more heterogeneous and differentiated and more like the complex society from which they had emanated. But though the New England colonies had become more atomistic, competitive, contentious, mobile, open, materialistic, and secular and less cohesive, settled, healthy, and self-confident, the Chesapeake colonies had grown less atomistic, competitive, contentious, mobile, open, materialistic, and secular and more cohesive, settled, healthy, and self-confident. To determine which, if either, of these two patterns was normative in the process of early modern British sociocultural development, this chapter and the two following will examine the histories of Britain, Ireland, and the other four main regions of colonial British America.

This chapter will cover Britain and Ireland from 1660 to 1760, Chapter 6 the Middle Colonies and the Lower South between 1710 and 1760, and Chapter 7 the Atlantic island and West Indian colonies from 1660 to 1760. This examination is intended to provide the necessary foundations for evaluating, at the end of Chapter 7, the third of the traditional basic working assumptions of colonial historiography listed at the beginning of Chapter 2, specifically, the assumption that the declension model abstracted from the New England experience provides an appropriate framework for analyzing the whole of the early modern British-American experience.

IF, as was suggested in the preceding chapter, the Chesapeake was becoming more like rural Britain between 1660 and 1760, an analysis of the social development of England or, after the union with Scotland in 1707, of Britain over the same period reveals that the developmental process followed in the Chesapeake was simply a colonial reflection of a metropolitan paradigm characterized by increasing economic dynamism and social and political consolidation. In sharp contrast to New England and in marked similarity to the Chesapeake, metropolitan Britain seems during the century following the Restoration to have been slowly cohering. Without losing any of the economic energy and creativity that had characterized it over the previous century, metropolitan Britain after 1660 moved steadily away from the social and political disarray of the first six decades of the seventeenth century toward an ever more settled and coherent society.

Of course, throughout this period, as before, British society was far more complex and dense than any of the simple colonial societies established in America. With a highly differentiated social status system and occupational structure, it exhibited a series of regional contrasts between the wealthier and more active southeast and the more slowly changing northwest, between coastal and inland areas, between the more arable and densely settled lowlands and the more wooded and thinly inhabited pastoral uplands, and between a growing number of towns and the country. Yet Britain, almost to as great an extent as the Chesapeake, remained throughout the century after 1660 predominantly rural and agricultural. Four out of five inhabitants still lived in the countryside, and almost nine out of ten "were employed either in agriculture or in processing rurally produced raw materials."[1]

After 1660, this essentially rural population grew far more slowly and moved about less extensively than it had over the previous century. The long period of population growth that had persisted throughout the century beginning in the 1540s brought the population to about 5.3 million in 1656 and then came to an abrupt halt. Over the next three decades, population actually declined to just over 4.9 million in 1690 before it began a slow but erratic increase. Not until 1720 did population again exceed 5.3 million, the figure achieved during the 1650s. Only after experiencing another decline to just under 5.3 million in 1730 did population again begin to rise relatively steadily: to almost 5.6 million in 1740, nearly 5.8 million in 1750, and over 6.1 million in 1760.[2]

Internal migration also changed character after the mid-seventeenth century. To be sure, population continued to "be very mobile geographically." Indeed, with just over six out of every ten town residents and nearly seven out of ten rural inhabitants having moved at least once in their lives, it is clear that after 1660, as before, "migration was not the exception but the social and demographic norm," the "usual way of life of most English people." Instead of the "fairly large-scale," "long-distance push migration found in the period before 1640," however, migration during the century after 1660 tended to be "localized and basically circular." There were two major exceptions to this trend. First were the numerous immigrants to London, which continued to draw people from all over England and, increasingly, from Scotland and Ireland as well. Second were the betterment migrants among "upper social groups—gentlemen and merchants, as well as professional men," who often moved long distances to urban centers.

Although the decline in long-distance subsistence migration in favor of localized population movement after 1660 may well have contributed to stabilizing post-Restoration society, migration was still sufficiently widespread to produce a high turnover of families within local communities: in just twelve years between 1676 and 1688 40 percent of the population of Clayworth in Nottinghamshire moved away. Such extensive population change necessarily meant that, in Roy Porter's words, the nostalgic "picture of a stable village England where the rude forefathers of the hamlet slept, where time stood still and generations of Hodges ploughed the patriarchal furrows," was as much of a myth after 1660 as it had been before. So was the related image of the English village as a "wholesome 'community'" characterized by peace, neighborliness, and harmony in which each "'peasant'" was "engaged on satisfying creative craft-work, . . . snug within the bosom of the extended family." English localities continued to be "highly disputacious" and the typical family simple, composed of a nuclear household of a married couple with small children who usually were apprenticed to a trade or sent out to service early in their teens.[3]

Whether or not the slowing of population growth and changes in migration patterns helped to bring a new stability to English society after 1660, historians of all persuasions seem to agree that the most conspicuous social development over the subsequent century was the extraordinary resurgence of the aristocracy. From the dark days of the Civil War and the Interregnum, when its very survival seemed to be at issue, the aristocracy underwent an "astonishing revival" over the next hundred years that, by the 1760s, had brought it to the apex of its prestige and power. In the intervening century, the land market was extremely active, with "a marked tendency for landed property to be concentrated in fewer and fewer hands" and an increase in the number, size, and proportion of the countryside taken up by large estates. These gains apparently were made at the expense of the smaller gentry and freeholders, and by 1800 members of the landed elite were both "absolutely and relatively wealthier and more united than their grand-fathers." The proportion of national landed wealth held by peers jumped from about 15 to 20 percent in 1700 to 20 to 25 percent in 1800, with the gentry at the latter date owning about 50 to 60 percent and freeholders the remaining 15 to 20 percent. Throughout the century from 1660 to 1760, this "tight, privileged ring of landowners," account-ing for no more than 1.2 percent of the population and composed of the peerage and upper levels of the landed gentry, had succeeded in gathering to themselves phenomenal social and economic power.[4]

One of the main costs of this development was an ever-widening gap between the elite and the substantial proportion of the popula-tion who lived near and below the poverty line. No less than in ear-lier centuries, British society continued to be characterized by a pro-nounced gulf "between ruler and ruled, rich and poor, propertied and unpropertied" and a highly "exploitative system of inversely sharing out work and rewards" that produced a large "pauper residuum" at the bottom of the socioeconomic order. This "labouring Poor" consisted not, as in some parts of Europe, of "peasants working tiny plots of land for which they paid feudal dues or labour services, but landless labourers earning wages for work on other men's land or materials, and at least half of them in 1760 worked for part of their time outside agriculture." Including paupers and vagrants, this group amounted in 1688 to about half of the population, and it subsisted on only about one-fifth of the annual national income. At some points during the eighteenth century, nearly one family out of five received relief from what one historian has called the "most elaborate and expensive poor-relief system in Europe." But together with continuing cheap food prices, at least before the 1760s, that system prevented the English poor from undergoing the periodic subsistence crises that had earlier visited England and were still common in continental Europe. More-over, by 1803 the opening up of new employment through the expan-sion of marketing and manufacturing had reduced the numbers of the laboring poor to just over a third of the population, who then lived on about one-sixth of the national income.

Notwithstanding this large reservoir of laborers, substantial numbers of black people, a few of whom had been present since the early days of English participation in the African slave trade in 1555, began to congregate in London, Liverpool, and Bristol during the eighteenth century. By the last quarter of the century, there may have been as many as twenty thousand in London alone. Although many of them were free and found employment as servants, dock workers, sailors, and laborers, few rose above the ranks of the poor, and a significant proportion were slaves, the legality of their enslavement resting upon a substantial body of case law. Despite these numbers, slavery never became an important institution in the British Isles. Nevertheless, despite vigorous efforts by antislavery spokesmen from the 1760s on, it continued to exist until general emancipation took effect throughout the British Empire in 1834.[5]

Elite and poor were merely the opposite ends of a hierarchical and complex social order in which, in the words of Harold Perkin, "men took their places in an accepted order of precedence, a pyramid stretching down from a tiny minority of the rich and powerful through ever larger and wider layers of lesser wealth and power to the great mass of poor and powerless." In this "finely graded" hierarchy, "men were acutely aware of their exact relation to those immediately above and below them" and proclaimed their differential status "by every outward sign: manner, speech, deportment, dress, liveried equipage, size of house and household, the kind and quantity of the food they ate." Bound together not by "horizontal solidarities of class" but by strong "vertical connections of dependency or patronage," British society was essentially a patronage society in which social relations were ostensibly governed by an accepted code of paternalism or stewardship, according to which the elite treated their social inferiors in a fatherly way with warmth, justice, benevolence, and patronage, and the lower orders accepted their subordinate clientage status and deferred to the sociopolitical leadership of their superiors. Although paternalism could certainly exhibit a harsh and "unbenevolent face" whenever elite property or hegemony seemed to be threatened and although the imperatives of subordination certainly did not command universal acceptance among all members of the lower orders, "almost everyone" before the late eighteenth century seems to have believed that "there should be a graded status hierarchy."[6]

As the ruling propertied elite gradually "knitted itself together" ever more tightly and as society, at least in rural areas, became ever "more hierarchical . . . as the eighteenth century progressed," the social power of the elite was enormously enhanced by two complementary developments in the public sphere. First was the effective monopolization by the elite of all "the inflexions of power: land, status, patronage, office and legal privilege within the state." Second was a growing unanimity among the elite. Neither of these developments came quickly. Indeed, during the years from 1679 to 1721 intense political conflict occurred in which the contending forces, representing opposing religious and political ideologies, struggled over the relative authority of crown and Parliament and which side should exercise hegemony over English public life. The length and intensity of these struggles led to a considerable expansion of the electorate.

By making the government financially dependent on annual parliamentary votes and by paving the way for a financial revolution that intimately linked the possessing classes to government credit, the Glorious Revolution of 1688–89 and the Revolutionary Settlement that followed over the subsequent quarter-century eventually made possible the establishment of both a national consensus around the desirability of maintaining the Protestant ascendancy and pride in the British Constitution. They also facilitated important structural changes that permitted the reigning administration to use patronage, pensions, and favors to build a powerful machine in support of government. By the late 1740s, party animosity had virtually disappeared, the electorate may even have contracted somewhat, political conflict largely revolved around the struggle for office within a narrow oligarchy, and established institutions at both the local and the national levels grew "more exclusive, oligarchic, and unrepresentative."[7]

All these developments endowed the existing social hierarchy with extraordinary "strength and resilience." "Presided over by a super-confident oligarchy . . . whose dominion was consolidated early in the century and [was] never—at least not until the 1790s—seriously challenged, let alone jeopardized," this hierarchy left the elite with a tight grip on most available forms of "power—capital, economic leverage, office, local influence, pervasive manipulation of patronage in state, Church, and armed forces." "Styles of politics and architecture, the rhetoric of the gentry and their decorative arts, all seem[ed] to proclaim stability, self-confidence, and a habit of managing all threats to their hegemony." Indeed, the entire British world stretching out even across the Atlantic and into the Indian Ocean and beyond seemed, like the increasingly contrived landscape gardens Britons were creating on their estates, to be potentially subject to their control.[8]

If, however, the revival of the aristocracy, the apparently growing strength and social and political dominance of the landed elite, and the achievement of a degree of political and social stability that was the envy of the rest of Europe were among the most visible and important developments in Britain between 1660 and 1760, the celebrated stability of British society was also certainly a "dynamic stability," built not on the suppression but on the stimulation of the creative socio-economic and cultural energy that had characterized English life for at least a century or more before 1660. At the same time that "political institutions and [the] . . . distribution of social power . . . were un-ashamedly hierarchichal, hereditary, and privileged," British society, as Roy Porter has remarked, was also "capitalist, materialist, market-oriented; worldly pragmatic, [and] responsive to economic pressures." No less than in the previous century, Britain continued to be an "acquisitive, restless society."[9]

Although it was so strikingly "inegalitarian and oozing with privilege (some of it hereditary)," the British social hierarchy never became "rigid and brittle." Manners, education, and money—not pedigree—determined status; people at all levels of society "could quite easily rise *towards* the portal of the next status group," and social mobility was probably even more substantial than it had been in the century before 1660. In comparison with the other major societies of Continental Europe, even the aristocracy was remarkably open. Lawrence and Jeanne Stone have shown that far fewer wealthy merchants, professionals, and officeholders actually succeeded in buying their way into the elite than has sometimes been claimed. But there were no legal restraints on their doing so. Indeed, except for the immunity from arrest for debt for peers and their right to be tried for felonies by the House of Lords, British society had no hereditary legal privilege, one of the most celebrated boasts of Englishmen being that all men, including even kings and magistrates, were "beneath the law" and equally subject to its benefits and penalties.

In addition, prevailing inheritance practices excluded all but the eldest son from inheriting a landed estate and thereby ensured that younger sons of the landed elite were frequently "sent out into the world to earn their living in trade and the professions." In combination, the "absence of legal or customary barriers between the landed aristocracy and the rest" of society; a persistent, if modest, "upflow of new men from trade and the professions into the landed class"; and a "continuous downflow of younger sons, with education, small capitals and great energy and determination to succeed, into the middle ranks" meant that British society during these years would remain "extraordinarily free and open . . . for those not too badly scarred by other people's freedom."[10]

As their willingness to send their younger sons into trade and the professions so powerfully attested, the landed elite had little scorn for the monied and professional classes. Like the Chesapeake gentry, they "revelled on their estates, building, landscaping, and so creating in the heart of the country a sanctum of civilization." But they also built townhouses in London and "made money enthusiastically and without shame" in any way available, investing in trade, government securities, and the new Bank of England as well as making efforts to enhance agricultural productivity and marketing potential in the countryside. Increasingly over the century after 1660, they endorsed the "acquisitiveness and opportunism" of the rapidly expanding market society, and they used the power of the state "to further the interests of the nation as a whole and the commercial bourgeosie" of bankers and large overseas merchants in particular. The result was an astonishing symbiosis among land, trade, and the professions in which the landed elite, again like the Chesapeake gentry, were mostly all "profit-hungry capitalists," and Britain was "the foremost capitalist society in Europe."[11]

This ethos of possessive individualism, shared by landed and monied interests alike, was supported throughout the period from 1660 to 1760 by a generally accelerating economy. Although this was certainly a period of "predatory . . . agrarian and commercial capitalism," the economy, as Porter has remarked, "worked well enough" not only "to profit the rich" but also "to keep practically everyone alive, to prevent sudden subsistence crises, and to give prospects of individual improvement" to a wide spectrum of society. The still basically agrarian system had long since produced in most years far more than was needed to sustain its population and had been deeply involved in a market economy. Stimulated by heavy military and naval spending—Britain was involved in foreign wars during thirty-eight of seventy-four years between 1689 and 1763—and by a consumer revolution that brought a growing range of material goods within the reach of an expanding segment of the population, the economy began to show a "new buzz of activity" during the closing decades of the seventeenth century and underwent a dramatic expansion and acceleration throughout the eighteenth century and especially after 1740.[12]

The effects of these developments were evident in virtually all aspects of British economic and social life. Increasingly "sensitive to market demand and aimed at cost effectiveness," agriculture expanded. Increased output in both cereal and livestock production, largely in response to the introduction of new fodder crops, higher expenditures for capital improvements, and a burgeoning urban market, were accompanied by attention to drainage, improving yields, and stock breeding. More and more, Britain was also becoming a trading nation. At the beginning of the eighteenth century, it had 3,300 ships with a carrying capacity of 260,000 tons, exported £6,470,000 worth of goods, and imported £6,000,000 worth. By 1770, these figures had risen steeply to 9,400 ships with a total tonnage of 695,000, exports valued at £14,300,000, and imports valued at £12,200,000. By the same time, the country had already experienced considerable industrial development in woolen, cotton, silk, and linen textiles, coal, iron, and brewing. Simultaneous developments in banking, investment, insurance, transport, and communications and the emergence of a complex economic infrastructure made the production and "exchange of goods and services easier, faster, and more reliable."[13]

These changes, which deeply involved Britain's innovative landed elite, were a consequence of and a profound stimulus to the rapid expansion of the "middling sort," which the Stones have referred to as "the most important social feature" of the period between 1660 and 1800. Dedicated to industry, success, and making money, and aspiring not to overturn but to assimilate to the elite by imitating its education, manners, and behavior, this "swelling and confident middle rank" consisted not only of yeomen and larger tenant farmers and clerics but also of a numerous group of commercial men ranging from petty tradesmen up to the great London bankers, stock managers, and overseas traders; an increasingly complex miscellany of men involved in producing goods for the market, including skilled craftsmen and artisans of all varieties, millers, butchers, and processers of food and other agricultural products, brewers, shipbuilders, building contractors, mine owners, and manufacturers of iron, porcelain, and clothing; an expanding and ever more highly differentiated group of professional and service people such as lawyers, doctors, architects, teachers, and clerks; and a growing number of government servants in civil administration and the army and navy.

By the late eighteenth century, this middle group, comprising what one historian has called a "long unbroken chain" between the elite and the lower orders and still proliferating in response to the needs of Britain's increasingly market-oriented society, probably consisted of as many as a half million families, many of whom were "well-educated, fashion conscious, and with money to burn on luxuries." Within this group, as Porter has remarked, the "urge to 'improve' and 'arrive' was irresistible," and the gentrification of its upper levels over the course of the eighteenth century "drove the wheels of [social] emulation and tyrant fashion faster and faster," contributing to the boom in private building in both towns and countryside, the growing demand for luxury goods and services, and the conspicuous consumption that, stimulated by status competition, supplied much of the fuel for the consumer revolution.[14]

Though a majority of these growing middle ranks lived in the country, they formed the strategic core of an expanding network of towns, which grew substantially in response to the dynamic expansion of market forces after 1660. The seat of both government and trade, London continued to be far and away the largest urban center. Despite the high mortality rate that claimed large numbers of people throughout the era, a continuing stream of immigrants drove the city's population constantly upward from 575,000 in 1700 to 675,000 in 1750 and about 950,000 by 1800, its proportion of the country's total population remaining fairly uniform at between 10 and 11 percent. Over the same period, however, the number of other towns with 2,500 or more inhabitants jumped from 67 in 1700 to 103 in 1750 and 187 in 1800, and the total proportion of the population living in towns moved slowly upward from 18.7 percent in 1700 to 22.6 percent in 1750 and 30 percent in 1800.

These towns served a variety of functions. They included county capitals like Durham, Lincoln, Salisbury, and York; marketing and manufacturing centers such as Manchester, Leeds, Sheffield, Birmingham, Norwich, and Taunton; ports and dockyard towns like Bristol, Liverpool, Hull, and Newcastle; and spas and resorts, the most important of which was Bath. These towns were not only economic centers but also "foci of polite society, consumption, communications, and the arts." Presided over by increasingly distinctive and independent urban patriciates who mimicked the genteel culture of the landed elite but lived in "small retreats or residential villas" near town, all of these towns saw a major boom in both private and public building, and many of them developed impressive cultural infrastructures, including clubs, societies, coffee houses, libraries, bookshops, and theaters.[15]

No less than in the previous century, English society from 1660 to 1760 had a dark underside, including the high mortality in the towns, the callous exploitation of the laboring poor, and a persistent undercurrent of the violence and disorder that, in Porter's words, was "as English as plum pudding." Yet the extended acceleration of the economy "put prosperity within the reach of many," and, at the same time that it "gave plenty of scope to those living comfortably above the breadline to explore new life-styles," it also provided more opportunity for at least the upper reaches of the bottom third of society. So far from being "opposed to the inroads of consumer capitalism," the "laboring poor," as Lawrence Stone has pointed out, "adapted readily to new market values and mass-produced goods." The falling incidence of crimes against property and the dramatic rise in population growth after 1740 provide some testimony to the wide diffusion of hopefulness associated with the new prosperity. As E. A. Wrigley has argued, the spurt in population seems to have been less the result of improved mortality than of rising fertility, the result of a sharp fall in the age of marriage between 1680 and 1800 from 26.5 years to 23.5 for women and from 27.5 to 25.5 for men, and a corresponding fall in the proportion of the unmarried from 18 to 6 percent of the population.[16]

These demographic changes heralded a new and widely diffused optimism that was also manifest in the rage for improvements; the celebration of innovation and a "collective desire for advance—rational, technical, scientific, and industrial"; lavish spending and liberal hospitality among the elite and middle orders; a new emphasis on politeness; and a new vitality in the arts. If, as it grew more fastidious and genteel, polite society was trying more and more to distance "itself from the dirty, pungent, and sometimes dangerous world of the hoi polloi, withdrawing from village and community activities, and [thereby] emasculating the culture of its inferiors," it also provided much of the energy behind the growing humanitarianism that was an important by-product of the rising stress on improvement.[17]

The optimism of the age was only slightly restrained by religious passion. Although most English people were nominally Christians and profoundly anti-Catholic and the elite was mostly nominally Anglican, most historians agree that religious fervor declined significantly among all segments of society during the century after the Restoration. The Restoration greatly "loosen[ed] the new bonds of discipline" that puritanism had only recently managed to establish; the "'magical command' of the [established] Church and of its rituals over the populace . . . was becoming very weak"; the church in general failed to perform "an effective, a psychologically compelling paternalist role"; and Methodism, like evangelical religion in the Chesapeake, did not become a powerful force until the last two decades of the century. Religious moderation was the watchword of the day, enthusiasm was suspect, and "Dissenters no less than Anglicans agreed that godliness should complement virtue and prudence, rather than demanding abandonment of this world as a vale of tears."[18]

The emphasis on moderation in religion was only one among many indications that Britain continued after 1660, as before, to be a highly permissive society with a "generally relaxed moral atmosphere." With no police force and only a small army, the elite had to tolerate considerable disorder on the part of the populace, and, notwithstanding an increasingly draconian criminal code, Britain was notorious among Europeans for the "licence permitted to the common people." In the countryside, the gentry relied heavily upon the force of custom and the cultivation of paternalistic behavior to maintain social control and enforce moral standards. As Robert Malcolmson has pointed out, however, paternalism necessarily implied "a large dose of toleration," and local squires "were little inclined to meddle with people's affairs on the grounds of religion or morality." Although the situation may not have been quite so loose in the countryside, a burgeoning rate of premarital conceptions, a growing number of bastard children, and a general loosening of sexual restraints beginning during the first half of the eighteenth century vividly underlined the reality that Britain was in general a "relaxed—or lax—society, in which neither state, Church, nor opinion was very vigilant in policing the morals of the community."[19]

In this increasingly permissive society, the growth of the economy and the accompanying rise of materialism enhanced traditional British individualism. As the "pursuit of personal gratification found expression in economic individualism, [in] the dictum that each [person] should use his own labour and capital to get on," enormous "premium came to be placed on self-management and presentation," more and more people "affirmed the right to self-fulfillment," and egoistic behavior, "even greed," came to be seen "not as sinful and anti-social but as natural and even admirable." Changes in family relations further accelerated this process. If, as Lawrence Stone has argued, the authority of fathers and husbands had, for various reasons, including the emergence of puritanism, been increasing through the sixteenth century and the first half of the seventeenth, it and the patriarchal ideal that sustained it declined rapidly over the next hundred years, as more affectionate attitudes within families and changes in inheritance practices combined to give individual family members more autonomy. As a result, children acquired greater control over their own lives, including the choices of whether to marry and to whom.[20]

In its broad outlines, the social development of Britain between 1660 and 1760 thus corresponded astonishingly closely to that of its oldest American settlements in the Chesapeake in the same period. The steady movement toward social consolidation and hegemony of the elite, the establishment of social and political stability, and the development of more sophisticated social and cultural institutions within a dynamic context provided by the interaction between a permissive and highly secular social order and an accelerating, flexible, and diversifying economy operating in a psychology of assertive individualism reflected, on the larger scale of an older and infinitely more complex society, the social process earlier described for the Chesapeake. The closeness of this correspondence at least raises the possibility that the developmental model illustrated by the Chesapeake may have had wide applicability in the greater Anglophone world.

CERTAINLY it was applicable to England's closest and oldest colony in Ireland. Just as in England and the Chesapeake, consolidation and growth were the twin themes of social development in Ireland between 1660 and 1760. From the renewal of English efforts at intensive colonization in Ireland during the late sixteenth and early seventeenth centuries, the two great questions confronting the colonizers were how to control the numerically superior and culturally advanced native Irish population and how to make the colony viable economically. The first problem was exacerbated by two basic social facts. First, the native population contained not just "wild Irish" but, especially in the pale around Dublin, a significant minority of Old English descendants from the several waves of earlier English conquerors. This last group was distinguished from the new immigrant settler population of the Elizabethan and early Stuart period not only by its long-term identification with Ireland but also by its Catholicism. Second, although they were united by their Protestantism and their common interest in subjugating the native Catholic population, the new settlers were strikingly heterogeneous in ethnic and religious composition. They included not just Englishmen, who were divided among Anglicans and dissenters, but also, especially in the northern province of Ulster, a substantial admixture of Scots Presbyterians. The social composition of the settler population presented the colony with still a third problem: how to weld such heterodox materials into a viable social order. At least for the short run, all three problems were resolved during the century after the Restoration.

The establishment of settler hegemony in Ireland was the product of two related developments. First was the effective subjugation of the native Irish population and the achievement of English military control as a result of Tudor expansion, the long war of the 1640s and early 1650s, and William III's victory over James II during the campaigns of 1689–91. These events paved the way for a settlement that placed the preponderance of economic and political power in the hands of Protestants. In 1641, Catholics still held 59 percent of the land, far and away the colony's most important economic resource. But the confiscations that followed the midcentury war drastically reduced this figure to only 22 percent in 1660, and the process continued over the subsequent century, the proportion of Catholic-owned land falling to 14 percent in 1703 and a mere 5 percent in 1776.

Similarly, whatever hopes Irish Catholics might have entertained for securing civil and religious rights under the later Stuarts entirely vanished in the 1690s as a consequence of the Williamite settlement. In the 1690s, the Protestant-controlled Irish Parliament passed a series of penal laws placing Catholics under severe disabilities. Many of the provisions of these laws proved to be unenforceable, and they failed miserably in their broadest goals "to eliminate Catholicism and to transform Ireland into a wholly or predominantly Protestant country." Although it enjoyed considerable power and wealth, the established Church of Ireland was "singularly ineffective as a religious organisation." "Lacking in proselytizing zeal," it does not seem to have had broad and enthusiastic support among the gentry and was regarded by the government very largely as an instrument of patronage. Despite the establishment of several charter schools in the 1730s and 1740s with the avowed purpose of bringing Catholic children into the fold of the established church, fewer than three thousand Irish actually converted between 1703 and 1761. By the latter date "any serious idea of persuading or compelling the bulk of the population to convert to the religion of the state had long been abandoned," and most people had accepted the existing tripartite religious order of Catholic, Anglican, and dissenters. Nevertheless, by barring Catholics from all participation in civil affairs and sharply restricting their social, economic, and religious activities, the penal laws helped to assure Protestant dominance.[21]

The second development that helped to establish settler control was the continuing immigration of English and Scots in substantial numbers down into the first decades of the eighteenth century. "On a scale which had no parallel in the rest of Europe," this immigration "probably equalled the entire flow from Britain to America" in the seventeenth century and was particularly high in the 1650s, when it probably exceeded eight thousand per annum, and again in the late 1670s and the 1690s. Changing in character from the sponsored immigration of the early seventeenth century to a more independent movement of individuals and families thereafter, this stream of immigrants was almost as much Scottish as it was English and was composed of a varied group ranging from younger sons of gentry and yeoman families to skilled artisans and "resourceless" people, all of whom were anxious to find a place where they could support themselves and find a field for their ambitions. This influx had a strong effect on the ethnic balance of the Irish population. Whereas people of Scottish and English descent constituted no more than 2 percent of the population in 1600, they made up roughly 18 percent in 1660 and 30 percent by the mid-1730s. Most numerous in Ulster, where they probably outnumbered Catholics, they "were strong in Leinster also, especially in and around Dublin, and in parts of Munster," and even Connacht, the most Catholic part of the colony, had "a much more substantial protestant population" than it would have in the nineteenth century.[22]

The rise in the proportion of the population of settler descent and the establishment of their hegemony over the Catholic population occurred in the context of extended demographic and economic

growth. The years from 1660 to 1760 were a period of "rapid population growth" in Ireland. Between 1600 and 1641, the number of inhabitants had grown by about 50 percent from 1.4 million to 2.1 million.
But population numbers declined sharply during the years of war,
famine, and plague between 1641 and 1660, a period when there was
also substantial outmigration. Although population began to climb
again thereafter, it had reached only about 1.7 million in 1672. Over the
following century, however, it doubled, rising to 2.2 million in 1687, 2.8
million in 1712, 3.2 million in 1754, and 3.5 million in 1767. As with
Britain's American colonies, some of this growth could be attributed
to immigration and some to falling mortality. But most of it seems to
have come from unusually high fertility produced by an exceptionally
low age of marriage. Typically, men married at age twenty-two and
women at age twenty, each about five years under the contemporary
European norm and well below even American norms.[23]

Demographic growth also betokened a generally upward trend in
the economy, which underwent a "remarkable expansion" during the
century after 1660. In this period, Ireland continued, as it had done
earlier, to be a highly exploitive society organized primarily with the
goals of producing profits for the settler population and enabling absentee landlords to skim off some of the cream. As L. M. Cullen has
remarked, "the orientation of this society was, from the outset . . .
highly commercialized." "Dominated by farmers holding leases from a
landlord or a middleman," its economy was primarily agricultural, the
main products being grains, which were typically grown on small
farms, and livestock, which was raised on larger units. Beginning during the late seventeenth century, there may have been a slight movement away from tillage to grazing, but this trend "was not progressive." Tillage was "still substantial in the 1750s," and cereal output
remained high. The most important feature of the Irish agricultural
economy, however, was that from very early on it usually yielded a
considerable surplus. As a result, "a very high proportion of output
was marketed," and both internal and external trade developed rapidly.
Indeed, as Cullen has concluded, Ireland seems to have had a considerably "more commercialised economy" and to have been "much more
export-oriented" than contemporary Scotland.[24]

Just how export-oriented Ireland was is revealed by the statistics,
which provide the most vivid available indication of the extent and
pace of Ireland's economic growth. Whereas exports were valued at

only about £400,000 in 1665, they grew at an average annual rate of about 2 percent over the next half-century and had passed £1 million by the 1710s. Growth was much slower over the next thirty years, but it began to acclerate markedly after 1740. Rising at an annual rate of 3.4 percent after 1740, the annual value of exports had reached about £3 million by 1770. From the beginning, this trade had been largely with two markets. In the 1650s and 1660s, the English market, which took cattle, sheep, wool, butter, and beef to meet the demands of a growing London population, had been particularly important, and even after the English Parliament had prohibited imports of Irish cattle, sheep, and beef by the Cattle Acts of 1663 and 1667 the metropolitan market, stimulated by an expanding woolen industry, continued to be the most significant destination of Irish exports. But the transatlantic trade in provisions, especially beef, butter, and pork, with the British and French West Indies became more and more important during the eighteenth century. Over the same period, Ireland also developed a thriv ing trade in textiles, with linen and wool yarn going almost wholly to the English market.[25]

The earnings from this "sustained rise in trade and output . . . laid the financial basis to support sustained changes" in the Irish economy. They paid for substantial agricultural improvements and stimulated the development of a significant domestic textile industry, which, as it "spread to a remarkable degree across the countryside in the eighteenth century," created much new employment in spinning and weaving. Linen was concentrated in the northern half of the island and in some "pockets farther afield," and wool was produced largely in the midlands and south. Export earnings also paid for an expanding volume of imports, mostly from Britain, which rose from just under £800,000 in value in 1700 to almost £2.3 million in 1766. They also fostered the development of banking institutions in Dublin and Cork and a sophisticated internal marketing and communications system throughout the country, including better roads and, beginning around midcentury, canals, and they helped pay for expanded port facilities in Dublin and Cork, where overseas trade increasingly tended to concentrate.[26]

Taken together, these developments and the economic growth and accompanying prosperity that underlay them also contributed to the consolidation of the settler-imposed social order. The structure of this predominantly rural society was articulated early. "Except in the southeast and the Pale . . . where some tradition of yeomen or comfortable farmers existed," the landscape was "dominated at the outset by large landowners and minute tenants," the former, few in number and almost entirely Protestant and of British descent, "receiving rent for the land" they held and the latter, composing the overwhelming majority of the inhabitants and very largely Gaelic and Catholic, "paying rent for the right of occupation." Out of a total population of about 2.5 million, there were only 26,000 landowners with thirty or more acres in 1705.[27]

In this "age of property and individualism," the Irish counterparts of the great tobacco magnates in the Chesapeake were the landlords. Recent historiography has shown that, powerful as it was, this group was "far less despotic than has often been represented." The "arbitrary dominion of landlords" and hard usage of tenants that characterized some estates in the early decades of the colony gradually gave way beginning in the late seventeenth century "to a highly regulated relationship, in which each tenant's place on the estate was first negotiated and thereafter determined by reference to a written contract." In this increasingly "commercial" relationship, landlord power was apparently considerably "more circumscribed than elsewhere" in contemporary Europe. By the early eighteenth century, tenants typically enjoyed long leases—three lives for Protestants and thirty-one years for Catholics, in the latter case the maximum time allowed by law—and owned their own farm animals, carts and wagons, and other equipment. In richer areas, they were often able to develop some savings; in poorer areas, they supplied labor or services in lieu of rents.[28]

If the landlord-tenant system was not "intrinsically oppressive," however, it was enormously—and of course disproportionately—profitable for the landlords. In the eighteenth century, rent to landlords siphoned off "at least a third of the net income of the rural community." Partly as a result of the landlords' ability to negotiate more profitable terms for improved leases and partly because of the general expansion of the economy, gross rentals for the country as a whole rose from £1.2 million in 1687 to £1.6 million to £2 million in the 1720s to approximately £2.5 million in the early 1750s, an increase of over 100 percent in just over sixty years. Some significant proportion of these rents flowed out of the colony as remittances to absentee landlords resident in England and Scotland. Estimates of these remittances put the amount at £100,000 in 1698 and £300,000 in the 1720s.

Yet, although absentee ownership was a serious problem and was condemned by contemporaries as a heavy drain on the colony's economic resources and a severe hindrance to improvement, it "was far from progressive." After rising at an alarming rate during the last decades of the seventeenth century, it "was in effect contained," and remittances fell steadily. Total rents tripled between the 1720s and the 1770s, but remittances to absentee owners only doubled, declining from about a fourth to a sixth of total rents in the 1720s to only about an eighth in the 1770s. Landlord residence was in fact "commonplace." Cork, Galway, and the Pale all had especially large resident gentry populations, and one scholar has estimated that at least half of those landlords who did not live on their estates were "internal" absentees who lived somewhere in Ireland, usually Dublin.[29]

Indeed, the new social and economic history of early modern Ireland has developed an altogether much deeper appreciation for what landlords put back into the society and has come to depict them as the chief agents of modernization during the century from 1660 to 1760. Prosperous, well-educated, and cognizant of metropolitan ideas, landlords, historians have shown, sponsored "much innovation," "engaged . . . in a wide variety of experiments in social engineering and economic improvement," and "financed and superintended" significant changes in the countryside. With "a serious interest in estate management" and "a keen interest in the social welfare of the ordinary inhabitants," they "financed enclosure, encouraged or recompensed tenant investment by rent abatements or the inducement of advantageous leases, improved their demesnes, and built new houses [for themselves] with enthusiasm." They also encouraged the systematic use of more advanced agricultural practices, including graveling, marling, and liming, and the planting of orchards, and in negotiating leases they "moved sensitively in recognition of social changes."

With the capital derived from greater rents after 1730, they took the leadership in "mining, large-scale enterprise in textiles and the promotion of canal and road building" and invested substantial sums in new housing and outbuildings for their tenants and in the new planned villages that sprang up all over the countryside in the 1730s and 1740s. As devices to foster the production of textiles, these villages, usually with straight streets, good houses, and a well-appointed market house and church, were, like most socially constructive efforts by landlords, the product not simply of a desire to promote economic development

and enhance private profits but also of a competitive "landlord ostentation." So also were the massive building and improvement programs
undertaken by many landlords on their estates. Following an extensive
wave of house building by landlords in the 1680s, there was a lull in
such construction until the 1730s and 1740s, when many landlords built
large country houses of a scale and quality comparable to those being
erected at the same time in rural England. Demonstrating increasing
refinement in decoration and furnishing, these new houses were frequently situated in improved demesnes with landscaped grounds,
elaborate gardens, and deer parks.[30]

If all of these activities betokened "a more permanent landed presence" and a stronger commitment to Irish society than has traditionally been supposed, the influence of landlords stretched far beyond
their estates. Their younger sons either went into trade or the professions or became large tenant farmers, and their daughters married into
the same groups. The connection between landlords and large tenant
farmers or "middlemen" was particularly close. Although some of the
people in this group were immigrants from England or Scotland,
many were native younger sons of gentry, including Catholics. For
such people "large tracts of land at low rents," which could be leased
out in smaller parcels to lower tenants, "offered the avenue to a gentry
style of life."

Especially during the half century after 1660, "when no other solvent
tenants offered," the development of many estates "depended heavily"
upon the efforts of this group. "With some economic resources, a
knowledge of farming and a strong commitment to the survival of
local Protestant institutions," its members became the "real backbone"
of rural society. Playing a "vital role" in helping to anglicize the countryside and then to maintain the viability of settler dominance, they
helped to finance "the spread of . . . stable" agricultural and marketing
structures and themselves often took an important part as brokers and
traders in the commercial networks through which Ireland's substantial agricultural produce was marketed.[31]

Below the middlemen was the enormous population of tenants,
among whom there was a basic division between those prosperous
enough to hire employed labor and "the labouring and cottage-tenant
families who were the reservoir for such employment." As many as 60
percent of these people lived close to subsistence in the 1670s and in
the many bad harvest years over the next half-century, and, although

there was apparently considerable charitable giving by the wealthy, at least during the eighteenth century, there was no poor law in Ireland to help tide the impoverished over such periods. According to Cullen, however, this situation improved considerably beginning in the 1730s. The last major famine of the century occurred in 1741, and the acceleration of the economy, particularly the opening up of new opportunities in spinning, weaving, and other aspects of textile production, resulted in a general rise in prosperity that reached even down to the laboring classes and enabled some tenants to build up greater resources. These developments in turn "created the comforting illusion" among landlords that their improving "initiative was responsible for the general rise in living standards."[32]

The rapid development of the countryside also helped to provide the base for the emergence of an expanding middling group and significant urbanization. As throughout the contemporary English-speaking world, there was a close interaction among land, trade, and the professions that was fostered by a continuous circulation of the children of landlords down into the ranks of commerce, finance, the army, law, medicine, and the church and of successful professionals and merchants up into the ranks of the gentry. Excluded from buying landed estates, wealthier Catholic families were especially attracted into trade and played a major role in overseas commerce. Although each of the major groups that composed the middling orders was nearly as complex and diversified in Ireland as its counterpart was in England, none was nearly so numerous. Nevertheless, they "provided much of the leadership both in cultural life and in schemes for social and economic betterment."[33]

Ireland remained a predominantly rural country throughout the period down to 1760, with only about a twelfth of its people living in towns in 1725, but it became much more highly urbanized during the eighteenth century. By the 1680s, Dublin had a population of 50,000 to 60,000 and, after London, was easily the second largest city in the Anglophone world, whereas Cork had a population of about 20,000. Only two other urban places, Limerick and Waterford, had as many as 5,000 people, however, and no other place exceeded 2,000. By 1760, Dublin had grown to 140,000, Cork to around 60,000 to 70,000, and Limerick to 20,000, and there were a dozen other towns with between 2,000 and 10,000 people. Although many of these towns were still crude and only enlarged versions of the many smaller market towns that had grown up over the countryside to service this market-oriented society, Dublin, and to a lesser extent Cork, with their sophisticated urban infrastructures in the trades and professions and their various social amenities and organizations, were developing an elegant face. As the capital and chief seaport, Dublin prided itself on being the Irish London. With its own "season" and university, it was the site of extensive private and public building, including before 1760 the magnificent Parliament House, completed in 1739, and the Trinity College library.[34]

Over the course of the century from 1660 to 1760, Ireland had undergone a profound sociocultural transformation under the direction of its new English and Scottish settler population. Historians have conventionally emphasized the considerable differences between Irish and English rural society during the early modern era, differences in the more extensive subdivision of landholdings, the smaller-sized agricultural units, the comparative rarity of yeoman farmers, and the extensive amount of land devoted to grazing in Ireland. As its laboring population became ever more sedentary, however, as "the gentleman's seat became the most conspicuous feature of the Irish rural scene," and as its impressive infrastructure of villages, towns, roads, and canals gradually took shape, it moved swiftly through the same general developmental process that characterized both the Chesapeake and old England during the same years, and this economically vital, dynamic, and ostensibly stable society seems, in fact, to have been becoming considerably more like provincial England. Although in retrospect it is easy to see that the Protestant establishment in Ireland was always on a "very precarious footing in most parts of the country" and that settler Ireland was a fundamentally unstable society, these developments explain why, more and more during the first six decades of the eighteenth century, confidence—"exemplified by the numbers, grandeur, and beauty of eighteenth-century buildings"—"radiated out from the landed class, both in the countryside and in the capital."[35]

THIS examination of the experiences of Britain and Ireland between 1660 and 1760 reveals that the New England declension model is not an appropriate conceptual device for understanding the thrust and character of the social development of either society during that period. Old England entered the era after 1660 in a state of socioeconomic, political, and religious disarray and only gradually during the following century developed a more coherent and settled society. Settler Ireland, like the Chesapeake, was in 1660 still a thoroughly materialistic, crudely exploitive, loosely structured, lax, and volatile society, whose English and Scottish inhabitants were still trying desperately to establish their hegemony over the native Irish population and only slowly during the following century managed to transform the island into a more cohesive and anglicized society. For both of the main British societies on the eastern side of the Atlantic, a developmental model of the kind formulated in the discussion of the Chesapeake seems best to describe the process of social change.

Chapter Six

VARIATIONS: THE MIDDLE
COLONIES AND THE
LOWER SOUTH, 1710–1760

During the half-century after 1710, the two newest of the six main regions of colonial British America, the Middle Colonies and the Lower South, each developed its own distinctive sociocultural configurations. At the same time, however, they also underwent a process of social development that, like that described in the previous chapter for Britain and Ireland from 1660 to 1760, was thoroughly compatible with the developmental model elaborated in Chapter 3 in reference to the Chesapeake. Like all of the other regions of the British Empire with the exception of New England, social change in both the Middle Colonies and the Lower South proceeded in the direction of greater elaboration, consolidation, and coherence within a broad framework of rapid economic expansion.

AFTER 1710, as before, the Middle Colonies of Delaware, Pennsylvania, New Jersey, and New York had two socioeconomic centers. The competing port towns of Philadelphia and New York each served as a focal point of trade for a largely discrete hinterland, the former drawing upon the Delaware River valley, including western and much of southern New Jersey, and the counties to the west, and the second serving Long Island Sound and the Hudson River valley, including eastern and most of northern New Jersey. This socioeconomic configuration has caused some historians to question the familiar assumption that these two areas constituted a common cultural area. Yet, throughout the colonial period, broad similarities in demographic patterns, ethnic composition, economic orientation, and social organization seem to argue strongly for treating the Middle Colonies as a single sociocultural unit.[1]

Just as the early experiences of these colonies showed more similarity to those of the Chesapeake than to those of New England, so also their social trajectories after 1710 conformed closely to the developmental model represented by the Chesapeake and were wholly incongruous with the declension model associated with New England. Like both New England and the Chesapeake, the Middle Colonies gradually became more heterogeneous, differentiated, and complex. Unlike New England and like the Chesapeake, however, the pluralistic, materialistic, individualistic, and contentious societies that had taken shape in the Middle Colonies between 1660 and 1710 became not less but more coherent and settled during the fifty years before the American Revolution.

Population growth was every bit as dramatic in the Middle Colonies as it was in both the Chesapeake and New England. From just over 63,000 in 1710, the white population of the region expanded to more than 200,000 in 1740 and more than 520,000 in 1770. More than an eightfold increase in just sixty years, this extraordinary growth was somewhat uneven. Whereas New York showed something more than a sevenfold increase and New Jersey just under a sixfold rise, the population of Pennsylvania and Delaware rose more than ten times. Throughout the Middle Colonies, however, this "long, powerful, sustained expansion," like that of the contemporary Chesapeake, was the result not merely of vigorous natural increase but also of continuing heavy immigration. Especially after 1730, the Philadelphia hinterland in particular attracted thousands of immigrants from Scotland, Ireland, and Germany as well as from England. With a burgeoning population, the extent of settled territory expanded to cover all of Delaware and New Jersey, most of eastern Pennsylvania, and much of the Hudson Valley. Only the French and their powerful Great Lakes Indian allies blocked expansion into central New York. Indeed, the immediate hinterland of Philadelphia served as a plentiful source of immigrants for places farther south and west in Maryland, Virginia, and the Carolinas.[2]

Demographic and territorial growth was accompanied by strong economic growth. Like that of the eighteenth-century Chesapeake, the economy of the Middle Colonies was "both diverse and balanced." Expanding agricultural productivity, which grew at roughly 2 to 3

percent per year between 1700 and 1770, was a major source of economic growth. As Duane Ball and Gary Walton have pointed out, this
increase in farm output scarcely matched "modern growth rates."
Founded on strong external and internal markets, regional specialization, and improvements in farming and processing techniques, it was
nevertheless extraordinarily impressive when compared to "the stagnation observed for most pre-industrial economies" of the time and certainly signaled a highly commercialized agricultural economy in which
farmers may have contributed up to 40 percent of their produce to the
marketplace.[3]

From the earliest settlement of these "bread colonies," wheat and
other grains and grain products had been almost as important to their
economies as tobacco was to the Chesapeake. Grain was a profitable
staple for which there was a high overseas demand, and its production
was especially stimulated after 1730 by growing markets in southern
Europe. In the late 1760s, grains and grain products accounted for
over 72 percent of the value of Middle-Colony exports to Europe, the
West Indies, and Africa. Although Great Britain and Ireland accounted
for just over 6 percent of this trade, most of it went to the West
Indies, traditionally the major market for Middle-Colony grain, and
southern Europe, the former accounting for over 47 percent of the
total and the latter for 46 percent. Of the other major agricultural
exports, flaxseed, which accounted for nearly 7 percent of the total
value of overseas exports, went almost entirely to Ireland, and livestock
and meat products, which composed about 5.5 percent of the total,
went primarily to the West Indies. These figures do not include a
burgeoning coastal trade with other continental colonies, which, by
1770, amounted to slightly more than 40 percent of the value of goods
exported from the region.[4]

Throughout the Middle Colonies, family farms were the primary
source of this large agricultural output. The predominant settlement
pattern among all national groups was the individual farm "under one
operator, in most cases under one owner," with "farmsteads placed
amidst contiguous fields" in "complex, open country neighborhoods
without certain edges or centers." Farms in excess of five hundred acres
were relatively common during the early generations of settlement.
But after 1730 in the oldest settled counties and by the third generation
in more recently occupied areas, growing population density and rising land prices had resulted in a steady decline in the median size of

farms to just over two hundred acres in New Jersey by the 1740s and to between eighty and two hundred acres in southeastern Pennsylvania by the 1760s. Because of the general shortage and high cost of labor, these smaller acreages were still highly profitable—and probably even more efficient—units of production than larger units. Although the growing demand for grain exports and expanding urban markets for foodstuffs in Philadelphia, New York, and several other smaller towns led to the development of some specialized agriculture, especially in the vicinity of towns, most farms throughout the region seem to have engaged in general mixed farming, producing a wide range of crops and livestock for both home consumption and sale.[5]

Advancing land prices and the rapid diminution of unoccupied land in the oldest settled areas combined through the middle decades of the eighteenth century to produce two results. First, they led to the opening up of new areas and the rapid spread of the Middle-Colony settlement pattern into new areas, a situation that proved to be a significant source of profits for land developers. These included both proprietary groups who had inherited control of vast tracts of land from the original charter grantees or purchasers—the Penn family in Pennsylvania and Delaware, the West Jersey Council of Proprietors, and the East Jersey Board of Proprietors—and speculators who acquired vast holdings from these proprietors or, in the case of New York after 1688, directly from the royal government. During the three decades between 1680 and 1710, influential public figures engrossed over 2 million acres of some of the best agricultural land in New York.[6]

A second result was an increase in tenancy, which has traditionally been associated primarily with New York, where since the Dutch period the largest landholders had endeavored to function as European-style landlords. By the early eighteenth century, New York had about thirty "great baronial estates" almost equally divided between non-manorial and manorial estates. In theory, manorial estates all carried privileges of feudal lordship, including the right to hold civil and criminal courts and to extract fowl and labor rents from tenants. In practice, as Sung Bok Kim has shown, neighboring local jurisdictions early swallowed up most of these privileges until by the 1720s only the erratically collected fowl and labor rents remained, and the latter were exacted from residents of all political jurisdictions of New York. Nevertheless, historians have often seen these great estates as a feudal anomaly in Middle-Colony society.[7]

As Kim's work reveals, however, these estates were "far more capital-istic . . . in character than feudal." Although they were leaseholds, the individual farms into which they were divided were of roughly the same size, organization, and orientation as those elsewhere in the Mid-dle Colonies and, even more important, were nearly as profitable to their commercially oriented operators as were the freehold properties of southeastern Pennsylvania. Increasing pressures on land resources in the old settlements and, between 1742 and 1763, warfare on the fron-tiers enabled landlords to achieve considerable success in luring ten-ants to their estates. By the 1770s, there were six to seven thousand tenants in New York. But the abundance of cheap land elsewhere in the Middle Colonies had always made it difficult for landlords to re-cruit tenants and had early forced them to offer unusually favorable rental terms.

These terms included material help such as a year's provisions, farm-ing equipment, seeds, livestock, and sometimes a house; secure leases with an initial rent-free period and low annual rents thereafter; local services such as gristmills, sawmills, and stores; and, most important, equity in whatever improvements tenants made to their holdings in the form of buildings, orchards, fences, cleared fields, and gardens. Not surprisingly, such enticements were especially appealing to those many people who lacked the resources necessary to purchase a free-hold and make the large capital outlay required to start an independent farm.[8]

Even though conflicting land claims between New York and Massa-chusetts led to several uprisings among tenants along the border in the 1750s and to an even more widespread revolt in 1766, these arrange-ments, Kim shows, produced a social order that for most of the eigh-teenth century and for all but a few of New York's large landed estates was stable, peaceful, and profitable for landlords and tenants alike. For landlords it was sufficiently successful that, whereas the founding and second generations of landlords were principally merchants, whose interest in their lands was clearly auxiliary to commercial enterprise, members of the third generation, which came into control after 1745, received enough money in rents that they could deemphasize their commercial activities and "settle down as rentiers and sedentary coun-try gentlemen." Although the fortunes of individual tenants varied, most managed under these favorable conditions to achieve consider-able prosperity. Some even obtained an equity in their leaseholds equal to that of the landlord, and many acquired the financial capability to purchase their own freeholds.[9]

The function of tenancy as a vehicle of opportunity for the impoverished and those just starting out in life and as an agency for the spread of the mixed-farming commercial agricultural economy that characterized the Middle Colonies and the eighteenth-century Chesapeake was by no means limited to New York. Rather, it was common to all the Middle Colonies, where, more and more after 1720, wealthy urban merchants and professionals who had invested in both undeveloped land and developed rural properties in hope of renting for a profit found many young families willing to become tenants. Leaseholding was widespread in New Jersey, and during the 1750s close to 50 percent of the landholders in Chester County, Pennsylvania, were renters rather than freeholders. As in New York, renting or leasing in Delaware, Pennsylvania, and New Jersey was a necessary first step for many who hoped to acquire an independent freehold in places where land prices were no longer cheap.[10]

The grains and livestock produced on the freeholds and leaseholds in the rich agricultural hinterlands of the Middle Colonies were the main foundation for an expanding export trade, but an increasingly numerous and differentiated group of innovative and industrious merchants provided the commercial, organizational, and distributional services essential to its development. Presiding over an enormous increase in the volume of exports after 1720, these merchants were always alert to new trading possibilities and were chiefly responsible for "the opening of a direct trade to Ireland, the growth of the immigrant traffic," the expansion of trade with southern Europe, the opening up of a modest slave trade with Africa, "and the rapid growth of the coastal trade," especially with New England and the Carolinas. They were responsible as well for the introduction of more efficient maritime practices, including shorter turnaround times, larger ships, smaller crews, and an "increasingly sophisticated insurance market." Finally, along with millers, carters, and haulers, they played the major role in stimulating technological advances in the milling industry, introducing innovations in transport, and organizing internal trading networks.[11]

The mercantile communities of the Middle Colonies were both large and diverse. Before 1720, a significant number of merchants could be found in smaller ports, Newcastle in Delaware and Salem,

Burlington, and Perth Amboy in New Jersey. Over the next four or five decades, however, they tended to concentrate in Philadelphia and New York. Although the New York merchant community was smaller, the number of merchants in Philadelphia grew from about 200 in 1750 to about 320 in 1774. During the early years of the eighteenth century, they were mostly general merchants with little tendency to specialize in any one branch of trade, and they engaged mostly only in direct trade back and forth between one of the Middle-Colony ports and one of the major trading areas, the West Indies, the North American coast, Ireland, Britain, or southern Europe and the Wine Islands.

As the scale of trade became larger and trading patterns became more complex after 1750, however, considerable geographical and functional specialization occurred within the merchant community, at least in Philadelphia. By the 1770s, exporting firms tended to trade mostly with only one of the main geographical sectors of Middle-Colony trade. At the same time, the provision trade, to take an important example, involved "three distinct types of merchants: shippers who employed their capital in importing and exporting; flour merchants and lumber merchants who supplied these shippers with their outward cargoes; and distributors who sold in the hinterland the shippers' inward cargoes of groceries."[12]

Middle-Colony merchants not only became more specialized during the middle decades of the eighteenth century, they also accumulated enough capital to own a substantial proportion of the ships employed in overseas trade. Earlier in the century, most of the tonnage seems to have been still British owned. By 1770, however, three out of every five ships clearing the port of New York and three out of every four clearing the port of Philadelphia were locally owned, and Pennsylvanians had around £500,000 tied up in their shipping industry. These figures reveal both the remarkable ability of Middle-Colony businessmen "to generate increasing amounts of investment capital" and the existence of a substantial shipbuilding industry that, in the Delaware valley alone, produced around ninety-five thousand tons of shipping between 1722 and 1776 in large annual amounts, ranging between 1746 and 1775 from twenty-five to fifty-five ships and fifteen hundred to thirty-seven hundred tons per year.[13]

In addition to shipbuilding and such associated industries as ship chandleries, ropewalks, and sail lofts, a variety of other industries—flour mills, meatpacking, and other food-processing industries—were important industrial activities in the Middle Colonies from the 1730s onward. Extractive industries involving wood, iron, and potash earned considerable capital both in local markets and in the export sector, wood products accounting for 5.5 percent, iron for 5.25 percent, and potash for 2.3 percent of Middle-Colony exports between 1768 and 1772. Wood exports consisting of lumber, casks, staves, and naval stores went in large quantities to the West Indies and in smaller ones to Ireland, southern Europe, and Britain, and potash and iron, composed mostly of raw pig iron, went almost entirely to Britain. Although some wood products and potash were collected from other colonies in the coastal trade, much was also produced locally, as was virtually all of the iron, which was manufactured on large "plantations" in all of the Middle Colonies. By the late colonial period, most of the output of the Middle-Colony iron industry was being consumed locally. Nevertheless, in the total volume of iron exports, the Middle Colonies were second only to the Chesapeake.[14]

The labor market in this burgeoning economy was usually vigorous and often almost "insatiable." In all probability free labor always predominated in the Middle Colonies as it did in New England. By the last decade of the colonial period, only about 15 percent of the labor force in Philadelphia and probably considerably less in the countryside was unfree. Nevertheless, indentured servants were always a vital part of the labor market, especially in Pennsylvania, Delaware, and western New Jersey. Though the Chesapeake continued to be the primary market for servants, taking between five and six times as many as any other group of colonies between 1773 and 1776, the Middle Colonies were the second largest importers of servants during those years.

In the Middle Colonies, as in the Chesapeake, servitude was primarily "a rural, agricultural institution." During the second half of the eighteenth century in the Middle Colonies, however, it was also evolving "into an urban, service sector institution" with many servants employed in the larger cities and surrounding towns. Whereas servants accounted for only 1 to 3 percent of laborers in surrounding counties in the early 1770s, they made up about 5 percent of the labor force in Philadelphia, where artisans, craftsmen, and other middle-level industrial, commercial, and service sector employers were the primary purchasers of servants in virtually every occupational category.[15]

Slavery was also an important institution in the Middle Colonies. The black population, only a tiny fraction of which was free, rose just under five times between 1710 and 1770 from a little over 6,000 in 1710 to about 16,500 in 1740 to just under 35,000 in 1770. Because immigration and natural increase among whites were so vigorous, the proportion of blacks in the total population fell gradually over this period from about 9 percent in 1710 to 7.25 percent in 1740 to 6.25 percent in 1770. But these aggregate figures understate the importance of slavery to some areas. Slaves were considerably more significant in the Hudson valley than in the Philadelphia hinterland. In New York and eastern New Jersey, they consistently accounted for 14 to 15 percent of the population, whereas in western New Jersey, Pennsylvania, and Delaware they constituted only between 2 and 5 percent.

There were further variations within these two broad interregional patterns. During the half-century before the American Revolution, Kings, Richmond, Queens, and Ulster counties in New York and Bergen County in New Jersey were all more than 20 percent slave, and Kings registered in excess of 30 percent even after 1749. Slaves made up about 30 percent of laborers in New York City in 1746. Next to Charleston, New York was the second largest "urban center of slavery in colonial, eighteenth-century British North America." Although the proportion of slaves in both New York City and Ulster County slowly declined to around 14 percent between 1756 and 1771, it was still rising in other New York counties during those years, from 14 percent to over 17 percent in Albany County and from just under 11 percent to almost 16 percent in Westchester.

By contrast, within the Philadelphia hinterland, for which population statistics are less precise, slavery seems to have been most prominent during the earlier eighteenth century, though it was still an expanding institution during the late colonial period. Although many Pennsylvania and some western New Jersey counties were no more than 2 to 3 percent slave, many jurisdictions, including Delaware, Philadelphia, several New Jersey counties—Hunterdon, Cape May, Burlington, and Salem—and perhaps even some south-central Pennsylvania counties, had slave populations in the 1760s and early 1770s ranging between 5 and 9 percent of the total number of inhabitants. Although slavery began to decline sharply in Philadelphia after 1770, it "actually showed signs of growing in [much of] rural Pennsylvania."[16]

Some iron plantations employed as many as thirty to fifty slaves in the production of charcoal and other aspects of the iron industry, but the Middle Colonies "produced no staples that required a plantation-style labor force," and most slaveholders owned relatively few slaves. Although many slaveowners had 5 or 6 slaves, the average number was only about 3 in rural areas of the Philadelphia hinterland and only 2.4 in Philadelphia. Figures for the Hudson valley were probably only slightly higher. Along with the concentration of slaves in wealthy households, this pattern of distribution strongly suggests, as Alan Tully has argued, that to some important extent slavery functioned as a status symbol for slaveowning families. In Jean Soderlund's words, "a staff of black servants clearly denoted the owner's power and wealth."[17]

But two other considerations make it clear that slavery was also a viable economic institution in the Middle Colonies. First, demand remained high throughout the last years of the colonial period. In particular, the port of New York seems always to have offered a lively market for slaves. Between 1700 and 1774, it imported around seventy-four hundred slaves representing a total capital outlay of roughly £238,000 sterling. "Highly seasonal" and far more "fragile," the Philadelphia market was "easily glutted . . . and required that . . . slaves be moved about for prospective buyers." Yet, toward the end of the Seven Years' War, when the loss of large numbers of servants to military service rendered servant labor less desirable, Philadelphia and its hinterland managed to absorb more than twelve hundred slaves in just six years between 1759 and 1762. Before midcentury, most slaves came in relatively small lots primarily from other British plantation colonies to the south. Beginning in 1748 in New York and in 1759 in Philadelphia, however, local merchants trading on their own imported slaves in much larger numbers directly from Africa.[18]

If the rising volume of slave imports during the 1750s and 1760s strongly argues for substantial continuing demand for slaves as laborers in the Middle Colonies, so also does the broad diffusion of slavery throughout the economy. During the first half of the eighteenth century, a majority of Middle-Colony slaves almost certainly were purchased in agricultural areas, where most slaveowners were wealthy farmers and most slaves were either farm laborers or domestics. Nor did slavery decline in rural areas after midcentury. Even in the Philadelphia hinterland, where developing opposition to slavery among Quakers after 1750 led to the withdrawal of most Quaker merchants from the slave trade and a powerful demand among Quakers for the manumission of slaves, slavery "continued to increase through the 1770s." In rural New York, New Jersey, Delaware, and south-central Pennsylvania, slaves still constituted a majority of unfree laborers on the eve of the American Revolution.[19]

But slaves were also present in large numbers in towns, where they served "as one significant source of labor" for urban homes, shops, and other commercial and industrial enterprises. In both New York and Philadelphia, they could be found working at virtually every conceivable task. They served as sailors, shipwrights, ropemakers, sailmakers, stevedores, teamsters, bakers, masons, carpenters, shoemakers, tailors, butchers, millers, hatters, skinners, brushmakers, distillers, sugar boilers, candlers, coopers, clockmakers, joiners, barbers, brewers, and domestics, as well as in a variety of still more specialized trades. More and more after 1730, craftsmen, lesser merchants, and shopkeepers were purchasing slaves to assist them in their work. By the 1750s, almost 70 percent of the wealthier craftsmen in Philadelphia had slaves. As the countryside in the Middle Colonies became more highly urbanized after 1760, moreover, craftsmen and merchants in growing towns such as Lancaster and New Brunswick employed slaves in a similarly wide variety of tasks. Although the slave population of Philadelphia declined rapidly after 1770, the expansion of slavery in that city in the 1750s and 1760s has led Gary Nash to observe that "slaveowning in Pennsylvania was [becoming] predominantly an urban phenomenon" during those years, albeit the same seems to have been less true of New York.[20]

Except perhaps on the iron plantations, slavery in the Middle Colonies, as in New England, was free from the harsh gang labor regimes present in many areas of plantation British America, but this organizational distinction did not make the institution any more palatable for slaves. Although sex ratios were nearly equal, the scattering of slaves in small numbers in many separate households precluded the achievement of a settled family life for most slaves, and only Philadelphia and New York City had a sufficient concentration of Afro-Americans to permit the emergence of a well-developed sense of community among them.[21]

Slave regulations in Pennsylvania, which, as a result of Quaker activities after 1750, became one of the earliest places in the English-speaking world to develop an organized movement to abolish slavery, were somewhat less draconian than those elsewhere in the Middle Colonies. But slave codes were severe everywhere and discontent and resistance among slaves widespread. The first major organized slave revolt in British North America occurred in 1712 in New York, which also experienced a second alleged plot in 1741. Authorities executed eighteen slaves in 1712 and thirty-one slaves and four whites in 1741, when they also banished seventy other slaves to the West Indies. These events dramatically revealed the extent of black discontent with the slave system, the depth of white fears of slave revolt, and the harsh character of Middle-Colony slavery.[22]

Demographic and territorial growth, economic expansion and diversification, and substantial investments in bound labor were not the only indications that the Middle Colonies were proceeding along developmental lines similar to those experienced earlier in the Chesapeake. Spreading urbanization; a more complex occupational structure; a rising number of professionals, especially lawyers; growing wealth and social stratification; and expanding consumption of English imports all revealed that, perhaps even to a greater extent than the Chesapeake colonies, the Middle Colonies were becoming more like Britain as they became more settled.

Through the middle decades of the eighteenth century, the Middle Colonies were rapidly achieving significant levels of urbanization. They contained the two largest and most important cities, first Philadelphia in the 1740s and then New York in the 1750s and 1760s overtaking Boston in both population and volume of economic activity. Despite a high death rate in both cities, by 1774 Philadelphia had grown to between twenty-seven and thirty thousand and New York to between twenty-two and twenty-five thousand. But urban development was not limited to these major centers. Especially after 1730, older and smaller administrative centers—the capital towns of Newcastle, Delaware, and Burlington and Perth Amboy, New Jersey—and secondary ports and trading centers—New Brunswick, Trenton, Elizabethtown, and Newark, New Jersey, and Albany, New York—increased in size and occupational specialization. Albany had nearly four thousand inhabitants by 1775. During the same period, many new towns emerged as county seats and as transport and processing centers. In Pennsylvania and Delaware alone, fifty-five such towns were founded between 1730 and 1775. Not all of them prospered, but the more successful ones, Wilmington, Lancaster, and Reading, had between a thousand and twenty-five hundred inhabitants by the mid-1770s, and at least a dozen others had from three hundred to a thousand. By 1765, almost one-fifth of Pennsylvanians lived in towns.[23]

As the employment of more and more servants and slaves in non-agricultural work suggests, growing urbanization combined with increasing population density in the countryside to stimulate the development of an increasingly complex occupational structure and the rise of a small but growing class of specialized professionals. Not just in Philadelphia and New York, both of which exhibited a full range of urban occupations and professions by the 1720s and 1730s, but also in the smaller towns and even in the oldest settled rural areas, a growing proportion of the population found opportunities outside of farming: a few as merchants, lawyers, doctors, ministers, and millers and many more as artisans, craftsmen, and laborers. In 1760 in Lancaster and Chester counties, Pennsylvania, "from 30 to 40 per cent of rural taxable persons were non-farmers," although most of them continued to produce some food for themselves. This diversification served to keep economic opportunity high even in areas where unoccupied land was no longer available.[24]

The social structure also became more differentiated. As was the case in both the Chesapeake and New England, wealth became significantly more concentrated and social stratification more marked. This was especially true in the cities, where by the early 1770s the wealthiest 10 percent controlled over 65 percent of the taxable wealth and the bottom 30 percent less than 2 percent. As the wealthy urban mercantile elites acquired more resources to spend on building elegant townhouses, purchasing urban rental properties and country estates, filling their houses and wardrobes with items made according to the latest English fashions, and otherwise imitating the genteel urban lifestyle of contemporary British cities, a growing class of people were permanently either on poor relief or "trapped in low-paying jobs that kept them close to the subsistence margin," albeit the extent of poverty was far lower than in London, Bristol, Liverpool, and other major British cities. In Philadelphia and New York, as in British cities, however, urban neighborhoods were beginning to be defined according to the economic resources of their inhabitants.[25]

Although social stratification was also increasing in rural areas and in smaller urban centers, property was much less unevenly distributed in the countryside. Though few other rural landowners could match the great landlords of New York in the extent of their fortunes, most older settled counties had several residents with estates valued in excess of £2,000 and even more with estates worth more than £1,000. But these rural elites owned a far smaller proportion of property than did their urban counterparts. Indeed, for the Middle Colonies as a whole at the end of the colonial period, property was significantly more equally divided than it was in either the Chesapeake or New England. Whereas the top 20 percent controlled almost 70 percent of the wealth in the Chesapeake and over 65 percent in New England, it owned just under 53 percent in the Middle Colonies. Throughout the Middle Colonies, "the rural prosperity that accompanied the expansion of the export sector . . . was widely shared and . . . did not lead to a sharp increase in inequality."[26]

As James Lemon has written about southeastern Pennsylvania, the Middle Colonies were "without doubt . . . one of the most affluent agricultural societies anywhere" in the eighteenth century. This affluence was reflected in the inhabitants' ability to pay for a rising volume of imports from Britain, the annual average value of which increased from just under £100,000 in the 1720s, to over £250,000 in the 1740s to almost £700,000 in the 1760s. It was reflected as well in a higher standard of living for the vast majority of the population, who lived in better and larger housing units and owned greater quantities of a wider range of consumer goods. For the society as a whole, this expanding wealth made possible the construction of elegant public buildings and churches; an improving network of roads, bridges, and ferries; the creation of a variety of new cultural institutions, including, after 1750, four separate institutions of higher learning located in Philadelphia, Princeton, New Brunswick, and New York; and the evolution of vigorous urban societies in both Philadelphia and New York.[27]

As most historians of the region have emphasized, this affluent and developing society continued throughout the middle decades of the eighteenth century to rest upon the same broad heterogeneous base that had characterized it from the beginning. More than any other region of colonial British America, the Middle Colonies were a pluralistic society containing a large variety of linguistic, ethnic, and religious groups. In this "patchwork of cultures," groups of the like-minded and the clannish could—and, like the Moravians in Bethlehem or the Scots in central New Jersey, often did—band together to form well-defined and clearly bounded communities in which they could pursue their own particular vision of happiness in the New World. The result was a mélange of cultural configurations in which modes of land use, community structures, strength and nature of religious ties, inheritance practices, and patterns of family and social relations varied considerably within the same political jurisdictions.[28]

Yet it is easy to exaggerate both the extent and the importance of these variations, many of which "were of superficial rather than [of] substantial nature." The rich cultural diversity of the Middle Colonies should not blind scholars to the emergence of a common cultural core as a result of a steady process of social amalgamation in which, especially during the last half-century of the colonial period, people of different backgrounds learned to live together at the same time that they were adapting themselves to a physical and political environment that was common to all of them. In their predominant pattern of settlement "on isolated farmsteads and in crossroads communities," in their housing and in their farm buildings, in their agricultural practices, in their diet, and in their willingness to move, they all displayed an astonishing similarity.[29]

The same can be said about family relations. With their "purified household environments, voluntary love marriages, financially independent conjugal households, and tender child rearing," Quaker families may very well have been somewhat in advance of other Middle-Colony residents in achieving the most important attributes of the modern family. Among almost every group, however, the nuclear family living together in an independent household and practicing partible inheritance was the norm. Although intergenerational ties were often strong and "families understood and accepted responsibility for their own members," sons routinely achieved early independence, parental authority over adult children was weak, and children showed little reluctance to move away from their parents in the quest to improve their material prospects. As land became less abundant, moreover, most groups showed a steady "linear progression to modern rates of low fertility" and a correspondingly smaller number of children per completed family. "More committed to individual prosperity than to the binding ties of kinship and Old World traditions," most Middle-Colony inhabitants shared in "a distinctively privatistic, pragmatic style of family experience."[30]

If this particular family experience served as a common foundation for the essentially "privatistic, middle-class social order" that developed throughout most of the Middle Colonies during the colonial era, that order was sustained by a broadly shared commitment to a set of values rooted in "the premises of possessive individualism." No less than the older society in the Chesapeake, Middle-Colony society showed a powerful tendency to embrace the "American obsession with acquiring and accumulating." Although relatively few people were "the single-minded maximizing materialists" depicted by some liberal historians, most displayed a "middle class faith in the right to seek success," very often placed "individual freedom and material gain over that of the public interest," and believed devoutly in "liberty, the sanctity of private property, the legitimacy of profit, family, and harmony."[31]

In a society with these priorities, communities and governments could only be regarded as "necessary evils to support individual fulfillment." The result was a deep and broadly diffused suspicion of established authority rooted in the powerful antiauthoritarian strain within the dominant Quaker population in Pennsylvania but also manifest in New York, where contempt of authority accounted for a significant proportion of criminal prosecutions. As in the Chesapeake, government at both the provincial and local levels, including the criminal justice system, was necessarily weak and limited in scope. With no professional police, a small amateur establishment to enforce judicial decisions, and widespread public aversion to serving on juries or performing other public obligations, local institutions were weak and remarkably inclusive. In Pennsylvania, a strong movement toward more popular control of local affairs had, by the 1730s, shifted responsibility for assessing taxes and administering many other local matters from the appointed justices of the peace to elected county commissioners. In all the Middle Colonies, in short, both provincial and local political institutions were too weak and too closely tied to the populace not to demonstrate a powerful "sensitivity to local and popular pressure."[32]

Borrowing uncritically from modern social science, several recent historians have stressed the extent to which the diversity and growth of the Middle Colonies were corrosive of social cohesion and stability. In the Middle Colonies, as in New England, the "general trend," in the words of Douglas Greenberg, "was away from tranquil social stability toward fragmentation and conflict of significant dimensions." But there are many problems with this characterization of Middle-Colony society, not the least of which is that, except perhaps for a few of the early puritan settlements on Long Island and in New Jersey and the still fewer utopian communities established by German sectarians in

Pennsylvania during the eighteenth century, none of the Middle Colonies ever seems to have enjoyed a "tranquil social stability" at any time during the early generations of settlement. Having "never known a time of tranquility" during their early histories, the Middle Colonies during the eighteenth century, like the Chesapeake and unlike New England, seem to have been moving not from coherence to incoherence but from incoherence to coherence.[33]

To be sure, during the last four decades of the colonial period, Middle-Colony elites were considerably less cohesive and commanded even less public deference than those in the Chesapeake colonies and perhaps even in some parts of New England, provincial politics was more "conflict-ridden" than in any other region of colonial British America, and large-scale violence was more frequent than elsewhere. As Michael Kammen, Sung Bok Kim, and Thomas L. Purvis, among others, have all pointed out, however, even the great land riots in New Jersey and New York between the mid-1740s and 1766 provided evidence of the strong regional commitment to the tenets of possessive individualism. So far from being "'levelers' eager to alter an unjust system of social class and vicious economic exploitation," the rioters were through their actions dramatically underlining their own attachment to those tenets. In New Jersey, they were conservative defenders of property rights who selectively employed extrainstitutional pressure in an effort to gain secure title to their lands. In New York, they were "landowners *manques* . . . who wanted a piece of the system more than they wanted to revise it."[34]

Many other developments during the mid-eighteenth century also powerfully revealed that Middle-Colony society was not falling apart but coming together. The emergence of "protoparties out of the older system of chaotic, impermanent factions" at the provincial level, the achievement of an underlying consensus on the basic nature of the political system, the increasing acceptance of the existence of an organized political opposition, the development—present from their early histories but further stimulated by the experience of the Great Awakening—of a broadly accepted religious toleration, the growing perception of society as a series of competing "economic interest blocs," the emergence of the courts as an "impersonal means for settling disputes and maintaining order" in societies with "no all-encompassing private institutions," the appearance of a more permissive attitude toward minor crime, the rise in social spending and civic consciousness represented by improvements in private and public buildings and public services, and the evident growth—reflected in the newspapers—"in provincial consciousness and native chauvinism" all suggest that residents of the Middle Colonies were rapidly coming to terms with their "extraordinarily heterogeneous society."[35]

All these developments indicate that in the Middle Colonies, as in the Chesapeake, a common devotion to the pursuit of family and individual happiness served as a powerful social cement that, in a society with many unexploited resources, enabled people to come to terms with their diversity and to develop attitudes and forms of behavior appropriate to it. In the process, they seem to have acquired a "preparedness for novelty," a psychology of accommodation, a receptivity to change, and a tolerance for diversity that provided the basis for an emerging cohesiveness and sense of identity that, though quite unlike those in many more homogeneous societies and still fragile in situations of conflict between material interests or competing ambitions, promoted habits of "social flexibility." These habits in turn both served as an important foundation for the emergence of social cohesion and coherence and enabled the Middle Colonies to pass "through the eighteenth century in [relative] peace and harmony amidst diversity." Coercive and homogenous community of the kind associated with early New England was neither a prerequisite for nor a preventive to the achievement of social order in the Middle Colonies.[36]

IN their socioeconomic development between 1713 and 1775, the lower southern colonies of South Carolina, North Carolina, and Georgia, like the Middle Colonies, also conformed to a developmental model similar to that in the Chesapeake. As, especially after 1745, the low countries of these colonies became increasingly more settled, coherent, and complex, they came more and more to resemble a well-established Old World society. Also similar to the Middle Colonies, the Lower South continued after 1713, as before, to be divided into two distinct regions. With its mixture of plantations and farms, the area from the Cape Fear River Valley north to the northern border of North Carolina continued to resemble the Chesapeake. Before the mid-1730s, settlement in this region was largely confined to a small area extending not more than fifty to one hundred miles inland from the coast. Well before 1750, however, this extension of the "greater Chesapeake" culture had begun to expand rapidly; by the 1770s, it had reached all the way to the Appalachian Mountains in the west and stretched south into the backcountries of South Carolina and Georgia, where it met and intermingled with a second, related, but quite distinct culture expanding west from the low country.

First articulated in the vicinity of Charleston between 1670 and 1720, the plantation, staple-producing culture of the low country spread rapidly thereafter throughout the coastal region of the Carolinas. By the late 1730s, it extended over a long strip reaching from the Savannah River north into the Cape Fear River valley of North Carolina. Even though the founders of Georgia had intended that colony to be free from slavery and plantation agriculture, this vigorous socioeconomic and cultural system spilled across the Savannah River into Georgia beginning in the late 1740s. From Georgia, it expanded after 1763 into the newly acquired colonies of East and West Florida.[37]

As elsewhere in continental colonial British America, territorial expansion was accompanied by vigorous demographic growth. Between 1710 and 1740, population in the Lower South increased more than four times, from just over 25,000 to around 110,000. During the next thirty years, it rose by more than a factor of three. By 1770, it had reached nearly 350,000. In contrast to other regions on the continent, however, relatively little of this growth was the result of natural increase. Throughout the coastal area of the Lower South, a malignant disease environment in which malaria and other fevers flourished kept mortality at levels only slightly more favorable than those of the seventeenth-century Chesapeake. In some areas, it may even have been worse. In Christ Church Parish outside Charleston, for example, 86 percent of those whose births and deaths were recorded died before the age of twenty, and fewer than 10 percent of those born before 1760 lived beyond age sixty. The survival rate was higher in St. Johns, Berkeley, where between 20 and 25 percent of those born during the same period lived beyond sixty. In Charleston itself mortality may have been even higher.

Although the white population was almost certainly self-sustaining by the 1730s and 1740s, and mortality may even have begun to decline considerably after midcentury, most of the population increase in the low country was the result of immigration. Especially after 1730, the Carolinas and Georgia, like the Middle Colonies, attracted large numbers of English, Scots, Ulster Scots, and Germans. Some of these arrived directly from Europe. Many more came through the colonies to the north. Only with the settlement of the backcountry starting in the 1740s and 1750s does the Lower South appear to have begun to exhibit the same high levels of vigorous natural population increase achieved elsewhere in eighteenth-century British North America.[38]

Throughout the half-century before the American Revolution, the population of the Lower South was far more heavily slave and black than that of other areas of contemporary continental British America. The black population rose sharply from less than 3,000 in 1700 to 6,600 in 1710, to slightly over 50,000 in 1730, and to more than 155,000 in 1770. A majority of these slaves were concentrated in low-country South Carolina and Georgia, where total numbers jumped from about 4,000 in 1710 to over 39,000 in 1740 to almost 86,000 in 1770. But the black population of North Carolina increased dramatically after mid-century, from around 10,000 in 1740 to nearly 70,000 in 1770. Before 1720, South Carolina's black population seems to have been able to generate a natural increase. But with the intensification of staple agriculture in the 1720s and 1730s and, probably much more important, the importation of large numbers of new slaves from Africa, it began, like its counterparts in the West Indian colonies, to experience a net annual decrease. Though the slave population seems to have again become self-sustaining after 1760, most of the enormous increase in slaves was the result of large imports, which, except for the decade of the 1740s, remained high throughout the colonial period.

The ratio of blacks to whites in the Lower South was always high. From about a quarter of the total population in 1710, it rose above 40 percent in the late 1730s and hovered between 42 and 45 percent for the rest of the colonial period. But these figures disguise important intra-regional variations. For most of the period after 1720 in both South Carolina and, after 1755, Georgia, the black-white ratio seems to have remained roughly at 2 to 2.5 to 1, and in some low-country parishes, the importation of blacks and the emigration of whites had, by the 1750s, raised the ratio as high as 9 to 1. This figure is far above that found in any other area of British North America, well above that found in colonial Barbados, and only slightly below that found in Jamaica. Such a racial distribution indeed made those parts of the low country seem, in the words of one contemporary, "more like a Negro country" than a settlement of people of European descent.[39]

The massive and rapidly expanding slave population of the Lower South amply testified to the vigor of its staple agricultural economy.

Rice was far and away the most important product. Following its first successful cultivation in the 1690s, rice production, as measured by exports, grew steadily during the first three decades of the eighteenth century from 1.5 million pounds in 1710 to nearly 20 million by 1730. By the 1720s, it had become South Carolina's most valuable export, a position it held throughout the colonial period. Between 1730 and 1750, the rice market was erratic, and exports increased slowly, except for a brief period in the late 1730s. Starting in the early 1750s, however, exports once again began to surge steadily upward, led by high external demand. Between 1768 and 1772, Britain took about two-thirds of the crop and southern Europe and the West Indies each about one-sixth. By the early 1770s, rice ranked fourth in total value among exports from Britain's American colonies behind only sugar, tobacco, and wheat.[40]

But the low country never became monocultural. Throughout the colonial period, it continued to export most of its earliest products: deerskins, naval stores, lumber and barrel staves, all of which went mostly to Britain, and grains and meat products, which went mostly to the West Indies. Beginning in the 1740s, the reintroduction of indigo by Eliza Lucas Pinckney and others and its successful production (almost wholly for the British market) provided the low country with a second highly profitable staple, albeit one whose quality was not sufficiently high to sustain it following the withdrawal of a British bounty after the American Revolution. Between 1768 and 1772, rice accounted for about 55 percent of the value of all exports, indigo for 20 percent, deerskins, naval stores, and lumber products each for between 5 and 7 percent, and grain and meat products each for about 2 percent. The diversity—and the latent capacity—of the low-country economy is illustrated by Robert M. Weir's calculation that the record rice crop of 1770 was grown by less than 50 percent of the slave population on no more than 3 percent of the land in private hands and that the largest harvest of indigo was grown by only about 13 percent of the slaves on less than 0.5 percent of such land.[41]

The economy of North Carolina was even more diverse. The production of rice and indigo was limited to a small area adjacent to South Carolina in the lower Cape Fear River valley, and the colony's pattern of exports closely resembled that of the Chesapeake. Tobacco, shipped mostly to Britain, and corn, wheat, livestock, and meat products, sent mostly to the West Indies, were relatively more important sources of export income than in the low country. But the most important exports were naval stores and wood products: sawn lumber, shingles, and staves. Indeed, in many areas of eastern North Carolina, the production of corn, tobacco, and rice was actually "ancillary to the production of naval stores and lumber." As H. Roy Merrens has noted, planters and farmers often reaped far "more profit from the trees on their land than they did from [their] patches of corn, rice, [tobacco], or indigo." Similar economic arrangements characterized the western areas of South Carolina and Georgia once they began to fill with population in the late 1750s.[42]

The society that grew up around this economy was highly stratified and became more so over time, though again there were significant differences between the southern and northern regions of the Lower South. In one rice-growing parish near Charleston in 1745, only 3 percent of white householders possessed no slaves, and, although the average number of slaves per household was forty-three, planters who had fifty or more owned more than two-thirds of all the slaves in the parish. Landowning patterns were similar. About a fifth of all householders owned no land, but the top third all possessed over a thousand acres, and more than 60 percent held over five hundred acres. Perhaps as many as a fifth of the total white population of South Carolina and Georgia belonged to these large slaveowning and landowning planting families. By contrast, with the exception of the rice-growing counties in the Cape Fear River valley, social stratification in North Carolina more closely resembled that of the Chesapeake during the early decades of the eighteenth century. Although the number of households with slaves increased over time, from 40 to 50 percent of most households had no slaves, almost two-thirds of those that did had only four or fewer slaves, less than a quarter had more than ten, and just 1 to 2 percent had more than twenty.[43]

In both areas of the Lower South, wealthy planters constituted the core of an emerging, increasingly creole, but still quite open elite. Merchants and lawyers, however, both of which were especially numerous in the low country, enjoyed equal status, intermarried freely with planting families, and were themselves often heavily involved in plantation agriculture. A few merchants and lawyers could be found in all of the smaller ports, towns, and hamlets of the Lower South. As the region's principal center of commercial activity, however, Charleston contained the largest concentration of both groups. By the 1730s, the bar was a significant source of income and status in Charleston, and continuing high mortality and a growing volume of business transactions combined to keep the demand for legal services high throughout the colonial period.

The mercantile community, on the other hand, was "small and financially weak" before the 1740s and did not begin to undergo substantial expansion until 1750. Over the next quarter-century, an "enterprising, aggressive, and seasoned" group of resident local merchants presided over the Lower South's "increasingly kinetic economic pace." Like its counterparts in the Middle Colonies and New England, this large and varied group seems to have handled a large proportion—perhaps as much as three-fourths—of the region's overseas trade. Although it may have owned less than 40 percent of the total tonnage involved in that trade, between 1735 and 1775 it probably invested as much as £100,000 sterling in shipping. During the middle decades of the century, it also fostered a significant shipbuilding industry.[44]

Like the Chesapeake, most of the Lower South did not begin to exhibit significant urbanization until late in the colonial period. To be sure, Charleston had long been a major town. With around twelve thousand inhabitants, it was the fourth largest town in British North America in 1775, the rapid expansion of overseas trade after 1745 having brought it an extraordinary prosperity that was reflected in the construction of several hundred new houses and commercial buildings, including several wharves, and some substantial public buildings. By the 1750s, it had most of the amenities of European provincial cities, including a wide assortment of crafts, services, and cultural activities.

Beginning in the 1750s, several smaller ports—Savannah, Georgia; Georgetown and Beaufort, South Carolina; and Wilmington, New Bern, and Edenton, North Carolina—experienced moderate demographic and commercial growth, and several new inland towns, the most important of which were Salisbury, North Carolina, Camden, South Carolina, and Augusta, Georgia, and a number of other still smaller places began to develop as distribution, service, and processing centers. Though linked together by an increasingly complex network of roads and other transportation facilities, these small "urban" centers were not yet large or numerous enough to satisfy all the demands for nonagricultural services in the extensive region of the Lower South. As in the Chesapeake, most artisans and craftsmen continued to reside in rural areas.[45]

By the 1750s and 1760s, white settlers in the low-country area of the Lower South were the wealthiest segment of the population of colonial British North America. Although well below the levels enjoyed by their counterparts in some of the Caribbean colonies, especially Jamaica, per capita wealth in the Charleston district of South Carolina in 1774 was an astonishing £2,337.7. This figure was more than four times that achieved by residents of the tobacco areas of the Chesapeake and nearly six times greater than that of people in New York and Philadelphia. Moving steadily upward after 1748, burgeoning imports, amounting by the early 1770s to almost £650,000 sterling per annum, provide still further testimony to the area's expanding wealth. Imports from Britain, southern Europe, and the Caribbean exceeded £10 sterling per capita of white population per annum, a figure that was considerably above those for the Chesapeake and far surpassed those for the Middle Colonies and New England. Nor did this figure include imported slaves, whose purchase annually accounted for a massive expenditure. So rich was the low country in the late colonial period that it was one of the few areas of colonial British America in which people had large sums of accumulated capital to lend at interest.[46]

The great wealth accumulated by the commercial gentry—the richest planters, merchants, and lawyers—of South Carolina and Georgia during the late colonial period enabled them to enjoy a luxurious and highly anglicized lifestyle comparable, within the British colonial world, only to those of similar groups in seventeenth-century Barbados and eighteenth-century Jamaica. Beginning in the 1740s, members of this group built, usually in the English style but sometimes with some West Indian modifications, several expensive public buildings and many sumptuous private houses. Though a few of them constructed elegant brick houses on their plantations, most wealthy planters chose Charleston or Savannah as the site for their principal, and most elegant, residence. With a large resident absentee planter class for much of the year, Charleston and increasingly Savannah became lively cultural centers. Charleston, in particular, had a wide assortment of urban cultural institutions such as could be found only in the most fully developed provincial cities in England. These included a library company, concerts, theater, horse races, and a variety of benevolent organizations, fraternal groups, and social clubs. By the 1770s, some Lower South families had become sufficiently wealthy that they were following the example of the West Indians and abandoning the colony altogether. In the early 1770s, as many as fifty absentee South Carolina proprietors were living in London.[47]

But absenteeism and high levels of consumption and materialism in the Lower South neither produced an immediate diminution in economic energy nor led to neglect of the public weal by the elite. At least through the end of the eighteenth century, the several elites in this dynamic region remained alive to new economic potentialities. The spread of plantation agriculture into new areas to the west and south, the introduction of indigo, the successful search for technological innovations in rice cultivation and processing, and an active interest in science, technology, and social and cultural improvements among the commercial gentry of the low country all revealed an active and expansive society that was receptive to changes that would enhance the economic well-being of its dominant population. Although the newer and less well-established elites in North Carolina—where corruption was in some parts rampant—and in Georgia had a considerably weaker record in this regard, the South Carolina gentry not only sponsored the development of a rich urban culture in Charleston but also, in the manner of its counterparts elsewhere in colonial British America, actively performed the duties of public office at both the provincial and local levels.[48]

If the commercial gentry of the low country was conscientious in fulfilling its public obligations, many of its members were ostensibly also notoriously self-indulgent and lacking in self-discipline, and the society they presided over may have been even looser and more permissive than those to the north. In a society in which high mortality inevitably meant small family size, families tended to be characterized not by strong patriarchal authority but by paternal indulgence, a child-rearing ethos that encouraged self-assertiveness and independence, and considerable autonomy for children in marriage choices. With so much wealth and so few surviving children, low-country inhabitants, in contrast to those in other regions in British North America, were able to devise an inheritance system that discriminated less against female heirs and emphasized the liquid and "commercial rather than the patrimonial character of wealth."[49]

Just as family and inheritance practices did little to encourage deference to parental authority, patterns of law enforcement were too slack to nourish deep respect for law, and depth of religious attachment and attention to education were similarly lax. Although inhabitants of older settled areas supported a considerable number of Anglican and dissenting churches, few people seem to have been compulsively religious, and the Great Awakening made little lasting impact. Perhaps because the wealthier members of the elite so often sent their children to Britain to be educated, the Lower South seems to have paid less attention to establishing educational institutions than any other region of British North America, though interest in local education may well have become stronger during the late colonial period.[50]

Astonishingly in this heavily slave society, the permissive attitude toward children, law enforcement, religion, and education also appears to have carried over into the institution of slavery. Because of the proximity of the Spanish in Florida, the French in Louisiana, and many powerful Indian tribes, the lower southern colonies, like those in the Caribbean, had always existed in recurrent danger of external attack, and the numerical preponderance of blacks in the rural rice-growing areas gave those colonies, again like those in the West Indies, a potentially powerful domestic enemy. To counteract this danger, whites early adopted a highly restrictive posture toward blacks. Based on that of Barbados, South Carolina's slave code was the most draconian on the continent. Masters and courts usually punished slave crime severely, slaves ran away in large numbers, and the specter of slave revolt always lurked in the background. Yet in contrast to seventeenth-century Barbados and to Jamaica throughout the colonial period, both of which were riven by slave revolts, the Lower South had only one major slave uprising, the Stono Rebellion of 1739 in South Carolina.[51]

The low country's unique labor regime, which to some extent appears to have mitigated some of the harshness that characterized slavery in the Caribbean colonies, may help to explain why slaves did not revolt more frequently. Most low-country slaves worked not in gangs, as did the sugar slaves in the West Indies, the tobacco slaves in the Chesapeake, or even the iron slaves in the Chesapeake and Middle Colonies, but by the task system, so that their time was their own after they had completed the specific jobs for which they were responsible. Many slaves, moreover, worked on plantations that contained few white and mainly black supervisors, they lived in their own separate houses with their families, and, no matter what their occupation, they had considerable geographical mobility.

Thus, despite the severity of the laws, slaves seem to have enjoyed some measure of autonomy in more areas than merely their work routines. Though many of them engaged in considerable "irreverent fraternizing" with whites, and the Lower South had a higher incidence of interracial sexual unions than any other region on the continent, the relatively greater distance of so much of the slave population from white society seems to have enabled them to preserve more of their African cultural heritage than did blacks elsewhere in British North America. Although it led to a tightening of the slave code and an ineffective effort to redress the population imbalance between whites and blacks, not even the Stono Rebellion fundamentally changed this slave system. After the rebellion, "as before, [white] citizens proved unwilling to engage in close surveillance of the slave population." As a consequence, a stringent new patrol act was only "casually enforced."⁵²

Not only did slaves have considerable latitude in the countryside, but they also exerted a profound influence on the shaping of the local economy, and not simply as field laborers. By enabling the more industrious slaves to grow their own produce and raise their own animals for sale to whites, the task system fostered the development by slaves of a domestic marketing system that, in its extent and economic importance, probably rivaled those of West Africa and Jamaica. Indeed, in Charleston, slaves virtually monopolized the local food market. "Although supposedly forbidden from earning wages, seeking profits, or organizing collectively," through these markets and through their involvement in virtually every artisanal, craft, and service occupation represented in the Lower South economy, slaves not only did the work but also, as Peter Wood has remarked, devised "ways to regulate that work" and, "quite literally," controlled "business in a number of avenues."⁵³

Despite the looseness of the societies of the Lower South, during the half-century before the American Revolution, the region, with its rapidly expanding demographic and economic base, had, like the Chesapeake and Middle Colonies, moved steadily from lesser to greater social coherence and complexity. If mortality remained high, it was slowly improving for both whites and blacks. If the countryside beyond Charleston and a few smaller seaport towns remained predominantly rural, significant urban development was well under way by the 1760s and 1770s. With increasing social stratification, mounting labor resources in the form of a steadily increasing number of black slaves, ever more sharply articulated elites, high levels of consumption, and, at least in the low country, a demonstrably more anglicized sociocultural life, the societies of the Lower South were passing through a developmental process that, in its general outlines, was remarkably similar to those experienced by the other continental colonies south of New England.

BETWEEN 1713 and 1760, the broad outlines and direction of social development in both the Middle Colonies and the Lower South thus conformed remarkably closely to those observed earlier for the Chesapeake, Britain, and Ireland during the century after 1660. In contrast to the orthodox puritan colonies of New England, they did not proceed from coherence to incoherence or, perhaps more accurately, from one form of coherent social order to another. Rather, they began this period in a state of considerable socioeconomic and political flux and slowly developed over the next half-century into more coherent and European-style social orders.

Chapter Seven

VARIATIONS: THE ATLANTIC AND CARIBBEAN ISLANDS, 1660–1760

During the century after 1660, all of Britain's older island colonies in America went through a process of social development that was remarkably similar to those found in the Chesapeake, England, Ireland, the Middle Colonies, and the Lower South. As was the case before 1660, these colonies fell into two dissimilar groups. Situated east of the North American continent in the Atlantic and only semitropical in climate, the small island colonies of Bermuda and the Bahamas never developed a staple agricultural system before the American Revolution. Lying farther south in the Caribbean, Barbados, Jamaica, and the four Leeward Islands of Antigua, Montserrat, Nevis, and St. Kitts concentrated on the production of staples, primarily sugar, with the large-scale use of African slave labor. Before the 1760s and 1770s in both regions, however, the direction of social development among the white settler populations was toward the establishment of an ever more coherent, settled, and Europeanized society.

BECAUSE of their small size and their unsuitability for the production of sugar, both Bermuda and the Bahamas achieved socioeconomic stasis fairly rapidly. Tobacco, the principal product of Bermuda during the first two generations of settlement, ultimately proved unable to compete with that grown in the Chesapeake and was being abandoned by the 1670s and 1680s. Thereafter, although the colony continued to produce some foodstuffs for internal consumption as well as onions, palmetto fronds, and cedarware for export, it directed its primary economic energies to building ships from its exceptionally fine cedar trees and to various seafaring activities, including fishing, whaling, smuggling, privateering (during wartime), and salt collecting in the Turks Islands.

First settled by immigrants from Bermuda in the mid-seventeenth century and consisting of hundreds of mostly small, low-lying, sandy islands, the Bahamas was a nest of pirates for much of the period before the crown took it over in 1717. Like Bermuda, it never found a highly profitable economic activity and depended heavily upon the sea for its sustenance, its exports being confined largely to relatively small amounts of dyewoods, salt, turtles and turtle shells, cotton, and fruit.[1]

Although a few people seem to have made surprisingly large fortunes from these activities during the eighteenth century, neither Bermuda nor the Bahamas offered enough economic opportunity to attract immigrants or to enable many people to acquire much wealth. Nevertheless, both were sufficiently healthy that they experienced substantial population increase during the eighteenth century. Despite considerable emigration, high losses of men at sea, and a declining birthrate among whites, the population of Bermuda almost doubled between 1698 and 1774, rising from 5,862 to 11,155. The Bahamas acquired only just over a thousand people during its first sixty or seventy years, but its population more than tripled during the half-century before 1773, when it numbered 4,293 people, over 65 percent of whom lived on the small capital island of New Providence. In both colonies, and in sharp contrast to the West Indian colonies, the black population was considerably more fecund than the white. Thus, although Bermuda imported few new slaves after the 1680s and 1690s, the proportion of blacks in the population grew from just over 38 percent in 1698 to about 45 percent in 1774. In the Bahamas, the increase was even more dramatic, from just over a quarter of the population in 1722 to almost 53 percent in 1773.[2]

In Bermuda, at least, this steadily expanding population put great pressure on the food supply. With fewer than 1.09 acres of land per inhabitant, the colony had to import a large amount of its food. There was a widespread feeling following the decline of tobacco production in the late seventeenth century that the colony had vastly more slaves than were needed to meet current labor demands, and a major slave rebellion was narrowly averted in 1761. For whatever reasons, however, families rarely parted with their slaves, and slaveownership was widely diffused. In one parish, as many as 85 percent of white families held slaves. Of an average of 9.7 members per household in 1764, 4.6 were black and 5.1 white. Although many slaves were profitably employed as shipwrights, sailors, and general laborers, many others seem to have been used within the household to perform domestic and farm chores.[3]

Despite its expanding size, the population of Bermuda was sufficiently small and persistent that, as Henry C. Wilkinson has remarked,
"by the early years of the eighteenth century nearly every family had
become related in some way to every other," and these "oldstanders,"
as descendants of the early colonists were called, formed the nucleus of
a stable social order of much the same character as could be found in
the older continental colonies at the same time. The same may have
been true for New Providence by the 1750s and 1760s. In one respect,
however, the population of Bermuda was unique in colonial British
America. Because at any one time as many as a fifth to a third of white
males were at sea and because both the emigration rate and the death
rate among the male seafaring population were high, Bermuda always
had a considerable surplus of women from the late seventeenth century
on. At the same time that its population was becoming more deeply
interconnected and more heavily female, Bermuda was both systematically attempting to make its legal and political institutions as much like
those of the metropolis as possible and, despite its partly puritan beginnings, was also becoming more Anglican. After 1720, as many as
seven-eighths of its population belonged to the established church.[4]

WHAT chiefly separated these small island colonies from those in the
Caribbean was the enormous profitability of sugar. With its exploitive
and materialistic orientation, concentration on sugar production, a
slave-powered plantation system, a highly stratified social structure,
great disparities in wealth and styles of life, a high ratio of blacks to
whites, little attention to the development of family life and other
traditional social institutions and cultural amenities, high levels of absenteeism among the wealthy, a rapid turnover among the elite, and
heavy mortality, the socioeconomic and cultural model first successfully articulated in Barbados slowly spread between 1660 and 1720 to
the four neighboring Leeward Island colonies and Jamaica. Though
historians have customarily linked together Barbados, the Leeward
Islands, and Jamaica as a single socioeconomic region, no two of them
followed precisely the same course during the eighteenth century.
Rather, each constituted a separate subregion, every bit as distinct
from the others as those that developed later within the Middle Colonies and the Lower South. Indeed, there were even significant variations among the four Leeward Island colonies.

Barbados always had a proportionately much larger white settler
population than either the Leeward Islands or Jamaica. For fifty years

after it had converted to a slave labor system in the 1650s and 1660s, Barbados experienced a steady absolute decline in white population, the result of a combination of large-scale migration—as many as 5 percent of the total number of slaveholders may have left the colony annually between 1675 and 1700—to other islands and to the North American mainland colonies and a rash of epidemic diseases that struck the island during the twenty years beginning around 1690. For fifty years after 1710, however, the number of whites in Barbados rose steadily. From a low of 13,000 in 1710, the white population grew by nearly 50 percent to around 18,500 in 1773.

A small part of this increase was probably the result of an excess of immigrants over emigrants, as Barbados continued over this period to attract some indentured servants and other whites employed as managers or in other service occupations. Perhaps somewhat more came from a small natural increase, but almost certainly not from a rising birthrate. Despite a roughly equal number of women and men, the number of children per family was rather low in 1715 and probably continued to be so. Rather, the growth in the number of whites seems to have been a consequence of improving health conditions. After 1710, all classes of whites in Barbados enjoyed more favorable health conditions than did settlers elsewhere in the West Indies, on the southern North American mainland, or even in continental cities such as Boston and Philadelphia.[5]

Over the same period, declining soil fertility and higher production costs considerably reduced the level of profits. Fixed capital costs in labor, buildings, and machinery, as well as depreciation costs (mainly the result of the high replacement cost for slaves), were higher for sugar than for any other colonial agricultural industry, and there were few important cost-saving changes in the technology and methods of cultivation, processing, or transportation during the eighteenth century. The result was that as soil fertility declined, more and more capital and labor were required to yield ever diminishing rates of return, which fell from an excess of 10 percent on total investment during the late seventeenth century to around 4 to 5 percent in the 1760s and 1770s. Barbados thus was forced inexorably in the direction of an ever greater "capital-intensive, power-intensive system of agriculture conducted on a sustain-yield basis," a system in which constantly rising costs raised serious doubts as to whether the island could continue to compete with newer colonies with more productive land, even on the protected British-American sugar market.

As a consequence of this economic squeeze, the drive toward intensive sugar monoculture and many of the tendencies associated with that drive either lost vigor or changed in character between 1720 and 1775. Already by the 1730s, Barbados was turning from sugar to livestock production, and the movement toward property consolidation that had been so evident in the first century of sugar production leveled off by the 1740s, with roughly a third of the proprietors owning somewhat more than half of the estates and sugar mills. After 1750, the colony, once again manifesting a spirit of innovation such as it had demonstrated a century earlier during the sugar revolution, was responding to its increasingly unfavorable place in the Atlantic sugar market by successfully developing methods to produce more sugar byproducts, methods that yielded almost 50 percent more rum than the British West Indian average.

Despite these innovations, neither the size of estates nor the rate of profit was high enough to support much absenteeism among the large planter families, and less favorable economic conditions combined with improved health to produce an increased emphasis on family development. All but a few of the large estate owners lived on their estates in elaborate "great houses" surrounded by increasingly manicured fields and gardens that were the envy of people from other West Indian colonies. Through the attention they devoted to their estates and through their domination of provincial and local offices, this planting elite exhibited a commitment to Barbados that defies the modern stereotype of early modern West Indian planter society. Nor did the large estate owners constitute more than about 20 to 25 percent of the island's whites. Another quarter belonged to an intermediate class of officeholders, small merchants, professionals, estate managers, and small estate owners who produced cotton and foodstuffs on less than one hundred acres or hired out slaves. The rest consisted of a numerous class of poor whites, families with ten acres or less, who lived, many of them in considerable poverty, on the margins of the plantation system, either in some of the drier areas of the countryside or in Bridgetown, the colony's capital and leading shipping and urban center.[6]

Along with the steady growth in white population between 1710 and 1775, the slave population continued to rise, increasing by nearly three-fourths over the same period to over 68,500. Slave imports remained fairly high, but they accounted for a declining proportion of the slave population. Like all of the West Indian colonies, Barbados experienced high slave mortality of from 2 to 6 percent annually throughout the eighteenth century and had to maintain imports at that level to keep the slave population from declining in absolute numbers. But mortality among Barbadian slaves seems to have fallen on the low side of these figures. With declining profits and most of their capital tied up in slaves, planters found it more economical to provide better diet and health care in an effort to breed slaves locally and so save the costs of high annual replacements. Better living conditions and a growing ratio of seasoned creoles to the total number of slaves combined to lower annual mortality rates among Barbadian slaves from about 6 percent during the first quarter of the eighteenth century to 3.8 percent during the third quarter of the century. The ratio of blacks to whites leveled off at around 4 to 1 between 1750 and 1780.[7]

If, after 1750, declining profits forced Barbadian slaveowners to provide better conditions for their slaves, the colony's slave system was by no means benign. Slaves continued to have a low caloric intake and to produce a small number of children who survived to adulthood, and before the early nineteenth century, there were few opportunities for them to become free. Nevertheless, a few avenues were open through which Barbadian slaves could escape the rigorous labor of the cane fields. Some men became skilled artisans or sugar processors; others worked in various service occupations in the towns. Members of both sexes were domestic house slaves, and, by the mid-eighteenth century, a sufficient number of slave women had become mistresses to white men to produce a visible mulatto population. Together, slaves and free people handled much of the internal marketing system in the island and thereby found the wherewithal to acquire modest amounts of property. For reasons never satisfactorily explained, moreover, Barbadian slaves offered considerably less overt resistance than did their counterparts in other British West Indian colonies. Following serious scares of slave uprisings in 1675, 1692, and 1701, Barbados went more than a century without a slave rebellion, trusted slaves were even incorporated into the militia, and white residents of the island celebrated the relative tranquillity of its race relations.[8]

In part because of the concentration of capital and labor in Barbados and in part because rivalries with the Dutch and French prevented English settlers from securing uncontested control over most of them until 1713, the Leeward Island colonies developed far more slowly than did Barbados and never attracted such a large white immigration. Not until the 1720s and 1730s did these colonies successfully emulate the experience of Barbados in the previous century. However, with profits remaining high—between 10 and 13 percent—down to 1775, the Leeward Islands, in contrast to Barbados, showed no tendency to turn away from the drive toward sugar monoculture and no reversal in the steady decline of white settlers. Nevis and Montserrat, the smallest of the four islands, steadily lost white population from the 1670s to a low point in 1745, followed by a slight rise over the next decade and a continuing downward trend thereafter. In St. Kitts and Antigua, which developed later, white population continued to climb into the 1720s and then dropped slowly thereafter. From a high of just over 9,000 in 1720, the number of whites in all four islands fell to around 8,700 in 1756 and 6,800 in 1775, with Antigua having about 2,500, St. Kitts, 1,900, Montserrat, 1,300, and Nevis, 1,000 at the later date.[9]

Between 1708 and 1775, the black population in all four islands tripled. Already numbering almost 36,000 in 1720, it rose to slightly more than 82,000 by 1775, with Antigua having nearly 38,000, St. Kitts, almost 23,500, Nevis, 11,000, and Montserrat, around 6,800. The ratio of blacks to whites was thus much higher than in Barbados—15 to 1 in Antigua, 12 to 1 in St. Kitts, 11 to 1 in Nevis, and 7.5 to 1 in Montserrat. Although the creole portion of the black inhabitants expanded slowly during the eighteenth century, most of this rise in slave numbers was the result of continuing heavy imports from Africa. Also in contrast to Barbados, the Leeward Islands manifested considerable slave unrest in the eighteenth century, the most important example of which was a massive conspiracy in 1736 in which Antiguan slaves planned to blow up the leading white inhabitants while they were attending a ball and then to seize the entire island. Smaller uprisings were put down in Nevis in 1761 and Montserrat in 1768.[10]

To some extent this slave unrest may have been stimulated by the declining proportion of whites in the population. All four islands, but especially Antigua and St. Kitts, continued to have a substantial population of resident merchants, lawyers, and doctors and to attract from England and Scotland immigrants who found opportunities in plantation management, trade, and the professions and often were rapidly absorbed into the local planter elite through intermarriage. Antigua at least, and probably the other three islands, also continued to be "a family-centered society where the great [planting] families were units of considerable permanence and power." To a much greater degree than Barbados, however, the Leeward Islands had "a growing number of absentees in the mid-century years of sugar prosperity." No doubt, the incidence of absenteeism varied among the four colonies, but fifty-two of sixty-five gentry families in Antigua "had members away from the island for protracted periods in the years from 1730 to 1775," and some plantations, perhaps as many as half in St. Kitts, were operated entirely by managers or estate attorneys for owners resident in Britain.

All four of the Leeward Islands were well on the way to becoming little more than a congeries of sugar factories with large concentrations of black slaves and small white populations consisting of only a handful of white settler families, a few plantation managers, and a small intermediate class of merchants, lawyers, and doctors. The Leeward Islands thus represented an extreme version of the Barbadian social model that by the late eighteenth century was perhaps beginning to resemble a nineteenth-century industrial enterprise more closely than it did the settler societies developing elsewhere in colonial British America. Far more than Barbados, the Leeward Islands were being transformed by the 1770s from colonies of settlement into colonies of exploitation with the impoverished cultural and political life usually associated with that category. The new colonies begun by the British in the West Indies after 1750—the Virgin Islands, Dominica, Grenada, St. Vincent, and Tobago—all conformed to the Leeward Island example."

Despite many similarities, Jamaica diverged considerably from the patterns exhibited by the smaller islands. With 4,411 square miles, it was twenty-six times the size of Barbados, which occupied only 166 square miles, and seventeen times larger than the Leeward Islands, which together covered 251 square miles. Jamaica's sugar industry continued to grow slowly during the first four decades of the eighteenth century because of a variety of factors, including the secular decline of the British sugar market, the engrossment of some of the best sugar lands by large landholders who did not have the labor to exploit them, an inadequate slave supply, and the fierce opposition of the Maroons, bands of runaway slaves who lived in the inaccessible interior and terrorized outlying areas of the colony, especially between 1725 and 1739.[12]

After the end of hostilities with the Maroons in 1739 and in response to a rising sugar market, Jamaica experienced spectacular economic growth from 1740 to 1775. The slave population more than doubled from about 100,000 to 197,000, and the number of sugar estates grew from 419 to 775, an increase of over 45 percent. By 1775, Jamaica had three times as many slaves as Barbados and was exporting ten times the quantity of sugar products. Over the same period, the aggregate value of its annual exports rose from £650,000 to £2.4 million, an almost fourfold increase, and the total value of the colony's economy rose almost five times, from just over £3.5 million to over £15.1 million. The annual rate of profit on sugar estates ranged from 10 to 13 percent. Jamaica was far and away Britain's most valuable American colony. Its net worth per free white person was an astonishing £12,000 in 1775, more than nine times that of the richest continental colonies in the Upper and Lower South.[13]

But this rapid expansion produced significantly different results from those arising from the similar development of Barbados a century earlier or of the Leeward Islands a half-century before. With much still uncultivated land remaining as late as 1775 and considerable land wastage, the plantation economy in Jamaica was more land-intensive and less labor- and capital-intensive than in the smaller islands. By British West Indian standards, sugar estates were large—according to one sample studied, about nine hundred acres in the 1760s—and the organization of many sugar estates "created a degree of internal self-sufficiency." Only about a third of total acreage in the 1760s and 1770s was planted in sugarcane. Another third was in woodland, nearly a fifth was in pasture, just under a tenth was in provision grounds on which slaves were required to produce their own food, and small acreages were devoted to guinea grass and plantains for general use on the estate.

Nor did Jamaica ever approach becoming a sugar monoculture. Sugar, molasses, and rum made up nearly three-fourths of the colony's exports by the 1770s, but four out of ten slaves were employed in production other than sugar, and more than half of the plantations were devoted to livestock, provisions, and minor staples. In 1774, the colony contained an estimated 193,000 head of livestock. Nor did Jamaica experience a loss of white population. Even though as high as 30 percent of the sugar plantations may have belonged to absentees by the mid-eighteenth century and the ratio of blacks to whites climbed from about 6.5 to 1 in 1703 to slightly more than 11 to 1 in 1775, white population rose slowly but steadily from seven thousand in 1703 to eighteen thousand in 1774. Between 1720 and 1740, one study estimates, Jamaica was the destination of almost 40 percent of white indentured servants leaving Britain. Only Maryland, with 27 percent of the total, came close to equaling that proportion.[14]

Neither, in contrast to that of the Leeward Islands, was the white population limited to a handful of resident managers of large sugar estates and a few professionals and local factors of London merchants. With land still available for settlement during the third quarter of the eighteenth century, those with enough capital could still establish sugar plantations from scratch, and those with fewer resources could begin with minor staples and build up sugar estates gradually from reinvested profits, a common form of estate building in the colony. Whatever the avenue of advancement, opportunities were sufficient to permit men to rise up from the lower or middle strata of society and acquire sugar estates. Many of those who did so, however, seem not to have been creoles but British immigrants, especially Scots, who came in large numbers after 1710.

The social structure of the white population was similar to that of Barbados. About a fifth of island whites were from large landholding or wealthy and substantial mercantile or professional families, some of whom were newcomers and some of whom, like the Prices, were from old established families who had been in Jamaica for three or four generations. Some of these families built up enormous fortunes. Over two-fifths of those who died between 1771 and 1775 had accumulated more than £1,000 worth of personal property by the time of death, more than 10 percent had acquired over £5,000, and more than 1 percent had vast fortunes ranging from £30,000 to as high as £120,000. The rest of the whites were either "middle-class mercantile and professional men [who] exerted an influence that was disproportionate to their numbers" or small planters, estate managers, urban artisans, craftsmen, clerks, and shopkeepers, many of whom lived in Jamaica's two principal towns. Spanish Town, with many sumptuous townhouses and expensive public buildings, was the colony's capital. Kingston, by far the largest urban place in the British West Indies, was by the mid-1770s Jamaica's chief port and numbered over eleven thousand inhabitants, including five thousand whites, twelve hundred free blacks and mulattoes, and five thousand slaves.[15]

Unlike the Leeward Islands but like Barbados, Jamaica thus managed, despite some absenteeism, to sustain a "self-conscious, articulate, cohesive social class of proprietor-administrators" well into the later eighteenth century. Just as settled "family life coexisted with bachelor-hood," so also "it was not unusual for families to remain in possession of plantations for many years." Like the wealthier groups in most of Britain's American colonies, the orientation of the Jamaican elite was much more practical than aesthetic, and its primary capital—and so-cial—investment in the island was in the form of material improve-ments such as roads, bridges, public buildings, and forts.

Like the Barbadian elite, however, the members of this class were by no means yet "passengers only." As Edward Brathwaite has shown, they were creoles in the fullest sense of the term. That is, they were "committed settlers" who, especially after 1750, constructed grand country—and also often town—houses in an emergent Jamaican ver-nacular style; invested heavily in capital improvements and labor for their estates; supported an active press; built churches, schools, and hospitals; and, through their service in dynamic and self-conscious local political institutions, demonstrated a devotion to public life and a degree of local patriotism that compared favorably with that of their counterparts in the continental colonies. All of these activities strongly suggest that certainly as late as the 1770s and 1780s many members of the Jamaican elite regarded Jamaica as their home and were making "considerable effort . . . to 'civilize the wilderness.'" One measure of their commitment to the island could be found in the amount of land set aside on their estates for the great house and its environs. This figure reached a high of 7.3 acres in the 1780s and only began to contract as absenteeism grew as a response to the growing threat of the abolition of slavery after 1790.[16]

No less than in the rest of the sugar colonies, slavery in Jamaica was harsh, and it was also given to more frequent revolts than in either Barbados or the Leeward Islands. Every year, moreover, thousands of new slaves imported from Africa, ranging between 1720 and 1774 from a low of two thousand to a high of almost sixteen thousand, had to be assimilated to the work demands of the local economy. Nevertheless, slave mortality seems to have been considerably lower than in the Leeward Islands, ranging from 4 percent down to 2 percent annually, the probable result of better dietary standards deriving from the local custom of allowing each slave a small plot of provision ground and one and one-half days per week for his or her own activities. By 1760, a combination of falling mortality and an increasing birthrate had finally produced a black population in which creoles outnumbered Africans.

This population was not only more creole but also highly creative and increasingly differentiated. The small number of whites on most plantations and the wide dispersal of estates on an island of such size probably permitted slaves far more cultural autonomy than could be found in the more congested social spaces of the smaller West Indian islands, and slaves used the produce grown on their provision grounds to develop a vigorous internal marketing system that supplied much of the food for the white as well as the black population. Nor, any more than in Barbados, were Jamaican blacks all confined to field labor. Not just domestics but skilled workers and drivers on most plantations were slaves. In urban areas slaves worked as mechanics, tradesmen, preachers, seamen, and higglers, often in a state of independence that provided them with considerable scope for privacy and individual autonomy.

After 1750, the size of the free black and colored population began to expand considerably until by the 1770s it probably exceeded that of Barbados by a factor of ten. Although many of these people lived in isolation near the borderline of poverty, others were small planters, fishermen, pilots, overseers, clerks, artisans, shopkeepers, schoolmasters, and builders, and a few, the offspring of an active sexual interchange between white males and black and colored mistresses, inherited substantial property from their white fathers. The increasing size of this "intermediate" population of free people strongly suggests that the slave system in Jamaica contained more and somewhat easier avenues of escape than was the case elsewhere in the British West Indies.[17]

However important the differences among Barbados, the Leeward Islands, and Jamaica, they all exhibited some profound similarities. Although Jamaica was much larger and had a much more diversified agricultural economy, they were all heavily involved in the production of agricultural staples, especially sugar and its by-products, for overseas markets. Importing vast numbers of African slaves, they quickly developed populations in which blacks were heavily predominant. At least in Barbados and Jamaica, local conditions may have made slavery slightly less onerous after 1750, but sugar production always involved a harsh labor regime and contained a latent threat of servile revolt.

Except for the Leeward Islands, where the number of whites was actually declining in absolute numbers and a considerable number of absentees had moved to Britain or to North America, each had a substantial and stable population of white settlers, who, as late as the mid-1770s, remained committed to the societies they had created in the

New World. The wealthiest people anywhere in the contemporary British overseas empire, the planting elite who presided over the vital political, legal, and social institutions that had taken deep root in all these colonies used a significant proportion of their vast economic resources in an effort to anglicize their societies as much as their tropical climates would permit. Thus they imported large quantities of British finished goods, built elaborate public buildings and private houses, created expensive social infrastructures and showy cultural institutions, and otherwise sought to live in the British manner. As mortality fell during the eighteenth century, they gradually achieved a more settled family life and, at least in Barbados and Jamaica, established stronger traditions of family continuity and ever greater identification with the local society. Notwithstanding the growing Africanization of society and culture as a result of the massive increase in the black population and its significant role in socioeconomic life, the settler population in both of those colonies in all these respects thus assimilated to the developmental model observed first in the Chesapeake and then in all the other major regions of colonial British America except New England.

THIS analysis of the experiences of the Atlantic island and West Indian colonies between 1660 and 1763 reveals that the New England declension model is not an appropriate conceptual device for understanding the thrust and character of their social development. Although segments of two of them, specifically Bermuda among the Atlantic islands and Barbados and perhaps the Leeward Islands in the Caribbean, experienced some economic decline or, more accurately, stasis during the late colonial period, no one of them replicated to any important degree the New England experience. Like the other new settler societies in the Chesapeake, Ireland, the Middle Colonies, and the Lower South, and unlike New England, these island colonies began without a powerful religious content and a well-organized sociocultural order that, like those associated with the orthodox New England colonies, went through a gradual process of attenuation and social reformulation until it finally emerged as a substantially different and much looser social entity a century or more later.

Rather, like the Chesapeake, all the new societies considered in this chapter began as highly materialistic, poorly defined, permissive, secular, and simple social entities, whose members, bound together by little more than their common British heritage and their eagerness to exploit their new environments in any way that would satisfy their own individual quests for the happiness of themselves and their families, had little common purpose and no unified social vision. Only over the following century did they gradually lose some of their harsh edge and begin, again like the Chesapeake, to develop into more coherent and elaborated societies. Despite many modifications dictated by the nature of the local ecosystem, the virulence of the disease environment, the organization of the economy, the ethnic composition of the population, and other variables, these societies all eventually managed to reproduce, to some recognizable degree, many of the more basic social features and processes of the metropolitan society to which they were attached.

THE perspective supplied by the experience, considered in this and the preceding chapters, of old England, Ireland, and all six major regions of colonial British America—the Chesapeake, New England, the Atlantic and West Indian island colonies, the Middle Colonies, and the Lower South—from their origins to the eve of the American Revolution makes it fully evident that New England was "no model for America." Although it may be unnecessarily hyperbolic to suggest, as G. R. Elton has done, that "as colonizers," New England puritans "were the freaks, not a main force," it can no longer be doubted that, in most respects, New England's experience was fundamentally dissimilar from that of every other area of the early modern British world.[18]

Indeed, from the perspective of the histories of all of those other areas, it becomes vividly clear just how atypical, peculiar, even anachronistic the New England experience was in British American colonial history during the seventeenth and eighteenth centuries, how weak were the pressures exerted by the New England environment in comparison with those at work everywhere else, how powerful and enduring were the religious and social restraints imposed by puritan culture upon all aspects of rural New England life, and how long it took for New England to assimilate to a pattern of behavior that, to a very significant degree, had dominated the societies of all the other colonial regions from their inceptions. At the same time, the peculiar vantage point supplied by the New England colonies makes it equally apparent just how weak the corporate impulse was in all the other major regions of British colonization, how great were the possibilities for material gain, how rapid and pervasive was the development of highly autonomous behavior, and how long they took to develop into well-delineated and stable social entities.

If, however, the developmental model exhibited in the Chesapeake, and not the declension model represented by New England, was thus normative in the larger British and colonial British-American experience before the Revolution and if the social history of New England was moving in a different direction from those of all the other regions of colonial British America, New England was, nevertheless, also developing in ways that, by the middle decades of the eighteenth century, were bringing it ever closer to patterns of social organization and behavior that long had been evident in all the other regions. New England society was still more religious and probably also had a stronger sense of community, and it had much lower levels of wealth concentration and far fewer black slaves.

As the social and religious coherence of the early puritan era slowly gave way during the late seventeenth and early eighteenth centuries under the pressures of growth and dispersion to a more diverse, contentious, and open society and as New England society slowly, if erratically, evolved in a generally libertarian, acquisitive, and individualistic direction, even rural New Englanders slowly adjusted to and participated in the behavioral revolution associated with the transition from a communal to an individualistic mentality, a mentality that had, of course, been evident from the beginnings of social formation in all the other regions of the colonial British world. With this development, New Englanders finally relinquished their grand vision of building a city upon a hill and both "rejoined the Western world" and finally worked themselves into the mainstream of British American social and cultural development.[19]

ALTHOUGH this and previous chapters have established that the New England colonial experience deviated considerably from the colonial British norm, Chapter 3 also suggests that it would be a serious mistake to carry this contrast too far. Indeed, it can be argued that the rapidity with and the extent to which the orthodox puritan colonies managed to achieve the initial goals of the founders and the declension model used by contemporaries and historians to describe that region's subsequent experience have obscured the considerable degree to which

FIGURE 7.1

A Model of Sociocultural Development in Early Modern New Societies

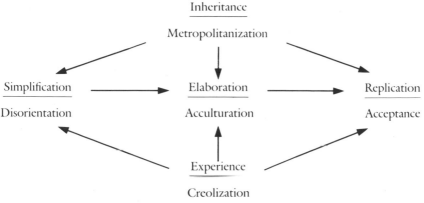

even New England participated in a common developmental process that took all of the new societies established by the English overseas after 1600 in the direction of an ever more complex, differentiated, and Old World–style society. For, notwithstanding the social complexity of early New England in comparison with other regions during their first generations of settlement, it still represented not just a highly selective but also a drastically simplified version of early seventeenth-century English society.

On the basis of the detailed characterizations presented in these chapters, this common developmental process can now be defined more explicitly. Figure 7.1 depicts it graphically. It consisted of three sequential stages. The first involved the *social simplification* of inherited forms that we have noted for the first generations in every new region of settlement. With the principal exception of New England, this early phase was characterized by much unsettledness and disorientation. Settlers were preoccupied with finding ways to manipulate their new environments for their own sustenance and advantage, and their early endeavors to recreate social arrangements that both bore some resemblance to those they had left behind and conformed to those prescriptive ideals of social order that underlay metropolitan society rarely met with much success.[20]

As social arrangements gradually became more settled, as population grew more dense and usually more heavily creole, and as the inhabitants acquired greater economic wherewithal, the simple social conditions that had obtained during the first stage of settlement gave way to more elaborate ones. This second stage of *social elaboration* was marked by the continuing articulation of socioeconomic, political, and cultural institutions, structures, and values that were usually at once highly creolized variants of those found in the more settled areas of Britain and sufficiently functional to enable local populations to assimilate to them with relatively little difficulty. If this second phase was characterized by a growing acculturation of the inhabitants to their local social environments, that acculturation was by no means so complete as to inhibit the articulation of demands, emanating largely from emerging elites and wealthy or strategically placed immigrants, for a restructuring of their societies along lines that would make them more recognizably British.[21]

As these regional overseas societies became more populous, provided opportunities for greater comfort and affluence, grew more settled (if not in all cases much more orderly), and became internally more complex—as they became, in the common language of the time, more "improved"—they approximated more closely to established societies of the Old World and entered into still a third phase of development, a stage of *social replication*. In this stage, members of the elite groups who, by the mid-eighteenth century, almost everywhere dominated and contributed disproportionately to their numbers to give tone and definition to their societies, displayed a strong desire to replicate British society in their regions, and took pride in the extent to which those societies were coming increasingly to resemble that of the metropolis. By no means all members of the less affluent ranks of these societies shared this desire so fully, however, and some of the instances of sharp conflict in the colonies over religion, economics, and politics during the three or four decades before the American Revolution were at least partly attributable to opposing notions about precisely what directions the process of subsequent social development should take. For this reason, this third stage cannot be depicted as one of harmonious solidification under an image of anglicized replication.[22]

If all the regions of colonial British America moved through this common developmental process, previous chapters have illustrated in detail the considerable extent to which its specific timing and results and the duration of each stage varied from region to region. The rate and character of population growth (including the changing ratios among the sexes, racial groups, and immigrants and creoles), economic growth, territorial expansion, and date of settlement seem to have been the central variables in determining differences in timing. Variations in results, on the other hand, were obviously a function of a much more numerous group of variables, including the nature of economic organization and the labor system, levels of socioeconomic differentiation, the depth and character of religious orientation, the goals of the populace, the healthfulness of the environment, the authority and responsiveness of local political leaders and institutions, and the degree of direct involvement with metropolitan Britain.

At every stage in this process of social development, however, these variables seem to have operated within a general framework of persisting tension between what can, for convenience, be referred to as experience and inheritance. *Experience* refers to the slowly accumulating expertise arising out of the inhabitants' learning through a process of trial and error how best to meet the complex demands made upon them by the need for their societies to function effectively within their specific physical and social environments. These demands pushed those societies strongly in the direction of creolization, which may be defined as the adjustment of inherited forms and practices to make them congruent with local conditions.

Inheritance signifies those traditions, cultural imperatives, and conceptions of the proper social order that settlers derived from the metropolis. Initially brought by them or their ancestors from the Old World, these traditions, imperatives, and conceptions were subsequently reinforced through a process of continuous interaction with that world. This process pulled colonial societies in the direction of metropolitanization or anglicization. The balance of force between experience and inheritance shifted from one phase of social development to the next according to local circumstances and the imperial and international context. The general direction of movement down to the 1760s, however, seems to have been toward the growing importance, though not necessarily in all cases the predominance, of inheritance. The major exception was New England, where the force of inheritance, however selectively interpreted and implemented by puritan leaders, was especially strong during the stage of social simplification and, after weakening considerably during the period of social elaboration, increased in power during the stage of social replication.

Chapter Eight

✻✻✻✻✻✻✻✻✻✻✻✻✻✻✻✻✻✻

CONVERGENCE: DEVELOPMENT

OF AN AMERICAN SOCIETY,

1720–1780

Down to the very eve of the American Revolution, contemporaries were far more impressed by the diversities than by the similarities among the several regions and colonies of British America. Benjamin Franklin expressed the predominant opinion in 1760, just sixteen years before the Declaration of Independence. Without counting any of the island colonies, Franklin informed British readers in a well-known pamphlet, Britain had by that date fourteen separate colonies on the North American continent, no two of which seemed to be much alike. Rather, Franklin emphasized, the colonies were "not only under different governors, but have different forms of government, different laws, different interests, and some of them different religious persuasions and different manners." This perception was not inaccurate. As previous chapters have emphasized, each of the major regions of the early modern colonial British American world quickly developed its own distinctive socioeconomic and cultural configurations. Yet, notwithstanding this fact and the observations of Franklin and most other contemporary commentators, there are strong reasons to suggest that the diversity among the several regions of colonial British America has been greatly overemphasized.[1]

Indeed, this chapter argues that at least on the continent these regions were becoming increasingly alike during the generations immediately preceding the American Revolution. Building on the material presented in previous chapters, it offers two principal contentions. The first is that the common developmental process described at the conclusion of Chapter 7 produced a slow but powerful cultural and social convergence that mitigated the sharp variations that had distinguished the several regions of colonial British America from one another during their early generations of settlement. The second is that out of this steady process of convergence emerged the beginnings of an American cultural order that was waiting to be defined during and immediately after the era of the American Revolution. An examination of these contentions will provide the materials for the evaluation of the last of the four underlying historiographical assumptions elaborated in Chapter 2, the assumption that American culture was in large part a derivative of puritan culture.

I F one underlying argument of the previous chapters has been that the several regions of overseas settlement in Britain's early modern empire exhibited a similar pattern of social development, a second has been that during the century after 1660 they also participated in a powerful process of social and cultural convergence that rendered the differences among them less and less pronounced. This process can be seen most dramatically in the contrasting histories of New England and the Chesapeake as they were elaborated in Chapters 3 and 4. On the surface at least, these two oldest groups of British continental colonies seemed to be moving further and further apart, as the Chesapeake acquired a strong biracial character with the proliferation of black slavery between 1680 and 1730. But closer examination reveals that in most areas during the century following 1660 the two regions became not less but more alike as a consequence of a congeries of developments that together gradually eroded the striking differences that had distinguished them during their early decades.

In New England, the deterioration of health conditions raised mortality to levels by the mid-eighteenth century not too much lower than those in the contemporary Chesapeake, and a variety of other developments pushed the region closer to patterns of behavior and values toward which people in the Chesapeake were moving. Thus, impressive population growth, the consequent scattering of people out from the original town centers to individual farms, an increasing differentiation of society and complexity of kinship networks, a growing diversity in many aspects of local life, the acceleration of the economy as a result of rapid internal population growth and the increasing integration of the New England economy into the larger Atlantic economy, the slow attenuation of the social and religious synthesis of the founders, a growing demand for and exhibition of autonomy among the sons of each successive generation, more individualism and more conflict in public life in the localities, and a marked rise in geographical mobility—all of these changes weakened the bonds of community and pushed New England in the direction of greater individualism, personal autonomy, and social fluidity.

Simultaneously, in the Chesapeake, the slow improvement of health conditions during the late seventeenth century had led by the first decades of the eighteenth century to a balance of sex ratios and a more typically European family structure. In addition, as tobacco profits settled down to less spectacular if somewhat steadier levels, few people continued to entertain much hope of being able to return to England, the commitment to the Chesapeake became stronger, settlement became more compact and expansion more measured, and the devotion to staple production was less exclusive. Concomitantly, as Chesapeake society cohered around an emergent and authoritative socioeconomic elite, members of which had all of the traditional attributes of social leadership as they strove successfully to emulate the powerful cultural model of the English country gentry, social, religious, and political institutions acquired more vigor, society became far more settled and cohesive, and the communal impulse was much more evident. The new sense of coherence and community that was so strikingly manifest in the Chesapeake after 1725 was, perhaps ironically, probably intensified among the free white population by the pressures toward racial solidarity created by the shift to a heavily African slave labor force.

Not just the Chesapeake and New England colonies but most of the other colonies as well were moving closer together in the configurations of their socioeconomic life. Like the Chesapeake, Ireland, the Middle Colonies, the Lower South, the Atlantic island colonies of Bermuda and the Bahamas, and even the Caribbean colonies of Barbados and Jamaica were all moving, like Britain itself during the same period, toward greater order, coherence, differentiation, and complexity. The reader will recall the hypothetical continuum employed as a heuristic device in Chapter 2. That continuum depicted a line running between two ideal types of society, one centrifugal and highly individualistic in its orientation and the other centripetal and strongly communal. A similar continuum for the years 1713 and 1763 would reveal, I submit, a steady convergence toward the center with all of the colonies south of New England moving from individualism toward

FIGURE 8.1

*Graphic Representation of the Process of Social Convergence
among Early Modern British Colonies*

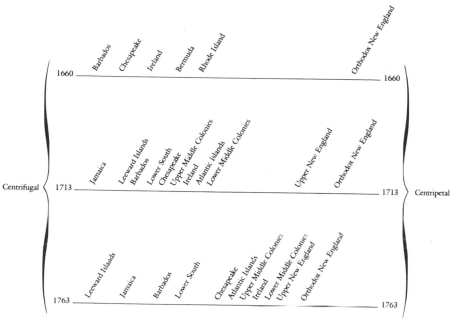

KEY: Atlantic Islands: Bermuda, Bahamas
Chesapeake: Virginia, Maryland, upper North Carolina
Lower Middle Colonies: Pennsylvania, Delaware, western New Jersey
Lower South: South Carolina, Georgia, lower North Carolina
Orthodox New England: Massachusetts, Connecticut
Upper New England: New Hampshire, Maine, Nova Scotia
Upper Middle Colonies: eastern New Jersey, New York

communalism and New England moving from communalism toward
individualism. This process is illustrated in Figure 8.1.

Only the four small Leeward Island colonies may have deviated
from this process. By the mid-eighteenth century, they may already
have begun to move toward a situation in which white society was
little more than a handful of loosely organized managers and other
people whose sole function was to preside over the extraction of tropical agricultural profits, who had no long-term commitment to those
societies, and whose impulse toward material gain was so predominant
as to stifle the urge to recreate British social forms in a colonial setting.
As a result, those colonies may already have been in the early stages of
a move away from the center in the direction of the pole of pure

individualism. But the experience of the Leeward Islands serves as the exception that underlines all the more pointedly the growing social and cultural convergence that between 1660 and 1760 had created, among all the British colonies in America, a common Anglophone cultural order in the western Atlantic. By the last half of the eighteenth century, that convergence had so blurred the differences among the colonies that they were more alike than they had ever been before. If, as was contended in Chapter 2, a broad cultural fault line separated orthodox puritan New England from all the rest of the English colonies in 1660, that line had been all but obliterated a century later. At least in terms of the general thrust of colonial social development, the Leeward Island colonies were by that time the exceptions.

The explanation for this growing convergence is to be found, I would argue, in the dialectical interplay between the same two sets of conditions—experience and inheritance—that provided the context for the common process of colonial social development discussed in the concluding section of Chapter 7. Several conditions—distance from the metropolis, the laxity of British controls, the relative breadth of economic opportunity not just in land but in occupations catering to the needs of an increasingly complex economy, and incorporation into the larger Atlantic economy—combined to produce levels of prosperity sufficient to support societies that were everywhere becoming more and more differentiated, pluralistic, and improved. They also operated to promote the high levels of individual activity and expansiveness that underlay the remarkable economic and demographic growth that characterized all of the continental colonies between 1710 and 1770.

If, as observed Samuel Williams, whose *History of Vermont*, published in 1794, was one of the first systematic attempts to analyze the main features of the emerging American society, a "similarity of situation and conditions" had gradually pushed the colonies toward a similitude of society and values, more specifically, toward "that natural, easy, independent situation, and spirit, in which the body of the [free] people were found, when the American war came on," still a second major influence—inheritance operating in the form of growing metropolitanization or anglicization—was important in helping to erode differences among the colonies. If this development was partly the result of efforts by metropolitan authorities to bring the colonies under closer political and economic control, it was also attributable to an ever more intense involvement between metropolis and colonies in virtually all spheres of life. Together with an increasing volume of contacts among individuals and the improved communications that accompanied them, this growing involvement drew the colonies more and more into the ambit of British life as the eighteenth century advanced and thereby tied them ever more closely to metropolitan culture.[2]

As the ties with the metropolis thus tightened and became more robust, the pull of metropolitan culture grew, and the standards of the metropolis increasingly came to be the primary model for colonial behavior, the one certain measure of cultural achievement for these provincial societies at the outermost peripheries of the British world. Throughout the colonies, and especially among the emergent elites, there was a self-conscious effort to anglicize colonial life through the deliberate imitation of metropolitan institutions, values, and culture. Thus, before the mid-1770s, British-Americans thought of themselves primarily as Britons, albeit Britons overseas. Contrary to the dominant opinion among earlier historians, colonial comparisons of the colonies with Britain rarely came out in favor of the colonies. The central cultural impulse among the colonists was not to identify and find ways to express and to celebrate what was distinctively American about themselves and their societies but, insofar as possible, to eliminate those distinctions so that they might—with more credibility—think of themselves and their societies—and be thought of by people in Britain itself—as demonstrably British.[3]

Among the several colonial regions, of course, there remained significant differences. In particular, the finite amount of land in the island colonies limited their growth and expansion to a degree unknown on the continent. Together with their comparatively heavier concentration on extractive agriculture, these limits were the early harbingers of a major divergence between the island and continental colonies. Similarly, the relatively greater affluence derived by the southern and West Indian colonies from staple agriculture had enabled them to purchase many more black slaves, to devote more time both to the pursuit of the good life and to politics and the law, to cultivate metropolitan cultural models more assiduously, to rely more heavily upon metropolitan cultural institutions rather than to develop their own, and to be more self-indulgent and less industrious. By contrast, New England still was considerably more religious, had much lower levels of wealth concentration, and, along with the Middle Colonies, was more heavily urbanized. The Middle Colonies were perhaps the least settled socially, were certainly more heterogeneous in the religious and ethnic composition of their free populations, and may have had the most highly developed social and commercial infrastructures. During the late eighteenth century, however, these differences were largely ones of degree.

Not even the presence of so many slaves in the southern and island colonies, certainly the most conspicuous difference between them and New England, was yet a crucial distinguishing feature among the colonies. In general, there was a steady diminution in the ratio of black slaves to the free population from the most southern to the most northern colonies. As late as 1770, however, slavery was still an expanding, not a contracting, institution in every one of the island and continental colonies except New Hampshire and Nova Scotia. New York, Rhode Island, New Jersey, and Pennsylvania all had populations with a higher proportion of slaves than did the Chesapeake as late as 1700 to 1710 during the early stages of that region's large-scale transition to a slave labor system, and no colony had acted to try to ban slavery, which would be legal in Britain itself for another sixty years. Slavery was everywhere an integral and accepted component of British American culture, and limitations of space were almost certainly more important than ratios of slaves to free people in contributing to the beginnings of a cultural rift between the island and continental colonies after 1750. Given the strong convergence of cultural development in colonial British America by the 1740s and 1750s, it is by no means preposterous to suggest that all of the colonies, including Massachusetts and Connecticut, would have used slavery as extensively as did the southern and West Indian colonies had they had the resources and the incentives to do so.[4]

As between 1660 and 1760 each of the regions of colonial British America became both more creole and more metropolitan, as they increasingly assimilated to a common American social and behavioral pattern and to British cultural models, they became more and more alike, and this powerful social convergence resulted in the emergence and articulation of a common cultural pattern that, though present to some degree throughout the British American world, was especially evident among the continental colonies. If the central features of this pattern were most powerfully manifest at the center of British North America, in the Chesapeake and Middle Colonies, they were also present to a conspicuous degree in the peripheries, in the Lower South and New England. This pattern can be discussed under three rubrics: growth, differentiation, and values.

As previous chapters have made clear, the growth of the colonies was genuinely impressive, and in each colonial region demographic growth was particularly dramatic. Table 8.1 provides population figures, broken down by whites, blacks, and total population for both individual colonies and regions for 1660, 1710, and 1760. Table 8.2 contains figures for percentage increases for each region and for all the colonies during each of these fifty-year intervals and over the entire century from 1660 to 1760. A sharp distinction can be drawn between the continental colonies and the islands. Once a solid base had been established in the former, as occurred in the Chesapeake and New England during the last half of the seventeenth century, population grew at a rapid rate, ranging between 200 and 300 percent every half-century. But in the latter, where the land supply was limited, the disease environment more virulent for newcomers, and the work regime much harsher for slaves, population grew at only around 40 percent of that on the continent. Nevertheless, every region, even the island colonies, showed a sustained increase in population during the century beginning in 1660, the continental colonies growing at about 2.6 percent per annum and the island colonies at about 1.5 percent.

This growth resulted from both immigration and natural increase. Perhaps as many as one out of five new whites were immigrants; a much higher proportion of new blacks, especially in the islands, derived from slave imports. By far the largest source of this vigorous demographic rise on the continent, however, was natural increase. This increase was primarily the result of three factors: declining mortality, younger ages at marriage of from four to five years for women than in Europe, and a bountiful food supply and high nutrition that already by the 1750s had operated to make male residents of the continental colonies three to three and one-half inches taller than their British counterparts.

Natural growth was, however, lower in cities and in coastal areas of the Chesapeake and Lower South, where, as in the West Indies, mortality was significantly higher. Nevertheless, in overall population trends, the mortality differential between northern and southern colo-

TABLE 8.1

Population of British Colonies in America, 1660, 1710, and 1760

Colony	1660			
	W	B	T	R
Virginia	26,070	950	27,020	27:1
Maryland	7,668	758	8,426	10:1
Chesapeake	33,738	1,708	35,446	20:1
Massachusetts	22,062	422	22,484	52:1
Connecticut	7,955	25	7,980	318:1
Rhode Island	1,474	65	1,539	23:1
New Hampshire	1,515	50	1,565	30:1
Nova Scotia				
New England	32,584	562	33,146	59:1
Bermuda	3,500	200	3,700	17:1
Bahamas				
Atlantic Islands	3,500	200	3,700	17:1
Barbados	26,200	27,100	53,300	1:1
Antigua	1,539	1,448	2,987	1:1
Montserrat	1,788	661	2,449	2.7:1
Nevis	2,347	2,566	4,913	0.9:1
St. Kitts	1,265	957	2,222	1.3:1
Virgin Islands				
Jamaica				
Caribbean	33,139	32,732	65,871	1:1
New York	4,336	600	4,936	7.7:1
New Jersey				
Pennsylvania				
Delaware	510	30	540	17:1
Middle Colonies	4,846	630	5,476	8:1
North Carolina	980	20	1,000	49:1
South Carolina				
Georgia				
Lower South	980	20	1,000	49:1
Totals	109,209	35,852	145,061	3:1

KEY: W White
   B Black
   T Total
   R Ratio of White to Black

	1710				1760		
W	B	T	R	W	B	T	R
5,163	23,118	78,281	2.3:1	199,156	140,470	339,726	1.4:1
4,796	7,945	42,741	4.4:1	113,263	49,004	162,267	2.3:1
9,959	31,063	121,022	3:1	312,419	189,574	501,993	1.7:1
1,080	1,310	62,390	47:1	217,734	4,866	222,600	45:1
3,700	750	39,450	52:1	138,687	3,783	142,470	37:1
7,198	375	7,573	19:1	42,003	3,468	45,471	12:1
5,531	150	5,681	37:1	38,493	600	39,093	64:1
				7,644	100	7,744	76:1
2,509	2,585	115,094	44:1	444,561	12,817	457,378	35:1
4,268	2,845	7,113	1.5:1	6,154	5,222	11,376	1.2:1
				2,000	2,000	4,000	1:1
4,268	2,845	7,113	1.5:1	8,154	7,222	15,376	1.1:1
3,000	52,300	65,300	0.25:1	17,800	86,600	104,400	0.2:1
2,892	12,960	15,852	0.2:1	3,451	34,863	38,314	0.1:1
1,545	3,570	5,115	0.4:1	1,429	8,854	10,283	0.16:1
1,104	3,676	4,780	0.3:1	1,120	8,377	9,497	0.13:1
1,670	3,294	4,964	0.5:1	2,706	21,898	24,604	0.12:1
				1,183	6,121	7,304	0.2:1
7,250	58,000	65,250	0.12:1	15,000	146,464	161,464	0.1:1
7,461	133,800	161,261	0.2:1	42,686	313,177	355,863	0.14:1
8,814	2,811	21,625	6.7:1	100,798	16,340	117,138	6:1
8,540	1,332	19,872	14:1	87,246	6,567	93,813	13:1
2,875	1,575	24,450	14:1	179,294	4,409	183,703	40:1
3,145	500	3,645	6.1	31,517	1,733	33,250	18:1
3,314	6,218	69,532	10:1	398,855	29,049	427,904	14:1
4,220	900	15,120	16:1	76,888	33,554	110,442	2.3:1
6,783	4,100	10,883	1.6:1	36,740	57,334	94,074	0.6:1
				6,000	3,578	9,578	1.7:1
21,003	5,000	26,003	4:1	119,628	94,466	214,094	1.3:1
8,574	181,511	500,025	1.7:1	1,326,306	646,305	1,972,608	2:1

TABLE 8.2

Percentage of Population Increase by Region, 1660–1760

Region	1660–1710			1710–1760			1660–1760		
	W	B	T	W	B	T	W	B	T
Chesapeake	167	1,719	214	247	510	315	826	10,999	1,316
New England	268	360	270	295	396	297	1,353	21,745	1,368
Atlantic Islands	22	1,322	92	91	154	116	133	3,511	316
Caribbean	−17	309	145	55	134	121	29	857	540
Middle Colonies	1,208	887	1,171	526	273	515	805	4,511	7,714
Lower South	—	—	—	470	1,789	723	—	—	—
All Colonies	201	407	253	316	256	294	1,153	1,704	1,293

KEY: W White
   B Black
   T Total

nies may have been at least partly offset by a more plentiful food and protein supply in the South, one indication of which was that the average height of militiamen during the Revolution increased from North to South. The special demographic vigor demonstrated by the continental colonies was no doubt also stimulated by the continuing availability of land and the high levels of economic opportunity to meet the demands of both the growing population and an expanding overseas commerce. Although the island colonies had about the same number of whites per household as in contemporary England, those on the continent averaged between five and seven people, the largest in the entire British world.[5]

The psychology of expansiveness implied by the demographic performance of the populations of colonial British America, especially on the continent, was also reflected in the extent of territorial expansion and the mobility of the population. At the conclusion of Queen Anne's War in 1713, the continental settlers were still clustered in a series of noncontiguous nuclei close to the Atlantic seaboard. There were two large centers of settlement, one in the Chesapeake and another covering the coastal regions of eastern and southern New England and reaching up the Connecticut River valley. Two smaller concentrations of population fanned out from Philadelphia and New York, and there were isolated groups of settlement on the central Maine coast, in the upper Connecticut River valley in what is now southeastern Vermont, around Albany on the Hudson River, on the upper Delaware River in the vicinity of Easton, Pennsylvania, on the lower Delaware, at three widely dispersed points in Tidewater North Carolina, and at Charleston and Port Royal in South Carolina.

During the next fifty years, population spilled out in all possible directions from these nuclei until by the 1760s and 1770s there was one long continuum of settlement stretching from Georgia to Maine and reaching inland for more than 150 miles, and new nuclei were building in East and West Florida and Nova Scotia. This rapid spread of settlement was one sign of the high levels of geographical mobility among settlers in all regions on the continent. Although southerners were somewhat more mobile than New Englanders, no region had a persistence rate much above 60 percent during the third quarter of the eighteenth century, and farmers everywhere showed an especially strong propensity to move. Residents from New York north tended to move longer distances north into upper New York and New England; those from Pennsylvania south tended to move west and south into the broad upland areas between the seacoast and the Appalachian Mountains.[6]

But the most impressive evidence of growth lies in the economic realm. "Led by a growing demand for colonial exports, linked to an expanding commercial empire, protected and promoted by a strong imperial system, and endowed with an abundance of natural resources," the economy of colonial British America, John McCusker and Russell Menard have observed, "became increasingly successful" between 1607 and 1775. As has been stressed in previous chapters, there were marked differences between the economies of the plantation colonies of the Chesapeake, the Lower South, and the West Indies and those of the farm colonies from Pennsylvania north. Those of the latter were less highly specialized, much less capital- and labor-intensive, less dependent on servile labor, especially the use of slaves, and somewhat less tied to external markets. At the same time, the economies of all the continental colonies were somewhat more complex and better balanced than those in the West Indies. Yet the economic performance of every region over time was impressive. Growth seems not to have been especially rapid before 1740, but every available indicator—numbers of slaves, rising levels of personal wealth, volume of agricultural production, amount of exports, value of imports from Britain, quantities shipped in the coastal trade—suggests extraordinary growth thereafter. McCusker and Menard estimate that the gross national product (GNP) multiplied about twenty-five times between 1650 and 1770, increasing at an annual average rate of 2.7 percent for British America as a whole and 3.2 percent for British North America. This increase, they posit, may have represented a real per capita growth rate of 0.6 percent, which was twice that of Britain and was "sufficient to double income" over that period.[7]

By the time of the American Revolution, this vigorous economic growth had produced a standard of living that may have been "the highest achieved for the great bulk of the [free] population in any country up to that time." In her massive study of the wealth of the continental colonies, Alice Hanson Jones has found that for the continental colonies as a whole in 1774 average per capita wealth—composed of land, slaves, livestock, nonagricultural productive goods, and consumer goods—was £60.2. This figure may have been lower than that of England and Wales, for which there is no reliable estimate of per capita wealth after 1688, the date for which Gregory King estimated that it was already about £55. But Jones concludes that it must nevertheless have been "of a very respectable order of magnitude in comparison" with that of the metropolis. There were, of course, marked regional variations. As McCusker and Menard have revised Jones's figures, New England with a net worth per free white person of £33 was the poorest region, followed by the Middle Colonies with a figure of £51 and the southern colonies—the Chesapeake and Lower South combined—with the striking amount of £132. No comparable figures are available for the island colonies, although McCusker and Menard cite the astounding figure of £1,200 per capita for the relatively small slaveowning white population of Jamaica in the early 1770s.[8]

The sources of this remarkable prosperity lay in a combination of the demands for food and other commodities on the part of the burgeoning population and in growing overseas markets for colonial products. Though the proportion of income gained through exports declined over time, it was still substantial in 1770. Exports of all varieties, including ships and shipping services and those vended in both overseas and coastal trades, may have contributed from 17 to 19 percent of total income. The annual average worth of the six highest-valued commodities exported over the five years 1768–72 were as follows:

TABLE 8.3

Exports and Imports for the Continental Colonies, 1768–1772

Region	Exports				Imports			
	A	B	C	D	E	F	G	H
Chesapeake	£1,181,000	£1.8	£3.0	42	£1,136,629	£1.7	£2.9	29
Lower South	614,000	1.8	3.2	21	533,953	1.6	2.8	13
Middle Colonies	572,000	1.0	1.1	20	1,204,474	2.1	2.3	31
New England	479,000	0.8	0.9	17	1,358,788	2.3	2.6	27
Totals	2,846,000			100	4,233,844			100

KEY: A Total value of annual average commodity exports
  B Annual value of exports per capita
  C Annual value of exports per free white resident
  D Percentage share of total commodity exports
  E Total value of annual average commodity imports
  F Annual value of imports per capita
  G Annual value of imports per free white resident
  H Percentage share of total commodity imports
Sources: James F. Shepherd and Gary M. Walton, "Trade, Distribution, and Economic Growth," *Journal of Economic History* 32 (1972): 133, 136, and *Shipping, Maritime Trade, and Economic Development of Colonial North America* (Cambridge, 1972), 160–65.

tobacco, £766,000; shipping earnings, £610,000; bread and flour, £412,000; rice, £312,000; dried fish, £287,000; and indigo, £117,000. As Table 8.3 reveals, the Chesapeake was responsible for 42 percent of total exports, twice the figure for the Lower South and the Middle Colonies and more than two and one-half times that for New England. The value of exports per capita and per free white resident increased from North to South, reflecting the greater per capita wealth of the free white populations of those regions.[9]

Along with the rising imports of slaves suggested by the burgeoning slave population figures in Table 8.1, the import totals in Table 8.3, which increased considerably after 1750, provide a further measure of a substantial rise in colonial buying power on the eve of the American Revolution. The Middle Colonies, the Chesapeake, and New England all took somewhat less than a third and the Lower South somewhat more than a tenth of total commodity imports into the continental colonies. The Chesapeake had the highest average value of imports per free white resident, followed by the Lower South, New England, and the Middle Colonies in that order. The Chesapeake and the Lower

South still had a favorable balance of exports over imports, but the Middle Colonies imported commodities worth more than twice as much as those they exported, and New England, which displayed a substantial deficit in food production during the late colonial period, imported nearly three times as much as it exported. Yet both the Middle Colonies and New England seem to have made up a considerable proportion of these deficits, perhaps as much as 60 percent, by invisible earnings derived from the sale of ships and shipping and other merchandizing services. Both import and export figures reflect the development of a considerable coastwise trade among the colonies. Though all four regions participated in this trade, it was dominated by New England and the Middle Colonies, and it marked the early stages in the articulation of an integrated "American" economy through which products from all regions were widely distributed for domestic consumption on a continental scale.[10]

As McCusker and Menard have remarked, these figures "describe a strong, flexible, and diverse economy . . . able to operate without a considerable metropolitan subsidy," at least in peace time. In stark contrast to the situation during the first generations of settlement, none of these continental regions relied heavily on foreign investment. Rather, they "accumulated most of their capital on their own" through the productivity of their inhabitants, savings, and capital improvements, developments that were also reflected in the emergence of a resident and highly skilled commercial sector. The impressive performance of the economies of every one of these regions in turn probably also heralded, to one degree or another, increased specialization of production and a consequent lowering of production costs; improvements in transportation and a resulting decline in distribution costs; advances in human capital, including rising technical expertise; improvements in economic organization; and at least some technological advances such as occurred in shipbuilding and shipping.[11]

THIS impressive demographic, territorial, and economic growth supported an increasingly complex society with an ever larger range, more dense distribution, and more deeply established agglomeration of social institutions. These included families and kinship groups; neighborhoods and hamlets; stores and artisanal establishments; local judicial and administrative institutions; churches; transportation facilities, including roads, bridges, ferries, and a few canals; and a variety of

cultural institutions, including schools, libraries, clubs, and other social organizations. Although many of these institutions were well represented in the countryside, others, including especially commercial
and artisanal establishments and cultural institutions, were most fully
developed in the towns.

The extensive spread of population and the continuing rustication
process it represented meant that as the eighteenth century proceeded,
a declining proportion of the population lived in towns. Yet substantial urbanization occurred in all of the older settled areas, especially
after 1720. Boston was the largest colonial town into the 1740s, when
its population leveled off to between fifteen and sixteen thousand,
where it remained for the rest of the colonial period. At some point
between 1745 and 1760, the populations of both Philadelphia and New
York passed that of Boston. By 1775 the population of Philadelphia was
perhaps as high as forty thousand, that of New York twenty-five thousand. Also by 1775, Charleston and Newport had populations ranging
between nine and twelve thousand; Baltimore and Norfolk, both of
which had developed primarily after 1750 in the Chesapeake, traditionally the least urbanized area of continental America, had around
six thousand; a dozen towns—New Haven, Norwich, New London,
Salem, Lancaster, Hartford, Middletown, Portsmouth, Marblehead,
Providence, Albany, Annapolis, and Savannah—had between three
and five thousand; and perhaps as many as fifty other places had between five hundred and three thousand people.

To an important extent, all of these towns, even those that doubled
as provincial capitals, were trading centers. The largest served as general trading marts and processing, communications, and financial centers for an extensive hinterland. Others were mere collection, distribution, and shipping points. But all provided a greater or lesser range
of services to surrounding areas. In the largest cities, roughly half
of the adult male population was employed in the service sector, of-
fering a wide variety of professional, commercial, building, transport,
and other skills. Of the remaining half of the adult male working
population, only around 2 percent were in a very small public sector;
about a quarter in the industrial sector, including textile and leather
trades, food and drink processing, shipbuilding and fitting crafts,
and metal and furniture trades; and just over a fifth in maritime commerce and fisheries, including mariners and merchants and supporting
personnel.[12]

The increasingly complex occupational structure of the towns, a trend that was also evident, if to a much less impressive extent, in the countryside, was one powerful indication of the results of the steady process of social differentiation that had been occurring in all the major regions of colonial British America during the century after 1660. For instance, the resident commercial sector of the population had developed during these years into an increasingly complex group ranging from petty retailers, peddlers, and hawkers at the lowest level up through primary traders composed mostly of country storekeepers and urban retailers, to secondary traders or wholesalers who collected local products from and distributed finished goods to retailers, to tertiary traders or large merchants who presided over the overseas trade and offered more and more sophisticated financial and insurance services to the commercial economy.

A similar development can be followed with regard to the professions, including the ministry, medicine, and the law. To an important extent, the law remained an unspecialized activity, though by mid-century in several colonies an important distinction had developed between those who practiced before provincial courts and those whose business was primarily local. Everywhere, however, the law became an increasingly self-conscious profession with a concern for maintaining standards, growing sophistication and expertise reflected in a large number of impressive legal libraries, and enhanced social status and respectability. The large volume of litigation over land and mercantile property made the law an especially lucrative activity that by the 1740s and 1750s was attracting not just, as earlier, immigrants but also native sons of the creole elites and middle orders.[13]

The process of social differentiation can also be observed in the development of a much more sharply articulated social structure. To be sure, even at the end of the colonial period, the emerging social hierarchies in the several regions of colonial British America were all much less finely developed and more open than in metropolitan Britain. Nowhere was there anything remotely resembling a legally privileged aristocracy. Indeed, colonial society was not yet divided into well-defined social classes but consisted of two broad and not always discrete social categories, independents and dependents. *Independents* were those with sufficient property in land, tools, or personal goods to make them theoretically free from external control by any other person; *dependents* were those whose wills, in Sir William Blackstone's phrase, were subject to the control of the people on whom they depended.[14]

By contemporary standards, the independent proportion of the population was very large. At the top of this category, the most successful planters, merchants, landlords, and lawyers were, by the 1720s and 1730s in the oldest colonies and by the 1740s and 1750s in the newer ones, a self-conscious and conspicuous elite that, though consisting of no more than two to three percent of colonial families, was distinguished from the rest of society by its substantially greater wealth and affluent and refined lifestyles. Manifest in their clothing, consumption patterns, housing, modes of transportation, education, cosmopolitan outlook, prominence in both public office and the emerging cultural infrastructures, and cultivation of the traditional values of the British rural and urban gentries, including liberality, civility, and stewardship, the superior social status of these developing elites was also evident in the large number of dependents their members could command and by the passive deference usually accorded them by other independent members of society. Yet this largely self-made group, as Richard Hofstadter has remarked, had "only a slender sense of the personal prerogative, the code of honor, or the grand extravagance" usually associated with its equivalents in Europe. Rather, it exhibited "the disciplined ethic of work, the individual assertiveness, the progressive outlook . . . and the calculating and materialistic way of life" associated with the burgeoning middle classes of contemporary Britain.[15]

Some scholars have linked the growing concentrations of property that sustained the several regional colonial elites and the increasing density of population in older settled areas with a decrease in opportunities for upward social mobility beginning during the middle decades of the eighteenth century. In support of these claims, they have cited the appearance of a considerable body of agricultural tenants in several colonies, an increase in the number of people of both sexes among the landless free laboring population, and a rise in the number of people on the poor rolls, especially in the larger cities. Yet it is by no means clear that the increase in poverty, which, even in the cities, still remained far below that in Britain, either was a linear process or was yet leading to the creation of a substantial underclass of residual poor among the free population. Several studies have shown that both tenancy and employment as free labor were very often merely stages in the life cycle, a way for young men to gather the resources necessary to achieve later in life an independent status as landowners or in nonagricultural employment. Similarly, for young women, a period in the labor market was frequently a temporary phase between leaving home and marriage. Moreover, if opportunities to acquire land were declining in long-occupied areas, they were still present in the many new settlements that after 1720 were formed at a phenomenal rate in every region of continental British America. A combination of the demands stimulated by a burgeoning population and the steady development of a more complex occupational structure created vast new and, for some people, obviously preferable opportunities for employment in service, industrial, and mercantile activities.[16]

Certainly in the 1760s and 1770s, as earlier, the most impressive aspect of the free population of Britain's American colonies was the extraordinarily large number of families of independent middling status, which was proportionately substantially more numerous than in any other contemporary Western society. Situated immediately below the elite and, like their counterparts in England, sharing, in many cases, the values and the orientations of those just above them, this vast and increasingly differentiated body of yeoman farmers, artisans, smaller traders, and lesser professionals included the great bulk of independent people in the colonies. In every region of continental colonial British America, their sheer numbers meant that the emerging American society would be "a preponderantly middle-class world" in which "the simpler agencies of the middle class" would be "in strong evidence: the little churches of the dissenting sects, the taverns . . . the societies for [social and] self-improvement and 'philosophical' inquiry, the increasingly eclectic little colleges, the contumacious newspapers, the county court houses and town halls, the how-to-do books, the *Poor Richard's Almanack*."[17]

In the developing American social schema, agricultural tenants and people employed with contracts in the service, industrial, and commercial sectors constituted an ambiguous intermediate group who, though they in many cases enjoyed sufficient resources in the form of their own skills and property to function and be regarded by the rest of society as independent people, were at least technically dependent on their landlords or employers. But such people formed only a small part of the social category of dependents. Because they were defined in the early modern British world as extensions of their husbands' and fathers' legal and social personalities, wives and children together were certainly the largest groups of dependents in colonial America. At least within the confines of the free population, however, most, if not the vast majority, of women and children were members of families whose male head was independent. As a consequence, they assumed his independent social status.[18]

When colonial Americans referred to *social* dependents, they were talking largely about people who fell into one or the other of three groups of laborers, all of whom were employed to provide a substantial amount of the extraordinary effort required to produce the food and the vendible commodities necessary to sustain this rapidly expanding and still highly exploitive society: free laborers, servants, and slaves. Although much of the labor in the farm colonies, especially in New England, where the pace of economic development was slower and the labor requirements much lower, had been supplied by family members, the demand for labor, as has been shown at length in previous chapters, was a persistent problem in the land- and resource-rich but labor-poor colonies from New York south to Barbados. Over time, first in New England and then in the Chesapeake and Middle Colonies, an expanding pool of free laborers, mostly younger men and women just getting started in life, slowly developed into a significant, if notoriously expensive, component of the labor market. By the mid-eighteenth century, male laborers in this category may have constituted as much as 10 percent of the adult male population of large towns and an even larger percentage of the inhabitants of smaller towns and long-established rural districts.[19]

From the Middle Colonies south, however, servitude, which was also present in New England, especially before 1720, had almost certainly been a more important means of supplying the demand for labor beyond what could be provided by family members, and the predominant form of servant labor was provided through indentured servitude, a new institution developed in the first half of the seventeenth century to meet the heavy labor requirements of the West Indian and Chesapeake colonies. Servitude was a transitional status that enabled people to secure passage to the colonies in return for selling their labor for a set period of time, at the end of which they hoped to move into a position from which they could acquire land and an independent status. With the substitution of blacks for whites as plantation laborers, beginning in the West Indies and extending to the continent during the closing decades of the seventeenth century, servitude changed from an institution that supplied primarily unskilled labor to one that furnished considerable amounts of skilled labor, albeit by the mid-eighteenth century throughout the colonies slaves were more and more being trained to perform skilled tasks formerly assigned to servants. Notwithstanding these changes in the institution and use of white servitude, however, the demand for unskilled servant labor remained high in all regions of continental British America except New England. The especially high demand for such labor in the Chesapeake and Middle Colonies was evidenced by the eagerness with which buyers snapped up as many as forty to fifty thousand largely young, male, and minimally skilled convicts transported from Britain between 1718 and 1775.[20]

Life was no picnic for servants, who had traditionally been and still in the mid-eighteenth century were often worked hard, but servitude at least held out an eventual promise of freedom and independence for the more ambitious and fortunate of those who survived their terms; the same could not be said for slaves. As Table 8.1 makes clear, blacks—of whom all except perhaps 1 to 2 percent were slaves—constituted the largest single category of the dependent population, over a third of the population of colonial British America as a whole and more than 20 percent in the continental colonies in 1760. These substantial numbers remind us of the extraordinary extent to which the growth and prosperity of the emerging society of free colonial British America as well as the high incidence of independent individuals who lived there were achieved as a result of slave labor, of the forced emigration from their widely dispersed homelands of thousands of people of African descent and their systematic subjugation to an intrinsically harsh and virtually inescapable labor regime based on racial discrimination and enforced by the full power of the law.[21]

To be sure, except in some rural parishes in low-country South Carolina and Georgia, slaves were nowhere nearly so numerous in any of the continental colonies as they were in the West Indies, where, in 1760, for the region as a whole, they outnumbered whites by about 7 to 1, ranging from 5 to 1 in Barbados up to almost 10 to 1 in Antigua and Jamaica. At the same time, among the continental colonies, whites exceeded blacks in every region, but there were striking differences between the regions heavily engaged in plantation agriculture and the farm colonies of the North. Thus, though the Lower South had only 1.3 and the Chesapeake colonies 1.7 whites for every slave, whites in the

Middle Colonies outnumbered blacks by 14 to 1 and in New England by 35 to 1. Moreover, the percentage of slaves in the population was only one of several important variables that produced substantial temporal and spatial variations in the nature of slavery and its impact upon those who were subjected to it. Others included the ways slaves were employed, the social distance between whites and slaves, and the proportion of newly imported Africans in the slave population.

Everywhere on the continent, however, the institution of slavery seems to have gone through a similar cycle. More open, less oppressive, and often more conducive to the formation of a stable family life among slaves during its earliest decades, it became more rigid, more differentiated, and often less congenial for slaves as they became more numerous and more integral to the culture and as the proportion of new male slaves imported directly from Africa increased. As Chapters 3, 4, and 6 have shown in some detail and as Ira Berlin has emphasized, the differential operation of the several variables affecting the institution had by the second half of the eighteenth century produced at least three distinctive slave systems among the continental colonies, one in each of the plantation areas of the Chesapeake and the Lower South and another in the farm colonies to the north.

In the Chesapeake, the first and oldest center of slavery on the continent, slaves, both those who lived on large plantations and the majority who resided on smaller units, mostly lived under the direct management of white families, were thoroughly subjected to the assimilative pressures of white paternalism, enjoyed relatively little autonomy, and had very few opportunities to obtain freedom. Having already acquired a more balanced sex ratio and a creole majority by the mid-eighteenth century, Chesapeake blacks early achieved a more stable family life; the proportion of new Africans, most of whom ended up on smaller units in newer areas, declined steadily; differences within the black population diminished more quickly; blacks developed no distinctive language and managed to retain relatively few African cultural survivals; and an Afro-American culture "evolved parallel with Anglo-American culture and with considerable congruence."

Slavery in the Lower South contrasted markedly with that in the Chesapeake. There, profitable staple agriculture developed later; the concentration of slaves on larger units with a minimum of white supervision and the widespread use of the task system tended to limit the effects of white paternalist ideology, to give blacks more autonomy in their daily lives, and to enable them, like West Indian slaves, to play a major role in the internal marketing system; Africans continued to be imported in substantial numbers throughout the eighteenth century; and a higher incidence of interracial sexual liaisons created the conditions for the appearance of at least a small black and mulatto free population. In such conditions, "the transformation of Africans into Afro-Americans . . . was a slow halting process that left most black people alienated from white society and fully equipped to establish their own distinctive culture," one that in language, patterns of familial descent, and work practices "incorporated more of West African culture into their new lives than any other black peoples on mainland North America."

Although there were outposts of the plantation system in the northern colonies, in the iron plantations of the Middle Colonies, and in the large stock-farming operations in the Narragansett country of Rhode Island, most blacks in the northern colonies tended to live and work either as agricultural workers on small units of production in the countryside or in small numbers as domestics, hired laborers, teamsters, and dock and maritime workers in towns. Indeed, as Berlin has remarked, the importance of slaves "to the growth of Northern cities increased during the eighteenth century" as urban slavery "moved steadily away from the household to the docks, warehouses and shops." A steady rise in the "importance of slaves to the work force" in the northern colonies after 1730 led to considerable importations directly from Africa, particularly into Rhode Island and the Middle Colonies, throughout the middle decades of the eighteenth century. This development enabled blacks to draw upon and to "remain acutely conscious of their African inheritance" at the same time that their emerging Afro-American culture was being increasingly "integrated into the larger Euro-American one."[22]

Notwithstanding the importance of these substantial differences among the slave systems of continental British North America, however, it is important to an understanding of the character of the emerging society and culture of British North America to emphasize certain basic similarities among them. No region displayed a manifest reluctance to employ slaves before the 1760s and 1770s. If only those colonies from New York south "had fairly elaborate slave codes," they all still "sanctioned slaveholding on the eve of the American Revolution" and "had at least the rudiments of a statutory law of slavery or race" that "defined slavery as a lifetime condition," made slave status "hereditable through the mother," identified it racially with people of African descent, defined slaves as property, and established a system of "racial etiquette" designed to maintain a clear and permanent distinction between the free white inhabitants and their black slaves. Everywhere, this well-established system of racial slavery was thus based on "the permanent, violent domination of natally alienated and generally dishonored persons" defined primarily on the basis of color and without "social existence" outside the persons of their free owners. Along with the continuing importance of the institution of servitude, the powerful presence, wide diffusion, and—except in Nova Scotia and New Hampshire—expanding use of slavery in the 1760s and 1770s throughout colonial British America provides a vivid reminder of just how fundamentally exploitive that society was.[23]

IF the emerging society of late colonial British America was at once expansive, mobile, prosperous, increasingly more differentiated, and exploitive of its least fortunate members, it fulfilled many of the most sanguine hopes of the first settlers. The extraordinary outpouring of people from the British Isles and continental Europe into the British colonies was the result not of "discontent and persecution at home," not of a determination "to enlarge the realm of English power," not of a desire "to reach the glories of the other world," and not even of "visions of liberty." Rather, what "stirred people into these extraordinary activities," as G. R. Elton has written, was "a drive for land and fortune." Lured to America by "promises of riches," they were primarily moved by "the common and acceptable human emotions of greed and the search for greater wealth." Except for the New England puritans, Perry Miller has noted, most immigrants "came for better advantage and for less danger, and to give their posterity the opportunity of success."[24]

Given this orientation among immigrants and settlers, the establishment and development of Britain's overseas empire rapidly turned into what D. A. Farnie has described as "a revolutionary cultural expansion wherein the energies of the littoral communities" in Ireland and America "were increasingly diverted into economic fields." As the "successive emergence of staple after staple made the Atlantic basin the sphere of a commercial empire unparalleled in the past in its nature" and "as a common economic civilization" emerged in which consumption became an increasingly powerful motor among people "in both transatlantic and cisatlantic lands" and "commerce became the great bond of unity in societies otherwise divided," these littoral societies increasingly became one of the most vivid "manifestation[s] of the efflorescent secular culture of western Europe," and the "'Great Tradition'" of the "emerging Atlantic civilizations became a secular rather than a sacred tradition, and in particular an economic, a commercial, a 'sensate' tradition" in which the major focus of the people who shared in it was upon production, profit, trade, and consumption.[25]

Notwithstanding the "serene rustic image of self-sufficient communities" invoked by some historians to characterize colonial British America, no group of colonists, as Carole Shammas has shown, were "commercial primitives" in the sense that they were entirely cut off from the secular market society of this broader Atlantic commercial world. Very few households had the resources necessary to be self-sufficient and therefore had both to supplement "homegrown products with textiles, flour, butter, and meat bought from tradesmen, peddlars, and neighboring producers" and to function in an environment in which the prices that were almost always "attached to their labor and goods" were invariably "affected by regional, continental, and international markets." Even in the most isolated areas of colonial New England, Shammas has found, colonial Americans "fully participate[d] in" this emerging commercial world. Although the extent of that participation varied according to wealth and accessibility to markets, there was no dual economic system as has been posited by some historians and "no stark dichotomy of market versus nonmarket activity" from one area or one social group to the next. Rather, there was only a "gradual reduction occurring as one moved from major seaport areas to minor, from coast to interior, from older settlements to the frontier." Indeed, not only did most households usually have to spend about "a quarter of per capita income on goods imported from outside the *colony*" in which they lived, but over time they also exhibited that same "voracious appetite . . . for new market commodities" manifested by consumers throughout the Atlantic world during the century after 1660. Indeed, the social depth and extent of British-American involvement in this consumer revolution provided a remarkable testimony to the breadth of economic well-being among colonists in all regions: the top two-thirds of the population participated in it, whereas only the top quarter did so in Britain.[26]

In this emerging secular and commercial culture, the central orientation of people in the littoral became the achievement of personal independence, a state in which a man and his family and broader dependents could live "at ease" rather than in anxiety, in contentment rather than in want, in respectability rather than in meanness, and, perhaps most important, in freedom from the will and control of other men. On the eastern side of the Atlantic, in Britain and in Ireland, and in the confined spaces of the small Atlantic and Caribbean island colonies, the proportion of independent men in the total male population was small. But in the continental colonies, the opportunity to acquire land, an independent trade, or both was so wide as to put the achievement of independence within the grasp of most able-bodied, active, and enterprising free men. The prospect for "a very comfortable and independent subsistence" held out by promotional writers, land developers, and government authorities contributed throughout the colonial era to act as a powerful magnet in attracting settlers to new colonies and newly opening areas.[27]

Moreover, although the achievement of genuine affluence and a gentle status was confined to a relatively small number of people, as it was in contemporary Britain, the comparatively widespread realization of independence by people whose beginnings were modest, a realization achieved mostly by the disciplined application of industry to the mastery of the soil, contributed to an equally broad diffusion of an expansive sense of self-worth throughout the independent, mostly landowning adult male population. In J. R. Pole's words, this expansive psychology in turn gave rise to "the very rapid advance of the more egocentric type of individualism" in which the ideal of the masterless man became associated with a variety of other values of "an individualising character." These values included a jealous regard for personal autonomy; "a hearty confidence in the individual['s] . . . ability to manage his own affairs"; a growing "respect for the integrity of individual character" and individual choice in such fundamental matters as decisions about when and whom to marry, what career to pursue, and where and what religious beliefs to profess; "a profound attachment to private property"; a deep "suspicion of government"; and high expectations for one's children.[28]

In this situation, the achievement and peaceful enjoyment of personal independence, the objective that had initially drawn so many of both the first settlers and later immigrants to the colonies, continued to be the most visible and powerful imperative in the emerging American culture, the principal aspiration and animating drive in the lives of colonists in all regions. The most popular cultural image in eighteenth-century British America was the biblical image of the independent farmer sitting contentedly and safely under his own shade trees in front of his own home in full view of his fields, his flocks, and his dependents, including slaves if he had them. This was precisely the image Thomas Jefferson evoked in the Declaration of Independence when he included among the inalienable rights of man not merely life and liberty but also the "pursuit of happiness," a phrase that had been defined more specifically three weeks earlier by Jefferson's fellow Virginian George Mason in the first article of the Virginia Declaration of Rights as "the enjoyment of life and liberty, with the means of acquiring and possessing property, and pursuing and obtaining happiness and safety."[29]

The pursuit of happiness and the expansive individualism that lay behind it have often been associated with the profit motive. "*The love of gain*," Samuel Miller noted in 1800 in his retrospective commentary on developments in America during the previous century, "particularly characterizes the inhabitants of the *United States*." But the considerable individuality Americans "were able to cultivate in their personal lives" and their devotion to personal independence should not be confused with "either the drive for profit maximization or the individualism of economic competition." If the "manifold opportunities for individualistic economic enterprise" everywhere fostered a social order that "was shot through with a restless mobility" and "a pervasive materialism," James Henretta is certainly correct to emphasize both the extent to which "the 'calculus of advantage' for these men and women was not mere pecuniary gain, but encompassed a much wider range of social and cultural goals." He is also right to stress the degree to which the expression of individual desires was mitigated by a prior concern with "meeting . . . household needs" and "maintaining . . . established social relationships within the community." Henretta does not deny that "economic gain was important to these men and women," but he correctly insists that it was usually "subordinate to (or encompassed by) two other goals: the yearly subsistence and the long-run financial security of the family unit." Indeed, it might be argued that precisely because "the family persisted as the basic unit of . . . production, capital formation, and property transmission," virtually all early Americans associated the drive for personal independence and the pursuit of happiness with the promotion and perpetuation of the welfare of the lineal family. For most colonial Americans the pursuit of self by definition also involved the fulfillment of family obligations.[30]

Certainly, the individual pursuit of happiness, the quest for personal independence, emphatically did not "whittle away at the foundations of the family, community, church, and other institutions of the social order." Largely an artifact of the puritan rhetoric of declension and of the subsequent "New Englandization of early North American history," this conception of the early American social process is almost wholly at variance with actual experience. For the people who created and perpetuated the new societies of colonial British America sought not merely personal independence as individuals and the welfare of their families but also the social goal of improved societies that would both guarantee the independence they hoped to achieve and enable them to enjoy its fruits. Indeed, demands and aspirations for improvement were nearly as prominent among settlers in these new societies as were those for independence and affluence.[31]

Ubiquitous in the economic writings of early modern Britain, the language of improvement as it took shape in Britain primarily referred to schemes, devices, or projects through which the economic position of the nation might be advanced, the estates or fortunes of individuals might be bettered, or existing resources might be made more productive. In the new societies of colonial British America, the term *improvement* carried similar connotations. Settlers sought to "improve" their situation by securing the necessary capital and labor to develop their lands and fortunes; towns that would provide them with local markets in which they could exchange the produce of their lands for finished goods; bounties that would encourage them to experiment with new crops; and roads, bridges, and ferries that would provide them with better access to wider markets and link them more closely to economic and administrative centers.[32]

In the new and relatively undeveloped societies of colonial British America, however, the term *improvement* acquired a much wider meaning: it was used to describe a state of society that was far removed from the savagery associated with the native Indians. An *improved* society was one defined by a series of positive and negative juxtapositions. Not wild, barbaric, irregular, rustic, or crude, it was settled, cultivated, civilized, orderly, developed, and polite. The primary model for an improved society was the emerging and more settled, orderly, and coherent society of contemporary Britain. For new frontier settlements within the colonies, it was the older occupied areas along the seacoast. With re-creation and not innovation as their aim, colonial British Americans generally aspired to a fully developed market society with credit, commercial agriculture, slavery, and a rapid circulation of money and goods. They wanted a settled and hierarchical social structure with social distinctions ranging from the genteel down to the vulgar. In particular, they wanted a social structure that would enable successful independent and affluent people, in conformity with the long-standing traditions of Western civilization (and probably all other highly developed civilizations), to exploit dependent people. They desired authoritative, if not very obtrusive, political institutions that could facilitate their socioeconomic and cultural development and would be presided over by people whose very success in the private realm testified to their merit and capacity and gave them a legitimate claim to political leadership. They wanted vital traditional social institutions that would contribute to and stand as visible symbols of their improvement, including churches, schools, and towns.[33]

If the concept of improvement thus enabled colonial British Americans to think of their societies in developmental terms and if their demographic vigor and material prosperity provided two impressive measures of the degree to which they were moving rapidly toward the achievement of an improved state, the changing character of public life offered still a third such measure. For during the century after 1660 all of the older colonies underwent a profound transformation in the political sphere. Because the colony, and not the region, was the unit of political organization, a regional framework such as I have used in this volume is inappropriate for an analysis of political developments. Indeed, each colony constituted an almost wholly discrete political environment with its own distinctive configurations of political activity, and this distinctiveness was reinforced because at least until the Seven Years' War and really until the crises that preceded the American Revolution there was virtually no common political life among the colonies. By the mid-eighteenth century, however, all but the very newest colonies of Georgia and Nova Scotia, in the islands as well as on the continent, had experienced a major expansion of political resources, which contributed to a significant increase in the capabilities of provincial political systems.

By the 1730s and 1740s in older colonies and by the 1740s and 1750s in the newer ones, both provincial and, except in the most recently settled areas, local politics were dominated by coherent, effective, acknowledged, and authoritative political elites with considerable social and economic power, extensive political experience, confidence in their capacity to govern, and—what crucially distinguished them from their European counterparts —broad public support. Second, they had viable governing institutions at both the local and provincial levels most of which were becoming more and more assimilated to those in metropolitan Britain, vigorous traditions of internal self-government, and extensive experience in coping with the socioeconomic and other problems peculiar to their own societies. Third, even though political participation was limited to white, independent, adult males, their political systems were almost certainly more inclusive and more responsive to public opinion than those of any other societies in the world at that time, and they were becoming more and more capable of permitting the resolution of conflict, absorbing new and diverse groups, and, as their recent histories had so amply attested, providing political stability in periods of rapid demographic, economic, and territorial expansion.

If the several colonial polities were becoming more expert, they were also becoming far more settled. By the mid-eighteenth century, levels of collective violence and civil disorder were ordinarily low, few colonies had outstanding issues that deeply divided the polity, society routinely accepted existing institutional and leadership structures, relations among the several branches and levels of government had been thoroughly regularized, rates of turnover among elected officials were low, changes in leadership followed an orderly process through regular constitutional channels without serious disruption of the polity, and factional and party strife was either being routinized or reduced to levels at which it was not dysfunctional within the political system. As was manifest in declining turnover among elected representatives to the colonial assemblies in most colonies, the electorate increasingly exhibited a passive and uncoerced deference toward the governing elite. With their attentions firmly concentrated on their own individual and family goals in the private realm, the vast bulk of the electorate seems, in ordinary times, to have had little interest in taking an active role in public life. Together, these developments brought a new stability and regularity to colonial political life in the three or four decades before 1760.

Notwithstanding these developments, the public realm everywhere

remained small. Citizens expected little from government; budgets
and taxes were low; paid officials were few; civil and judicial establishments were small, part-time, and unprofessional; and the maintenance
of order devolved very largely upon local units of government, which
had few coercive resources vis-à-vis the free population. Thus, despite
efforts by elites to enforce stricter moral standards in communities
during the mid-eighteenth century and attempts by provincial governments to deal with a possible rise in crime by adopting more severe
penal measures during the last half of the century, local governments,
bowing to local opinion, remained relatively permissive in dealing
with minor offenses involving violations of morality and punished all
but the most heinous crimes with whippings and fines rather than
imprisonment, banishment, or execution. Indeed, possessing limited
powers, colonial governments necessarily exerted only weak authority
and were heavily dependent upon public opinion, which sharply limited the scope for action among political leaders. Government in these
always potentially highly participatory polities was necessarily consensual. Always open to challenge from dissatisfied elements among the
free population, the several polities of late colonial British America
invariably contained a latent potential for widespread popular mobi-
lization.[34]

If many of the features of these emerging American political systems
revealed a growing capacity for accommodation among increasingly
differentiated and complex social populations within the several colonial polities, the same can be said for developments in other areas of
cultural life. The societies of all regions of colonial British America
remained predominantly English. But the substantial immigration of
non-English groups after 1713 and, notwithstanding the strong predis-
position of people from many of these groups to settle in communities
of their own kind, the consequent intermingling of peoples of diverse
cultural and national backgrounds and competing religious persuasions slowly edged people toward a habit of compromise and an enhanced capacity for the toleration and acceptance of ethnic, cultural,
and religious diversity. At the same time, the overwhelming cultural
preoccupation with the pursuit of individual and family happiness in
the socioeconomic area seems everywhere to have weakened the impulse to try to enforce a coercive religious uniformity.

But this is not to suggest that pluralism was necessarily pushing
people in the direction of ever greater secularism. Using New England

as a surrogate for the whole of colonial America, many historians have interpreted the weakening of the puritan religious synthesis as an indication of growing secularism. Although they have admitted that this process was temporarily reversed by the series of mid-eighteenth-century religious revivals known as the Great Awakening, they have argued that it accelerated after midcentury and that by the 1770s and 1780s, British America, as Hofstadter has remarked, may well have been one of "the most unchurched regions in all of Christendom."[35]

But this interpretation seems to have the process of religious development backward. Except for the early puritan settlers of New England and, to a considerably lesser extent, the Quaker founders of Pennsylvania, the vast majority of early colonists seem to have had a profoundly secular orientation from the beginning. If they were almost all nominally Protestant, they seem to have had neither a deep religiosity nor, perhaps, even very strong attachments to any specific doctrine or form of religion. So pervasive and powerful, in fact, was the secular bias of the early settlers outside New England that it is highly probable that, contrary to the traditional interpretation, the inhabitants of British America were becoming, if not less secular, at least no less and possibly even somewhat more religious during the last century of the colonial period.

Although it is difficult to sustain the argument that any of the several regions of colonial British America south of New England had yet become deeply religious before the so-called second Great Awakening at the end of the eighteenth century, it is also true that interest in religion was substantial throughout the first eight decades of the eighteenth century and that, as Patricia Bonomi has argued, the trend toward social consolidation during the same period everywhere resulted in the emergence of religious organizations "as significant centers of stability and influence" and in the enhancement of religious authority. In short supply in many colonies as late as the 1720s and 1730s, ministers by the mid-eighteenth century "were visibly present in every section except the far frontier, and ecclesiastical consolidation was well under way in all denominations." As Bonomi and Peter Eisenstadt have shown, the number of churches in the seven largest Protestant denominations increased more than seven times between 1700 and 1780, an overall rate of congregation formation that rose in much closer ratio to population growth than has commonly been supposed. Whereas the white population increased 888 percent between 1700 and

1780, the number of churches rose by 632 percent, and one suspects that the gap would have been even smaller if the authors had used an earlier baseline of 1660 or 1680. With one church for every 467 whites, the Middle Colonies had the highest ratio of churches to population in 1750. New England came next with one church for every 606 whites, and the southern colonies—the Chesapeake and the Lower South combined—were last with only one church for every 1,046 whites. Bonomi and Eisenstadt also show that church adherence as measured by estimated church attendance declined relatively steadily from 80 percent of the white population in 1700 to 78 percent in 1720, around 75 percent in the 1740s and 1750s, 69 percent in 1765, and 59 percent in 1780. But they argue that everywhere in continental British North America during the eighteenth century, the churched population, which ranged from about 80 percent of whites in New England down to about 56 percent in the Chesapeake, considerably exceeded the unchurched.[36]

If, however, most people were both nominally Christian and occasional church attendants, if the religious needs of the population were not nearly so badly served as historians have often suggested, if the changing religious landscape outside New England contains "little that accords with the notion of declension," and if, perhaps, by the late colonial period interest in religion may even have been considerably more extensive than during the earliest generations of settlement in all regions except New England, still religious life remained in many respects fragile and unsettled. Church hierarchies in the colonies were undeveloped, clerical authority in most major denominations was weak, lay control over religious matters was extensive and relations between ministers and congregations often conflicted, anticlericalism was widespread, and a shortage of trained ministers among several denominations left many newly settled areas without ministers.

These conditions may not have been sufficiently severe to create the "breakdown of church religion" that some historians have suggested was responsible for making people "unusually susceptible" to the evangelical revivals that swept so many congregations at various times during the middle decades of the eighteenth century. As Jon Butler has persuasively argued, moreover, those revivals were probably far too heterogeneous, too disconnected in time and space, and insufficiently general to constitute a continentwide "Great" Awakening of the sort invented by modern historians. Nevertheless, the widespread appeal of evangelical religion represented by those revivals strongly suggests that existing religious institutions were failing in important respects to meet the spiritual needs of colonial populations, who in significant numbers turned to an alternative and, for them, more emotionally satisfying form of religious belief that emphasized the importance of conversion, the centrality of the individual in the conversion experience, and the primacy of religious beliefs in daily life.[37]

For New England, the attraction of evangelicalism, as several scholars have suggested, may well have represented a reaction to the rapid assimilation of the region to the dominant patterns of behavior in the rest of colonial British America. As New Englanders became more and more preoccupied with the worldly concerns involved in the individual pursuit of happiness, as they became less attentive to religion and more materialistic, more consumption-oriented, and less deferential to authority in both the religious and civil realms, they also seem to have longed for a return to the older, simpler, and more pious and coherent communal social order that by the 1730s and 1740s mostly survived only in the region's collective memory. In other regions, the appeal of evangelicalism may have been rooted in a profound disquiet arising out of an inability of many people to adjust to the extreme good fortune and prosperity they enjoyed and a corresponding sense of their own unworthiness.

Whatever their source, these many spiritual awakenings have been seen by some historians as occasions and vehicles for the revival and intensification within New England of the "special themes of New England providential thought" and their "spread . . . to other sections of America." The idea of national election, of the chosenness of the American people, has certainly been a highly visible and at times powerful component of American culture. Indeed, as Sacvan Bercovitch has argued, the idea that *"In the beginning was the word, and the word was with the New England Way, and the word became 'America'"* may well have been the most important ingredient in what he calls "the myth of America." As his formulation suggests, however, notwithstanding efforts by Cotton Mather and other Congregational clergymen to generalize and promote this conception of America as "sacred space," the idea that any segment of colonial British America had a special relationship with God and a providential destiny was almost wholly confined to New England before the second half of the eighteenth century. The inhabitants of all regions of colonial British America "believed in an absolute, intervening deity who controlled and directed all the natural and human developments within the universe." Yet, as John Berens has emphasized, "no . . . section outside New England [ever] considered itself to be the New Israel or to have a world-affecting divine mission to perform."[38]

By the 1770s, however, this ancient New England theme, the intellectual roots of which—in America—may be found in the puritans' ambition of erecting a city upon a hill and in their conception of themselves as God's chosen people, was becoming an American theme. Bercovitch may well be correct in arguing that the puritans "provided the scriptural basis for what we have come to call the myth of America." But it is far less certain that the concept of America as an elect nation that became so powerfully evident during the era of the American Revolution can be traced so directly and so completely to "the influence of New Englanders on other sections of America in the course of the Awakening" and later. If it obviously owed something to the conception, articulated especially strongly by New England clergymen, of the Seven Years' War as a providential struggle against popery and absolutism, it certainly also had important secular roots. Indeed, an important element in the emerging idea of Americans as a chosen people was the optimistic prediction, set forth by American writers from all regions, including John Trumbull, Hugh Henry Brackenridge, and Philip Freneau, that America not only might have a special place in secular history but also might soon be transformed "into a new Athens."

As Joseph Ellis has contended, this "effusive vision" was to an important degree "the result of a straightforward and conscious extrapolation from the visible and much discussed maturation of colonial society," particularly from its phenomenal demographic and economic performance over the previous century. Attributing that performance less to the special regard of the Almighty than to the favorable effects of the weakness of traditional economic, social, political, and religious constraints in America, exponents of this vision linked America's special future role to the expected further development "of a liberal mentality that exalted the untapped power that would be generated within individuals and society at large when [all] traditional impediments to thought and action were obliterated." Not Providence per se but the manifold, undirected, and unfettered actions of free individuals each pursuing his or her own happiness and operating in an unrestrained field of action would propel America to its special destiny. During the era of the Revolution, this idea was infused with ever more power by an emerging sense of the possibility of national greatness deriving out of the successful prosecution of the War for Independence and the creation of the American republic.[39]

HISTORIANS have repeatedly assigned New England the primary role in the creation of American culture. Two explicit assumptions underlie this assignment: first, that New England's sociocultural development was emblematic of the development of the rest of British colonial America, and, second, that the most important basic concepts animating the emerging American culture of the late eighteenth and early nineteenth centuries derived directly and immediately out of New England culture. But neither of these assumptions seems to be correct. An analysis of the process of sociocultural development for the several other regions of colonial British America reveals that New England was in many respects exceptional and that what has been traditionally characterized as the American tradition turns out on closer examination to be little more than what Michael Zuckerman has referred to as the "regional tradition of New England," a tradition that during the colonial period scarcely penetrated into the area west and south of the Hudson River.

The argument that American culture was very largely a derivative of New England culture rests mostly on New England's undeniable contribution to the theological foundations of the idea of national election. Important though it has sometimes been, however, the concept of national election seems never to have been so pervasively and persistently influential in shaping American culture as the notion of America as a place peculiarly favorable for the quest for the good life, defined as the pursuit of individual happiness and material achievement. During the colonial period, this quest was powerfully evident throughout all regions of colonial British America, including New England, but on the North American continent it was most conspicuous in the colonies south of New England. Moreover, to the important extent to which the American idea of national election had secular as well as theological roots, it derived not narrowly out of New England but out of the material achievements and expansive character of the broadly developing American culture of the eighteenth century, a culture that was strongly manifest in the early histories of the Chesapeake, Middle

Colonies, and Lower South and to which New England had to assimilate before it could fully participate in it.

If, as Zuckerman has remarked, it now "seems increasingly clear that the configuration of American civilization first found its essential contours in the mid- and South-Atlantic regions," it is also obvious, as has been argued here, that the Chesapeake continued at least through the first decades of the American republic to be the "center of gravity" of the American population and to occupy a prominent place in the process of social convergence involved in the creation of that civilization. In 1770, the Chesapeake included "the mainland colonies most prized in the mother country," contained almost a third of the population of the continental colonies, and had by far the most valuable export trade. For another sixty years, moreover, until the third decade of the nineteenth century, it would continue to be the most populous region of the United States. That Virginia, in particular, played such a paramount role in the American Revolution and the foundation of the United States and that four of the first five presidents of the United States were from the Chesapeake were no accidents. Rather, they were vivid indications of the continuing centrality of the Chesapeake in the early development of the American nation and the emerging national culture.[40]

EPILOGUE

During the first 150 years of their existence, the southern colonies were not distinctive. Not only did they stand at the center rather than on the peripheries of colonial British American cultural and social development, but they were also, for their free populations, the very embodiment of what was arguably the single most important element in the emerging American mind—the ideal of the pursuit of happiness by independent people in a setting that provided significant opportunities for success. Comprehension of the normative character of the experience of the southern colonies in the process of colonization and their centrality in the formation of an American culture makes it clear that the really important questions about southern distinctiveness are thus when and how this region came to be perceived not as the highest expression but as the very denial of many of the main tenets of American life.

These questions are beyond the scope of this volume. Yet the prominence of the southern colonies and states in the major events of the Revolution as well as in the establishment and early years of the American republic clearly reveals that their inhabitants had not yet come to think of their regions or to be thought of by people from other areas as outside the mainstream of American development. No less than residents of the states to the north, the inhabitants of the Chesapeake and Lower South thought of themselves as genuine republicans and of their regions as the epitomes of American republicanism. Americans of the revolutionary generation were certainly aware that there were still significant divergencies among the several states and regions of the new United States. From the perspective of their common experience in mounting and carrying out a successful war for independent nationhood, however, they had found it possible to perceive their commonalities as much more impressive than their differences and to think of themselves as all part of "a common culture that transcended sectional differences." Few could have found incredible George Washington's assertion in his Farewell Address in 1796 that "with *slight* shades of difference" Americans had "the same religion, manners, habits and political principles."[1]

At the very time Washington spoke, of course, some people were beginning to glimpse and to understand the potential seriousness of the many remaining fissures in this infant American society, especially as they were manifest in the northern commitment to abolition and the southern devotion to the preservation of a slave labor system. In an oration on March 5, 1776, Peter Thatcher, the Boston lawyer, had told his audience that America faced a dilemma as to whether "the rising empire of America" should "be an empire of slaves *or* of freemen." The particular choice he had in mind, of course, was the one between political slavery under Britain or political freedom with independence. But the dilemma he posed for America was not actually resolved by the Revolution, and it slowly became clear following the gradual evaporation of abolitionist sentiment in the Upper South after 1785 that the "rising empire of America" would be an empire of slaves *and* freemen.[2]

With the phased abolition of slavery in the British Empire and the spread of disdain for slavery throughout the northern areas of the United States after 1820, the South's continuing commitment to a slave labor system resulted in a growing divergence between its patterns of social organization and values and those of the increasingly urban and industrialized societies of the North. In their obvious "hierarchy, the cult of chivalry—the unmachined civilization, the folk society, the rural character of life, the clan values rather than the commercial values," the southern states, as the late David Potter has argued, seemed to have acquired a "*distinctiveness* of a deeply significant kind," one that was both less and less congruent with the social character and orientation of the states to the north and out of step with the rest of the civilized world. Notwithstanding their economic origins, the southern states seemed to have developed "a climate that was uncongenial" to the capitalist spirit that still thrived in the North.[3]

Some scholars have argued vigorously, of course, that by the middle of the nineteenth century the United States actually comprised two discrete cultures, one northern and one southern. But one does not have to subscribe to this extreme conception of the problem to recognize that by 1860 the divergencies between the northern and the southern states were perhaps as great as they had ever been and certainly greater than they had been at any time since the beginning of the eighteenth century.[4]

Insofar as it already existed, however, this southern distinctiveness did not appear to be of overwhelming importance to the revolutionary generation. Only after the northern states had both abandoned slavery and defined it as morally reprehensible were the cultural divergencies that had arisen out of the relatively more profuse material abundance of the southern colonies defined as distinctive and labeled, by critics, as deviant. Only thereafter were the southern colonies denied the central role they had occupied in the process of British-American colonization and the creation of not just the American nation but, more fundamentally, American culture as well.

NOTES

PREFACE

1. On the intellectual genealogy and deficiencies of this model, see the stimulating analysis in Joyce Appleby, "Value and Society," in Jack P. Greene and J. R. Pole, eds., *Colonial British America: Essays in the New History of the Early Modern Era* (Baltimore, 1984), 290–316.

2. Marc Bloch, *The Historian's Craft* (New York, 1959), 29–35.

3. Jack P. Greene, "Autonomy and Stability: New England and the British Colonial Experience in Early Modern America: A Review Essay," *Journal of Social History* 7 (1974): 171–94, "Economy and Society in the British Caribbean during the Seventeenth and Eighteenth Centuries: A Review Essay," *American Historical Review* 79 (1974): 1499–1517.

PROLOGUE

1. The quotation is from Richard Price, *Observations on the Importance of the American Revolution* (London, 1784), 5–7.

2. Duncan J. MacLeod, *Slavery, Race and the American Revolution* (Cambridge, 1974).

3. Far and away the most penetrating exploration of these developments is to be found in William R. Taylor, *Cavalier and Yankee: The Old South and American National Character* (New York, 1961). But see also Charles S. Sydnor, *The Development of Southern Sectionalism, 1819–1848* (Baton Rouge, 1948); Carl Degler, *Place over Time: The Continuity of Southern Distinctiveness* (Baton Rouge, 1977); and Thomas P. Govan, "Americans Below the Potomac," in Charles Grier Sellers, Jr., ed., *The Southerner as American* (Chapel Hill, 1960), 19–39.

4. See Degler, *Place over Time*, 99–132; C. Vann Woodward, *The Burden of Southern History* (Baton Rouge, 1960); Paul M. Gaston, *The New South Creed: A Study in Southern Mythmaking* (New York, 1970); and George B. Tindall, *The Ethnic Southerners* (Baton Rouge, 1976).

5. Significant exceptions are John R. Alden, *The First South* (Baton Rouge, 1961), and Carl Bridenbaugh, *Myths and Realities: Societies of the Colonial South* (Baton Rouge, 1952).

6. The fullest and most intelligent presentation of this view is perhaps Sacvan Bercovitch, *The Puritan Origins of the American Self* (New Haven, 1975). For an implicit endorsement by a prominent historian of the South of the assumptions that lie behind this view and in particular of the notion that the colonial world was principally defined by the puritans, see C. Vann Woodward, "The Southern Ethic in a Puritan World," *William and Mary Quarterly* 3d ser., 25 (1968): 343–70.

CHAPTER ONE

1. The most recent and systematic analysis of emigrants to America is Henry A. Gemery, "Emigration from the British Isles to the New World, 1630–1700: Inferences from Colonial Populations," *Research in Economic History* 5 (1980): 179–231; see esp. p. 215.

2. Kenneth R. Andrews, *Trade, Plunder, and Settlement: Maritime Enterprise and the Genesis of the British Empire, 1480–1630* (Cambridge, 1984), 5, 9.

3. Carole Shammas, "English Commercial Development and American Colonization, 1560–1620," in K. R. Andrews, N. P. Canny, and P. E. H. Hair, eds., *The Westward Enterprise: English Activities in Ireland, the Atlantic, and America, 1480–1650* (Detroit, 1979), 151–74. See also James O'Mara, "Town Founding in Seventeenth-Century North America: Jamestown in Virginia," *Journal of Historical Geography* 8 (1982): 1–11.

4. Sigmund Diamond, "From Organization to Society: Virginia in the Seventeenth Century," *American Journal of Sociology* 63 (1958): 457–75; Edmund S. Morgan, *American Slavery, American Freedom: The Ordeal of Colonial Virginia* (New York, 1975), 44–91; Andrews, *Trade, Plunder, and Settlement*, passim.

5. Morgan, *American Slavery, American Freedom*, 92–130.

6. Diamond, "From Organization to Society," 457–75.

7. See Wesley Frank Craven, *White, Red, and Black: The Seventeenth-Century Virginian* (Charlottesville, 1971), 1–37; Edmund S. Morgan, "Headrights and Head Counts: A Review Article," *Virginia Magazine of History and Biography* 80 (1972): 361–71; Morgan, *American Slavery, American Freedom*, 395–432; Mildred Campbell, "Social Origins of Some Early Americans," in James Morton Smith, ed., *Seventeenth-Century America: Essays in Colonial History* (Chapel Hill, 1959), 63–89; David W. Galenson, "'Middling People' or 'Common Sort'?: The Social Origins of Some Early Americans Reexamined," with "Rebuttal by Mildred Campbell," *William and Mary Quarterly* 3d ser., 35 (1978): 499–540; David Souden, "'Rogues, Whores and Vagabonds'? Indentured Servant Emigrants to North America, and the Case of Mid-Seventeenth Century Bristol," *Social History* 3 (1978): 23–38; Anthony Salerno, "The Social Background of Seventeenth-Century Emigration to America," *Journal of British Studies* 19 (1979): 31–52; and James Horn, "Servant Emigration to the Chesapeake in the Seventeenth Century," in Thad W. Tate and David L. Ammerman, eds., *The Chesapeake in the Seventeenth Century: Essays on Anglo-American Society* (Chapel Hill, 1979), 51–95.

8. Morgan, *American Slavery, American Freedom*, 118.

9. Perry Miller, "Religion and Society in the Early Literature of Virginia," in *Errand into the Wilderness* (Cambridge, Mass., 1956), 99–140.

10. Miller, *Errand into the Wilderness*, 108; Morgan, *American Slavery, American Freedom*, 106–30; T. H. Breen, "Looking Out for Number One: Conflicting Cultural Values in Early Seventeenth-Century Virginia," *South Atlantic Quarterly* 78 (1979): 342–60.

11. Carl Bridenbaugh, *Jamestown, 1544–1699* (New York, 1980), 44–45; Carville V. Earle, "Environment, Disease, and Mortality in Early Virginia," in Tate and Ammerman, eds., *Chesapeake in the Seventeenth Century*, 96–125; Nicholas Canny,

"The Permissive Frontier: The Problem of Social Control in English Settlements in Ireland and Virginia, 1550–1650," in Andrews, Canny, and Hair, eds., *Westward Enterprise*, 29–35; Morgan, *American Slavery, American Freedom*, 106–30.

12. Irene W. D. Hecht, "The Virginia Muster of 1624/5 as a Source for Demographic History," *William and Mary Quarterly* 3d ser., 30 (1973): 64–92.

13. Morgan, *American Slavery, American Freedom*, 133–57; Terry L. Anderson and Robert Paul Thomas, "Economic Growth in the Seventeenth-Century Chesapeake," *Explorations in Economic History* 15 (1978): 368–87; Russell R. Menard, "The Tobacco Industry in the Chesapeake Colonies, 1617–1730: An Interpretation," *Research in Economic History* 5 (1980): 110–16.

14. See Bernard Bailyn, "Politics and Social Structure in Virginia," in Smith, ed., *Seventeenth-Century America*, 90–115.

15. Craven, *White, Red, and Black*, 15; Russell R. Menard, "Immigration to the Chesapeake Colonies in the Seventeenth Century: A Review Essay," *Maryland Historical Magazine* 68 (1973): 323–29; Menard, "Tobacco Industry in the Chesapeake," 116–56.

16. Russell R. Menard, "From Servant to Freeholder: Status Mobility and Property Accumulation in Seventeenth-Century Maryland," *William and Mary Quarterly* 3d ser., 30 (1973): 37–64, quotations on pp. 55, 57.

17. See William A. Reavis, "The Maryland Gentry and Social Mobility, 1627–1676," *William and Mary Quarterly* 3d ser., 14 (1957): 418–28, quotation on p. 422.

18. Menard, "Tobacco Industry in the Chesapeake," 118.

19. Earle, "Environment, Disease, and Mortality." See also Karen Ordahl Kupperman, "Apathy and Death in Early Jamestown," *Journal of American History* 66 (1979): 24–40.

20. Craven, *White, Red, and Black*, 39–72; Morgan, *American Slavery, American Freedom*, 98–100, 149; Bernard W. Sheehan, *Savagism and Civility: Indians and Englishmen in Colonial Virginia* (Cambridge, 1980), 144–82; Gary B. Nash, "The Image of the Indian in the Southern Colonial Mind," *William and Mary Quarterly* 3d ser., 29 (1972): 197–230. See also Karen Ordahl Kupperman, "English Perceptions of Treachery, 1583–1640: The Case of the American Savages," *Historical Journal* 20 (1977): 283–87, and *Settling with the Indians: The Meeting of English and Indian Cultures in America, 1580–1640* (Totowa, N.J., 1980), esp. 169–88; J. Frederick Fausz, "Profits, Pelts, and Power: English Culture in the Early Chesapeake, 1620–1652," *Maryland Historian* 14 (1983): 15–30; William L. Shea, *The Virginia Militia in the Seventeenth Century* (Baton Rouge, 1983).

21. Morgan, *American Slavery, American Freedom*, 409–10; Terry L. Anderson and Robert Paul Thomas, "The Growth of Population and Labor Force in the 17th-Century Chesapeake," *Explorations in Economic History* 15 (1978): 290–312.

22. Morgan, *American Slavery, American Freedom*, 158–85; Darrett B. Rutman and Anita H. Rutman, "Of Agues and Fevers: Malaria in the Early Chesapeake," *William and Mary Quarterly* 3d ser., 33 (1976): 31–60; Lorena S. Walsh and Russell R. Menard, "Death in the Chesapeake: Two Life Tables for Men in Early Colonial Maryland," *Maryland Historical Magazine* 69 (1974): 211–27.

23. Lois Green Carr and Lorena S. Walsh, "The Planter's Wife: The Experience of White Women in Seventeenth-Century Maryland," *Maryland Historical Maga-*

zine 34 (1977): 542–71; Lorena S. Walsh, "'Till Death Us Do Part': Marriage and Family in Seventeenth-Century Maryland," in Tate and Ammerman, eds., *Chesapeake in the Seventeenth Century*, 126–52.

24. Walsh, "'Till Death Us Do Part'"; Darrett B. Rutman and Anita H. Rutman, "'Now-Wives and Sons-in-Law': Parental Death in a Seventeenth-Century Virginia County," in Tate and Ammerman, eds., *Chesapeake in the Seventeenth Century*, 153–82.

25. Morgan, *American Slavery, American Freedom*, 133–211; Breen, "Looking Out for Number One," 342–60; Russell R. Menard, P. M. G. Harris, and Lois Green Carr, "Opportunity and Inequality: The Distribution of Wealth on the Lower Western Shore of Maryland, 1638–1705," *Maryland Historical Magazine* 69 (1974): 169–84.

26. James Russell Perry, "The Formation of a Society on Virginia's Eastern Shore, 1615–1655" (Ph.D. dissertation, Johns Hopkins University, 1980); Rutman and Rutman, "Of Agues and Fevers," 57–60; Rutman and Rutman, "'Now-Wives and Sons-in-Law.'" See also Darrett B. Rutman, "The Social Web: A Prospectus for the Study of the Early American Community," in William L. O'Neill, ed., *Insights and Parallels: Problems and Issues of American Social History* (Minneapolis, 1973), 57–88; Darrett B. Rutman, Charles Wetherell, and Anita H. Rutman, "Rhythms of Life: Black and White Seasonality in the Early Chesapeake," *Journal of Interdisciplinary History* 11 (1980): 29–53; and Darrett B. Rutman and Anita H. Rutman, *A Place in Time: Middlesex County, Virginia, 1650–1750*, 2 vols. (New York, 1984), 1:19–35.

27. Warren M. Billings, "English Legal Literature as a Source of Law and Legal Practice for Seventeenth-Century Virginia," *Virginia Magazine of History and Biography* 87 (1979): 403–16, esp. 406; William H. Seiler, "The Anglican Parish in Virginia," in Smith, ed., *Seventeenth-Century America*, 119–42; Babette M. Levy, "Early Puritanism in the Southern and Island Colonies," *Proceedings of the American Antiquarian Society* 70 (1961): 69–163; William H. Seiler, "The Church of England as the Established Church in Seventeenth-Century Virginia," *Journal of Southern History* 15 (1949): 478–508; Virginia Bernhard, "Poverty and the Social Order in Seventeenth-Century Virginia," *Virginia Magazine of History and Biography* 85 (1977): 141–55, esp. 146.

28. See Warren M. Billings, "The Growth of Political Institutions in Virginia, 1634–1676," *William and Mary Quarterly* 3d ser., 31 (1974): 225–42; Steven D. Crow, "'Your Majesty's Good Subjects': A Reconsideration of Royalism in Virginia, 1642–1652," *Virginia Magazine of History and Biography* 87 (1979): 158–73; George B. Curtis, "The Colonial County Court, Social Forum and Legislative Precedent: Accomack County, Virginia, 1633–1639," ibid. 85 (1977): 274–88; J. Mills Thornton III, "The Thrusting Out of Governor Harvey: A Seventeenth-Century Rebellion," ibid. 76 (1968): 11–26; Perry, "Formation of a Society," 184–255; Jon Kukla, "Order and Chaos in Early America: Political and Social Stability in Pre-Restoration Virginia," *American Historical Review* 90 (1985): 275–98.

29. See John C. Rainbolt, *From Prescription to Persuasion: Manipulation of Eighteenth Century Virginia Economy* (Port Washington, N.Y., 1974), 35–54, and "The Absence of Towns in Seventeenth-Century Virginia," *Journal of Southern History* 35

(1969): 343–60; Sister Joan de Lourdes Leonard, "Operation Checkmate: The Birth and Death of a Virginia Blueprint for Progress, 1660–1676," *William and Mary Quarterly* 3d ser., 24 (1967): 44–74; Lois Green Carr, "'The Metropolis of Maryland': A Comment on Town Development along the Tobacco Coast," *Maryland Historical Magazine* 69 (1974): 124–45.

30. John Demos, *A Little Commonwealth: Family Life in Plymouth Colony* (New York, 1970); George D. Langdon, Jr., *Pilgrim Colony: A History of New Plymouth, 1620–1691* (New Haven, 1966); Douglas R. McManis, *Colonial New England: A Historical Geography* (New York, 1975), 68–69; Darrett B. Rutman, *Husbandmen of Plymouth: Farms and Villages in the Old Colony, 1620–1692* (Boston, 1967); J. M. Bumsted, "A Well-Bounded Toleration: Church and State in the Plymouth Colony," *Journal of Church and State* 10 (1968): 265–79.

31. Carl Bridenbaugh, "Right New-England Men; or The Adaptable Puritans," *Proceedings of the Massachusetts Historical Society* 88 (1976): 5, 13–14; Terry L. Anderson and Robert Paul Thomas, "White Population, Labor Force and Extensive Growth of the New England Economy in the Seventeenth Century," *Journal of Economic History* 33 (1973): 639–41; T. H. Breen and Stephen Foster, "Moving to the New World: The Character of Early Massachusetts Immigration," *William and Mary Quarterly* 3d ser., 30 (1973): 189–222; Virginia Dejohn Anderson, "Migrants and Motives: Religion and the Settlement of New England, 1630–1640," *New England Quarterly* 68 (1985): 340, 346–67; N. C. P. Tyack, "The Humbler Puritans of East Anglia and the New England Movement: Evidence from the Court Records of the 1630s," *New England Historical and Genealogical Register* 138 (1984): 79–106; Richard S. Dunn, "Experiments Holy and Unholy 1630–1," in Andrews, Canny, and Hair, eds., *Westward Enterprise*, 271–89; Harry Stout, "The Morphology of Re-Migration: New England University Men and Their Return to England, 1640–1660," *Journal of American Studies* 10 (1975): 151–72; Andrew Delbanco, "Looking Homeward, Going Home: The Lure of England for the Founders of New England," *New England Quarterly* 59 (1986): 358–86.

32. Anderson and Thomas, "White Population," 639–42; McManis, *Colonial New England*, 66–68; Philip J. Greven, Jr., *Four Generations: Population, Land, and Family in Colonial Andover, Massachusetts* (Ithaca, 1970), 21–40; Kenneth Lockridge, "The Population of Dedham, Massachusetts, 1636–1736," *Economic History Review* 2d ser., 19 (1966): 318–44.

33. Douglas Edward Leach, *The Northern Colonial Frontier, 1607–1763* (New York, 1966), 33–37; McManis, *Colonial New England*, 41–48; Alden T. Vaughan, *New England Frontier: Puritans and Indians, 1620–1675*, 2d ed. (New York, 1979), v–xlv, 93–154. For a contrary view, see Francis Jennings, *The Invasion of America: Indians, Colonialism, and the Cant of Conquest* (Chapel Hill, 1975), 177–227.

34. Perry Miller, *Orthodoxy in Massachusetts, 1630–1650* (Cambridge, Mass., 1933), *The New England Mind: The Seventeenth Century* (Cambridge, Mass., 1954), and *Errand into the Wilderness*, 48–98, remain the classic adumbrations of the religious orientation of the New England colonies. For more recent assessments, see the excellent short discussion by David D. Hall, "Understanding the Puritans," in Herbert Bass, ed., *The State of American History* (Chicago, 1970), 330–49; Michael McGiffert, "American Puritan Studies in the 1960's," *William and Mary Quarterly*

3d ser., 27 (1970): 36–67; and Anderson, "Migrants and Motives," 367–83. David D. Hall, "A World of Wonders: The Mentality of the Supernatural in Seventeenth-Century New England," in Hall and David Grayson Allen, eds., *Seventeenth-Century New England* (Boston, 1984), 239–74, William K. B. Stoever, *"A Faire and Easie Way to Heaven": Covenant Theology and Antinomianism in Early Massachusetts* (Middletown, Conn., 1978), and Philip F. Gura, *A Glimpse of Sion's Glory: Puritan Radicalism in Seventeenth-Century New England, 1620–1660* (Middletown, Conn., 1984), stress the religious diversity among puritan settlers. See also Stephen Foster, "New England and the Challenge of Heresy, 1630 to 1660: The Puritan Crisis in Transatlantic Perspective," *William and Mary Quarterly* 3d ser., 38 (1981): 624–60, "The Godly in Transit: English Popular Protestantism and the Creation of a Puritan Establishment in America," in Hall and Allen, eds., *Seventeenth-Century New England*, 185–238, and "English Puritanism and the Progress of New England Institutions, 1630–1660," in David D. Hall, John M. Murrin, and Thad W. Tate, eds., *Saints and Revolutionaries: Essays on Early American History* (New York, 1984), 3–37; J. F. Maclear, "New England and the Fifth Monarchy: The Quest for the Millennium in Early American Puritanism," *William and Mary Quarterly* 3d ser., 32 (1975): 223–60; and Sacvan Bercovitch, *The American Jeremiad* (Madison, 1978), 3–61. Relations between church and state, ministry and magistracy in early New England are treated in David D. Hall, *The Faithful Shepherd: A History of the New England Ministry in the Seventeenth Century* (Chapel Hill, 1972); George Selement, *Keepers of the Vineyard: The Puritan Ministry and Collective Culture in Colonial New England* (Lanham, Md., 1984); and B. Katherine Brown, "The Controversy over the Franchise in Puritan Massachusetts, 1954 to 1974," *William and Mary Quarterly* 3d ser., 33 (1976): 228. Other works on the complex issue of the franchise are T. H. Breen, "Who Governs: The Town Franchise in Seventeenth-Century Massachusetts," *William and Mary Quarterly* 3d ser., 27 (1970): 460–74; Stephen Foster, "The Massachusetts Franchise in the Seventeenth Century, " ibid. 24 (1967): 613–23; Arlin I. Ginsberg, "The Franchise in Seventeenth Century Massachusetts: Ipswich," ibid. 34 (1977): 444–52; Robert E. Wall, "The Franchise in Seventeenth Century Massachusetts: Dedham and Cambridge," ibid., 453–58, and "The Decline of the Massachusetts Franchise, 1647–1666," *Journal of American History* 59 (1972): 303–10; and James A. Thorpe, "Colonial Suffrage in Massachusetts," *Essex Institute Historical Collections* 106 (1970): 169–81.

35. T. H. Breen, "Transfer of Culture: Chance and Design in Shaping Massachusetts Bay, 1630–1660," *New England Historical and Genealogical Register* 132 (1978): 3–17, and "Persistent Localism: English Social Change and the Shaping of New England Institutions," *William and Mary Quarterly* 3d ser., 32 (1975): 3–28; Andrew Delbanco, "The Puritan Errand Re-Viewed," *Journal of American Studies* 18 (1984): 342–60; Allen Cardin, "The Communal Ideal in Puritan New England, 1630–1700," *Fides et Historia* 17 (1984): 25–38. The clearest and most perceptive discussion of puritan social goals in New England is Stephen Foster, *Their Solitary Way: The Puritan Social Ethic in the First Century of Settlement in New England* (New Haven, 1971).

36. See Alan Heimert, "Puritanism, the Wilderness, and the Frontier," *New England Quarterly* 26 (1953): 361–82; Peter N. Carroll, *Puritanism and the Wilderness:*

The Intellectual Significance of the New England Frontier, 1629–1700 (New York, 1969); Michael Zuckerman, "Pilgrims in the Wilderness: Community, Modernity, and the Maypole at Merry Mount," *New England Quarterly* 50 (1977): 255–77; James Axtell, *The School upon a Hill: Education and Society in Colonial New England* (New Haven, 1974), 245–81; Richard P. Gildrie, "Francis Higginson's New World Vision," *Essex Institute Historical Collections* 106 (1970): 182–89.

37. Diversity among New England towns is admirably treated in David Grayson Allen, *In English Ways: The Movement of Societies and the Transferal of English Local Law and Custom to Massachusetts Bay in the Seventeenth Century* (Chapel Hill, 1981). See also Joseph S. Wood, "Village and Community in Early Colonial New England," *Journal of Historical Geography* 8 (1982): 333–46; Sumner Chilton Powell, *Puritan Village: The Formation of a New England Town* (Middletown, Conn., 1964); Kenneth A. Lockridge, *A New England Town, The First Hundred Years: Dedham, Massachusetts, 1636–1736* (New York, 1970); Greven, *Four Generations*; John J. Waters, "Hingham, Massachusetts, 1631–1661: An East Anglian Oligarchy in the New World," *Journal of Social History* 1 (1968): 351–70, and "The Traditional World of the New England Peasants: A View from Seventeenth-Century Barnstable," *New England Historical and Genealogical Register* 130 (1976): 3–21.

38. Foster, *Their Solitary Way*, 11–64, 99–152; Timothy H. Breen and Stephen Foster, "The Puritans' Greatest Achievement: A Study of Social Cohesion in Seventeenth-Century Massachusetts," *Journal of American History* 60 (1973): 5–22; Breen, "Transfer of Culture," 3–17, and "Persistent Localism," 3–28; Lockridge, *New England Town*, 1–36; Mary Jeanne Anderson Jones, *Congregational Commonwealth: Connecticut, 1636–1662* (Middletown, Conn., 1968), 99–137; Emil Oberholzer, Jr., *Delinquent Saints: Disciplinary Action in the Early Congregational Churches of Massachusetts* (New York, 1956); Kai T. Erikson, *Wayward Puritans: A Study in the Sociology of Deviance* (New York, 1966); David Thomas Konig, *Law and Society in Puritan Massachusetts, 1629–1692* (Chapel Hill, 1979), 1–34; Eric G. Nellis, "Labor and Community in Massachusetts Bay: 1630–1660," *Labor History* 18 (1977): 525–44.

39. Greven, *Four Generations*, 41–99. See also Edmund S. Morgan, *The Puritan Family: Religion and Domestic Relations in Seventeenth-Century New England* (New York, 1966).

40. Hugh Kearney, "The Problem of Perspective in the History of Colonial America," in Andrews, Canny, and Hair, eds., *Westward Enterprise*, 296–99; Axtell, *School upon a Hill*, 166–244; Kenneth A. Lockridge, *Literacy in Colonial New England: An Enquiry into the Social Context of Literacy in the Early Modern West* (New York, 1974). For a contrary view, see Bernard Bailyn, *Education in the Forming of American Society* (Chapel Hill, 1960). On the subsequent demand for the liberalization and modernization of the curriculum at Harvard College, see Norman Fiering, *Moral Philosophy at Seventeenth-Century Harvard: A Discipline in Transition* (Chapel Hill, 1981), 239–94.

41. Robert Emmet Wall, Jr., *Massachusetts Bay: The Crucial Decade, 1640–1650* (New Haven, 1972), esp. 21–40; Foster, *Their Solitary Way*, 67–98, 155–72; T. H. Breen, *The Character of the Good Ruler: A Study of Puritan Political Ideas in New England, 1630–1730* (New York, 1970), 1–86; Breen and Foster, "Puritans' Greatest

Achievement," 9–10, and "Moving to the New World," 220; Selement, *Keepers of the Vineyard*; Stout, "Morphology of Re-Migration," 151–72; Brown, "Controversy over the Franchise," 212–41; Richard C. Simmons, "Godliness, Property, and the Franchise in Puritan Massachusetts: An Interpretation," *Journal of American History* 55 (1968): 495–511, esp. 496; Hall, *Faithful Shepherd*, esp. 121–55.

42. Terry Lee Anderson, *The Economic Growth of Seventeenth Century New England: A Measurement of Regional Income* (New York, 1975); Anderson and Thomas, "White Population," 661; Bernard Bailyn, *The New England Merchants in the Seventeenth Century* (Cambridge, Mass., 1955), 1–111; Daniel Vickers, "Work and Life on the Fishing Periphery of Essex County, Massachusetts, 1630–1675," in Hall and Allen, eds., *Seventeenth-Century New England*, 83–117; William Cronon, *Changes in the Land: Indians, Colonists, and the Ecology of New England* (New York, 1983), 127–56; Charles F. Carroll, *The Timber Economy of Puritan New England* (Providence, 1973); Darrett B. Rutman, *Winthrop's Boston: A Portrait of a Puritan Town, 1630–1649* (Chapel Hill, 1965), 164–201; William I. Davisson and Dennis J. Dugan, "Commerce in Seventeenth-Century Essex County, Massachusetts," *Essex Institute Historical Collections* 107 (1971): 113–18; William I. Davisson, "Essex County Wealth Trends: Wealth and Economic Growth in 17th Century Massachusetts," ibid. 103 (1967): 291–342; Donald W. Koch, "Income Distribution and Political Structure in Seventeenth-Century Salem, Massachusetts," ibid. 105 (1969): 50–71; Terry L. Anderson, "Wealth Estimates for the New England Colonies, 1650–1709," *Explorations in Economic History* 12 (1975): 151–76; Richard Waterhouse, "Reluctant Emigrants: The English Background of the First Generation of the New England Clergy," *Historical Magazine of the Protestant Episcopal Church* 44 (1975): 473–88; Breen, "Transfer of Culture," 3–17; Stephen Innes, "Land Tenancy and Social Order in Springfield, Massachusetts, 1652 to 1702," *William and Mary Quarterly* 3d ser., 35 (1978): 33–56.

43. Breen and Foster, "Moving to the New World," 209–13; David Grayson Allen, "Both Englands," in Hall and Allen, eds., *Seventeenth-Century New England*, 77–80; Linda Auwers Bissell, "From One Generation to Another: Mobility in Seventeenth-Century Windsor, Connecticut," *William and Mary Quarterly* 3d ser., 31 (1974): 79–110; W. R. Prest, "Stability and Change in Old and New England: Clayworth and Dedham," *Journal of Interdisciplinary History* 6 (1976): 359–74; John M. Murrin, "Review Essay," *History and Theory* 11 (1972): 231.

44. See Konig, *Law and Society in Puritan Massachusetts*; Paul R. Lucas, *Valley of Discord: Church and Society along the Connecticut River, 1636–1725* (Hanover, 1976), 1–57; Carla Pestana, "The City upon a Hill under Siege: The Puritan Perception of the Quaker Threat to Massachusetts Bay, 1656–1661," *New England Quarterly* 56 (1983): 323–53; Breen and Foster, "Puritans' Greatest Achievement," esp. 5–6.

45. Robert D. Mitchell, "American Origins and Regional Institutions: The Seventeenth-Century Chesapeake," *Annals of the Association of American Geographers* 73 (1983): 407.

CHAPTER TWO

1. Carl Bridenbaugh, "Right New-England Men; or The Adaptable Puritans," *Proceedings of the Massachusetts Historical Society* 88 (1976): 15; John J. Waters, "Hingham, Massachusetts, 1631–1661: An East Anglian Oligarchy in the New World," *Journal of Social History* 1 (1968): 370; T. H. Breen, "Transfer of Culture: Chance and Design in Shaping Massachusetts Bay, 1630–1660," *New England Historical and Genealogical Register* 132 (1978): 3–17, "Persistent Localism: English Social Change and the Shaping of New England Institutions," *William and Mary Quarterly* 3d ser., 32 (1975): 27, and "Looking Out for Number One: Conflicting Cultural Values in Early Seventeenth-Century Virginia," *South Atlantic Quarterly* 78 (1979): 344; John M. Murrin, review of Thad W. Tate and David L. Ammerman, eds., *The Chesapeake in the Seventeenth Century: Essays on Anglo-American Society* (Chapel Hill, 1971), in *William and Mary Quarterly* 3d ser., 38 (1981): 121.

2. Keith Wrightson, *English Society, 1580–1680* (London, 1982), 24, 31, 40–41, 58; Alan Macfarlane, *The Origins of English Individualism: The Family, Property and Social Transition* (New York, 1978), 62–79. See also L. A. Clarkson, *The Pre-Industrial Economy in England, 1500–1750* (London, 1971), 45–74; B. A. Holderness, *Pre-Industrial England: Economy and Society, 1500–1750* (London, 1976), 45–82. Detailed examinations of regional variations in the metropolitan domestic agricultural economy may be found in Joan Thirsk, ed., *The Agrarian History of England and Wales*, Vol. 4, *1500–1640* (Cambridge, 1967), and Eric Kerridge, *The Agricultural Revolution* (London, 1967).

3. Macfarlane, *Origins of English Individualism*, 68–79; Wrightson, *English Society*, 17, 22, 26–27, 35, 51, 128–29, 134–35, 140, 223; D. C. Coleman, *The Economy of England, 1450–1750* (Oxford, 1977), 48–90; Holderness, *Pre-Industrial England*, 27–45, 83–170; Clarkson, *Pre-Industrial Economy*, 210–38; Carole Shammas, "Food Expenditures and Economic Well-Being in Early Modern England," *Journal of Economic History* 43 (1983): 90; Mildred Campbell, *The English Yeoman under Elizabeth and the Early Stuarts* (New Haven, 1942), 103–4; Lawrence Stone, "Social Mobility in England, 1500–1700," *Past and Present*, no. 33 (1966): 16–55; Lawrence Stone and Jeanne C. Fawtier Stone, *An Open Elite? England, 1540–1880* (Oxford, 1984), 276–81, 289–92, 397–405; E. A. Wrigley, "A Simple Model of London's Importance in Changing English Society and Economy, 1650–1750," *Past and Present*, no. 37 (1967): 44–70; Margaret Spufford, *Contrasting Communities: English Villagers in the Sixteenth and Seventeenth Centuries* (Cambridge, 1974), 65–85; David Cressy, "Describing the Social Order of Elizabethan and Stuart England," *Literature and History*, no. 3 (March 1976): 29–44.

4. Macfarlane, *Origins of English Individualism*, 68–71; Wrightson, *English Society*, 43–44; Wrigley, "Simple Model," 44–50; Spufford, *Contrasting Communities*, 21–22; Peter Clark, "The Migrant in Kentish Towns, 1580–1640," in Peter Clark and Paul Slack, eds., *Crisis and Order in English Towns, 1500–1700: Essays in Urban History* (London, 1972), 117–63, and "Migration in England during the Late Seventeenth and Early Eighteenth Centuries," *Past and Present*, no. 83 (1979): 57–90; E. E. Rich, "The Population of Elizabethan England," *Economic History Review* 2d ser., 2 (1949–50): 247–65; John Harrison and Peter Laslett, "Clayworth and

Coggenhoe," in H. E. Bell and R. L. Ollard, eds., *Historical Essays, 1600–1750, Presented to David Ogg* (London, 1963), 157–84; Julian Cornwall, "Evidence of Population Mobility in the Seventeenth Century," *Bulletin of the Institute of Historical Research* 40 (1967): 143–52; Anthony Salerno, "The Social Background of Seventeenth-Century Emigration to America," *Journal of British Studies* 19 (1979): 37–52; James Horn, "Servant Emigration to the Chesapeake in the Seventeenth Century," in Thad W. Tate and David L. Ammerman, eds., *The Chesapeake in the Seventeenth Century: Essays on Anglo-American Society* (Chapel Hill, 1979), 31–52; J. P. Cooper, "Social Distribution of Land and Men in England, 1436–1700," *Economic History Review* 2d ser., 20 (1967): 419–40.

5. Peter Laslett and Richard Wall, eds., *Household and Family in Past Time* (Cambridge, 1972), 10–11, 26–30, 40, 72–73; Wrightson, *English Society*, 45–50, 112–18; Macfarlane, *Origins of English Individualism*, 86–88, 174–75, 198; Spufford, *Contrasting Communities*, 85–87, 104–11, 159–61; Thirsk, ed., *Agrarian History*, 9–12; Joan Thirsk, "Younger Sons in the Seventeenth Century," *History* 54 (1969): 358–77; Stone, "Social Mobility," 37–38.

6. Wrightson, *English Society*, 55, 61–62, 174, 182; Lawrence Stone, *The Crisis of the Aristocracy, 1558–1641* (Oxford, 1965), 191, 240–42; Peter Clark, *English Provincial Society from the Reformation to the Revolution: Religion, Politics and Society in Kent, 1500–1640* (London, 1977), 111–48, 279–84; Peter Laslett, *The World We Have Lost* (London, 1971), 96–100, 130–58, 168–72; Hugh Kearney, "The Problem of Perspective in the History of Colonial America," in K. R. Andrews, N. P. Canny, and P. E. H. Hair, eds., *The Westward Enterprise: English Activities in Ireland, the Atlantic, and America, 1480–1650* (Detroit, 1979), 293–94; Keith Thomas, *Religion and the Decline of Magic* (New York, 1971), 3–173, 631–40; E. A. Wrigley and R. S. Schofield, *The Population History of England, 1541–1871* (Cambridge, Mass., 1981), 310–42.

7. Macfarlane, *Origins of English Individualism*, 5, 62–66, 78–79, 165–66, 170–79; Wrightson, *English Society*, 223; C. B. Macpherson, *The Political Theory of Possessive Individualism: Hobbes to Locke* (Oxford, 1962); Joyce Appleby, *Economic Thought and Ideology in Seventeenth-Century England* (Princeton, 1978), esp. 52–72; Joan Thirsk, *Economic Policy and Projects: The Development of a Consumer Society in Early Modern England* (Oxford, 1978); Kenneth R. Andrews, *Trade, Plunder, and Settlement: Maritime Enterprise and the Genesis of the British Empire, 1480–1630* (Cambridge, 1984), 5, 9, 31, 356–62; Theodore K. Rabb, *Enterprise and Empire: Merchant and Gentry Investment in the Expansion of England, 1575–1630* (Cambridge, Mass., 1967), 1–101; Robert Brenner, "The Social Basis of English Commercial Expansion, 1550–1650," *Journal of Economic History* 32 (1972): 361–84, and "The Civil War Politics of London's Merchant Community," *Past and Present*, no. 58 (1973): 53–107; Coleman, *Economy of England*, 48–90; Holderness, *Pre-Industrial England*, 83–170; Joan Thirsk, "Patterns of Agriculture in Seventeenth-Century England," in David D. Hall and David Grayson Allen, eds., *Seventeenth-Century New England* (Boston, 1984), 39–54. E. P. Thompson, "The Moral Economy of the English Crowd in the Eighteenth Century," *Past and Present*, no. 50 (1971): 76–136, is the classic account of traditional notions of moral economy.

8. Charles Wilson and Bruce Lenman, "The British Isles," in Charles Wilson and Geoffrey Parker, eds., *An Introduction to the Sources of European Economic History,*

1500–1800 (Ithaca, 1977), 153; W. G. Hoskins, *Provincial England: Essays in Social and Economic History* (London, 1964), 68–114; Wrigley, "Simple Model," 44–70; Clark and Slack, eds., *Crisis and Order*, 1–56; Kerridge, *Agricultural Revolution*; Holderness, *Pre-Industrial England*, 109–14; Clarkson, *Pre-Industrial Economy*, 15–16, 105–58; Lawrence Stone, "The Educational Revolution in England, 1560–1640," *Past and Present*, no. 28 (1964): 41–80; Wrightson, *English Society*, 188–89.

9. Kearney, "Problem of Perspective," 294; Wrightson, *English Society*, 47–48; Macfarlane, *Origins of English Individualism*, 71–79.

10. Michael Walzer, "Puritanism as a Revolutionary Ideology," *History and Theory* 3 (1963): 59–90, and *The Revolution of the Saints: A Study in the Origins of Radical Politics* (Cambridge, Mass., 1965), esp. 148–231; Michael McGiffert, "God's Controversy with Jacobean England," *American Historical Review* 88 (1983): 1151–74; Kearney, "Problem of Perspective," 301.

11. See Darrett B. Rutman, *Winthrop's Boston: A Portrait of a Puritan Town, 1630–1649* (Chapel Hill, 1965), 164–201, and Richard P. Gildrie, *Salem, Massachusetts, 1626–1683: A Covenanted Community* (Charlottesville, 1975), 105–78.

12. Mark A. Kishlansky, "Community and Continuity: A Review of Selected Works on English Local History," *William and Mary Quarterly* 3d ser., 37 (1980): 146. David Grayson Allen, *In English Ways: The Movement of Societies and the Transferal of English Local Law and Custom to Massachusetts Bay in the Seventeenth Century* (Chapel Hill, 1981), discusses the many continuities between modes of life in old and New England.

13. See the following works by Nicholas P. Canny: *The Formation of the Old English Elite* (Dublin, 1975), *The Elizabethan Conquest of Ireland: A Pattern Established, 1565–76* (New York, 1976), "The Ideology of English Colonization: From Ireland to America," *William and Mary Quarterly* 3d ser., 30 (1973): 575–98, and "Dominant Minorities: English Settlers in Ireland and Virginia, 1550–1650," in A. C. Hepburn, ed., *Minorities in History* (London, 1978), 51–52; those by David Beers Quinn: *The Elizabethans and the Irish* (Ithaca, 1966), "Ireland and Sixteenth-Century Expansion," *Historical Studies* 1 (1958): 20–32, and "The Munster Plantation: Problems and Opportunities," *Cork Historical and Archaeological Society Journal* 71 (1966): 19–41; J. C. Beckett, *The Anglo-Irish Tradition* (Ithaca, 1976), 13–27; Aidan Clarke, *The Old English in Ireland, 1625–42* (London, 1966); R. A. Butlin, "Land and People, c. 1600," in T. W. Moody, F. X. Martin, and F. J. Byrne, eds., *A New History of Ireland*, Vol. 3: *Early Modern Ireland, 1534–1691* (Oxford, 1976), 142–67; T. W. Moody, *The Londonderry Plantation, 1609–41* (Belfast, 1939).

14. Kearney, "Problem of Perspective," 299; Raymond Gillespie, *Colonial Ulster: The Settlement of East Ulster, 1600–1641* (Cork, 1985), 221; Philip S. Robinson, *The Plantation of Ulster: British Settlement in an Irish Landscape, 1600–1670* (Dublin, 1984), 112, 150–51; M. Perceval-Maxwell, *The Scottish Migration to Ulster in the Reign of James I* (London, 1973), 267–73.

15. Nicholas Canny, "The Permissive Frontier: The Problem of Social Control in English Settlements in Ireland and Virginia, 1550–1650," in Andrews, Canny, and Hair, eds., *Westward Enterprise*, 37–38, and "Dominant Minorities," 53–54; Perceval-Maxwell, *Scottish Migration*, 126–27, 289; Robinson, *Plantation of Ulster*, 91–128; Gillespie, *Colonial Ulster*, 28–35, 51–53; Michael McCarthy-Morrogh, *The*

Munster Plantation, 1580–1641 (Oxford, 1985), 177–222; C. R. Mayes, "The Early Stuarts and the Irish Peerage," *English Historical Review* 73 (1958): 227–51.

16. Aidan Clarke, "The Irish Economy, 1600–60," and "Pacification, Plantation, and the Catholic Question, 1603–23," in Moody, Martin, and Byrne, eds., *New History of Ireland*, 3:168–232; Karl S. Bottigheimer, "Kingdom and Colony: Ireland in the Westward Enterprise, 1536–1660," in Andrews, Canny, and Hair, eds., *Westward Enterprise*, 45–64, and *English Money and Irish Land: The "Adventurers" in the Cromwellian Settlement of Ireland* (Oxford, 1971); Canny, "Permissive Frontier," 17–44, and "Dominant Minorities," 51–69; T. C. Barnard, "Planters and Policies in Cromwellian Ireland," *Past and Present*, no. 61 (1973): 31–69; Perceval-Maxwell, *Scottish Migration*, 60, 135, 209–11, 273, 277–78; Robinson, *Plantation of Ulster*, 150–94; Gillespie, *Colonial Ulster*, 113–224; McCarthy-Morrogh, *Munster Plantation*, 223–86; W. H. Crawford, "Landlord-Tenant Relations in Ulster, 1609–1820," *Irish Economic and Social History* 7 (1975): 5–12; Quinn, "Munster Plantation," 35–40; R. J. Hunter, "Towns in the Ulster Plantation," *Studia Hibernica* 7 (1971): 40–79.

17. Babette M. Levy, "Early Puritanism in the Southern and Island Colonies," *Proceedings of the American Antiquarian Society* 70 (1961): 164–200; Wesley Frank Craven, "An Introduction to the History of Bermuda," *William and Mary Quarterly* 2d ser., 17 (1937): 176–215, 317–62, 437–65, 18 (1938): 13–63; Henry C. Wilkinson, *The Adventurers of Bermuda* (Oxford, 1933), 104, 280–81, 303, 313, 359–62.

18. Wilkinson, *Adventurers of Bermuda*, 81, 137–38, 158–60, 222, 230, 246–47, 261–63, 266, 308, 329, 348–50; Virginia Bernhard, "Bermuda and Virginia in the Seventeenth Century: A Comparative View," *Journal of Social History* 19 (1985): 57–70.

19. Bernhard, "Bermuda and Virginia," 61. On population trends, see the analysis for the late seventeenth and early eighteenth centuries in Robert V. Wells, *The Population of the British Colonies in America before 1776: A Survey of Census Data* (Princeton, 1975), 172–81. See also Wilkinson, *Adventurers of Bermuda*, 362.

20. Henry C. Wilkinson, *Bermuda in the Old Empire* (Oxford, 1950), 1–27; Richard S. Dunn, "The Downfall of the Bermuda Company: A Restoration Farce," *William and Mary Quarterly* 3d ser., 20 (1963): 487–512.

21. F. C. Innes, "The Pre-Sugar Era of European Settlement in Barbados," *Journal of Caribbean History* 1 (1970): 1–22; Robert Carlyle Batie, "Why Sugar? Economic Cycles and the Changing of Staples on the English and French Antilles, 1624–54," ibid. 8 (1976): 1–41; Richard S. Dunn, *Sugar and Slaves: The Rise of the Planter Class in the English West Indies, 1624–1713* (Chapel Hill, 1972), 46–59, "Experiments Holy and Unholy, 1630–1," in Andrews, Canny, and Hair, eds., *Westward Enterprise*, 272–75, and "Masters, Servants, and Slaves in the Colonial Chesapeake and the Caribbean," in David B. Quinn, ed., *Early Maryland in a Wider World* (Detroit, 1982), 242–66; Richard B. Sheridan, *Sugar and Slavery: An Economic History of the British West Indies, 1623–1775* (Baltimore, 1974), 75–96; Richard Pares, *Merchants and Planters* (Cambridge, 1960), 1–25.

22. Dunn, *Sugar and Slaves*, 263–334; Levy, "Early Puritanism in the Southern and Island Colonies," 278–307; Hilary McD. Beckles, "Rebels and Reactionaries: The Political Responses of White Labourers to Planter-Class Hegemony in Seventeenth-Century Barbados," *Journal of Caribbean History* 15 (1981): 1–19; Batie, "Why Sugar?" 22.

23. Carl Bridenbaugh and Roberta Bridenbaugh, *No Peace Beyond the Line: The English in the Caribbean, 1624–1690* (New York, 1972), 165–305; Dunn, *Sugar and Slaves*, 59–83, 117–26, 188–264, "Experiments Holy and Unholy," 285–89, and "The English Sugar Islands and the Founding of South Carolina," *South Carolina Historical Magazine* 72 (1971): 82; Batie, "Why Sugar?" 1; Sheridan, *Sugar and Slavery*, 128–40; Beckles, "Rebels and Reactionaries," 1–19, "The Economic Origins of Black Slavery in the British West Indies, 1640–1680: A Tentative Analysis of the Barbados Model," *Journal of Caribbean History* 16 (1982): 36–56, *Black Rebellion in Barbados: The Struggle against Slavery, 1627–1838* (Bridgetown, 1984), 9–51, and "From Land to Sea: Runaway Barbados Slaves and Servants, 1630–1700," *Slavery and Abolition* 6 (1985): 79–94; Beckles and Andrew Downes, "The Economic Transition to the Black Labor System in Barbados, 1630–1680," *Journal of Interdisciplinary History*, 18 (1987): 225–47; J. H. Galloway, "The Sugar Industry in Barbados during the Seventeenth Century," *Journal of Tropical Geography* 19 (1964): 35–41; Gary A. Puckrein, *Little England: Plantation Society and Anglo-Barbadian Politics, 1627–1700* (New York, 1984), 56–87; John J. McCusker and Russell R. Menard, *The Economy of British-America, 1607–1789* (Chapel Hill, 1985), 151–53.

24. Sydney V. James, *Colonial Rhode Island: A History* (New York, 1975), 1–100.

25. David E. VanDeventer, *The Emergence of Provincial New Hampshire, 1623–1741* (Baltimore, 1976), 3–39, 181–86.

26. Dunn, *Sugar and Slaves*, 149–87; Sheridan, *Sugar and Slavery*, 92–96, 208–16; Orlando Patterson, *The Sociology of Slavery: An Analysis of the Origins, Development and Structure of Negro Slave Society in Jamaica* (Rutherford, N.J., 1969), 15–69; Nuala Zahedieh, "Trade, Plunder, and Economic Development in Early English Jamaica, 1655–89," *Economic History Review* 2d ser., 39 (1986): 205–22, and "The Merchants of Port Royal, Jamaica, and the Spanish Contraband Trade, 1655–1692," *William and Mary Quarterly* 3d ser., 43 (1986): 570–93.

27. Joseph E. Illick, *Colonial Pennsylvania: A History* (New York, 1976), 1–112; Gary B. Nash, *Quakers and Politics: Pennsylvania, 1681–1726* (Princeton, 1968), 3–88; James T. Lemon, *The Best Poor Man's Country: A Geographical Study of Early Southeastern Pennsylvania* (Baltimore, 1972), 150–83; Carl Bridenbaugh, "The Old and New Societies of the Delaware Valley in the Seventeenth Century," *Pennsylvania Magazine of History and Biography* 100 (1976): 143–72; Stephanie Grauman Wolf, *Urban Village: Population, Community, and Family Structure in Germantown, Pennsylvania, 1683–1800* (Princeton, 1976), 3–95.

28. Lemon, *Best Poor Man's Country*, 1–117; Nash, *Quakers and Politics*, 48–305; Jon Butler, "Into Pennsylvania's Spiritual Abyss: The Rise and Fall of the Later Keithians, 1693–1703," *Pennsylvania Magazine of History and Biography* 101 (1977): 151–70; Wolf, *Urban Village*, 155–202.

29. Van Cleaf Bachman, *Peltries or Plantations: The Economic Policies of the Dutch West India Company in New Netherland, 1623–1639* (Baltimore, 1969); Thomas J. Condon, *New York Beginnings: The Commercial Origin of New Netherland* (New York, 1968); George L. Smith, *Religion and Trade in New Netherland* (Ithaca, 1973); Adrian C. Leiby, *The Early Dutch and Swedish Settlers of New Jersey* (Princeton, 1964), together provide an excellent portrait of Dutch North American settlements on the eve of English conquest. See also Amandus Johnson, *The Swedish Settle-*

ments on the Delaware, 1638–1664, 2 vols. (New York, 1911), and Sally Schwartz, "Society and Culture in the Seventeenth-Century Delaware Valley," *Delaware History* 20 (1982): 98–122.

30. See Michael Kammen, *Colonial New York: A History* (New York, 1975), 73–127; Robert C. Ritchie, *The Duke's Province: A Study of New York Politics and Society, 1664–1691* (Chapel Hill, 1977), 9–152; Donna Merwick, "Becoming English: Anglo-Dutch Conflict in the 1670s in Albany, New York," *New York History* 62 (1981): 389–414.

31. Peter O. Wacker, *Land and People: A Cultural Geography of Preindustrial New Jersey: Origins and Settlement Patterns* (New Brunswick, 1975), 121–220; Wesley Frank Craven, *New Jersey and the English Colonization of North America* (Princeton, 1964); John E. Pomfret, *Colonial New Jersey: A History* (New York, 1973), 92–122; Kammen, *Colonial New York*, 73–160; Lemon, *Best Poor Man's Country*, 19–23; John A. Munroe, *Colonial Delaware: A History* (Millwood, N.Y., 1978), 59–101; Ned C. Landsman, "The Scottish Proprietors and the Planning of East New Jersey," in Michael Zuckerman, ed., *Friends and Neighbors: Group Life in America's First Plural Society* (Philadelphia, 1982), 65–89, and *Scotland and Its First American Colony, 1683–1765* (Princeton, 1985). Some of the religious effects of this pluralism are discussed in J. William Frost, "Religious Liberty in Early Pennsylvania," *Pennsylvania Magazine of History and Biography* 105 (1981): 419–52.

32. Lemon, *Best Poor Man's Country*, 118–30; Thomas J. Archdeacon, *New York City, 1664–1710: Conquest and Change* (Ithaca, 1976), 1–96; Gary B. Nash, *The Urban Crucible: Social Change, Political Consciousness, and the Origins of the American Revolution* (Cambridge, Mass., 1979), 3–25, 54–75, and "The Early Merchants of Philadelphia: The Formation and Disintegration of a Founding Elite," in Richard S. Dunn and Mary Maples Dunn, eds., *The World of William Penn* (Philadelphia, 1986), 337–62; James H. Levitt, *For Want of Trade: Shipping and the New Jersey Ports, 1680–1783* (Newark, 1981), 1–138.

33. Lemon, *Best Poor Man's Country*, 42–70, 98–117; Wacker, *Land and People*, 221–330; Munroe, *Colonial Delaware*, 149–67; Sung Bok Kim, *Landlord and Tenant in Colonial New York: Manorial Society, 1664–1775* (Chapel Hill, 1978), 1–161; Jessica Kross, *The Evolution of an American Town: Newtown, New York, 1642–1775* (Philadelphia, 1983), 3–178; Landsman, *Scotland and Its First American Colony*, 99–162; Langdon Wright, "In Search of Peace and Harmony: New York Communities in the Seventeenth Century," *New York History* 61 (1980): 5–21; Donna Merwick, "Dutch Townsmen and Land Use: A Spatial Perspective on Seventeenth-Century Albany, New York," *William and Mary Quarterly* 3d ser., 37 (1980): 53–78.

34. Kammen, *Colonial New York*, xvi, 161–90; James T. Lemon, "The Weakness of Place and Community in Early Pennsylvania," in James R. Gibson, ed., *European Settlement and Development in North America: Essays on Geographical Change in Honour and Memory of Andrew Hill Clark* (Toronto, 1978), 190–207; Wacker, *Land and People*, 409–12; Michael Zuckerman, "Introduction: Puritans, Cavaliers, and the Motley Middle," in Zuckerman, ed., *Friends and Neighbors*, 3–25; Barry Levy, "The Birth of the 'Modern Family' in Early America: Quaker and Anglican Families in the Delaware Valley, Pennsylvania, 1681–1750," in ibid., 26–64; Valerie G. Gladfelter, "Power Challenged: Rising Individualism in the Burlington, New

Jersey, Friends Meeting, 1678–1720," in ibid., 116–44; Milton M. Klein, "New York in the American Colonies: A New Look," *New York History* 53 (1972): 132–56, and "Shaping the American Tradition: The Microcosm of Colonial New York," ibid. 59 (1978): 173–97; Douglas Greenberg, "The Middle Colonies in Recent American Historiography," *William and Mary Quarterly* 3d ser., 36 (1979): 396–427; Wells, *Population of the British Colonies*, 110–43.

35. Harry Roy Merrens, *Colonial North Carolina in the Eighteenth Century: A Study in Historical Geography* (Chapel Hill, 1964), 18–31; Hugh T. Lefler and William S. Powell, *Colonial North Carolina: A History* (New York, 1973), 29–80; Lindley S. Butler, "The Early Settlement of Carolina," *Virginia Magazine of History and Biography* 79 (1971), 20–28.

36. M. Eugene Sirmans, *Colonial South Carolina, 1663–1763* (Chapel Hill, 1966), 1–100; Richard S. Dunn, "English Sugar Islands and the Founding of South Carolina," 81–93; Richard Waterhouse, "England, the Caribbean, and the Settlement of Carolina," *Journal of American Studies* 9 (1975): 259–81; Wells, *Population*, 166–69.

37. H. Roy Merrens and George D. Terry, "Dying in Paradise: Malaria, Mortality, and the Perceptual Environment in Colonial South Carolina," *Journal of Southern History* 50 (1984): 533–50; H. Roy Merrens, "The Physical Environment of Early America: Images and Image Makers in Colonial South Carolina," *Geographical Review* 59 (1969): 530–56; Converse D. Clowse, *Economic Beginnings in Colonial South Carolina, 1670–1730* (Columbia, 1971); Peter H. Wood, *Black Majority: Negroes in Colonial South Carolina from 1670 through the Stono Rebellion* (New York, 1974), 3–194; Clarence L. Ver Steeg, *Origins of a Southern Mosaic: Studies of Early Carolina and Georgia* (Athens, Ga., 1975), 103–32; Philip M. Brown, "Early Indian Trade in the Development of South Carolina: Politics, Economics, and Social Mobility during the Proprietary Period, 1670–1719," *South Carolina Historical Magazine* 76 (1975): 118–28; Stuart O. Stumpf, "A Case of Arrested Development: Charles Town's Commercial Life, 1670–1690," *Southern Studies* 20 (1981), 361–77; John S. Otto, "The Origins of Cattle-Ranching in Colonial South Carolina, 1670–1715," *South Carolina Historical Magazine* 87 (1986): 117–24; Lawrence Lee, *The Lower Cape Fear in Colonial Days* (Chapel Hill, 1965), 1–106, 117–60.

38. See the suggestive analysis by Robert D. Mitchell, "The Formation of Early American Cultural Regions: An Interpretation," in Gibson, ed., *European Settlement and Development*, 66–90.

39. Michael Craton, *A History of the Bahamas* (London, 1962), 47–135.

40. John Bartlett Brebner, *New England's Outpost: Acadia before the Conquest of Canada* (New York, 1927), and *The Neutral Yankees of Nova Scotia: A Marginal Colony during the Revolutionary Years* (New York, 1937); Andrew Hill Clark, *Acadia: The Geography of Early Nova Scotia to 1760* (Madison, 1968), 168–261, 330–69.

41. Paul S. Taylor, *Georgia Plan, 1732–1752* (Berkeley, 1972); Kenneth Coleman, *Colonial Georgia: A History* (New York, 1976).

42. Dunn, "Experiments Holy and Unholy," 282; John M. Murrin, "Review Essay," *History and Theory*, 11 (1972): 231.

43. Breen, "Looking Out for Number One," 344; Nicholas Canny, "The Anglo-American Colonial Experience," *Historical Journal* 24 (1981): 486.

CHAPTER THREE

1. Henry A. Gemery, "Emigration from the British Isles to the New World, 1630–1700: Inferences from Colonial Populations," *Research in Economic History* 5 (1980): 193, 195; James H. Cassedy, *Demography in Early America* (Cambridge, Mass., 1969), 40, 175; Clifford K. Shipton, "Immigration to New England, 1680–1740," *Journal of Political Economy* 44 (1936): 225–39; Philip J. Greven, Jr., "The Average Size of Families and Households in the Province of Massachusetts in 1764 and the United States in 1790: An Overview," in Peter Laslett and Richard Wall, eds., *Household and Family in Past Time* (Cambridge, 1972), 545–60, and *Four Generations: Population, Land, and Family in Colonial Andover, Massachusetts* (Ithaca, 1970), 185–97; Terry L. Anderson and Robert Paul Thomas, "White Population, Labor Force and Extensive Growth of the New England Economy in the Seventeenth Century," *Journal of Economic History* 33 (1973): 639, 647–48; Daniel Scott Smith, "The Demographic History of Colonial New England," ibid. 32 (1972): 165–83; Maris A. Vinovskis, "Mortality Rates and Trends in Massachusetts before 1860," ibid., 195–202; Kenneth A. Lockridge, "The Population of Dedham, Massachusetts, 1636–1736," *Economic History Review* 2d ser., 19 (1966): 324–26, 332–39; Susan L. Norton, "Population Growth in Colonial America: A Study of Ipswich, Massachusetts," *Population Studies* 25 (1971): 433–52; Douglas R. McManis, *Colonial New England: A Historical Geography* (New York, 1975), 66–72; Robert Higgs and H. Louis Stettler III, "Colonial New England Demography: A Sampling Approach," *William and Mary Quarterly* 3d ser., 27 (1970): 282–94; Stettler, "The New England Throat Distemper and Family Size," in H. E. Klarman, ed., *Empirical Studies in Health Economics* (Baltimore, 1970), 17–27; Rose Lockwood, "Birth, Illness, and Death in 18th Century New England," *Journal of Social History* 12 (1978): 111–28.

2. McManis, *Colonial New England*, 46–66; Douglas E. Leach, *Flintlock and Tomahawk: New England in King Philip's War* (New York, 1966); Charles E. Clark, *The Eastern Frontier: The Settlement of Northern New England, 1610–1763* (New York, 1970); Bruce C. Daniels, *The Connecticut Town: Growth and Development, 1635–1790* (Middletown, Conn., 1979), 8–44, and *Dissent and Conformity on Narragansett Bay: The Colonial Rhode Island Town* (Middletown, Conn., 1983), 23–47; Eric H. Christiansen, "The Emergence of Medical Communities in Massachusetts, 1700–1794: The Demographic Factors," *Bulletin of the History of Medicine* 54 (1980): 66; Jere R. Daniell, *Colonial New Hampshire: A History* (Millwood, N.Y., 1981), 133–64; David E. Van Deventer, *The Emergence of Provincial New Hampshire, 1623–1741* (Baltimore, 1976), 62–82; Andrew Hill Clark, *Acadia: The Geography of Early Nova Scotia to 1760* (Madison, 1968), 330–69. William Cronon, *Changes in the Land: Indians, Colonists, and the Ecology of New England* (New York, 1983), 54–81, 127–70, suggestively discusses the changing social landscape of New England during the colonial era.

3. Joseph H. Wood, "Village and Community in Early New England," *Journal of Historical Geography* 8 (1982): 333–46; Greven, *Four Generations*, 41–71, 175–221; Kenneth A. Lockridge, *A New England Town, The First Hundred Years: Dedham, Massachusetts, 1636–1736* (New York, 1970), 79–118, and "Land, Population, and the Evolution of New England Society, 1630–1790," *Past and Present*, no. 39 (1968):

62–80; Linda Auwers Bissell, "From One Generation to Another: Mobility in Seventeenth-Century Windsor, Connecticut," *William and Mary Quarterly* 3d ser., 31 (1974): 79–110; Thomas R. Cole, "Family, Settlement, and Migration in Southeastern Massachusetts, 1650–1805: The Case for Regional Analysis," *New England Historical and Genealogical Register* 132 (1978): 171–81; John W. Adams and Alice Bee Kasakoff, "Migration and the Family in Colonial New England: The View from Geneaologies," *Journal of Family History* 9 (1984): 24–44, and "Migration at Marriage in Colonial New England: A Comparison of Rates Derived from Genealogies with Rates from Vital Records," in Bennett Dyke and Warren T. Morrill, eds., *Genealogical Demography* (New York, 1980), 115–38; Darrett B. Rutman, "People in Process: The New Hampshire Towns of the Eighteenth Century," *Journal of Urban History* 1 (1975): 268–92; Douglas Lamar Jones, *Village and Seaport: Migration and Society in Eighteenth-Century Massachusetts* (Hanover, N.H., 1981); John J. Waters, "Patrimony, Succession, and Social Stability: Guilford, Connecticut in the Eighteenth Century," *Perspectives in American History* 10 (1976): 131–60; Charles S. Grant, "Land Speculation and the Settlement of Kent, 1738–1760," *New England Quarterly* 27 (1955): 51–71.

4. Robert G. Pope, *The Half-Way Covenant: Church Membership in Puritan New England* (Princeton, 1969), 128–36, 210–11, 233–35, 276; Gerald F. Moran, "Religious Renewal, Puritan Tribalism, and the Family in Seventeenth-Century Milford, Connecticut," *William and Mary Quarterly* 3d ser., 36 (1979): 236–54; Moran Vinovskis and Maris A. Vinovskis, "The Puritan Family and Religion: A Critical Reappraisal," ibid. 39 (1982): 32–42; David M. Scobey, "Revising the Errand: New England's Ways and the Puritan Sense of the Past," ibid. 41 (1984): 3–31; Charles E. Hambrick-Stowe, *The Practice of Piety: Puritan Devotional Disciplines in Seventeenth-Century New England* (Chapel Hill, 1982), 242; George Selement, *Keepers of the Vineyard: The Puritan Ministry and Collective Culture in Colonial New England* (Lanham, Md., 1984), 43–59; Perry Miller, "Declension in a Bible Commonwealth," in *Nature's Nation* (Cambridge, Mass., 1967), 25–30, and *The New England Mind: From Colony to Province* (Cambridge, Mass., 1953); Joseph J. Ellis, *The New England Mind in Transition: Samuel Johnson of Connecticut, 1696–1772* (New Haven, 1973), 11.

5. E. Brooks Holifield, *The Covenant Sealed: The Development of Puritan Sacramental Theology in Old and New England, 1570–1720* (New Haven, 1974), 169–230; Scobey, "Revising the Errand," 19, 30; Paul R. Lucas, *Valley of Discord: Church and Society along the Connecticut River, 1636–1725* (Hanover, 1976), 205; Lilian Handlin, "Dissent in a Small Community," *New England Quarterly* 58 (1985): 193–220; Sydney V. James, "Ecclesiastical Authority in the Land of Roger Williams," ibid. 57 (1984): 323–46; Pope, *Half-Way Covenant*, 260.

6. Stephen Foster, "The Godly in Transit: English Popular Protestantism and the Creation of a Puritan Establishment in America," in David D. Hall and David Grayson Allen, eds., *Seventeenth-Century New England* (Boston, 1984), 237; Lucas, *Valley of Discord*, xiii; James W. Schmotter, "Ministerial Careers in Eighteenth-Century New England: The Social Context, 1700–1760," *Journal of Social History* 9 (1975): 249–67; David D. Hall, *The Faithful Shepherd: A History of the New England Ministry in the Seventeenth Century* (Chapel Hill, 1972), 181.

7. Miller, "Declension in a Bible Commonwealth," 23, 43; Sacvan Bercovitch,

The American Jeremiad (Madison, 1978), 16; Stephen Foster, *Their Solitary Way: The Puritan Social Ethic in the First Century of Settlement in New England* (New Haven, 1971), xiv–xv; Pope, *Half-Way Covenant*, 261, 275–76, and "New England versus the New England Mind: The Myth of Declension," *Journal of Social History* 3 (1969–70), 95–108.

8. Foster, "Godly in Transit," in Hall and Allen, eds., *Seventeenth-Century New England*, 214; Miller, "Declension in a Bible Commonwealth," 25; Timothy H. Breen and Stephen Foster, "The Puritans' Greatest Achievement: A Study of Social Cohesion in Seventeenth-Century Massachusetts," *Journal of American History* 60 (1973): 20; Pope, "New England versus the New England Mind," 105; Kai T. Erikson, *Wayward Puritans: A Study in the Sociology of Deviance* (New York, 1966), 157; J. F. Maclear, "New England and the Fifth Monarchy: The Quest for Millennium in Early American Puritanism," *William and Mary Quarterly* 3d ser., 32 (1975): 258; Bruce Tucker, "The Reinterpretation of Puritan History in Provincial New England," *New England Quarterly* 54 (1981): 481–98, and "The Reinvention of New England, 1691–1770," ibid. 59 (1986): 315–40.

9. Emory Elliott, *Power and the Pulpit in Puritan New England* (Princeton, 1975), 8; Erikson, *Wayward Puritans*, 157–59, 163–81; John Demos, "Underlying Themes in the Witchcraft of Seventeenth-Century New England," *American Historical Review* 75 (1970): 1319–22, "John Godfrey and His Neighbors: Witchcraft and the Social Web in Colonial Massachusetts," *William and Mary Quarterly* 3d ser., 33 (1973): 242–65, and *Entertaining Satan: Witchcraft and the Culture of Early New England* (New York, 1982). See also David D. Hall, "Witchcraft and the Limits of Interpretation," *New England Quarterly* 58 (1985): 253–81.

10. J. William T. Youngs, Jr., *God's Messengers: Religious Leadership in Colonial New England, 1700–1750* (Baltimore, 1976); Laura L. Becker, "Ministers vs. Laymen: The Singing Controversy in Puritan New England, 1720–1740," *New England Quarterly* 55 (1982): 77–96; Ellis, *New England Mind in Transition*, 55–122, and "Anglicans in Connecticut, 1725–1750: The Conversion of the Missionaries," *New England Quarterly* 44 (1971): 66–81; Bruce E. Steiner, "New England Anglicanism: A Genteel Faith?" *William and Mary Quarterly* 3d ser., 27 (1970): 122–35.

11. McManis, *Colonial New England*, 86–122; John J. McCusker and Russell R. Menard, *The Economy of British America, 1607–1789* (Chapel Hill, 1985), 91–110; William I. Davisson and Dennis J. Dugan, "Commerce in Seventeenth-Century Essex County, Massachusetts," *Essex Institute Historical Collections* 107 (1971): 113–42; David Grayson Allen, *In English Ways: The Movement of Societies and the Transferal of English Local Law and Custom to Massachusetts Bay in the Seventeenth Century* (Chapel Hill, 1981), 228; Bruce C. Daniels, "Economic Development in Colonial and Revolutionary Connecticut: An Overview," *William and Mary Quarterly* 3d ser., 37 (1980): 429–34; Charles F. Carroll, *The Timber Economy of Puritan New England* (Providence, 1973), 57–128; Van Deventer, *Emergence of Provincial New Hampshire*, 93–106.

12. Terry Lee Anderson, *The Economic Growth of Seventeenth Century New England: A Measurement of Regional Income* (New York, 1975), 21, 23; McCusker and Menard, *Economy of British America*, 107. Bernard Bailyn, *The New England Merchants in the Seventeenth Century* (Cambridge, Mass., 1955), is the classic study of the role of the merchants in the developing New England economy.

13. Theodore B. Lewis, "Land Speculation and the Dudley Council of 1686," *William and Mary Quarterly* 3d ser., 31 (1974): 255–72; Stephen Innes, *Labor in a New Land: Economy and Society in Seventeenth-Century Springfield* (Princeton, 1983), and "Land Tenancy and Social Order in Springfield, Massachusetts, 1652 to 1702," *William and Mary Quarterly* 3d ser., 35 (1978): 33–56.

14. Innes, *Labor in a New Land*, 72–122; Jackson Turner Main, *Society and Economy in Colonial Connecticut* (Princeton, 1985), 68–69; Anderson, *Economic Growth of Seventeenth Century New England*, 114–19, "Economic Growth in Colonial New England: 'Statistical Renaissance,'" *Journal of Economic History* 39 (1979): 243–47, and Terry L. Anderson, "Wealth Estimates for the New England Colonies, 1650–1709," *Explorations in Economic History* 12 (1975): 151–76; William I. Davisson, "Essex County Wealth Trends: Wealth and Economic Growth in 17th Century Massachusetts," *Essex Institute Historical Collections* 103 (1967): 291–342; Donald W. Koch, "Income Distribution and Political Structure in Seventeenth-Century Salem, Massachusetts," ibid. 105 (1969): 50–71; Richard P. Gildrie, *Salem, Massachusetts, 1626–1683: A Covenanted Community* (Charlottesville, 1975), 155–69; James A. Henretta, "Economic Development and Social Structure in Colonial Boston," *William and Mary Quarterly* 3d ser., 22 (1965): 75–92.

15. See, in this connection, Paul Boyer and Stephen Nissenbaum, *Salem Possessed: The Social Origins of Witchcraft* (Cambridge, Mass., 1974), 60–109; Gildrie, *Salem, Massachusetts*, 145–69; Innes, *Labor in a New Land*, 123–50.

16. Bailyn, *New England Merchants*, 139–42; Innes, *Labor in a New Land*, 151–70; T. H. Breen, *The Character of the Good Ruler: A Study of Puritan Political Ideas in New England, 1630–1730* (New York, 1970), 87–202, "Who Governs: The Town Franchise in Seventeenth-Century Massachusetts," *William and Mary Quarterly* 3d ser., 27 (1970): 473, and "War, Taxes, and Political Brokers: The Ordeal of Massachusetts Bay, 1675–1692," in Breen, *Puritans and Adventurers: Change and Persistence in Early America* (New York, 1980), 81–105; Richard P. Gildrie, "Salem Society and Politics in the 1680s," *Essex Institute Historical Collections* 114 (1978): 185–206; Robert deV. Brunkow, "Officeholding in Providence, Rhode Island, 1646–1686: A Quantitative Analysis," *William and Mary Quarterly* 3d ser., 37 (1980): 242–60. Richard R. Johnson, *Adjustment to Empire: The New England Colonies, 1675–1715* (New Brunswick, 1981), provides an excellent account of the imperial context of these developments.

17. Daniels, *Dissent and Conformity on Narragansett Bay*, 22; Foster, *Their Solitary Way*, 7; David Thomas Konig, *Law and Society in Puritan Massachusetts, 1629–1692* (Chapel Hill, 1979), xii–xiii, 89–116, 188–89. That the enforcement of law became less exacting during the seventeenth century is suggested by R. W. Roetger, "The Transformation of Sexual Morality in 'Puritan' New England: Evidence from New Haven Court Records, 1639–1698," *Canadian Review of American Studies* 15 (1984): 243–57.

18. Edward M. Cook, Jr., *Fathers of the Towns: Leadership and Community Structure in Eighteenth-Century New England* (Baltimore, 1976), 179; Main, *Society and Economy in Colonial Connecticut*, 87–88; Michael Zuckerman, *Peaceable Kingdoms: New England Towns in the Eighteenth Century* (New York, 1970); Christopher M. Jedrey, *The World of John Cleaveland: Family and Community in Eighteenth-Century New England* (New York, 1979).

19. Carole Shammas, "How Self-Sufficient Was Early America?," *Journal of Interdisciplinary History* 13 (1982): 247–72; Bettye Hobbs Pruitt, "Self-Sufficiency and the Agricultural Economy of Eighteenth-Century Massachusetts," *William and Mary Quarterly* 3d ser., 41 (1984): 333–64; Winifred B. Rothenberg, "The Market and Massachusetts Farmers, 1750–1855," *Journal of Economic History* 41 (1981): 283–314.

20. Pruitt, "Self-Sufficiency and the Agricultural Economy," 349; Gary M. Nash, *The Urban Crucible: Social Change, Political Consciousness, and the Origins of the American Revolution* (Cambridge, Mass., 1979), 111–18, 172–76, 180–97, 244–47; G. B. Warden, "Inequality and Instability in Eighteenth-Century Boston: A Reappraisal," *Journal of Interdisciplinary History* 6 (1976): 585–620; Lynne Withey, *Urban Growth in Colonial Rhode Island: Newport and Providence in the Eighteenth Century* (Albany, 1984); Daniels, *Connecticut Town*, 140–80, and "Emerging Urbanism and Increasing Social Stratification in the Era of the American Revolution," in John Ferling, ed., *The American Revolution: The Home Front* (Carrollton, Ga., 1976), 15–30; Cook, *Fathers of the Towns*, 172–79; Jones, *Village and Seaport*; Christine Leigh Heyrman, *Commerce and Culture: The Maritime Communities of Colonial Massachusetts, 1690–1750* (New York, 1984).

21. McCusker and Menard, *Economy of British America*, 107–10; James G. Lydon, "Fish for Gold: The Massachusetts Fish Trade with Iberia, 1700–1773," *New England Quarterly* 54 (1981): 539–82; David C. Klingaman, "The Coastwise Trade of Colonial Massacusetts," *Essex Institute Historical Collections* 108 (1972): 217–33.

22. Pruitt, "Self-Sufficiency and the Agricultural Economy," 362, 364; Rothenberg, "Market and Massachusetts Farmers."

23. Pruitt, "Self-Sufficiency and the Agricultural Economy," 359–61, 364; Van Deventer, *Emergence of Provincial New Hampshire*, 93–106, 159–78; Daniels, "Economic Development in Colonial and Revolutionary Connecticut," 429–50; Elinor F. Oakes, "A Ticklish Business: Dairying in New England and Pennsylvania, 1750–1812," *Pennsylvania History* 47 (1980): 195–212; Karen J. Friedmann, "Victualling Colonial Boston," *Agricultural History* 47 (1973): 189–205; William D. Miller, "The Narragansett Planters," *Proceedings of the American Antiquarian Society* 43 (1934): 49–115; Christian McBurney, "The South Kingstown Planters: Country Gentry in Colonial Rhode Island," *Rhode Island History* 45 (1986): 81–93.

24. Richard L. Bushman, "Family Security in the Transition from Farm to City, 1750–1850," *Journal of Family History* 6 (1981): 240; Main, *Society and Economy in Colonial Connecticut*, 151, 241–56, 381; Daniels, "Economic Development in Colonial and Revolutionary Connecticut," 438–43.

25. Main, *Society and Economy in Colonial Connecticut*, 262–65, 278–313, 370, and "The Distribution of Property in Colonial Connecticut," in James Kirby Martin, ed., *The Human Dimensions of Nation Making: Essays on Colonial and Revolutionary America* (Madison, 1976), 64–70; Withey, *Urban Growth in Colonial Rhode Island*, 123–32; Elaine F. Crane, *A Dependent People: Newport, Rhode Island, in the Revolutionary Era* (New York, 1985), 16–46; Jay Coughtry, *The Notorious Triangle: Rhode Island and the African Slave Trade, 1700–1807* (Philadelphia, 1981); Alison Jones, "The Rhode Island Slave Trade: A Trading Advantage in Africa," *Slavery and Abolition* 3 (1981): 226–44; Van Deventer, *Emergence of Provincial New Hampshire*,

78–82, 174–78, 215; Christiansen, "Emergence of Medical Communities in Massachusetts," 64–77; John M. Murrin, "The Legal Transformation: The Bench and Bar of Eighteenth-Century Massachusetts," in Stanley N. Katz, ed., *Colonial America: Essays in Politics and Social Development* (Boston, 1971), 415–49; David H. Flaherty, "Criminal Practice in Provincial Massachusetts," *Publications of the Colonial Society of Massachusetts* 62 (1984): 191–242; McManis, *Colonial New England*, 132–39; Grant, "Land Speculation and the Settlement of Kent," 51–71, and *Democracy in the Connecticut Frontier Town of Kent* (New York, 1972), 55–65; Richard L. Bushman, *From Puritan to Yankee: Character and the Social Order in Connecticut, 1690–1765* (Cambridge, Mass., 1967), 73–82; Julian Gwyn, "Money Lending in New England: The Case of Admiral Sir Peter Warren and His Heirs, 1739–1805," *New England Quarterly* 44 (1971): 117–34.

26. Main, *Society and Economy in Colonial Connecticut*, 122, 132–33, 278–366, 368, 381, and "Distribution of Property in Colonial Connecticut," 77–90; Bruce C. Daniels, "Long Range Trends of Wealth Distribution in Eighteenth Century New England," *Explorations in Economic History* 11 (1973–74): 123–35, "Defining Economic Classes in Colonial New Hampshire, 1700–1770," *Historic New Hampshire* 28 (1973): 53–62, "Money-Value Definitions of Economic Classes in Colonial Connecticut, 1700–1776," *Histoire Sociale* 7 (1974): 346–52, and "Defining Economic Classes in Colonial Massachusetts, 1700–1776," *Proceedings of the American Antiquarian Society* 83 (1973): 251–59; Alice Hanson Jones, "Wealth Estimates for the New England Colonies about 1770," *Journal of Economic History* 32 (1972): 98–127, and *The Wealth of a Nation to Be: The American Colonies on the Eve of the Revolution* (New York, 1980), 50–194; G. B. Warden, "The Distribution of Property in Boston, 1692–1775," *Perspectives in American History* 10 (1976): 81–128, and "Inequality and Instability in Eighteenth-Century Boston," 585–620; Withey, *Urban Growth in Colonial Rhode Island*, 123–32; Crane, *Dependent People*, 25–29; Van Deventer, *Emergence of Provincial New Hampshire*, 173–78.

27. See Robert J. Dinkin, "Seating in the Meeting House in Early Massachusetts," *New England Quarterly* 43 (1970): 450–64; Anthony G. Roeber, "'Her Merchandize . . . Shall Be Holiness To The Lord': The Progress and Decline of Puritan Gentility at the Brattle Street Church, Boston, 1715–1745," *New England Historical and Genealogical Register* 131 (1977): 175–91; Christine Leigh Heyrman, "The Fashion among More Superior People: Charity and Social Change in Provincial New England, 1700–1740," *American Quarterly* 34 (1982): 107–24, and *Commerce and Culture*, 143–81, 330–65; Withey, *Urban Growth in Colonial Rhode Island*, 13–50; Crane, *Dependent People*, 47–62; Van Deventer, *Emergence of Provincial New Hampshire*, 217–25; Main, *Society and Economy in Colonial Connecticut*, 278–366.

28. Cook, *Fathers of the Towns*; Michael Zuckerman, "The Social Context of Democracy in Massachusetts," *William and Mary Quarterly* 3d ser., 25 (1968): 523–44; Van Deventer, *Emergence of Provincial New Hampshire*, 218–23; Main, *Society and Economy in Colonial Connecticut*, 317–66; Bruce C. Daniels, "Family Dynasties in Connecticut's Largest Towns, 1700–1760," *Canadian Journal of History* 8 (1973): 99–110, "Large Town Officeholding in Eighteenth-Century Connecticut: The Growth of Oligarchy," *Journal of American Studies* 9 (1975): 1–12, and "Democracy

and Oligarchy in Connecticut Towns: General Assembly Officeholding, 1701–1790," *Social Science Quarterly* 56 (1975): 460–75; Withey, *Urban Growth in Colonial Rhode Island*, 9–11, 130–31; G. B. Warden, "Officeholding and Officials in Boston, 1692–1775," *New England Historical and Genealogical Register* 131 (1977): 267–90; Robert M. Zemsky, "Power, Influence, and Status: Leadership Patterns in the Massachusetts Assembly, 1740–1755," *William and Mary Quarterly* 3d ser., 26 (1969): 502–20, and *Merchants, Farmers, and River Gods* (Boston, 1971); Heyrman, *Commerce and Culture*, 143–81, 330–65; Bruce E. Steiner, "Anglican Officeholding in Pre-Revolutionary Connecticut: The Parameters of New England Community," *William and Mary Quarterly* 3d ser., 31 (1974): 369–406.

29. Robert C. Twombly and Robert H. Moore, "Black Puritan: The Negro in Seventeenth-Century Massachusetts," *William and Mary Quarterly* 3d ser., 24 (1967): 224–41; "Estimated Population of the American Colonies, 1610–1780," in Jack P. Greene, ed., *Settlements to Society, 1584–1763: A Documentary History of the American Colonies* (New York, 1966), 238–39; Daniels, *Dissent and Conformity on Narragansett Bay*, 57–59; Withey, *Urban Growth in Colonial Rhode Island*, 71–73; Crane, *Dependent People*, 76–83; Miller, "Narragansett Planters," 67–71; McBurney, "South Kingstown Planters," 81–93; Main, *Society and Economy in Colonial Connecticut*, 129–30, 176–82, 309, 378; Louis P. Masur, "Slavery in Eighteenth-Century Rhode Island: Evidence from the Census of 1774," *Slavery and Abolition* 6 (1985): 140–50; Van Deventer, *Emergence of Provincial New Hampshire*, 113–14. On conditions of slavery in New England and the black response to it, see Robert C. Twombly, "Black Resistance to Slavery in Massachusetts," in William L. O'Neill, ed., *Insights and Parallels: Problems and Issues of American Social History* (Minneapolis, 1973), 11–32, and Lorenzo J. Greene, *The Negro in Colonial New England* (New York, 1942). On the decline of slavery in Massachusetts after 1770, see Elaine MacEacheren, "Emancipation of Slavery in Massachusetts: A Reexamination, 1770–1790," *Journal of Negro History* 55 (1970): 289–306.

30. Grant, *Democracy in the Connecticut Frontier Town*, 83–103; Lockridge, "Land, Population, and the Evolution of New England Society," 62–80; Main, *Society and Economy in Colonial Connecticut*, 149–51, 377–78, and "Standards of Living and the Life Cycle in Colonial Connecticut," *Journal of Economic History* 43 (1983): 159–65; Gloria L. Main, "The Standard of Living in Colonial Massachusetts," ibid., 101–8; Jones, *Village and Seaport*, 103–21; Nancy R. Folbre, "The Wealth of the Patriarchs: Deerfield, Massachusetts, 1760–1840," *Journal of Interdisciplinary History* 16 (1985): 208; Sarah F. McMahon, "A Comfortable Subsistence: The Changing Diet in Rural New England, 1620–1840," *William and Mary Quarterly* 3d ser., 42 (1985): 26–65.

31. Charles R. Lee, "Public Poor Relief and the Massachusetts Community, 1620–1715," *New England Quarterly* 55 (1982): 564–85; Douglas Lamar Jones, "The Strolling Poor: Transiency in Eighteenth-Century Massachusetts," *Journal of Social History* 8 (1975): 28–54, and "Poverty and Vagabondage: The Process of Survival in Eighteenth-Century Massachusetts," *New England Historical and Genealogical Register* 133 (1979): 243–54; Daniels, *Dissent and Conformity on Narragansett Bay*, 57–59; Withey, *Urban Development in Colonial Rhode Island*, 51–71, 133–36; Nash, *Urban Crucible*, 71–74, 88, 125–27, 185–89, 217, 245–46, 253–55, 263, 310, 326–28, 337; Allan Kulikoff, "The Progress of Inequality in Revolutionary Boston," *William and*

Mary Quarterly 3d ser., 28 (1971): 375–412; David H. Flaherty, "Crime and Social Control in Provincial Massachusetts," *Historical Journal* 24 (1981): 352–53.

32. Roger Thompson, *Sex in Middlesex: Popular Mores in a Massachusetts County, 1649–1699* (Amherst, 1986), 194, 198; Flaherty, "Crime and Social Control," 339–60; Hendrik Hartog, "The Public Law of a County Court: Judicial Government in Eighteenth Century Massachusetts," *American Journal of Legal History* 20 (1976): 282–329.

33. William E. Nelson, *Dispute and Conflict Resolution in Plymouth County, Massachusetts, 1725–1825* (Chapel Hill, 1981), 13–75, and *Americanization of the Common Law: The Impact of Legal Change on Massachusetts Society, 1760–1830* (Cambridge, Mass., 1975), 13–63; John M. Murrin, "Review Essay," *History and Theory* 11 (1972): 250–51; David Grayson Allen, "The Zuckerman Thesis and the Process of Legal Rationalization in Provincial Massachusetts," *William and Mary Quarterly* 3d ser., 29 (1972): 456–59; L. Kinvin Wroth, "Possible Kingdoms: The New England Town from the Perspective of Legal History," *American Journal of Legal History* 15 (1971): 318–27; Flaherty, "Crime and Social Control," 355; Bruce H. Mann, "Rationality, Legal Change, and Community in Connecticut, 1690–1760," *Law and Society Review* 14 (1980): 187–221.

34. Greven, *Four Generations*, 125–258; John J. Waters, "Family, Inheritance, and Migration in Colonial New England: The Evidence from Guilford, Connecticut," *William and Mary Quarterly* 3d ser., 39 (1982): 64–86; Jedrey, *World of John Cleaveland*, 58–94; Daniel Scott Smith, "Parental Power and Marriage Patterns: An Analysis of Historical Trends in Hingham, Massachusetts," *Journal of Marriage and the Family* 35 (1973): 419–39, and "Child-Naming Practices, Kinship Ties, and Change in Family Attitudes in Hingham, Massachusetts, 1641 to 1880," *Journal of Social History* 18 (1985): 541–66; Daniel Scott Smith and Michael Hindus, "Premarital Pregnancy in America, 1640–1966," *Journal of Interdisciplinary History* 6 (1975): 537–70; David H. Flaherty, *Privacy in Colonial New England* (Charlottesville, 1972), 26–27, 34–35, 38; Nancy F. Cott, "Divorce and the Changing Status of Women in Eighteenth-Century Massachusetts," *William and Mary Quarterly* 3d ser., 33 (1976): 586–614, and "Eighteenth-Century Family and Social Life Revealed in Massachusetts Divorce Records," *Journal of Social History* 10 (1976): 20–43; Folbre, "Wealth of the Patriarchs," 199–220; C. Dallett Hemphill, "Women in Court: Sex-Role Differentiation in Salem, Massachusetts, 1636 to 1683," *William and Mary Quarterly* 3d ser., 39 (1982): 164–75; Lyle Koehler, *A Search for Power: The "Weaker Sex" in Seventeenth-Century New England* (Urbana, Ill., 1980), 345–46, 361, 366; James A. Henretta, *The Evolution of American Society, 1700–1815: An Interdisciplinary Analysis* (Lexington, Mass., 1973), 30–31; Winifred B. Rothenberg, "Markets, Values and Capitalism: A Discourse on Method," *Journal of Economic History* 44 (1984): 175–76. Thompson, *Sex in Middlesex*, 190–200, has persuasively questioned the coerciveness of patriarchical authority in late seventeenth-century Middlesex County, Massachusetts.

35. Bushman, *From Puritan to Yankee*. See also Richard S. Dunn, *Puritans and Yankees: The Winthrop Dynasty of New England, 1630–1717* (Princeton, 1962). The quotation is from Fred Weinstein and Gerald M. Platt, *The Wish to Be Free: Society, Psyche, and Value Change* (Berkeley, 1969), 31.

36. Toby L. Ditz, *Property and Kinship: Inheritance in Early Connecticut, 1750–1820*

(Princeton, 1986), 159; Zuckerman, *Peaceable Kingdoms*; Jedrey, *World of John Cleaveland*, 58–94; Heyrman, *Commerce and Culture*, 15–19, 407–14. Laurel Ulrich, *Good Wives: Image and Reality in the Lives of Women in Northern New England, 1650–1750* (New York, 1982), emphasizes the role of women in sustaining the communal impulse in New England communities.

37. Maclear, "New England and the Fifth Monarchy," 259; Pope, "New England versus the New England Mind," 107; Bushman, *From Puritan to Yankee*. See also James Axtell, *The School Upon a Hill: Education and Society in Colonial New England* (New Haven, 1974), on the role of schools in perpetuating puritan social ideology and Kenneth A. Lockridge, *Literacy in Colonial New England: An Enquiry into the Social Context of Literacy in the Early Modern West* (New York, 1974), on one of the unintended modernizing effects of the widespread schooling.

38. Bushman, *From Puritan to Yankee*, ix, 276, 279; Harry S. Stout and Peter Onuf, "James Davenport and the Great Awakening in New London," *Journal of American History* 71 (1983): 577; Onuf, "New Lights in New London: A Group Portrait of the Separatists," *William and Mary Quarterly* 3d ser., 37 (1980): 627–43; Stout, "The Great Awakening in New England Reconsidered: The New England Clergy," *Journal of Social History* 8 (1974): 21–47; James Walsh, "The Great Awakening in the First Congregational Church of Woodbury, Connecticut," *William and Mary Quarterly* 3d ser., 28 (1971): 543–62; James W. Schmotter, "The Irony of Clerical Professionalism: New England's Congregational Ministers and the Great Awakening," *American Quarterly* 31 (1979): 148–68; Robert D. Rossel, "The Great Awakening: An Historical Analysis," *American Journal of Sociology* 75 (1970): 907–25; James W. Jones, *The Shattered Synthesis: New England Puritanism before the Great Awakening* (New Haven, 1973); Patricia J. Tracy, *Jonathan Edwards, Pastor: Religion and Society in Eighteenth-Century Northampton* (New York, 1979); Gregory H. Nobles, *Divisions throughout the Whole: Politics and Society in Hampshire County, Massachusetts, 1740–1775* (Cambridge, 1983), 36–106.

39. Miller, "Declension in a Bible Commonwealth," 25; McCusker and Menard, *Economy of British America*, 92.

CHAPTER FOUR

1. T. H. Breen, "Looking Out for Number One: Conflicting Cultural Values in Early Seventeenth-Century Virginia," *South Atlantic Quarterly* 78 (1979): 359.

2. Wesley Frank Craven, *White, Red, and Black: The Seventeenth-Century Virginian* (Charlottesville, 1971), 29–30; Russell R. Menard, "Immigrants and Their Increase: The Process of Population Growth in Early Colonial Maryland," in Aubrey C. Land, Lois Green Carr, and Edward C. Papenfuse, eds., *Law, Society, and Politics in Early Maryland* (Baltimore, 1977), 88–110, "Population, Economy, and Society in Seventeenth-Century Maryland," *Maryland Historical Magazine* 79 (1984): 71–74, and "The Tobacco Industry in the Chesapeake Colonies, 1617–1730: An Interpretation," *Research in Economic History* 5 (1980): 120–21; Terry L. Anderson and Robert Paul Thomas, "The Growth of Population and Labor Force in the 17th-Century Chesapeake," *Explorations in Economic History* 15 (1978): 300–

301; Russell R. Menard, P. M. G. Harris, and Lois Green Carr, "Opportunity and Inequality: The Distribution of Wealth on the Lower Western Shore of Maryland, 1638–1705," *Maryland Historical Magazine* 69 (1974): 169–84; Daniel Blake Smith, "Mortality and Family in the Colonial Chesapeake," *Journal of Interdisciplinary History* 8 (1978): 403–28; Darrett B. Rutman and Anita H. Rutman, *A Place in Time: Middlesex County, Virginia, 1650–1750*, 2 vols. (New York, 1984), 1:76–77, 2:25–69. See also James M. Gallman, "Mortality among White Males: Colonial North Carolina," *Social Science History* 4 (1980): 295–316.

3. Russell R. Menard, "From Servants to Slaves: The Transformation of the Chesapeake Labor System," *Southern Studies* 16 (1977): 355–90, "The Maryland Slave Population, 1658 to 1730: A Demographic Profile of Blacks in Four Counties," *William and Mary Quarterly* 3d ser., 32 (1975): 29–54, and "Tobacco Industry," 119–22. See also Anderson and Thomas, "Growth of Population," 300–306; Craven, *White, Red, and Black*, 73–109; David W. Galenson, "British Servants and the Colonial Indenture System in the Eighteenth Century," *Journal of Southern History* 44 (1978): 41–66, and "White Servitude and the Growth of Black Slavery in Colonial America," *Journal of Economic History* 41 (1981): 39–47; Allan Kulikoff, *Tobacco and Slaves: The Development of Southern Cultures in the Chesapeake, 1680–1800* (Chapel Hill, 1986), 37–43; Gloria L. Main, "Maryland and the Chesapeake Economy, 1670–1720," in Land, Carr, and Papenfuse, eds., *Law, Society, and Politics*, 134–52; Margaret M. R. Kellow, "Indentured Servitude in Eighteenth-Century Maryland," *Histoire Sociale* 17 (1984): 229–55; and Carville V. Earle, "A Staple Interpretation of Slavery and Free Labor," *Geographical Review* 68 (1978): 51–65.

4. Edmund S. Morgan, *American Slavery, American Freedom: The Ordeal of Colonial Virginia* (New York, 1975), 180–362; T. H. Breen, "A Changing Labor Force and Race Relations in Virginia, 1660–1710," *Journal of Social History* 7 (1973): 3–25; John C. Rainbolt, "The Alteration in the Relationship between Leadership and Constituents in Virginia, 1660–1720," *William and Mary Quarterly* 3d ser., 27 (1970): 411–34.

5. T. H. Breen and Stephen Innes, *"Myne Owne Ground": Race and Freedom on Virginia's Eastern Shore, 1640–1676* (New York, 1980); Winthrop D. Jordan, *White over Black: American Attitudes toward the Negro, 1550–1812* (Chapel Hill, 1968), 44–175. See also Alden T. Vaughan, "Blacks in Virginia: A Note on the First Decade," *William and Mary Quarterly* 3d ser., 29 (1972): 469–78; Warren M. Billings, "The Case of Fernando and Elizabeth Key: A Note on the Status of Blacks in Seventeenth Century Virginia," ibid. 30 (1973): 467–74; Jonathan L. Alpert, "The Origin of Slavery in the United States—The Maryland Precedent," *American Journal of Legal History* 14 (1970): 189–221; Whittington B. Johnson, "The Origin and Nature of African Slavery in Seventeenth Century Maryland," *Maryland Historical Magazine* 73 (1978): 236–45; Ross M. Kimmel, "Free Blacks in Seventeenth-Century Maryland," ibid. 71 (1976): 19–25; Menard, "Maryland Slave Population," 29–54.

6. See especially Bernard Bailyn, "Politics and Social Structure in Virginia," in James M. Smith, ed., *Seventeenth-Century America: Essays in Colonial History* (Chapel Hill, 1959), 90–115; David W. Jordan, "Maryland's Privy Council, 1637–1715," in Land, Carr, and Papenfuse, eds., *Law, Society, and Politics*, 65–87, and

"Political Stability and the Emergence of a Native Elite in Maryland," in Thad W. Tate and David L. Ammerman, eds., *The Chesapeake in the Seventeenth Century: Essays on Anglo-American Society* (Chapel Hill, 1979), 243–73; Carole Shammas, "English-Born and Creole Elites in Turn-of-the-Century Virginia," ibid., 274–96; Breen, "Looking Out for Number One," 359; Lois Green Carr and David W. Jordan, *Maryland's Revolution of Government, 1689–1692* (Ithaca, 1974); John C. Rainbolt, *From Prescription to Persuasion: Manipulation of Eighteenth Century Virginia Economy* (Port Washington, N.Y., 1974), 142–71, and "The Absence of Towns in Seventeenth-Century Virginia," *Journal of Southern History* 35 (1969): 343–60; Warren M. Billings, "The Causes of Bacon's Rebellion: Some Suggestions," *Virginia Magazine of History and Biography* 78 (1970): 412–35.

7. Jordan, "Maryland's Privy Council," 80; Charles Wetherell, "'Boom and Bust' in the Colonial Chesapeake Economy," *Journal of Interdisciplinary History* 15 (1984): 185–210; and a series of works by Jacob M. Price: "The Economic Growth of the Chesapeake and the European Market, 1697–1775," *Journal of Economic History* 24 (1964): 496–511; *France and the Chesapeake: A History of the French Tobacco Monopoly, 1674–1791, and of Its Relationship to the British and American Tobacco Trades,* 2 vols. (Ann Arbor, 1973), 1:649–77; "Capital and Credit in the British-Chesapeake Trade, 1750–1775," in Virginia Bever Platt and David Curtis Skaggs, eds., *Of Mother Country and Plantations: Proceedings of the Twenty-Seventh Conference in Early American History* (Bowling Green, Ohio, 1971), 7–36; and *Capital and Credit in British Overseas Trade: The View from the Chesapeake 1700–1776* (Cambridge, Mass., 1980). The figures on trade volume are calculated from Price, *Capital and Credit,* 158–62, and *Historical Statistics of the United States, Colonial Times to 1957* (Washington, 1960), 757.

8. David Klingaman, "The Significance of Grain in the Development of the Tobacco Colonies," *Journal of Economic History* 29 (1969): 268–78, and "The Development of the Coastwise Trade of Virginia in the Late Colonial Period," *Virginia Magazine of History and Biography* 77 (1969): 26–45; Gloria L. Main, *Tobacco Colony: Life in Early Maryland, 1650–1720* (Princeton, 1982), 74–76, and "Maryland and the Chesapeake Economy"; Paul G. E. Clemons, "The Operation of an Eighteenth-Century Chesapeake Tobacco Plantation," *Agricultural History* 49 (1975): 526, "Economy and Society on Maryland's Eastern Shore, 1689–1733," in Land, Carr, and Papenfuse, eds., *Law, Society, and Politics,* 153–170, and *The Atlantic Economy and Colonial Maryland's Eastern Shore: From Tobacco to Grain* (Ithaca, 1980), 111–224; Allan Kulikoff, "The Economic Growth of the Eighteenth-Century Chesapeake Colonies," *Journal of Economic History* 39 (1979): 275–88; Harold B. Gill, Jr., "Wheat Culture in Colonial Virginia," *Agricultural History* 52 (1978): 380–93; Carville V. Earle and Ronald Hoffman, "Staple Crops and Urban Development in the Eighteenth-Century South," *Perspectives in American History* 10 (1976): 28–31.

9. See G. Terry Sharrer, "Flour Milling in the Growth of Baltimore, 1750–1830," *Maryland Historical Magazine* 71 (1976): 322–33; Ronald L. Lewis, *Coal, Iron, and Slaves: Industrial Slavery in Maryland and Virginia, 1715–1865* (Westport, Conn., 1979), 11–14, 243–45, and "The Use and Extent of Slave Labor in the Chesapeake Iron Industry: The Colonial Era," *Labor History* 17 (1977): 388–405; Keach John-

son, "The Genesis of the Baltimore Iron Works," *Journal of Southern History* 19 (1953): 157–79, and "The Baltimore Company Seeks English Markets: A Study of The Anglo-American Iron Trade, 1731–1755," *William and Mary Quarterly* 3d ser., 16 (1959): 37–60; Klingaman, "Development of the Coastwise Trade," 33–35; Earle and Hoffman, "Staple Crops and Urban Development," 26–51; Carville V. Earle, *The Evolution of a Tidewater Settlement System: All Hallow's Parish, Maryland, 1650–1783* (Chicago, 1975), 2–3.

10. *Historical Statistics of the United States*, 756; Robert V. Wells, *The Population of the British Colonies in America before 1776: A Survey of Census Data* (Princeton, 1975), 144–66; Menard, "Maryland Slave Population"; Allan Kulikoff, "A 'Prolifick' People: Black Population Growth in the Chesapeake Colonies, 1700–1790," *Southern Studies* 16 (1977): 391–428. Herbert S. Klein, "Slaves and Shipping in Eighteenth-Century Virginia," *Journal of Interdisciplinary History* 5 (1975): 383–412; Darold D. Wax, "Black Immigrants: The Slave Trade in Colonial Maryland," *Maryland Historical Magazine* 73 (1978): 30–45; Susan Westbury, "Slaves of Colonial Virginia: Where They Came From," *William and Mary Quarterly* 3d ser., 42 (1985): 228–37; Donald M. Sweig, "The Importation of African Slaves to the Potomac River, 1732–1772," ibid., 507–24. Figures for total slave imports were calculated by adding a half (the proportion of Virginia's slave imports imported by Maryland as estimated by Wax, p. 35) of the figures given either by Klein (pp. 384–85) or Westbury (p. 235) to those figures. On the relation between population growth and economic expansion, see the suggestive piece by P. M. G. Harris, "Integrating Interpretations of Local and Regionwide Change in the Study of Economic Development and Demographic Growth in the Colonial Chesapeake, 1630–1775," *Working Papers from the Regional Economic History Research Center* 1 (1978): 35–71.

11. Astonishingly, there is no systematic modern study of the process of westward expansion or land speculation in the Chesapeake colonies. But see Robert D. Mitchell, "American Origins and Regional Institutions: The 17th-Century Chesapeake," *Annals of the Association of American Geographers* 73 (1983): 49, and Richard L. Morton, *Colonial Virginia*, 2 vols. (Chapel Hill, 1960), 2:444–53, 536–98. See also the excellent studies by Robert D. Mitchell, *Commercialism and Frontier: Perspectives on the Early Shenandoah Valley* (Charlottesville, 1977); Sarah S. Hughes, *Surveyors and Statesmen: Land Measuring in Colonial Virginia* (Richmond, 1979); and Richard R. Beeman, *The Evolution of the Southern Backcountry: A Case Study of Lunenburg County, Virginia, 1746–1832* (Philadelphia, 1984). The effects of expansion upon older settled areas are treated in Earle, *Evolution of a Tidewater Settlement*, 53–54, 193–203, and Clemons, *Atlantic Economy*, 161–67. On the activities of land speculators, see the brief remarks in Robert E. Brown and B. Katherine Brown, *Virginia, 1705–1786: Democracy or Aristocracy?* (East Lansing, 1964), 16–19; Aubrey C. Land, "Economic Base and Social Structure: The Northern Chesapeake in the Eighteenth Century," *Journal of Economic History* 25 (1965): 648–49, and "Economic Behavior in a Planting Society: The Eighteenth-Century Chesapeake," *Journal of Southern History* 33 (1967): 479–81; Jackson Turner Main, "The One Hundred," *William and Mary Quarterly* 3d ser., 11 (1954): 354–84.

12. See esp. Clemons, *Atlantic Economy*, 218–19, and Earle and Hoffman, "Staple Crops and Urban Development," 29–32. For evidence that a similar specialization

began to take place within traditional tobacco-growing areas during the early eighteenth century, see Main, "Maryland and the Chesapeake Economy," 141–43.

13. See Daniel Blake Smith, *Inside the Great House: Planter Family Life in Eighteenth-Century Chesapeake Society* (Ithaca, 1980), 150–51, 175–78; Rutman and Rutman, *A Place in Time*, 1:94–127; and Michael Zuckerman, "Fate, Flux, and Good Fellowship: An Early Virginia Design for the Dilemma of American Business," in Harold Sharlin, ed., *The Freedoms of Enterprise: Business and Its Environment* (Westport, Conn., 1983), 161–84.

14. Earle and Hoffman, "Staple Crops and Urban Development," 51–57; Earle, *Evolution of a Tidewater Settlement*, 53–54, 61–91, 142–57, 193–203; Mitchell, *Commercialism and Frontier*, 149–60; Clemons, *Atlantic Economy*, 161–67, and "Operation of an Eighteenth-Century Chesapeake Tobacco Plantation," 527–28; Main, *Tobacco Colony*, 77–78, and "Maryland and the Chesapeake Economy," 142–43; Jean B. Russo, "Free Workers in a Plantation Economy: Talbot County, Maryland, 1690–1759" (Ph.D. dissertation, Johns Hopkins University, 1983); Kulikoff, "Economic Growth," 277–79; Alan F. Day, "A Social Study of Lawyers in Maryland, 1660–1775," 3 vols. (Ph.D. dissertation, Johns Hopkins University, 1976), vol. 1, and "Lawyers in Colonial Maryland, 1660–1715," *American Journal of Legal History* 17 (1973): 145–65; A. G. Roeber, *Faithful Magistrates and Republican Lawyers: Creators of Virginia Legal Culture, 1680–1810* (Chapel Hill, 1981), 32–137; Gwenda Morgan, "The Hegemony of the Law: Richmond County, 1692–1776" (Ph.D. dissertation, Johns Hopkins University, 1980), 183–230.

15. Earle and Hoffman, "Staple Crops and Urban Development," 7–78; Joseph A. Ernst and H. Roy Merrens, "'Camden's turrets pierce the skies!': The Urban Process in the Southern Colonies during the Eighteenth Century," *William and Mary Quarterly* 3d ser., 30 (1973): 569–73. John Reps, *Town Planning in Frontier America* (Columbia, 1980), 73–99, analyzes earlier urban development in the Chesapeake.

16. Land, "Economic Base and Social Structure," 642–54, "Economic Behavior," 472–73, and "The Tobacco Staple and the Planter's Problems: Technology, Labor, and Crops," *Agricultural History* 43 (1969): 79; Brown and Brown, *Virginia*, 13–14, 73–77; Clemons, *Atlantic Economy*, 121, 144–49, 161, "Operation of an Eighteenth-Century Chesapeake Tobacco Plantation," 523–24, and "Economy and Society," 166–67; Earle, *Evolution of a Tidewater Settlement*, 202–14; Gregory A. Stiverson, "Landless Husbandmen: Proprietary Tenants in Maryland in the Late Colonial Period," in Land, Carr, and Papenfuse, eds., *Law, Society, and Politics*, 197–211, and *Poverty in a Land of Plenty: Tenancy in Eighteenth-Century Maryland* (Baltimore, 1977); Kulikoff, "Economic Growth," 280, "The Colonial Chesapeake: Seedbed of Antebellum Southern Culture," *Journal of Southern History* 45 (1979): 513–23, and *Tobacco and Slaves*, 131–41; Mitchell, "American Origins and Regional Institutions," 414–17; Richard R. Beeman, "Social Change and Cultural Conflict in Virginia: Lunenburg County, 1746 to 1776," *William and Mary Quarterly* 3d ser., 35 (1978): 464, and *Evolution of the Southern Backcountry*, 64–66, 172–75; Robert E. Gallman, "Influences on the Distribution of Landholdings in Early North Carolina," *Journal of Economic History* 42 (1982): 549–75.

17. Price, *Capital and Credit*, 158–62; James W. Deen, Jr., "Patterns of Testation: Four Tidewater Counties in Colonial Virginia," *American Journal of Legal History* 16 (1972): 169; Land, "Tobacco Staple," 76–77, and "Economic Base and Social Structure," 653–55; Main, *Tobacco Colony*, 140–266; Russell R. Menard, Lois Green Carr, and Lorena S. Walsh, "A Small Planter's Profits: The Cole Estate and the Growth of the Early Chesapeake Economy," *William and Mary Quarterly* 3d ser., 40 (1983): 171–96; Carr and Walsh, "Inventories and the Analysis of Wealth and Consumption Patterns in St. Mary's County, Maryland, 1658–1777," *Historical Methods* 13 (1980): 81–104; Walsh, "Urban Amenities and Rural Sufficiency: Living Standards and Consumer Behavior in the Colonial Chesapeake, 1643–1777," *Journal of Economic History* 43 (1983): 109–17; Clemons, *Atlantic Economy*, 206; Beeman, *Evolution of the Southern Backcountry*, 66–67, 76–77; Kulikoff, *Tobacco and Slaves*, 141–61; Henry Glassie, *Folk Housing in Middle Virginia* (Knoxville, 1975); Cary Carson, Norman F. Barka, William M. Kelso, Garry Wheeler Stone, and Dell Upton, "Impermanent Architecture in the Southern American Colonies," *Winterthur Portfolio* 16 (1981): 135–96; Stiverson, *Poverty in a Land of Plenty*, 1–55; Howard Mackey, "Social Welfare in Colonial Virginia: The Importance of the English Old Poor Law," *Historical Magazine of the Protestant Episcopal Church* 36 (1967): 357–82; Brown and Brown, *Virginia*, 46–54. That the growth in wealth was not constant over time is argued by Kulikoff, "Economic Growth," 279–80.

18. Menard, Harris, and Carr, "Opportunity and Inequality," 174, 180–84; Menard, "From Servants to Slaves," 388; Gloria L. Main, "Inequality in Early America: The Evidence from Probate Records of Massachusetts and Maryland," *Journal of Interdisciplinary History* 7 (1977): 570–72, "Maryland and the Chesapeake Economy," 144–50, and *Tobacco Colony*, 206–66; Clemons, *Atlantic Economy*, 121–49, "Operation of an Eighteenth-Century Chesapeake Tobacco Plantation," 525–26, and "Economy and Society," 164; Brown and Brown, *Virginia*, 13–14; Earle, *Evolution of a Tidewater Settlement*, 101–41, 220; Stiverson, "Landless Husbandmen," 207–8, and *Poverty in a Land of Plenty*, 143–49; Land, "Economic Base and Social Structure"; Beeman, "Social Change and Cultural Conflict," 464–65; Main, "One Hundred," and "The Distribution of Property in Post-Revolutionary Virginia," *Mississippi Valley Historical Review* 41 (1954): 24–58; Kulikoff, *Tobacco and Slaves*, 131–41.

19. See Rhys Isaac, *The Transformation of Virginia, 1740–1790* (Chapel Hill, 1982), 34–42, 74–79, 58–138; Rutman and Rutman, *A Place in Time*, 1:152–63; Kulikoff, *Tobacco and Slaves*, 261–313; Carr and Walsh, "Inventories," 83–96; Carson, Barka, Kelso, Stone, and Upton, "Impermanent Architecture," 135–96; Wayne M. S. Rasmussen, "Designers, Builders, and Architectural Traditions in Colonial Virginia," *Virginia Magazine of History and Biography* 90 (1982): 198–212; Wayne Craven, "Virginia Portraits: Iconography, Style, and Social Context," ibid. 92 (1984): 201–25; Dell Upton, *Holy Things and Profane: Anglican Parish Churches in Colonial Virginia* (Boston, 1986); Louis B. Wright, *The First Gentlemen of Virginia: Intellectual Qualities of the Early Colonial Ruling Class* (San Marino, Calif., 1940); J. A. Leo Lemay, *Men of Letters in Colonial Maryland* (Knoxville, 1972); Richard Beale Davis, *Intellectual Life in the Colonial South, 1585–1763*, 3 vols. (Knoxville, 1978),

1:352–78, 2:526–79, 3:1147–63, 1173–92, 1212–17, 1229–49; Charles S. Sydnor, *Gentle-men Freeholders: Political Practices in Washington's Virginia* (Chapel Hill, 1952); Lois Green Carr, "The Foundations of Social Order: Local Government in Colonial Maryland," in Bruce C. Daniels, ed., *Town and Country: Essays on the Structure of Local Government in the American Colonies* (Middletown, Conn., 1978), 72–110; Robert Wheeler, "The County Court in Colonial Virginia," in ibid., 111–33; William H. Seiler, "The Anglican Church: A Basic Institution of Local Government in Colonial Virginia," in ibid., 134–59; Roeber, *Faithful Magistrates and Republican Lawyers*, 32–159; Donnel M. Owings, *His Lordship's Patronage: Offices of Profit In Colonial Maryland* (Baltimore, 1953); Morgan, "Hegemony of the Law," 72–230; C. Ray Keim, "Primogeniture and Entail in Colonial Virginia," *William and Mary Quarterly* 3d ser., 25 (1968): 545–86; Joan R. Gunderson and Gwen Victor Gampel, "Married Women's Legal Status in Eighteenth-Century New York and Virginia," ibid. 39 (1982): 114–34. Kenneth A. Lockridge, *The Diary, and Life, of William Byrd II of Virginia, 1674–1744* (Chapel Hill, 1987), and Jack P. Greene, *Landon Carter: An Inquiry into the Personal Values and Social Imperatives of the Eighteenth-Century Virginia Gentry* (Charlottesville, 1967), are two case studies of prominent men who were deeply involved in the effort to create a genteel culture in Virginia.

20. T. H. Breen, "Horses and Gentlemen: The Cultural Significance of Gambling among the Gentry of Virginia," *William and Mary Quarterly* 3d ser., 34 (1977): 239–57; Isaac, *Transformation of Virginia*, 94–114; Jack P. Greene, "Society, Ideology, and Politics: An Analysis of the Political Culture of Mid-Eighteenth-Century Virginia," in Richard M. Jellison, ed., *Society, Freedom, and Conscience* (New York, 1975), 14–57, "*Virtus et Libertas*': Political Culture, Social Change, and the Origins of the American Revolution in Virginia, 1763–1766," in Jeffrey J. Crow and Larry E. Tise, eds., *The Southern Experience in the American Revolution* (Chapel Hill, 1978), 55–65, and "Character, Persona, and Authority: A Study of Alternative Styles of Political Leadership in Revolutionary Virginia," in W. Robert Higgins, ed., *The Revolutionary War in the South: Power, Conflict, and Leadership* (Durham, N.C., 1979), 3–42; Jan Lewis, *The Pursuit of Happiness: Family and Values in Jeffer-son's Virginia* (Cambridge, 1983), 1–39; Sydnor, *Gentlemen Freeholders*; Charles A. Barker, *The Background of the Revolution in Maryland* (New Haven, 1940). See also David Curtis Skaggs, *Roots of Maryland Democracy, 1753–1776* (Westport, Conn., 1973), 13–140; Tommy R. Thompson, "The Court and Country Parties in Eighteenth Century Maryland," *North Dakota Quarterly* 47 (1979): 43–53.

21. Smith, *Inside the Great House*, 25–27, 44–54, 79–81, 124–25, 128–29, 175–230, 243–44, 284–86; Michael Zuckerman, "William Byrd's Family," *Perspectives in American History* 12 (1979): 255–311, "Penmanship Exercises for Saucy Sons: Some Thoughts on the Colonial Southern Family," *South Carolina Historical Magazine* 84 (1983): 152–66, and "Fate, Flux, and Good Fellowship," 173–76; Harold B. Gill, Jr., and George M. Curtis III, "Virginia's Colonial Probate Policies and the Pre-conditions for Economic History," *Virginia Magazine of History and Biography* 87 (1979): 71; Gunderson and Gampel, "Married Women's Legal Status," 114–34; Isaac, *Transformation of Virginia*, 20–21, 70–71, 76–79, 135–36; James M. Gallman, "Determinants of Age of Marriage in Colonial Perquimans County, North Caro-lina," *William and Mary Quarterly* 3d ser., 39 (1982): 176–91; Jan Lewis, "Domestic

Tranquility and the Management of Emotion among the Gentry of Pre-Revolutionary Virginia," ibid., 135–49. See also Kulikoff, *Tobacco and Slaves*, 165–220.

22. Gerald W. Mullin, *Flight and Rebellion: Slave Resistance in Eighteenth-Century Virginia* (New York, 1972), viii, 1–123, 161; Isaac, *Transformation of Virginia*, 30–32, 305–10; Morgan, "Hegemony of the Law," 136–52; Zuckerman, "William Byrd's Family," 279–81; Allan Kulikoff, "The Origins of Afro-American Society in Tidewater Maryland and Virginia, 1700 to 1790," *William and Mary Quarterly* 3d ser., 35 (1978): 226–59, "The Beginnings of the Afro-American Family in Maryland," in Land, Carr, and Papenfuse, eds., *Law, Society, and Politics*, 171–96, "Black Society and the Economics of Slavery," *Maryland Historical Magazine* 70 (1975): 207–8, and *Tobacco and Slaves*, 317–420; Jean Butenhoff Lee, "The Problem of Slave Community in the Eighteenth-Century Chesapeake," *William and Mary Quarterly* 3d ser., 43 (1986): 333–61; Carole Shammas, "Black Women's Work and the Evolution of Plantation Society in Virginia," *Labor History* 26 (1985): 5–28; Andrew Fede, "Legitimized Slave Abuse in the American South, 1619–1865: A Case Study of Law and Social Changes in Six Southern States," *American Journal of Legal History* 29 (1985): 93–150; Michael Anesko, "So Discreet a Zeal: Slavery and the Anglican Church in Virginia, 1680–1730," *Virginia Magazine of History and Biography* 93 (1985): 247–78; Mark J. Stegmaier, "Maryland's Fear of Insurrection at the Time of Braddock's Defeat," *Maryland Historical Magazine* 71 (1976): 467–83; Earle, *Evolution of a Tidewater Settlement*, 160–61; Rutman and Rutman, *A Place in Time*, 1:164–203; Ronald L. Lewis, "Slave Families at Early Chesapeake Ironworks," *Virginia Magazine of History and Biography* 86 (1978): 178–79; Darold D. Wax, "Negro Import Duties in Colonial Virginia: A Study of British Commercial Policy and Local Public Policy," ibid. 79 (1971): 29–44; Michael R. Bradley, "The Role of the Black Church in the Colonial Slave Society," *Louisiana Studies* 14 (1975): 413–21.

23. See Greene, "Society, Ideology, and Politics," 65–75; Breen, "Looking Out for Number One," 359–60; C. Vann Woodward, "The Southern Ethic in a Puritan World," *William and Mary Quarterly* 3d ser., 25 (1968): 343–70; Emory G. Evans, "Planter Indebtedness and the Coming of the Revolution in Virginia," ibid. 19 (1962): 511–33, and "The Rise and Decline of the Virginia Aristocracy in the Eighteenth Century: The Nelsons," in Darrett B. Rutman, ed., *The Old Dominion: Essays for Thomas Perkins Abernathy* (Charlottesville, 1964), 62–78; Zuckerman, "Fate, Flux, and Good Fellowship," 161–84; T. H. Breen, *Tobacco Culture: The Mentality of the Great Tidewater Planters on the Eve of the Revolution* (Princeton, 1985).

24. See Lee A. Gladwin, "Tobacco and Sex: Some Factors Affecting Non-Marital Sexual Behavior in Colonial Virginia," *Journal of Social History* 12 (1978): 57–75; Beeman, "Social Change and Cultural Conflict," 468; Morgan, "Hegemony of the Law," 231–84.

25. Isaac, *Transformation of Virginia*, 59–68, 120–21, 154–57, 161–77; J. Stephen Kroll-Smith, "Transmitting a Revival Culture: The Organizational Dynamic of the Baptist Movement in Colonial Virginia, 1760–1777," *Journal of Southern History* 50 (1984): 551–68; Joan R. Gunderson, "The Search for Good Men: Recruiting Ministers in Colonial Virginia," *Historical Magazine of the Protestant Episcopal Church* 48 (1979): 453–64; James P. Walsh, " 'Black Cotted Raskells': Anti-Anglican

Criticism in Colonial Virginia," *Virginia Magazine of History and Biography* 88 (1980): 21–36; Nelson Rightmeyer, *Maryland's Established Church* (Austin, 1957); Greene, "Society, Ideology, and Politics," 65–75, and "'*Virtus et Libertas*,'" 55–65.

26. See Michael Greenberg, "William Byrd II and the World of the Market," *Southern Studies* 16 (1977): 429–56; Woodward, "Southern Ethic," 355; Land, "Economic Behavior," 471–72; Clemons, *Atlantic Economy*, 164–65, 222–23; Douglas Greenberg, "The Middle Colonies in Recent American Historiography," *William and Mary Quarterly* 3d ser., 36 (1979): 422–23; Breen, "Changing Labor Force," 4; Zuckerman, "Fate, Flux, and Good Fellowship," 161–84; Douglas R. Littlefield, "Eighteenth-Century Plans to Clear the Potomac River," *Virginia Magazine of History and Biography* 93 (1985): 291–322.

27. Harold J. Perkin, *The Origins of Modern English Society, 1780-1880* (London, 1969), 17–62; Clemons, *Atlantic Economy*, 166–67; Kulikoff, "Colonial Chesapeake," 536; Breen, "Looking Out for Number One," 359–60.

CHAPTER FIVE

1. See Roy Porter, *English Society in the Eighteenth Century* (New York, 1982), 25, 56–58, 61–62.

2. See E. A. Wrigley, "Marriage, Fertility and Population Growth in Eighteenth-Century England," in R. B. Outhwaite, ed., *Marriage and Society: Studies in the Social History of Marriage* (London, 1981), 137–41, and E. A. Wrigley and R. S. Schofield, *The Population History of England, 1541-1871* (Cambridge, Mass., 1981), 160–215.

3. Peter Clark, "Migration in England during the Late Seventeenth and Early Eighteenth Centuries," *Past and Present*, no. 83 (1979): 57–90; John Wareing, "Migration to London and Transatlantic Emigration of Indentured Servants, 1683–1775," *Journal of Historical Geography* 7 (1981): 356–78; John Patten, *Rural-Urban Migration in Pre-Industrial England* (Oxford, 1973); Porter, *English Society*, 52–53, 159, 171.

4. Lawrence Stone, "The New Eighteenth Century," *New York Review of Books* 31 (Mar. 29, 1984): 44; John Cannon, "The Isthmus Repaired: The Resurgence of the Aristocracy, 1660–1760," *Proceedings of the British Academy* 68 (1982): 431–53; J. P. Cooper, "Social Distribution of Land and Men in England, 1436–1700," *Economic History Review* 2d ser., 20 (1967): 419–40; Christopher Clay, "Marriage, Inheritance, and the Rise of Large Estates in England, 1660–1815," ibid. 21 (1968): 503–18, and "Property Settlements, Financial Provisions for the Family, and Sale of Land by the Great Landowners," *Journal of British Studies* 21 (1981): 18–38; G. E. Mingay, *English Landed Society in the Eighteenth Century* (London, 1963), 19–107, 259–63; Porter, *English Society*, 69, 81–84; Lawrence Stone and Jeanne C. Fawtier Stone, *An Open Elite? England, 1540–1880* (Oxford, 1984).

5. Porter, *English Society*, 62, 98–112, 148, 160; Stone, "New Eighteenth Century," 44; Harold J. Perkin, "The Social Causes of the British Industrial Revolution," *Transactions of the Royal Historical Society* 5th ser., 18 (1968): 127, and *The Origins of Modern English Society, 1780-1880* (London, 1969), 19–22; Peter Mathias, *The Trans-*

formation of England: Essays in the Economic and Social History of England in the Eighteenth Century (London, 1979), 186–89; James Walvin, *The Black Presence: A Documentary History of the Negro in England, 1555–1860* (London, 1971), 12–31. See also Robert W. Malcolmson, *Life and Labour in England, 1700–1780* (London, 1981).

6. Porter, *English Society*, 64, 67; Perkin, *Origins of Modern English Society*, 17, 24–25, 49, and "Social Causes of the British Industrial Revolution," 129; Stone and Stone, *Open Elite*, 412–19; E. P. Thompson, "Patrician Society, Plebeian Culture," *Journal of Social History* 7 (1974): 387, and "Eighteenth-Century English Society: Class Struggle without Class?" *Social History* 3 (1978): 136–37.

7. Porter, *English Society*, 17, 129, 141, 358; J. C. D. Clark, *English Society, 1688–1832* (Cambridge, 1985), 68; J. H. Plumb, *The Origins of Political Stability in England, 1675–1725* (Boston, 1967); W. A. Speck, *The Divided Society: Party Conflict in England, 1694–1716* (New York, 1968); Cannon, "Isthmus Repaired," 440–50.

8. Porter, *English Society*, 301, 358; Thompson, "Patrician Society, Plebeian Culture," 387.

9. Perkin, "Social Causes of the British Industrial Revolution," 136–37; Porter, *English Society*, 16, 362.

10. Porter, *English Society*, 64–65, 149, 359; Stone and Stone, *Open Elite*, 402–3, 407–8, 415; Perkin, "Social Causes of the British Industrial Revolution," 127, 136–57.

11. Porter, *English Society*, 17, 59–60, 73, 379; Stone and Stone, *Open Elite*, 400–403, 420.

12. Thompson, "Eighteenth-Century English Society," 139; Porter, *English Society*, 201–22, 358; A. H. John, "War and the English Economy, 1700–1763," *Economic History Review* 2d ser., 7 (1955): 329–44; Neil McKendrick, John Brewer, and J. H. Plumb, *The Birth of a Consumer Society: The Commercialization of Eighteenth-Century England* (Bloomington, Ind., 1982), 1–33.

13. E. L. Jones, "Agriculture and Economic Growth in England, 1660–1750: Agricultural Change," *Journal of Economic History* 25 (1965): 1–18; A. H. John, "Agricultural Productivity and Economic Growth in England, 1700–1760," ibid., 19–34, and "The Course of Agricultural Change, 1660–1760," in L. S. Presnell, ed., *Studies in the Industrial Revolution* (London, 1960), 122–55; H. C. Darby, "The Age of the Improver, 1600–1800," in Darby, ed., *A New Historical Geography of England* (Cambridge, 1973), 302–88; M. W. Flinn, "The Growth of the English Iron Industry, 1660–1760," *Economic History Review* 2d ser., 11 (1958–59): 144–53; Charles Wilson and Bruce Lenman, "The British Isles," in Charles Wilson and Geoffrey Parker, eds., *An Introduction to the Sources of European Economic History* (Ithaca, 1977), 115–54; Porter, *English Society*, 205–23.

14. Stone, "New Eighteenth Century," 44; Stone and Stone, *Open Elite*, 408–9, 411, 419; Porter, *English Society*, 92–97, 240; Perkin, "Social Causes of the British Industrial Revolution," 128; Geoffrey Holmes, *Augustan England: Professions, State and Society, 1680–1730* (London, 1982); Michael Reed, *The Georgian Triumph, 1700–1800* (London, 1983), 50–174; McKendrick, Brewer, and Plumb, *Birth of a Consumer Society*, 34–202, 265–85.

15. P. J. Corfield, *The Impact of English Towns, 1700–1800* (Oxford, 1982), 7–145, 168–85; Peter Clark, ed., *The Transformation of English Provincial Towns, 1600–1800*

(London, 1984); Reed, *Georgian Triumph*, 143–74; R. S. Neale, *Bath, 1680–1850: A Social History* (London, 1981); Nicholas Rogers, "Money, Land and Lineage: The Big Bourgeoisie of Hanoverian London," *Social History* 4 (1979): 437–54; Porter, *English Society*, 53–61, 225; Stone and Stone, *Open Elite*, 403–4; Stone, "New Eighteenth Century," 44–46.

16. Porter, *English Society*, 114–20, 218, 223, 328; Derek Jarrett, *England in the Age of Hogarth* (London, 1974), 12–63, 86–113, 172–234; Stone, "New Eighteenth Century," 45–46; J. M. Beattie, "The Pattern of Crime in England, 1660–1800," *Past and Present*, no. 62 (1974): 47–95; E. A. Wrigley, "The Growth of Population in Eighteenth-Century England: A Conundrum Resolved," ibid., no. 98 (1983): 121–50, and "Marriage, Fertility and Population Growth," 137–85.

17. Porter, *English Society*, 232, 260–68, 287, 292, 302–7, 365.

18. Thompson, "Patrician Society, Plebeian Culture," 390–91; Porter, *English Society*, 184–98, 275. For a contrary assessment of the English religious climate, see Clark, *English Society*, esp. 119–89.

19. Porter, *English Society*, 118–20, 149–58, 164, 283, 328; Stone and Stone, *Open Elite*, 413–14; Stone, "New Eighteenth Century," 46–47; Robert W. Malcolmson, *Popular Recreations in English Society, 1700–1850* (Cambridge, 1973), 70–71, 158–59.

20. Porter, *English Society*, 275–76, 328; Lawrence Stone, *The Family, Sex and Marriage in England, 1500–1800* (London, 1977), 145–46, 149–299.

21. Karl S. Bottigheimer, "The Restoration Land Settlement in Ireland," *Irish Historical Studies* 18 (1972): 1–21; T. W. Moody, F. X. Martin, and F. J. Byrne, eds., *A New History of Ireland*, Vol. 3, *Early Modern Ireland, 1534–1691* (Oxford, 1976), 426–29, 453, and Vol. 4, *Eighteenth-Century Ireland, 1691–1800* (Oxford, 1985), xlviii–xlix, liv, 34, 38, 237; S. J. Connolly, "Religion and History," *Irish Economic and Social History* 10 (1983): 76–79.

22. L. M. Cullen, *The Emergence of Modern Ireland, 1600–1900* (London, 1981), 83–88; Moody et al., *New History of Ireland*, 4:xliv, 34.

23. Cullen, *Emergence of Modern Ireland*, 25, 29, 55, 83, 91, 95–96; Moody et al., *New History of Ireland*, 3:388, 391, 4:161. See also K. H. Connell, "Land and Population in Ireland, 1780–1845," *Economic History Review* 2d ser., 2 (1950): 278–89, and W. Macafee and V. Morgan, "Population in Ulster, 1660–1760," in Peter Roebuck, ed., *Plantation to Partition: Essays in Ulster History in Honour of J. L. McCracken* (Belfast, 1981), 46–63. See also Michael Drake, "The Irish Demographic Crisis of 1740–41," *Historical Studies* 6 (1968): 104–64, and "Marriage and Population Growth in Ireland, 1750–1845," *Economic History Review* 2d ser., 16 (1963): 301–13, for an alternative explanation of the sources of Irish population growth.

24. Cullen, *Emergence of Modern Ireland*, 15–16, *An Economic History of Ireland since 1660* (London, 1972), 68, 80, "Problems in the Interpretation and Revision of Eighteenth-Century Irish Economic History," *Transactions of the Royal Historical Society* 5th ser., 17 (1967): 19, and "Incomes, Social Classes and Economic Growth in Ireland and Scotland, 1600–1900," in T. M. Devine and David Dickson, eds., *Ireland and Scotland, 1600–1850* (Edinburgh, 1983), 251–55; Moody et al., *New History of Ireland*, 3:441–42, 4:130.

25. Cullen, *Emergence of Modern Ireland*, 39, and *Economic History of Ireland*, 11–25, 53–66; Moody et al., *New History of Ireland*, 3:390–91, 4:248; Francis G. James,

"Irish Colonial Trade in the Eighteenth Century," *William and Mary Quarterly* 3d ser., 20 (1963): 574–84, and *Ireland in the Empire, 1688–1770: A History of Ireland from the Williamite Wars to the Eve of the American Revolution* (Cambridge, Mass., 1973), 198–207; R. C. Nash, "Irish Atlantic Trade in the Seventeenth and Eighteenth Centuries," *William and Mary Quarterly* 3d ser., 42 (1985): 329–56. On the dimensions of the smuggling trade, see Cullen, "The Smuggling Trade in the Eighteenth Century," *Proceedings of the Royal Irish Academy* 67 (1969): 149–75.

26. Cullen, *Emergence of Modern Ireland*, 29, 93–94, and *Economic History of Ireland*, 18–19, 65, 73, 87–89; James, *Ireland in the Empire*, 198–207; Moody et al., *New History of Ireland*, 4:151–58; G. Kirkham, "Economic Diversification in a Marginal Economy: A Case Study," in Roebuck, ed., *Plantation to Partition*, 64–81; Patrick O'Flanagan, "Settlement Development and Trading in Ireland, 1600–1800," in Devine and Dickson, eds., *Ireland and Scotland*, 146–50.

27. Cullen, *Emergence of Modern Ireland*, 17, 98–99; James, *Ireland in the Empire*, 225, 232.

28. Moody et al., *New History of Ireland*, 4:166–68, 236; Cullen, *Emergence of Modern Ireland*, 35–36, 49, and *Economic History of Ireland*, 20; W. H. Crawford, "The Influence of the Landlord in Eighteenth-Century Ulster," in L. M. Cullen and T. C. Smout, eds., *Comparative Aspects of Scottish and Irish Economic History, 1600–1900* (Edinburgh, 1977), 193–203, and "Landlord-Tenant Relations in Ulster, 1609–1820," *Irish Economic and Social History* 7 (1975): 5–21.

29. Moody et al., *New History of Ireland*, 4:36, 167; Cullen, *Emergence of Modern Ireland*, 41, 45–46, *Economic History of Ireland*, 44–45, 83, and "Problems in the Interpretation," 17; A. P. W. Malcolmson, "Absenteeism in Eighteenth Century Ireland," *Irish Economic and Social History* 1 (1974): 15–35.

30. Cullen, *Emergence of Modern Ireland*, 13, 15, 23, 29, 41–44, 47–48, 61–78, 98–99, 172, 204; Moody et al., *New History of Ireland*, 4:44–46, 177–80, 471–88, 499–508; D. G. Lockhart, "Planned Village Development in Scotland and Ireland, 1700–1850," in Devine and Dickson, eds., *Ireland and Scotland*, 132–45.

31. Cullen, *Emergence of Modern Ireland*, 17, 21–22, 41, 46, 98–101; Moody et al., *New History of Ireland*, 4:173–77.

32. Moody et al., *New History of Ireland*, 3:150, 169–70, 4:50; Cullen, *Emergence of Modern Ireland*, 15, 17, 40, 89–93, and *Economic History of Ireland*, 22–23; James, *Ireland in the Empire*, 223.

33. Cullen, *Emergence of Modern Ireland*, 16, 41, 115; James, *Ireland in the Empire*, 229; Moody et al., *New History of Ireland*, 4:lviii–lix.

34. Cullen, *Emergence of Modern Ireland*, 13, 29, and *Economic History of Ireland*, 84–86; Moody et al., *New History of Ireland*, 3:390, 451–53, 4:44–45, 49–50, 181–82, 261; David Dickson, "The Place of Dublin in the Eighteenth-Century Irish Economy," in Devine and Dickson, eds., *Ireland and Scotland*, 177–92.

35. Moody et al., *New History of Ireland*, 3:453, 4:lvii, 43–53, 130, 180, 466–67; Cullen, *Emergence of Modern Ireland*, 13, 21–22, 88–93.

CHAPTER SIX

1. On the appropriateness of the Middle Colonies as an analytical category, see Patricia U. Bonomi, "The Middle Colonies: Embryo of the New Political Order," in Alden T. Vaughan and George Athan Billias, eds., *Perspectives on Early American History: Essays in Honor of Richard B. Morris* (New York, 1973), 63–94; Douglas Greenberg, "The Middle Colonies in Recent American Historiography," *William and Mary Quarterly* 3d ser., 36 (1979): 396–427; Michael Zuckerman, "Introduction: Puritans, Cavaliers, and the Motley Middle," in Zuckerman, ed., *Friends and Neighbors: Group Life in America's First Plural Society* (Philadelphia, 1982), 3–25; and Robert J. Gough, "The Myth of the 'Middle Colonies': An Analysis of Regionalization in Early America," *Pennsylvania Magazine of History and Biography* 103 (1983): 392–419.

2. John J. McCusker and Russell R. Menard, *The Economy of British America, 1607–1789* (Chapel Hill, 1985), 202–3, 218–26, 228–29; Robert V. Wells, *The Population of the British Colonies in America before 1776: A Survey of Census Data* (Princeton, 1975), 110–43; Ian C. C. Graham, *Colonists from Scotland: Emigration to North America, 1707–1783* (Ithaca, 1956); Audrey Lockhart, *Some Aspects of Emigration from Ireland to the North American Colonies between 1660 and 1775* (New York, 1976); R. J. Dickson, *Ulster Immigration to Colonial America, 1718–1775* (London, 1966); Marianne Wokeck, "The Flow and the Composition of German Immigration to Philadelphia, 1727–1775," *Pennsylvania Magazine of History and Biography* 105 (1981): 249–78.

3. McCusker and Menard, *Economy of British America*, 198; Duane E. Ball and Gary M. Walton, "Agricultural Productivity Change in Eighteenth-Century Pennsylvania," *Journal of Economic History* 36 (1976): 102, 110, 114; James T. Lemon, "Household Consumption in Eighteenth-Century America and Its Relationship to Production and Trade: The Situation among Farmers in Southeastern Pennsylvania," *Agricultural History* 16 (1967): 60.

4. McCusker and Menard, *Economy of British America*, 198–99, 202–3.

5. Peter O. Wacker, *Land and People: A Cultural Geography of Preindustrial New Jersey: Origins and Settlement Patterns* (New Brunswick, 1975), 399–403; James T. Lemon, *The Best Poor Man's Country: A Geographical Study of Early Southeastern Pennsylvania* (Baltimore, 1972), 98, 150–51, 167, 180, 220–21; Ball and Walton, "Agricultural Productivity Change," 105–6. By the mid-1770s in some areas, average acreages may have fallen to a point at which many farmers did not have sufficient land to support themselves comfortably. See Dennis P. Ryan, "Landholding, Opportunity, and Mobility in Revolutionary New Jersey," *William and Mary Quarterly* 3d ser., 36 (1979): 571–78.

6. Lemon, *Best Poor Man's Country*, 30, 40, 43, 49, 51–55, 62, 65, 89–90, 144; Wacker, *Land and People*, 301–3, 321; Sung Bok Kim, *Landlord and Tenant in Colonial New York: Manorial Society, 1664–1775* (Chapel Hill, 1978), 4–43; William Chazanof, "Land Speculation in Eighteenth-Century New York," in Joseph R. Frese and Jacob Judd, eds., *Business Enterprise in Early New York* (Tarrytown, N.Y., 1979), 55–76.

7. Kim, *Landlord and Tenant*, vii, 87–128; Gough, "Myth of the 'Middle Colonies,'" 408.

8. Kim, *Landlord and Tenant*, vii, 129–280.

9. Ibid., 161, 235–415.

10. Ned C. Landsman, *Scotland and Its First American Colony, 1683–1765* (Princeton, 1985), 128–30, 144, 196–98, 214, 218–19, 223–24; Lucy Simler, "The Township: The Community of the Rural Pennsylvanian," *Pennsylvania Magazine of History and Biography* 106 (1982): 67–68, and, esp., "Tenancy in Colonial Pennsylvania: The Case of Chester County," *William and Mary Quarterly* 3d ser., 43 (1986): 542–69.

11. James G. Lydon, "Philadelphia's Commercial Expansion, 1720–1739," *Pennsylvania Magazine of History and Biography* 91 (1967): 401–18, and "New York and the Slave Trade, 1700 to 1774," *William and Mary Quarterly* 3d ser., 35 (1978): 375–94; Darold D. Wax, "Africans on the Delaware: The Pennsylvania Slave Trade, 1759–1765," *Pennsylvania History* 50 (1983): 38–49; Arthur L. Jensen, *The Maritime Commerce of Colonial Philadelphia* (Madison, 1963), 42–106; Thomas M. Doerflinger, "Commercial Specialization in Philadelphia's Merchant Community, 1750–1791," *Business History Review* 57 (1983): 47–49, and *A Vigorous Spirit of Enterprise: Merchants and Economic Development in Revolutionary Philadelphia* (Chapel Hill, 1986), 1–134; John F. Walzer, "Colonial Philadelphia and Its Backcountry," *Winterthur Portfolio* 7 (1972): 161–73; David E. Dauer, "Colonial Philadelphia's Intraregional Transportation System: An Overview," *Working Papers from the Regional Economic History Research Center* 2 (1979): 1–16, and "The Hinterland Commercial System and the Port of Philadelphia: Business Development in Colonial America" (Ph.D. dissertation, Johns Hopkins University, 1986).

12. James H. Levitt, *For Want of Trade: Shipping and the New Jersey Ports, 1680–1783* (Newark, 1981), 21–44, 57–75, 107–38; Bruce M. Wilkenfeld, "The New York City Shipowning Community, 1715–1764," *American Neptune* 37 (1977): 50–65; Doerflinger, "Commercial Specialization," 24–26, 48–49; William I. Davisson and Lawrence J. Bradley, "New York Maritime Trade: Ship Voyage Patterns, 1715–1765," *New-York Historical Society Quarterly* 55 (1971): 309–17; Philip L. White, *The Beekmans of New York in Politics and Commerce, 1647–1877* (New York, 1956), 533–49; McCusker and Menard, *Economy of British America*, 194–97; Marc Egnal, "The Changing Structure of Philadelphia's Trade with the West Indies, 1750–1775," *Pennsylvania Magazine of History and Biography* 99 (1975): 156–79.

13. Lydon, "Philadelphia's Commercial Expansion," 405; McCusker and Menard, *Economy of British America*, 191–92; Wilkenfeld, "New York City Shipowning Community," 62; John J. McCusker, "Sources of Investment Capital in the Colonial Philadelphia Shipping Industry," *Journal of Economic History* 32 (1972): 146–57; Simeon J. Crowther, "The Shipbuilding Output of the Delaware Valley, 1722–1776," *Proceedings of the American Philosophical Society* 117 (1973): 90–104.

14. McCusker and Menard, *Economy of British America*, 198–99; Paul F. Paskoff, *Industrial Evolution: Organization, Structure, and Growth of the Pennsylvania Iron Industry, 1750–1860* (Baltimore, 1983); Arthur C. Bining, "The Iron Plantations of Early Pennsylvania," *Pennsylvania Magazine of History and Biography* 57 (1933): 117–37, and "Early Ironmasters of Pennsylvania," *Pennsylvania History* 18 (1951): 93–103; Irene D. Neu, "The Iron Plantations of Colonial New York," *New York History* 33 (1952): 3–24, and "Hudson Valley Extractive Industries before 1815," in Frese and Judd, eds., *Business Enterprise in Early New York*, 133–65; Theodore W. Kury, "Iron

as a Factor in New Jersey Settlement," *New Jersey History Symposium Papers* 2 (1971): 63–76; Edward S. Rutsch, "The Colonial Plantation Settlement Pattern in New Jersey: Iron and Agricultural Examples," ibid., 5 (1973): 11–23.

15. Sharon V. Salinger, "Colonial Labor in Transition: The Decline of Indentured Servitude in Late Eighteenth-Century Philadelphia," *Labor History* 22 (1981): 165–91; Farley Grubb, "The Incidence of Servitude in Trans-Atlantic Migration, 1771–1804," *Explorations in Economic History* 22 (1985): 316–39, "Immigrant Servant Labor: Their Occupational and Geographic Distribution in the Late Eighteenth-Century Mid-Atlantic Economy," *Social Science History* 9 (1985): 249–75, and "The Market for Indentured Immigrants: Evidence on the Efficiency of Forward-Labor Contracting in Philadelphia, 1745–1773," *Journal of Economic History* 45 (1985): 855–68; Robert O. Heavner, "Indentured Servitude: The Philadelphia Market, 1771–1773," ibid. 38 (1978): 701–13.

16. "Estimated Population of the American Colonies, 1610–1780," in Jack P. Greene, ed., *Settlements to Society, 1584–1763: A Documentary History of the American Colonies* (New York, 1966), 238–39; Edgar J. McManus, *A History of Negro Slavery in New York* (Syracuse, 1970), 197–99, and *Black Bondage in the North* (Syracuse, 1973), 207–14; Wacker, *Land and People*, 190; Gary B. Nash, *The Urban Crucible: Social Change, Political Consciousness, and the Origins of the American Revolution* (Cambridge, Mass., 1979), 107–10; Thomas J. Davis, *A Rumor of Revolt: The "Great Negro Plot" in Colonial New York* (New York, 1985), ix; Grubb, "Immigrant Servant Labor," 254; Simon F. Moss, "The Persistence of Slavery and Involuntary Servitude in a Free State (1685–1866)," *Journal of Negro History* 35 (1950): 293–94, 310–11; Frances D. Pingeon, "Slavery in New Jersey on the Eve of Revolution," in William C. Wright, ed., *New Jersey in the American Revolution: Political and Social Conflict* (Trenton, 1974), 48–64; Gary B. Nash, "Slaves and Slaveowners in Colonial Philadelphia," *William and Mary Quarterly* 3d ser., 30 (1973): 231–37; Jean R. Soderlund, "Black Women in Colonial Pennsylvania," *Pennsylvania Magazine of History and Biography* 103 (1983): 52, and *Quakers and Slavery: A Divided Spirit* (Princeton, 1985), 57–59, 75.

17. Rutsch, "Colonial Plantation Settlement Pattern," 18; Wacker, *Land and People*, 191, 200; Moss, "Persistence of Slavery," 290; Joseph E. Walker, "Negro Labor in the Charcoal Industry of Southeastern Pennsylvania," *Pennsylvania Magazine of History and Biography* 93 (1969): 466–86; Lydon, "New York and the Slave Trade," 387; Wax, "Africans on the Delaware," 38, 41; Alan Tully, "Patterns of Slaveholding in Colonial Pennsylvania: Chester and Lancaster Counties, 1729–1758," *Journal of Social History* 6 (1973): 284–305; Soderlund, *Quakers and Slavery*, 64, 70, 80.

18. Lydon, "New York and the Slave Trade," 375–94; Darold D. Wax, "Quaker Merchants and the Slave Trade in Colonial Philadelphia," *Pennsylvania Magazine of History and Biography* 86 (1962): 143–59, "Negro Imports into Pennsylvania, 1720–1766," *Pennsylvania History* 32 (1965): 254–87, "The Demand for Slave Labor in Colonial Pennsylvania," ibid. 34 (1967): 331–45, and "Africans on the Delaware," 38–49.

19. Jessica Kross, *The Evolution of an American Town: Newtown, New York, 1642–1775* (Philadelphia, 1983), 231–33; Lydon, "New York and the Slave Trade," 387; Wax, "Demand for Slave Labor," 334, and "Quaker Merchants and the Slave Trade,"

143–45, 159; Soderland, *Quakers and Slavery*, 75, 87–187, and "Black Women in Colonial Pennsylvania," 52; Grubb, "Immigrant Servant Labor," 272; A. J. Williams-Myers, "Hands That Picked No Cotton: An Exporatory Examination of African Slave Labor in the Colonial Economy of the Hudson River Valley to 1800," *Afro-Americans in New York Life and History* 11(1987): 25–53.

20. Wax, "Demand for Slave Labor," 334–36; Soderlund, *Quakers and Slavery*, 64–65, 74–75; Nash, "Slaves and Slaveowners in Colonial Philadelphia," 242–45, and *Urban Crucible*, 320; Tully, "Patterns of Slaveholding in Colonial Pennsylvania," 294.

21. Wax, "Africans on the Delaware," 44–45; Soderlund, "Black Women in Colonial Philadelphia," 49–68; Merle G. Brouwer, "Marriage and Family Life among Blacks in Colonial Pennsylvania," *Pennsylvania Magazine of History and Biography* 99 (1975): 368–72.

22. Wax, "Quaker Merchants and the Slave Trade," 143–59; Soderlund, *Quakers and Slavery*, 54–187; Carl Nordstrom, "The New York Slave Code," *Afro-Americans in New York Life and History* 1 (1980): 7–25; McManus, *History of Negro Slavery in New York*, 59–140, and *Black Bondage in the North*, 85–159; Kenneth Scott, "The Slave Insurrection in New York in 1712," *New-York Historical Quarterly* 45 (1961): 43–74; Davis, *Rumor of Revolt*, passim; T. Wood Clarke, "The Negro Plot of 1741," *New York History* 25 (1941): 167–81; Ferenc M. Szasz, "The New York Slave Revolt of 1741: A Re-examination," ibid. 48 (1967): 215–30.

23. Billy G. Smith, "Death and Life in a Colonial Immigrant City: A Demographic Analysis of Philadelphia," *Journal of Economic History* 37 (1977): 863–89; Nash, *Urban Crucible*, 102–3, 120, 179, 194, 313; Gary B. Nash and Billy G. Smith, "The Population of Eighteenth-Century Philadelphia," *Pennsylvania Magazine of History and Biography* 99 (1975): 362–68; John K. Alexander, "The Philadelphia Numbers Game: An Analysis of Philadelphia's Eighteenth-Century Population," ibid. 98 (1974): 314–24; Sharon V. Salinger and Charles Wetherell, "A Note on the Population of Pre-Revolutionary Philadelphia," ibid. 109 (1985): 369–86; McCusker and Menard, *Economy of British America*, 187, 203; James T. Lemon, "Urbanization and the Development of Eighteenth-Century Southeastern Pennsylvania and Adjacent Delaware," *William and Mary Quarterly* 3d ser., 24 (1967): 501–42; Richard Pillsbury, "The Urban Street Pattern as a Culture Indicator: Pennsylvania, 1682–1815," *Annals of the Association of American Geographers* 60 (1970): 428–46; John A. Munroe, *Colonial Delaware: A History* (New York, 1978), 153–60; John E. Pomfret, *Colonial New Jersey: A History* (New York, 1973), 196–202; Michael Kammen, *Colonial New York: A History* (New York, 1975), 293–94; Laura L. Becker, "The People and the System: Legal Activities in a Colonial Pennsylvania Town," *Pennsylvania Magazine of History and Biography* 105 (1981): 136.

24. Lemon, *Best Poor Man's Country*, 7–8, 141, and "Urbanization," 527–28; Lydon, "Philadelphia's Commercial Expansion," 417; Jacob M. Price, "Economic Function and the Growth of American Port Towns in the Eighteenth Century," *Perspectives in American History* 8 (1974): 123–86; Duane E. Ball, "Dynamics of Population and Wealth in Eighteenth-Century Chester County, Pennsylvania," *Journal of Interdisciplinary History* 6 (1976): 621–44; Alan Tully, "Economic Opportunity in Mid-Eighteenth Century Rural Pennsylvania," *Histoire Sociale* 9 (1976): 11–

28; Stephanie Grauman Wolf, *Urban Village: Population, Community, and Family Structure in Germantown, Pennsylvania, 1683–1800* (Princeton, 1976), 104–11, and "Artisans and the Occupational Structure of an Industrial Town: 18th-Century Germantown, Pa.," *Working Papers from the Regional Economic History Research Center* 1 (1977): 33–56; Milton M. Klein, "From Community to Status: The Development of the Legal Profession in Colonial New York," *New York History* 60 (1979): 133–56; Kross, *Evolution of an American Town*, 215–16; Laura L. Becker, "Diversity and Its Significance in an Eighteenth-Century Pennsylvania Town," in Zuckerman, ed., *Friends and Neighbors*, 198, 215.

25. McCusker and Menard, *Economy of British America*, 271; Raymond A. Mohl, "Poverty in Early America, a Reappraisal," *New York History* 50 (1969): 5–27; Gary B. Nash, "Up from the Bottom in Franklin's Philadelphia," *Past and Present*, no. 77 (1977): 57–83, "Urban Wealth and Poverty in Pre-Revolutionary America," *Journal of Interdisciplinary History* 6 (1976): 545–84, and "Poverty and Poor Relief in Pre-Revolutionary Philadelphia," *William and Mary Quarterly* 3d ser., 33 (1976): 3–30; Billy G. Smith, "The Material Lives of Laboring Philadelphians, 1750 to 1800," ibid. 38 (1981): 162–202, and "Inequality in Late Colonial Philadelphia: A Note on Its Nature and Growth," ibid. 41 (1984): 537–65; Sharon V. Salinger and Charles Wetherell, "Wealth and Renting in Prerevolutionary Philadelphia," *Journal of American History* 71 (1985): 826–40; Frederick B. Tolles, *Meeting House and Counting House: The Quaker Merchants of Colonial Philadelphia* (Chapel Hill, 1948), 109–43; Stephen J. Brobeck, "Revolutionary Change in Colonial Philadelphia: The Brief Life of the Proprietary Gentry," *William and Mary Quarterly* 3d ser., 30 (1976): 410–34; Bruce M. Wilkenfeld, "New York City Neighborhoods, 1730," *New York History* 67 (1976): 165–82; Carl Abbott, "The Neighborhoods of New York, 1760–1775," ibid. 55 (1974): 35–54.

26. See Thomas L. Purvis, "'High-Born, Long-Recorded Families': Social Origins of New Jersey Assemblymen, 1703 to 1776," *William and Mary Quarterly* 3d ser., 37 (1980): 592–95; Sung Bok Kim, "A New Look at the Great Landlords of Eighteenth-Century New York," ibid. 27 (1970): 581–614; Alice Hanson Jones, "Wealth Estimates for the American Middle Colonies, 1774," *Economic Development and Cultural Change* 18 (1970): 54, "La fortune privée en Pennsylvanie, New Jersey, Delaware (1774)," *Annales* 24, pt. 1 (1969): 235–49, and *The Wealth of a Nation to Be: The American Colonies on the Eve of the Revolution* (New York, 1980), 164–65, 185; McCusker and Menard, *Economy of British America*, 206.

27. Lemon, *Best Poor Man's Country*, xiii; Lemon and Gary B. Nash, "The Distribution of Wealth in Eighteenth-Century America," *Journal of Social History* 2 (1968): 1–24; Ball, "Dynamics of Population and Wealth," 621–44; "Value of Exports to, and Imports from, England, 1697–1776," in Greene, ed., *Settlements to Society*, 274–75; Jack Michel, "'In a Manner and Fashion Suitable to Their Degree': A Preliminary Investigation of the Material Culture of Early Rural Pennsylvania," *Working Papers from the Regional Economic History Research Center* 5 (1981): 1–83; Tolles, *Meeting House and Counting House*, 109–229; Munroe, *Colonial Delaware*, 169–84; Joseph E. Illick, *Colonial Pennsylvania: A History* (New York, 1976), 137–63; Pomfret, *Colonial New Jersey*, 218–46; Kammen, *Colonial New York*, 242–77.

28. Edward H. Tebbenhoff, "Tacit Rules and Hidden Family Structure: Naming

Practices and Godparentage in Schenectady, New York, 1680–1800," *Journal of Social History* 18 (1985): 583; Greenberg, "Middle Colonies in Recent American Historiography," 425; Gillian Lindt Gollin, *Moravians in Two Worlds: A Study of Changing Communities* (New York, 1967); Landsman, *Scotland and Its First American Colony*; David E. Narrett, "Preparation for Death and Provision for the Living: Notes on New York Wills (1665–1760)," *New York History* 57 (1976): 417–37; Daniel Snydacker, "Kinship and Community in Rural Pennsylvania, 1749–1820," *Journal of Interdisciplinary History* 13 (1982): 41–61.

29. Narrett, "Preparation for Death," 425; Zuckerman, "Introduction," 13; James T. Lemon, "The Agricultural Practices of National Groups in Eighteenth-Century Southeastern Pennsylvania," *Geographical Review* 56 (1966): 467–96; Peter O. Wacker, "New Jersey's Cultural Landscape before 1800," *New Jersey Historical Society Papers* 2 (1971): 35–61; Wolf, *Urban Village*.

30. Barry Levy, "Birth of the 'Modern Family' in Early America," in Zuckerman, ed., *Friends and Neighbors*, 26–64, and "'Tender Plants': Quaker Farmers and Children in the Delaware Valley, 1681–1735," *Journal of Family History* 3 (1978): 116–35; Tebbenhoff, "Tacit Rules and Hidden Family Structure," 583; Donald J. Mrozek, "Problems of Social History and Patterns of Inheritance in Pre-Revolutionary New Jersey, 1751–1770," *Journal of the Rutgers University Library* 36 (1972): 1–19; Robert V. Wells, "Quaker Marriage Patterns in Colonial Perspective," *William and Mary Quarterly* 3d ser., 39 (1972): 415–42; Susan Klepp, "Five Early Pennsylvania Censuses," *Pennsylvania Magazine of History and Biography* 106 (1982): 500; Louise Kantrow, "Philadelphia Gentry: Fertility and Family Limitation among an American Aristocracy," *Population Studies* 34 (1980): 21–30; Daniel Blake Smith, "The Study of the Family in Early America: Trends, Problems, and Prospects," ibid. 36 (1982): 8; Wolf, *Urban Village*.

31. Levy, "'Tender Plants,'" 133; Zuckerman, "Introduction," 6, 13; Lemon, *Best Poor Man's Country*, xv, 13; Kammen, *Colonial New York*, xvi, 189–90, 230; Kross, *Evolution of an American Town*, xv.

32. Lemon, *Best Poor Man's Country*, xv; Douglas Greenberg, *Crime and Law Enforcement in the Colony of New York, 1691–1776* (Ithaca, 1976), 59, 65, 154–213; Alan Tully, *William Penn's Legacy: Politics and Social Structure in Provincial Pennsylvania, 1726–1755* (Baltimore, 1977), 103–21; Patricia U. Bonomi, "Local Government in Colonial New York: A Base for Republicanism," in Jacob Judd and Irwin H. Polishook, eds., *Aspects of Early New York Society and Politics* (Tarrytown, N.Y., 1974), 29–50, 136–39; Clair W. Keller, "The Pennsylvania County Commission System, 1712 to 1740," *Pennsylvania Magazine of History and Biography* 93 (1969): 372–82; Frederick R. Black, "Provincial Taxation in Colonial New Jersey, 1704–1735," *New Jersey History* 95 (1977): 21–47; Nicholas Varga, "The Development and Structure of Local Government in Colonial New York," in Bruce C. Daniels, *Town and County: Essays on the Structure of Local Government in the American Colonies* (Middletown, Conn., 1978), 186–215; Wayne L. Bockelman, "Local Government in Colonial Pennsylvania," ibid., 216–37.

33. Greenberg, "Middle Colonies in Recent American Historiography," 411; Kammen, *Colonial New York*, xvi, 63, 127, 348; Bonomi, "Middle Colonies," 84–85; Zuckerman, "Introduction," 7–8.

34. Greenberg, "Middle Colonies in Recent American Historiography," 425–27; Thomas L. Purvis, "Origins and Patterns of Agrarian Unrest in New Jersey, 1735 to 1754," *William and Mary Quarterly* 3d ser., 39 (1982): 600–627; Kim, *Landlord and Tenant*; Kammen, *Colonial New York*, 302.

35. Kammen, *Colonial New York*, 192–93, 241, 244, 279; Patricia U. Bonomi, *A Factious People: Politics and Society in Colonial New York* (New York, 1971) and "Middle Colonies," 74–90; Hermann Wellenreuther, "The Quest for Harmony in a Turbulent World: The Principle of 'Love and Unity' in Colonial Pennsylvania Politics," *Pennsylvania Magazine of History and Biography* 107 (1983): 537–76; Sydney E. Ahlstrom, *A Religious History of the American People* (New Haven, 1972), 200–279; Jon Butler, "Power, Authority, and the Origins of the American Denominational Order: The English Churches in the Delaware Valley, 1680–1730," *Transactions of the American Philosophical Society* 68, pt. 2 (1978): 5–85; Martin E. Lodge, "The Crisis of the Churches in the Middle Colonies, 1720–1750," *Pennsylvania Magazine of History and Biography* 95 (1971): 195–210; John B. Frantz, "Religion in the Middle Colonies: A Model for the Nation," *Journal of Regional Cultures* 2 (1982): 9–22; Becker, "People and the System," 146; G. S. Rowe, "Women's Crime and Criminal Administration in Pennsylvania, 1763–1790," *Pennsylvania Magazine of History and Biography* 109 (1985): 335–68; Greenberg, *Crime and Law Enforcement*, 32, 188–213; David S. Shields, "The Wits and Poets of Pennsylvania: New Light on the Rise of Belles Lettres in Provincial Pennsylvania, 1720–1740," *Pennsylvania Magazine of History and Biography* 109 (1985): 99–143; Zuckerman, "Introduction," 5.

36. Zuckerman, "Introduction," 7; Becker, "Diversity and Its Significance," 213–14; Tully, *William Penn's Legacy*, 53–78; Milton M. Klein, "New York in the American Colonies: A New Look," *New York History* 53 (1972): 132–56, and "Shaping the American Tradition: The Microcosm of Colonial New York," ibid. 59 (1978): 173–97.

37. Harry Roy Merrens, *Colonial North Carolina in the Eighteenth Century: A Study in Historical Geography* (Chapel Hill, 1964), 19–31; Robert W. Ramsey, *Carolina Cradle: Settlement of the Northwest Carolina Frontier, 1747–1762* (Chapel Hill, 1964), 1–170; Robert L. Meriwether, *The Expansion of South Carolina, 1729–1765* (Kingsport, Tenn., 1940); David M. Potter, Jr., "The Rise of the Plantation System in Georgia," *Georgia Historical Quarterly* 16 (1932): 114–35; Willard Range, "The Agricultural Revolution in Royal Georgia, 1752–1775," *Agricultural History* 21 (1947): 250–55; Betty Wood, *Slavery in Colonial Georgia, 1730–1775* (Athens, Ga., 1984), 1–109; Jack P. Greene, "Travails of an Infant Colony: The Search for Viability, Coherence, and Identity in Colonial Georgia," in Harvey H. Jackson and Phinizy Spaulding, eds., *Forty Years of Diversity: A Symposium on Colonial Georgia* (Athens, Ga., 1984), 278–309.

38. McCusker and Menard, *Economy of British America*, 172; H. Roy Merrens and George D. Terry, "Dying in Paradise: Malaria, Mortality, and the Perceptual Environment in Colonial South Carolina," *Journal of Southern History* 50 (1984): 541–49; Peter A. Coclanis, "Death in Early Charleston: An Estimate of the Crude Death Rate for the White Population of Charleston, 1722–32," *South Carolina Historical Magazine* 85 (1984): 280–91; John E. Crowley, "Family Relations and

Inheritance in Early South Carolina," *Histoire Sociale* 17 (1984): 35–57; Gerald L. Cates, "'The Seasoning': Disease and Death among the First Colonists of Georgia," *Georgia Historical Quarterly* 64 (1980): 146–58; Thomas C. Parramore, "The 'Country Distemper' in Colonial North Carolina," *North Carolina Historical Review* 48 (1971): 44–52; Robert M. Weir, *Colonial South Carolina: A History* (Millwood, N.Y., 1983), 205–11; Merrens, *Colonial North Carolina*, 53–81, 196–201.

39. McCusker and Menard, *Economy of British America*, 172; Peter H. Wood, *Black Majority: Negroes in Colonial South Carolina from 1670 through the Stono Rebellion* (New York, 1974), 131–66; Merrens, *Colonial North Carolina*, 74–81; "Estimated Population of the American Colonies," 238–39; Philip D. Morgan, "Black Slavery in the Lowcountry, 1760–1810," in Ira Berlin and Ronald Hoffman, eds., *Slavery and Freedom in the Age of the American Revolution* (Charlottesville, Va., 1983), 85–96, and "Black Life in Eighteenth-Century Charleston," *Perspectives in American History*, n.s., 1 (1984): 188; Daniel C. Littlefield, *Rice and Slaves: Ethnicity and the Slave Trade in Colonial South Carolina* (Baton Rouge, 1981), and "Charleston and Internal Slave Redistribution," *South Carolina Historical Magazine* 87 (1986): 93–105; W. Robert Higgins, "The Geographical Origins of Negro Slaves in Colonial South Carolina," *South Atlantic Quarterly* 70 (1971): 34–47; Converse D. Clowse, *Measuring Charleston's Overseas Commerce, 1717–1767: Statistics from the Port's Naval Lists* (Washington, D.C., 1981), 31–34; Ralph Gray and Betty Wood, "The Transition from Indentured to Involuntary Servitude in Colonial Georgia," *Explorations in Economic History* 13 (1976): 353–70; Wood, *Slavery in Colonial Georgia*, 74–109.

40. McCusker and Menard, *Economy of British America*, 175–80, 186–87; Littlefield, *Rice and Slaves*, 74–114; James M. Clifton, "The Rice Industry in Colonial America," *Agricultural History* 55 (1981): 266–83; Henry C. Dethloff, "The Colonial Rice Trade," ibid. 56 (1982): 231–43; Sam B. Hillard, "Antebellum Tidewater Rice Culture in South Carolina and Georgia," in James R. Gibson, ed., *European Settlement and Development in North America: Essays on Geographical Change in Honour and Memory of Andrew Hill Clark* (Toronto, 1978), 91–115; Douglas C. Wilms, "The Development of Rice Culture in 18th Century Georgia," *Southeastern Geographer* 12 (1972): 45–57; William B. Lees, "The Historical Development of Limerick Plantation, a Tidewater Rice Plantation in Berkeley County, South Carolina, 1683–1945," *South Carolina Historical Magazine* 82 (1981): 44–62; Peter A. Coclanis, "Rice Prices in the 1720s and the Evolution of the South Carolina Economy," *Journal of Southern History* 48 (1982): 531–44, and "Bitter Harvest: The South Carolina Low Country in Historical Perspective," *Journal of Economic History* 45 (1985): 251–59; Julia Floyd Smith, *Slavery and Rice Culture in Low Country Georgia, 1750–1860* (Knoxville, 1985), 15–29.

41. Charles Jones Gayle, "The Nature and Volume of Exports from Charleston, 1624–1772," *Proceedings of the South Carolina Historical Association, 1937* (1940), 25–33; W. O. Moore, Jr., "The Largest Exporters of Deerskins from Charles Town, 1735–1775," *South Carolina Historical Magazine* 74 (1973): 144–50; Gary S. Dunbar, "Colonial Carolina Cowpens," *Agricultural History* 25 (1961): 125–31; G. Melvin Herndon, "Naval Stores in Colonial Georgia," *Georgia Historical Quarterly* 52 (1968): 426–33, and "Timber Products of Colonial Georgia," ibid. 57 (1973): 56–62;

G. Terry Sharrer, "The Indigo Bonanza in South Carolina, 1740–1790," *Technology and Culture* 12 (1971): 447–55, and "Indigo in Carolina, 1671–1796," *South Carolina Historical Magazine* 72 (1971): 94–103; David L. Coon, "Eliza Pinckney and the Reintroduction of Indigo Culture in South Carolina," ibid. 80 (1979): 61–76; John J. Winberry, "Reputation of Carolina Indigo," ibid., 242–50; McCusker and Menard, *Economy of British America*, 174; Weir, *Colonial South Carolina*, 172.

42. Merrens, *Colonial North Carolina*, 85–141; James M. Clifton, "Golden Grains of White: Rice Planting on the Lower Cape Fear," *North Carolina Historical Review* 50 (1973): 365–93; Justin Williams, "English Mercantilism and Carolina Naval Stores, 1705–1776," *Journal of Southern History* 1 (1935): 169–85; Alan D. Watson, "Society and Economy in Colonial Edgecombe County," *North Carolina Historical Review* 50 (1973): 231–55; Carl Bridenbaugh, *Myths and Realities: Societies of the Colonial South* (Baton Rouge, 1952), 119–96.

43. Philip D. Morgan, "A Profile of a Mid-Eighteenth Century South Carolina Parish: The Tax Return of Saint James', Goose Creek," *South Carolina Historical Magazine* 81 (1980): 51–65, "Black Slavery in the Lowcountry," 93–97, and "Black Life in Eighteenth-Century Charleston," 190; Bridenbaugh, *Myths and Realities*, 65; Richard Waterhouse, "South Carolina's Colonial Elite: A Study in the Social Structure and the Political Culture of a Southern Colony, 1670–1760" (Ph.D. dissertation, Johns Hopkins University, 1973), 161–77, and "The Responsible Gentry of Colonial South Carolina: A Study in Local Government, 1670–1760," in Bruce C. Daniels, ed., *Town and Country: Essays on the Structure of Local Government in the American Colonies* (Middletown, Conn., 1978), 160–85; Alan D. Watson, "Household Size and Composition in Pre-Revolutionary North Carolina," *Mississippi Quarterly* 31 (1978): 551–69, "Society and Economy in Colonial Edgecombe County," 231–55, and "Public Poor Relief in Colonial North Carolina," *North Carolina Historical Review* 54 (1977): 347–66; Merrens, *Colonial North Carolina*, 74–81.

44. Converse D. Clowse, "Shipowning and Shipbuilding in Colonial South Carolina: An Overview," *American Neptune* 64 (1984): 221–44; Stuart O. Stumpf, "South Carolina Importers of General Merchandise, 1735–1765," *South Carolina Historical Magazine* 84 (1983): 1–11, and "Implications of King George's War for the Charleston Mercantile Community," ibid. 77 (1976): 161–88; Moore, "Largest Exporters of Deerskins," 144–50; Jeanne A. Calhoun, Martha A. Zierden, and Elizabeth A. Paysinger, "The Geographic Spread of Charleston's Mercantile Community, 1732–1767," *South Carolina Historical Magazine* 86 (1985): 182–220; Peter A. Coclanis, "The Sociology of Architecture in Colonial Charleston: Pattern and Process in an Eighteenth-Century Southern City," *Journal of Social History* 18 (1985): 610; McCusker and Menard, *Economy of British America*, 185, 192; Weir, *Colonial South Carolina*, 257–60.

45. Coclanis, "Sociology of Architecture," 607–23; Calhoun, Zierden, and Paysinger, "Geographic Spread of Charleston's Mercantile Community," 182–220; Price, "Economic Function and the Growth of American Port Towns," 160–63, 176; Merrens, *Colonial North Carolina*, 142–72; Ramsey, *Carolina Cradle*, 171–78, 208–10; Harold E. Davis, *The Fledgling Province: Social and Cultural Life in Colonial Georgia, 1733–1776* (Chapel Hill, 1976), 95–124; Joseph A. Ernst and H. Roy Merrens, "'Camden's turrets pierce the skies,': The Urban Process in the Southern

Colonies during the 18th Century," *William and Mary Quarterly* 3d ser., 30 (1973): 549–74; Carville Earle and Ronald Hoffman, "Staple Crops and Urban Development in the Eighteenth-Century South," *Perspectives in American History* 10 (1976): 53–55; Alan D. Watson, "The Ferry in Colonial North Carolina: A Vital Link in Transportation," *North Carolina Historical Review* 51 (1974): 247–60, "Regulation and Administration of Roads and Bridges in Colonial Eastern North Carolina," ibid. 45 (1968): 399–417, and "Ordinaries in Colonial Eastern North Carolina," ibid., 67–83; Marvin L. Michael Kay and William S. Price, Jr., "'To Ride the Wood Mare': Road Building and Militia Service in Colonial North Carolina, 1740–1775," ibid. 57 (1980): 361–409.

46. Jones, *Wealth of a Nation to Be*, 357; James F. Shepherd and Gary M. Walton, *Shipping, Maritime Trade and the Economic Development of Colonial North America* (Cambridge, 1972), 228, 230, 235–36; McCusker and Menard, *Economy of British America*, 280–82; Clowse, *Measuring Charleston's Overseas Commerce*, 25–48; Lewis P. Frisch, "The Fraternal and Charitable Societies of Colonial South Carolina" (B.A. thesis, Johns Hopkins University, 1969); Morgan, "Profile of a Mid-Eighteenth Century South Carolina Parish," 57–65.

47. Bridenbaugh, *Myths and Realities*, 56–118; Richard Waterhouse, "The Development of Elite Culture in the Colonial American South: A Study of Charles Town, 1670–1770," *Australian Journal of Politics and History* 28 (1982): 391–404; Coclanis, "Sociology of Architecture," 607–23; Weir, *Colonial South Carolina*, 238–48; Crowley, "Family Relations and Inheritance," 55–56; Caroline Wyche Dixon, "The Miles Brewton House: Ezra Waite's Architectural Books and Other Possible Design Sources," *South Carolina Historical Magazine* 82 (1981): 118–42; Frisch, "Fraternal and Charitable Societies"; Diane Sydenham, "'Going Home': South Carolinians in England, 1745–1775" (seminar paper, Johns Hopkins University, 1975); Davis, *Fledgling Province*, 145–92. For the spread of elite culture outside the low country, see Alan D. Watson, "Luxury Vehicles and Elitism in Colonial North Carolina," *Southern Studies* 19 (1980): 147–56. For the opposite end of the economic spectrum, see Walter J. Fraser, "Controlling the Poor in Colonial Charles Town," *Proceedings of the South Carolina Historical Association, 1980*, 13–30.

48. Hillard, "Antebellum Tidewater Rice Culture," 91–115; Clifton, "Rice Industry in Colonial America," 266–83; A. Roger Ekirch, *Poor Carolina: Politics and Society in Colonial North Carolina, 1729–1776* (Chapel Hill, 1981); Waterhouse, "Development of Elite Culture," 391–404, "Responsible Gentry of Colonial South Carolina," 160–85, and "South Carolina's Colonial Elite"; Weir, *Colonial South Carolina*, 261–63; Joyce E. Chaplin, "An Anxious Pursuit: Innovation in Commercial Agriculture in South Carolina, Georgia, and British East Florida, 1740–1815" (Ph.D. dissertation, Johns Hopkins University, 1986).

49. Michael Zuckerman, "Penmanship Exercises for Saucy Sons: Some Thoughts on the Colonial Southern Family," *South Carolina Historical Magazine* 84 (1983): 152–66; Crowley, "Family Relations and Inheritance," 35–57; James Matthew Gallman, "Relative Ages of Colonial Marriage," *Journal of Interdisciplinary History* 14 (1984): 609–17; Marylynn Salmon, "Women and Property in South Carolina: The Evidence from Marriage Settlements, 1730 to 1830," *William and Mary Quarterly* 3d ser., 39 (1982): 655–85; Alan D. Watson, "Orphanage in Colonial North Carolina:

Edgecombe County as Case Study," *North Carolina Historical Review* 52 (1975): 105–19, and "Women in Colonial North Carolina: Overlooked and Underestimated," ibid. 58 (1981): 1–22; Lee Ann Caldwell, "Women Landholders of Colonial Georgia," in Jackson and Spaulding, eds., *Forty Years of Diversity*, 183–97.

50. Donna J. Spindel, "The Administration of Justice in North Carolina, 1720–1740," *American Journal of Legal History* 25 (1981): 141–62; Spindel and Stuart W. Thomas, Jr., "Crime and Society in North Carolina, 1663–1740," *Journal of Southern History* 49 (1983): 223–44; Michael Stephen Hindus, *Prison and Plantation: Crime, Justice, and Authority in Massachusetts and South Carolina, 1767–1878* (Chapel Hill, 1980); Waterhouse, "Development of Elite Culture," 291–404; Weir, *Colonial South Carolina*, 219–23, 237–38, 248–53, 260; David T. Morgan, "The Great Awakening in South Carolina, 1740–1775," *South Atlantic Quarterly* 70 (1971): 595–606; Davis, *Fledgling Province*, 193–250.

51. M. Eugene Sirmans, "The Legal Status of the Slave in South Carolina, 1670–1740," *Journal of Southern History* 28 (1962): 462–73; Wood, *Black Majority*, 239–306; Wood, *Slavery in Colonial Georgia*, 110–30, 169–206; Hindus, *Prison and Plantation*, 132–45; Alan D. Watson, "North Carolina Slave Courts, 1715–1785," *North Carolina Historical Review* 60 (1983): 24–36; Marvin L. Michael Kay and Lorin Lee Cary, "'The Planters Suffer Little or Nothing': North Carolina Compensations for Executed Slaves, 1748–1772," *Science and Society* 40 (1976): 288–306; Daniel E. Meaders, "South Carolina Fugitives as Viewed through Local Colonial Newspapers with Emphasis on Runaway Notices, 1732–1801," *Journal of Negro History* 60 (1975): 288–319; Philip D. Morgan, "En Caroline du Sud: Marronage et culture servile," *Annales*, no. 3 (1982): 574–90; Morgan and George D. Terry, "Slavery in Microcosm: A Conspiracy Scare in Colonial South Carolina," *Southern Studies* 21 (1982): 121–45.

52. Philip D. Morgan, "Work and Culture: The Task System and the World of Lowcountry Blacks, 1700 to 1880," *William and Mary Quarterly* 3d ser., 39 (1982): 563–99, and "Colonial South Carolina Runaways: Their Significance for Slave Culture," *Slavery and Abolition* 6 (1985): 57–78; Morgan and Terry, "Slavery in Microcosm," 121–45; John C. Inscoe, "Carolina Slave Names: An Index to Acculturation," *Journal of Southern History* 49 (1983): 527–54; Winthrop D. Jordan, "American Chiaroscuro: The Status and Definition of Mulattoes in the British Colonies," *William and Mary Quarterly* 3d ser., 19 (1962): 183–200; Wood, *Slavery in Colonial Georgia*, 131–206; Darold D. Wax, "'The Great Risque We Run': The Aftermath of Slave Rebellion at Stono, South Carolina, 1739–1745," *Journal of Negro History* 77 (1982): 136–47; John E. Fleming, "The Stono Rebellion and Its Impact on the South Carolina Slave Code," *Negro History Bulletin* 42 (1979): 66–68.

53. Morgan, "Work and Culture," 563–99, "Black Slavery in the Lowcountry," 97–104, and "Black Life in Eighteenth-Century Charleston," 187–232; Peter H. Wood, "'Taking Care of Business' in Revolutionary South Carolina: Republicanism and the Slave Society," *South Atlantic Urban Studies* 2 (1978): 53–57.

CHAPTER SEVEN

1. Henry C. Wilkinson, *Bermuda in the Old Empire* (Oxford, 1950), 340; Michael Craton, *A History of the Bahamas* (London, 1962), 111; Robert V. Wells, *The Population of the British Colonies in America before 1776: A Survey of Census Data* (Princeton, 1975), 180–81; Elaine Forman Crane, "Paradise Lost: Bermuda in the Eighteenth Century," unpublished paper.

2. Wilkinson, *Bermuda in the Old Empire*, 143–44, 285–86, 322–25; Wells, *Population of the British Colonies*, 172–84.

3. Wells, *Population of the British Colonies*, 172–81; Wilkinson, *Bermuda in the Old Empire*, 242–59; Crane, "Paradise Lost."

4. Wilkinson, *Bermuda in the Old Empire*, 84–85, 267, 299; Crane, "Paradise Lost"; Wells, *Population of the British Colonies*, 177–79.

5. John J. McCusker and Russell R. Menard, *The Economy of British America, 1607–1789* (Chapel Hill, 1985), 153–54; Richard B. Sheridan, *Sugar and Slavery: An Economic History of the British West Indies, 1623–1775* (Baltimore, 1974), 123, and "The Role of the Scots in the Economy and Society of the West Indies," in Vera Rubin and Arthur Tuden, eds., *Comparative Perspectives on Slavery in New World Plantation Societies* (New York, 1977), 94 106; David W. Galenson, "Population Turnover in the English West Indies in the Late Seventeenth Century: A Comparative Perspective," *Journal of Economic History* 45 (1985): 227–39, *Traders, Planters, and Slaves: Market Behavior in Early English America* (Cambridge, 1986), 115–42; and "British Servants and the Colonial Indenture System in the Eighteenth Century," *Journal of Southern History* 44 (1978): 44–45, 62–65; Patricia A. Molen, "Population and Social Patterns in Barbados in the Early Eighteenth Century," *William and Mary Quarterly* 3d ser., 28 (1971): 287–300; Wells, *Population of the British Colonies*, 236–51; Gary A. Puckrein, *Little England: Plantation Society and Anglo-Barbadian Politics, 1627–1700* (New York, 1984), 181–94.

6. Sheridan, *Sugar and Slavery*, 124–47, 264–69; J. R. Ward, "The Profitability of Sugar Planting in the British West Indies, 1650–1834," *Economic History Review* 2d ser., 31 (1978): 204 7; McCusker and Menard, *Economy of British America*, 165–67; Karl Watson, *The Civilised Island Barbados: A Social History, 1750–1816* (Bridgetown, 1979), 30–125; Wells, *Population of the British Colonies*, 236–51; Molen, "Population and Social Patterns in Barbados," 292–94; Keith Hunte, "The Maintenance of White Power in Eighteenth Century Barbados" (Paper presented at the Fourteenth Conference of Caribbean Historians, 1982); Jack P. Greene, "Changing Identity in the British Caribbean: Barbados as a Case Study," in Nicholas Canny and Anthony Pagden, eds., *Colonial Identity in the Atlantic World, 1500–1800* (Princeton, 1987), 213–66.

7. Sheridan, *Sugar and Slavery*, 124–47, 505; Hilary McD. Beckles, *Black Rebellion in Barbados: The Struggle against Slavery, 1627–1838* (Bridgetown, 1984), 52–85; David W. Galenson, "The Atlantic Slave Trade and the Barbados Market, 1673–1723," *Journal of Economic History* 42 (1982): 491–511; J. Harry Bennett, Jr., "The Problem of Slave Labor Supply at the Codrington Plantations," *Journal of Negro History* 36 (1951): 406–41, 37 (1952): 115–41, and *Bondsmen and Bishops: Slavery and Apprenticeship on the Codrington Plantations of Barbados, 1710–1838* (Berkeley, 1958).

8. Kenneth E. Kiple, *The Caribbean Slave: A Biological History* (Cambridge, 1984), 67, 106, 114, 118–19; Jerome S. Handler and Robert S. Corruccini, "Plantation Slave Life in Barbados: A Physical Anthropological Analysis," *Journal of Interdisciplinary History* 14 (1983): 65–90, and "Weaning among West Indian Slaves: Historical and Bioanthropological Evidence from Barbados," *William and Mary Quarterly* 3d ser., 43 (1986): 111–17; Richard N. Bean, "Food Imports into the British West Indies, 1680–1845," in Rubin and Tuden, eds., *Comparative Perspectives on Slavery*, 581–90; Hunte, "Maintenance of White Power," 9–17; Barbara Bush, "White 'Ladies,' Coloured 'Favorites' and Black 'Wenches': Some Considerations on Sex, Race and Class Factors in Social Relations in White Creole Society in the British Caribbean," *Slavery and Abolition* 2 (1981): 245–62; Beckles, *Black Rebellion*, 25–85; Jerome S. Handler, "Slave Revolts and Conspiracies in Seventeenth-Century Barbados," *Nieuwe West-Indische Gids* 56 (1982): 5–42, "Freedmen and Slaves in the Barbados Militia," *Journal of Caribbean History* 19 (1984): 1–25, *The Unappropriated People: Freedmen in the Slave Society of Barbados* (Baltimore, 1974), and "Joseph Rachell and Rachel Pringle-Polgreen: Petty Entrepreneurs," in David G. Sweet and Gary B. Nash, eds., *Struggle and Survival in Colonial America* (Berkeley, 1981), 376–91; Handler and John T. Pohlmann, "Slave Manumissions and Freedmen in Seventeenth-Century Barbados," *William and Mary Quarterly* 3d ser., 41 (1984): 390–408.

9. Sheridan, *Sugar and Slavery*, 150, and "Samuel Martin, Innovating Sugar Planter of Antigua, 1750–1776," *Agricultural History* 24 (1960): 161–86; Ward, "Profitability of Sugar Planting," 207; Wells, *Population of the British Colonies*, 207–36.

10. Sheridan, *Sugar and Slavery*, 150; Wells, *Population of the British Colonies*, 207–36; David Barry Gaspar, *Bondmen and Rebels: A Study of Master-Slave Relations in Antigua* (Baltimore, 1985); Howard A. Fergus, "The Early Laws of Montserrat (1660–1680): The Legal Schema of a Slave Society," *Caribbean Quarterly* 24 (1978): 34–43; D. W. Thoms, "Slavery in the Leeward Islands in the Mid-Eighteenth Century: A Reappraisal," *Bulletin of the Institute of Historical Research* 22 (1969): 76–85; Elsa V. Goveia, *Slave Society in the British Leeward Islands at the End of the Eighteenth Century* (New Haven, 1965).

11. Sheridan, *Sugar and Slavery*, 148–207, "The Rise of a Colonial Gentry: A Case Study of Antigua, 1730–1775," *Economic History Review* 2d ser., 13 (1961): 342–57, and "Role of the Scots in the Economy and Society of the West Indies," 94–106; Margaret Deane Rouse-Jones, "St. Kitts, 1713–1763: A Study of the Development of a Plantation Society" (Ph.D. dissertation, Johns Hopkins University, 1977); J. R. V. Johnston, "The Stapleton Sugar Plantations in the Leeward Islands," *Bulletin of the John Rylands Library* 48 (1965): 175–206; Richard Pares, *A West India Fortune* (London, 1950).

12. Sheridan, *Sugar and Slavery*, 123, 208–21; Mavis C. Campbell, "Marronage in Jamaica: Its Origin in the Seventeenth Century," in Rubin and Tuden, eds., *Comparative Perspectives on Slavery*, 389–419; Orlando Patterson, "Slavery and Slave Revolts: A Sociohistorical Analysis of the First Maroon War, Jamaica, 1655–1740," *Social and Economic Studies* 19 (1970): 289–325; Barbara Kopytoff, "The Early Political Development of the Jamaican Maroon Societies," *William and Mary Quarterly* 3d ser., 25 (1978): 287–307.

13. Sheridan, *Sugar and Slavery*, 216–23, and "The Wealth of Jamaica in the Eighteenth Century," *Economic History Review* 18 (1965): 292–311; Ward, "Profitability of Sugar Planting," 207–9; McCusker and Menard, *Economy of British America*, 61.

14. B. W. Higman, "The Spatial Economy of Jamaican Sugar Plantations: Cartographic Evidence from the Eighteenth and Nineteenth Centuries," *Journal of Historical Geography* 13 (1987): 24–26; Sheridan, *Sugar and Slavery*, 216–33, and "Wealth of Jamaica," 297; Wells, *Population of the British Colonies*, 194–207; Galenson, "British Servants and the Colonial Indenture System," 44–45.

15. Edward Brathwaite, *The Development of Creole Society in Jamaica, 1770–1820* (Oxford, 1971), 105–50; Sheridan, *Sugar and Slavery*, 216–32, 364, "Wealth of Jamaica," 296–303, and "Role of the Scots in the Economy and Society of the West Indies," 94–106; Michael Craton and James Walvin, *A Jamaican Plantation: The History of Worthy Park, 1670–1970* (Toronto, 1970); Edward Long, *The History of Jamaica*, 3 vols. (London, 1774), 2:3–22, 103.

16. Brathwaite, *Development of Creole Society*, xiv, 8–175, 266–95; Craton and Walvin, *Jamaican Plantation*; Sheridan, *Sugar and Slavery*, 231, 360–88; Higman, "Spatial Economy of Jamaican Sugar Plantations," 30.

17. Sheridan, *Sugar and Slavery*, 502–4, and "The Jamaican Slave Insurrection Scare of 1776 and the American Revolution," *Journal of Negro History* 61 (1976): 290–308; Brathwaite, *Development of Creole Society*, 151–76, 193–239; Barry W. Higman, *Slave Population and Economy in Jamaica* (London, 1976), 129; Kiple, *Caribbean Slave*, 106–8; Orlando Patterson, *The Sociology of Slavery: An Analysis of the Origins, Development and Structure of Negro Slave Society in Jamaica* (Cranbury, N.J., 1969); J. R. Ward, "A Planter and His Slaves in Eighteenth-Century Jamaica," in T. C. Smout, ed., *The Search for Wealth and Stability: Essays in Economic and Social History Presented to M. W. Flinn* (London, 1979), 1–20; David Barry Gaspar, "A Dangerous Spirit of Liberty: Slave Rebellion in the West Indies during the 1730s," *Cimarrons* 1 (1981), 79–91.

18. Michael Zuckerman, "Introduction: Puritans, Cavaliers, and the Motley Middle," in Zuckerman, ed., *Friends and Neighbors: Group Life in America's First Plural Society* (Philadelphia, 1982), 11; G. R. Elton, "Contentment and Discontent on the Eve of Colonization," in David B. Quinn, ed., *Early Maryland in a Wider World* (Detroit, 1982), 113.

19. T. H. Breen and Stephen Foster, "The Puritan's Greatest Achievement: A Study of Social Cohesion in Seventeenth-Century Massachusetts," *Journal of American History* 60 (1973): 22.

20. See R. Cole Harris, "The Simplification of Europe Overseas," *Annals of the Association of American Geographers* 67 (1977): 469–83; Robert D. Mitchell, "The Simplification of Europe Overseas," ibid. 69 (1979): 474–76; Adrian Pollock, "Commentary—Europe Simplified," ibid., 476–77; Harris, "Comment in Reply," ibid., 478–80.

21. See Robert D. Mitchell, "The Formation of Early American Culture Regions: An Interpretation," in James R. Gibson, ed., *European Settlement and Development in North America: Essays on Geographical Change in Honour and Memory of Andrew Hill Clark* (Toronto, 1978), 66–90.

22. For a fuller development of this argument, see Jack P. Greene, "Indepen-

dence, Improvement and Authority: Toward a Framework for Understanding the Histories of the Southern Backcountry during the Era of the American Revolution," in Ronald Hoffman, Thad W. Tate, and Peter J. Albert, eds., *An Uncivil War: The Southern Backcountry during the American Revolution* (Charlottesville, 1985), 3–36.

CHAPTER EIGHT

1. Benjamin Franklin, *The Interest of Great Britain Considered* (London, 1760), in Leonard W. Labaree et al., eds., *The Papers of Benjamin Franklin*, 21 vols. to date (New Haven, 1959–), 9:90.

2. Samuel Williams, *The Natural and Civil History of Vermont*, 2 vols. (Walpole, N.H., 1794), 2:429–31.

3. A fuller discussion of several aspects of this subject may be found in Ian K. Steele, *The English Atlantic, 1675–1740: An Exploration of Communication and Community* (New York, 1986); Richard L. Bushman, "American High-Style and Vernacular Cultures," in Jack P. Greene and J. R. Pole, eds., *Colonial British America: Essays in the New History of the Early Modern Era* (Baltimore, 1984), 345–83; and Jack P. Greene, "Search for Identity: An Interpretation of the Meaning of Selected Patterns of Social Response in Eighteenth-Century America," *Journal of Social History* 3 (1970): 189–224. A contrary view emphasizing the celebration of the uniquely American among the continental colonists is succinctly put forth in Max Savelle, "Nationalism and Other Loyalties in the American Revolution," *American Historical Review* 67 (1962): 904.

4. See Table 8.1. Full decennial population figures for the continental colonies may be found in *Historical Statistics of the United States*, 756.

5. Jim Potter, "Demographic Development and Family Structure," in Greene and Pole, eds., *Colonial British America*, 123–56, and "The Growth of Population in America, 1700–1860," in D. V. Glass and D. E. C. Eversley, eds., *Population in History* (London, 1965), 631–88; Robert V. Wells, *Population of the British Colonies in America before 1776: A Survey of Census Data* (Princeton, 1975), 45–333, and "Household Size and Composition in the British Colonies in America, 1675–1775," *Journal of Interdisciplinary History* 4 (1974): 543–70; John J. McCusker and and Russell R. Menard, *The Economy of British America, 1607–1789* (Chapel Hill, 1985), 212–35; Henry A. Gemery, "European Emigration to North America, 1700–1820: Numbers and Quasi-Numbers," *Perspectives in American History* n.s., 1 (1984): 283–342; Kenneth L. Sokoloff and Georgia C. Villaflor, "The Early Achievement of Modern Stature in America," *Social Science History* 4 (1982): 453–81. Bernard Bailyn's suggestive *The Peopling of British North America: An Introduction* (New York, 1986) and his masterful *Voyagers to the West: A Passage in the Peopling of America on the Eve of the American Revolution* (New York, 1986), came to hand after this volume was written, but they are obviously relevant to this subject.

6. The statements about mobility are based on the excellent article by Georgia C. Villaflor and Kenneth L. Sokoloff, "Migration in Colonial America: Evidence from the Muster Rolls," *Social Science History* 6 (1984): 539–70. See also Darrett B.

Rutman, "People in Process: The New Hampshire Towns of the Eighteenth Century," *Journal of Urban History* 1 (1975): 268–92, and D. W. Meinig, *The Shaping of America: A Geographical Perspectiove on 500 Years of History*, Vol. 1, *Atlantic America, 1492–1800* (New Haven, 1986), 91–109, 119–90, 213–54.

7. McCusker and Menard, *Economy of British America*, 51–60.

8. Ibid., 55, 59–61; Alice Hanson Jones, "Wealth Estimates for the American Middle Colonies, 1774," *Economic Development and Cultural Change* 18 (1970): 130, *The Wealth of a Nation to Be: The American Colonies on the Eve of the Revolution* (New York, 1980), 302–3, and "Wealth and Growth of the Thirteen Colonies: Some Implications," *Journal of Economic History* 44 (1984): 250–52. See also Jeffrey G. Williamson and Peter H. Lindert, *American Inequality: A Macroeconomic History* (New York, 1980), 9–31; and James A. Henretta, "Wealth and Social Structure," in Greene and Pole, eds., *Colonial British America*, 262–89.

9. McCusker and Menard, *Economy of British America*, 85–86; James F. Shepherd and Gary M. Walton, "Trade, Distribution, and Economic Growth in Colonial America," *Journal of Economic History* 32 (1972): 130–31, 144.

10. Menard and McCusker, *Economy of British America*, 280–81; Shepherd and Walton, "Trade, Distribution, and Economic Growth," 136, and "Estimates of 'Invisible' Earnings in the Balance of Payments of the British North American Colonies, 1768–1772," *Journal of Economic History* 29 (1969): 553–69; James F. Shepherd and Samuel H. Williamson, "The Coastal Trade of the British North American Colonies, 1768–1772," ibid. 32 (1972): 783–810; William S. Sachs, "Interurban Correspondents and the Development of a National Economy before the Revolution: New York as a Case Study," *New York History* 36 (1955): 320–35. On developments within the import-export sector of the economy of the continental colonies, see also Marc Egnal, "The Economic Development of the Thirteen Continental Colonies," *William and Mary Quarterly* 3d ser., 32 (1975): 191–222; John R. Hanson II, "The Economic Development of the Thirteen Colonies, 1720 to 1775: A Critique," ibid. 37 (1980): 165–75; James F. Shepherd, "Commodity Exports from the British North American Colonies to Overseas Areas, 1768–1772: Magnitudes and Patterns of Trade," *Explorations in Economic History* 8 (1970): 5–76; David Klingaman, "Food Surpluses and Deficits in the American Colonies, 1768–1772," *Journal of Economic History* 31 (1971): 553–69; Gary M. Walton and James F. Shepherd, *The Economic Rise of Early America* (Cambridge, 1979); and Edwin J. Perkins, *The Economy of Colonial America* (New York, 1980). On the emergence of an American domestic economy, see Richard B. Sheridan, "The Domestic Economy," in Greene and Pole, eds., *Colonial British America*, 43–85.

11. McCusker and Menard, *Economy of British America*, 84, 266, 270, 310–27; Gary M. Walton, "Sources of Productivity Change in American Colonial Shipping, 1675–1775," *Economic History Review* 2d ser., 20 (1967): 67–78; James F. Shepherd and Garry M. Walton, *Shipping, Maritime Trade, and Economic Development of Colonial North America* (Cambridge, 1972), 158–59, 166, and "Trade, Distribution, and Economic Growth," 128–29, 144. See also Jacob M. Price, "The Transatlantic Economy," in Greene and Pole, eds., *Colonial British America*, 18–42.

12. Jacob M. Price, "Economic Function and the Growth of American Port Towns in the Eighteenth Century," *Perspectives in American History* 8 (1974): 123–

86; Carl Bridenbaugh, *Cities in the Wilderness: The First Century of Urban Life in America, 1625–1742* (New York, 1938), and *Cities in Revolt: Urban Life in America, 1743–1776* (New York, 1955); James T. Lemon, "Urbanization and the Development of Eighteenth-Century Southeastern Pennsylvania and Adjacent Delaware," *William and Mary Quarterly* 3d ser., 24 (1967): 501–42; Joseph A. Ernst and H. Roy Merrens, "'Camden's turrets pierce the skies!': The Urban Process in the Southern Colonies during the Eighteenth Century," ibid. 30 (1973): 549–74; Hermann Wellenreuther, "Urbanization in the Colonial South: A Critique," ibid. 31 (1974): 653–71. See also Gary B. Nash, *The Urban Crucible: Social Change, Political Consciousness, and the Origins of the American Revolution* (Cambridge, Mass., 1979), for information on the changing distribution of wealth in Boston, New York, and Philadelphia.

13. Price, "Economic Function and Growth of American Port Towns," 138–39, 177–83; Daniel J. Boorstin, *The Americans: The Colonial Experience* (New York, 1958), 189–239; Stephen Botein, "The Legal Profession in Colonial North America," in Wilfrid Prest, ed., *Lawyers in Early Modern Europe and America* (London, 1981), 129–46; John M. Murrin, "The Legal Transformation: The Bench and Bar of Eighteenth-Century Massachusetts," in Stanley N. Katz, ed., *Colonial America: Essays in Politics and Social Development* (Boston, 1971), 415–49; Alan F. Day, "A Social Study of Lawyers in Maryland, 1660–1775," 3 vols. (Ph.D. dissertation, Johns Hopkins University, 1976); A. G. Roeber, *Faithful Magistrates and Republican Lawyers: Creators of Virginia Legal Culture, 1680–1810* (Chapel Hill, 1981), 32–137; Milton M. Klein, "From Community to Status: The Development of the Legal Profession in Colonial New York," *New York History* 60 (1979): 133–56.

14. A fuller discussion of the nature and meaning of these social categories may be found in Jack P. Greene, *All Men Are Created Equal: Some Reflections on the Meaning of the American Revolution* (Oxford, 1976). See also Richard Bushman, "'This New Man': Dependence and Independence, 1776," in Bushman, et al., eds., *Uprooted Americans: Essays in Honor of Oscar Handlin* (Boston, 1979), 77–96.

15. See Jackson Turner Main, *The Social Structure of Revolutionary America* (Princeton, 1965); Philip Greven, *The Protestant Temperament: Patterns of Child-Rearing, Religious Experience, and the Self in Early America* (New York, 1977), 265–334; Bushman, "American High-Style and Vernacular Cultures," 345–83; Richard Hofstadter, *America at 1750: A Social Portrait* (New York, 1971), 131–79.

16. The case for constricting society is put most forcefully by Kenneth A. Lockridge, "Social Change and the Meaning of the American Revolution," *Journal of Social History* 6 (1972–73): 403–39; James A. Henretta, *The Evolution of American Society, 1700–1815* (Lexington, Mass., 1973); and Nash, *Urban Crucible*. But see also Jack P. Greene, "The Social Origins of the American Revolution: An Evaluation and an Interpretation," *Political Science Quarterly* 58 (1973): 1–22. Evidence in support of the contrary view, which is put forward here, may be found in Jackson Turner Main, *Society and Economy in Colonial Connecticut* (Princeton, 1985); Sung Bok Kim, *Landlord and Tenant in Colonial New York: Manorial Society, 1664–1775* (Chapel Hill, 1978); Lucy Simler, "Tenancy in Colonial Pennsylvania: The Case of Chester County," *William and Mary Quarterly* 3d ser., 43 (1986): 542–69; and Hermann Wellenreuther, "Labor in the Era of the American Revolution: A Discussion of Recent Concepts and Theories," *Labor History* 22 (1981): 573–600.

17. Hofstadter, *America at 1750*, 131–79.

18. Simler, "Tenancy in Colonial Pennsylvania," 542–69; Mary Beth Norton, "The Evolution of White Women's Experience in Early America," *American Historical Review* 89 (1984): 593–614.

19. Wellenreuther, "Labor in the Era of the American Revolution," 579–83; Simler, "Tenancy in Colonial Pennsylvania," 562–69; Richard S. Dunn, "Servants and Slaves: The Recruitment and Employment of Labor," in Greene and Pole, eds., *Colonial British America*, 180–88.

20. David W. Galenson, *White Servitude in America: An Economic Analysis* (Cambridge, 1981), "White Servitude and the Growth of Black Slavery in Colonial America," *Journal of Economic History* 41 (1981): 39–47, and "The Rise and Fall of Indentured Servitude in the Americas: An Economic Analysis," ibid. 44 (1984): 1–13; Farley Grubb, "Immigrant Servant Labor: Their Occupational and Geographic Distribution in the Late Eighteenth-Century Mid-Atlantic Economy," *Social Science History* 9 (1985): 249–75, and "The Market for Indentured Immigrants: Evidence on the Efficiency of Forward-Labor Contracting in Philadelphia, 1745–1773," *Journal of Economic History* 45 (1985): 855–68; Dunn, "Servants and Slaves," 157–72; Wellenreuther, "Labor in the Era of the American Revolution," 585; A. Roger Ekirch, "Bound for America: A Profile of British Convicts Transported to the Colonies, 1718–1775," *William and Mary Quarterly* 3d ser., 42 (1985): 184–200.

21. See Philip D. Curtin, *The Atlantic Slave Trade: A Census* (Madison, 1969).

22. Ira Berlin, "Time, Space, and the Evolution of Afro-American Society on British Mainland North America," *American Historical Review* 85 (1980): 44–78, and "The Slave Trade and the Development of Afro-American Society in English Mainland North America, 1619–1775," *Southern Studies* 20 (1981): 122–36; Dunn, "Servants and Slaves," 165–94; T. H. Breen, "Creative Adaptations: Peoples and Cultures," in Greene and Pole, eds., *Colonial British America*, 210–12. On the process by which an Afro-American culture was created in the early modern American slave societies, see Sidney W. Mintz and Richard Price, "An Anthropological Approach to the Afro-American Past: A Caribbean Perspective," *Institute for the Study of Human Issues, Occasional Papers*, no. 2 (Philadelphia, 1976). Peter H. Wood, "'I Did the Best I Could for My Day': The Study of Early Black History during the Second Reconstruction, 1960 to 1976," *William and Mary Quarterly* 3d ser., 35 (1978): 185–225, comprehensively and penetratingly analyzes literature on early American slavery and blacks written before 1976.

23. William M. Wiecek, "The Statutory Law of Slavery and Race in the Thirteen Mainland Colonies of British America," *William and Mary Quarterly* 3d ser., 34 (1977): 258–80; Rhett S. Jones, "Structural Differentiation and the Status of Blacks in British Colonial America, 1630–1755," *Journal of Human Relations* 3 (1971): 322–46; Orlando Patterson, *Slavery and Social Death: A Comparative Study* (Cambridge, Mass., 1982), 13, 38.

24. G. R. Elton, "Contentment and Discontent," in David B. Quinn, ed., *Early Maryland in a Wider World* (Detroit, 1982), 114–15; Perry Miller, *Errand into the Wilderness* (Cambridge, Mass., 1956), 4; Hofstadter, *America at 1750*.

25. D. A. Farnie, "The Commercial Empire of the Atlantic, 1607–1783," *Economic History Review* 2d ser., 15 (1962): 212–13.

26. Carole Shammas, "How Self-Sufficient Was Early America?," *Journal of In-*

terdisciplinary History 13 (1982): 252, 258, 263, 267–68, "The Domestic Environment in Early Modern England and America," *Journal of Social History* 14 (1980): 18, "Consumer Behavior in Colonial America," *Social Science History* 6 (1982): 68, 79–80, 83.

27. Samuel Williams, *Natural and Civil History of Vermont*, 2:354.

28. J. R. Pole, *American Individualism and the Promise of Progress* (Oxford, 1980), 6, 8, 12–14, 17.

29. The Virginia Declaration of Rights is conveniently reprinted in Jack P. Greene, ed., *Colonies to Nation, 1763–1789: A Documentary History of the American Revolution* (New York, 1975), 333.

30. Samuel Miller, *A Brief Retrospect of the Eighteenth Century*, 2 vols. (New York, 1803), 2:407; Pole, *American Individualism*, 13–14; Rowland Berthoff, *An Unsettled People: Social Order and Disorder in American History* (New York, 1971), 124; James A. Henretta, "Families and Farms: *Mentalité* in Pre-Industrial America," *William and Mary Quarterly* 3d ser., 35 (1978): 5, 14–16, 18–19, 25–26.

31. Berthoff, *Unsettled People*, 124; Wood, "'I Did the Best I Could for My Day,'" 187.

32. See esp., Joan Thirsk, *Economic Policy and Projects: The Development of a Consumer Society in Early Modern England* (Oxford, 1978); Joyce Appleby, *Economic Thought and Ideology in Seventeenth-Century England* (Princeton, 1978); and Robert D. Mitchell, *Commercialism and Frontier: Perspectives on the Early Shenandoah Valley* (Charlottesville, 1977), 133–240; Harry Roy Merrens, *Colonial North Carolina in the Eighteenth Century: A Study in Historical Geography* (Chapel Hill, 1964), 85–172.

33. See Roy Harvey Pearce, *The Savages of America: A Study of the Indian and the Idea of Civilization* (Baltimore, 1953); Louis B. Wright, *Culture on the Moving Frontier* (Bloomington, 1955), 11–45; Leo Marx, *The Machine in the Garden: Technology and the Pastoral Ideal in America* (New York, 1964), 75–144; Kenneth S. Lynn, *Mark Twain and Southwestern Humor* (Boston, 1959), 3–22; and Greene, "Search for Identity," 189–220.

34. See Jack P. Greene, "The Growth of Political Stability: An Interpretation of Colonial Political Development in the Anglo-American Colonies, 1660–1760," in John Parker and Carol Urness, eds., *The American Revolution: A Heritage of Change* (Minneapolis, 1975), 26–72, and "Legislative Turnover in British America, 1696 to 1775: A Quantitative Analysis," *William and Mary Quarterly* 3d ser., 38 (1981): 442–63; John M. Murrin, "Political Development," in Greene and Pole, eds., *Colonial British America*, 408–56; Katherine Preyer, "Penal Measures in the American Colonies: An Overview," *American Journal of Legal History* 26 (1982): 326–53; Douglas Greenberg, "Crime, Law Enforcement, and Social Control in Colonial America," ibid., 293–325.

35. David D. Hall, "Religion and Society: Problems and Reconsiderations," in Greene and Pole, eds., *Colonial British America*, 317–44; Hofstadter, *America at 1750*, 3–32, 180–216, 217–92.

36. Patricia U. Bonomi, *Under the Cope of Heaven: Religion, Society, and Politics in Colonial America* (New York, 1986), 1–27; Bonomi and Peter B. Eisenstadt, "Church Adherence in the Eighteenth-Century British American Colonies," *William and Mary Quarterly* 3d ser., 39 (1982): 245–86.

37. Among a vast literature on this subject, much of which is cited in previous chapters, see Bonomi, *Under the Cope of Heaven*, 131–60; Martin E. Lodge, "The Crisis of the Churches in the Middle Colonies, 1720–1750," *Pennsylvania Magazine of History and Biography* 95 (1971): 195–220; Jon Butler, "Enthusiasm Described and Decried: The Great Awakening as Interpretive Fiction," *Journal of American History* 69 (1982): 305–25; and Hall, "Religion and Society," 317–38.

38. John F. Berens, *Providence and Patriotism in Early America, 1640–1815* (Charlottesville, 1978), 29; Sacvan Bercovitch, "Rhetoric as Authority: Puritanism, the Bible, and the Myth of America," *Social Science Information* 21 (1982): 5–6, "Colonial Puritan Rhetoric and the Discovery of American Identity," *Canadian Review of American Studies* 6 (1975): 148. See also Bercovitch, *The Puritan Origins of the American Self* (New Haven, 1975), and *The American Jeremiad* (Madison, 1978).

39. Berens, *Providence and Patriotism*, 29; Bercovitch, "Rhetoric as Authority," 5; Nathan O. Hatch, *The Sacred Cause of Liberty: Republican Thought and the Millennium in Revolutionary New England* (New Haven, 1977); Joseph J. Ellis, "Culture and Capitalism in Pre-Revolutionary America," *American Quarterly* 31 (1979): 176–77, 180, 184; Jack P. Greene, "Paine, America, and the 'Modernization' of Political Consciousness," *Political Science Quarterly* 93 (1978): 73–92.

40. Michael Zuckerman, "Introduction: Puritans, Cavaliers, and the Motley Middle," in Zuckerman, ed., *Friends and Neighbors: Group Life in America's First Plural Society* (Philadelphia, 1982), 4, 11; Price, "Economic Function and the Growth of American Port Towns," 163; Hofstadter, *America at 1750*.

EPILOGUE

1. Joseph F. Kett and Patricia A. McClung, "Book Culture in Post-Revolutionary Virginia," *Proceedings of the American Antiquarian Society* 94 (1984): pt. 1, 136; Robert E. Shalhope, "Thomas Jefferson's Republicanism and Antebellum Southern Thought," *Journal of Southern History* 42 (1976): 529–56. The Washington quotation is taken from Yehoshua Arieli, *Individualism and Nationalism in American Ideology* (Cambridge, Mass., 1964), 27.

2. The quotation from Thatcher is from Max Savelle, "Nationalism and Other Loyalties in the American Revolution," *American Historical Review* 67 (1962): 919. See also John R. Alden, *The First South* (Baton Rouge, 1961), which argues for the existence of a conscious awareness of a broad South-North dichotomy within American society from the very beginning of the new nation.

3. David M. Potter, "The Historians' Use of Nationalism and Vice Versa," *American Historical Review* 67 (1962): 943; C. Vann Woodward, "The Southern Ethic in a Puritan World," *William and Mary Quarterly* 3d ser., 25 (1968): 343–70.

4. A compelling argument for the continuing similarities between North and South as late as the Civil War may be found in Carl Degler, *Place over Time: The Continuity of Southern Distinctiveness* (Baton Rouge, 1977), 67–97.

INDEX

colonies, 43–45, 161–64
Concentration. *See* Social differentiation
Congregationalists: in Middle Colonies, 49. *See also* Puritanism
.Connecticut: emigration from England and Scotland to, 8; as English colony, 8; settlement and early development, 20–27. *See also* New England
Connecticut River, 63
Connecticut River valley, 180–81
Conquest, by English forces: of Ireland, 114; of Jamaica, 46; of New York, 48
Constitution, English, 106
Consumer revolution: in England, 108–9
Continuum. *See* Social continuum
Cook, Edward M., 65
Cork, Ire., 117, 119, 121–22
Cotton: in West Indian colonies, 43
Creolization, role of in process of social convergence, 174
Crime: in England, 111; in Middle Colonies, 140; in New England, 74
Cullen, L. M., 116, 121
Cultural development: of Atlantic island colonies, 42, 154; of Chesapeake, 16–18, 84–85, 92–94; of Ireland, 39–40, 119–22; of Lower South, 148–49; of Middle Colonies, 137; of New England, 23–24, 66–67; of West Indian colonies, 44–45, 161–64

Dairying industry: in New England, 68
Declaration of Independence, 170, 196
Declension model. *See* Model—declension
Deerskin trade: in Lower South, 51, 144
Deference: in New England, 25
Delaware: settlement and early development, 47–50. *See also* Middle Colonies

Delaware River, 124, 181
Demography: of Atlantic island colonies, 153–54; of Barbados, 44; of Chesapeake, 10, 12–18, 27, 81–82, 87–88; of colonial British America, 177–80; of England, 31, 34, 103, 111; of Ireland, 115–16; of Lower South, 51–52, 142–43; of Middle Colonies, 125; of New England, 18, 20, 27, 56–57, 72; of South Carolina, 51–52; of West Indian colonies, 154–58, 160–61
Dependency: in England, 31
Dependents: as social category in colonial British America, 186–87, 189–93
Development. *See* Community formation; Cultural development; Economy—growth and development of; Family; Financial development; Political development; Social development
Developmental model. *See* Model—developmental
Diet: in New England, 73
Differentiation. *See* Social differentiation
Dispersion, of population in New England, 57–58
Distilling industry: in New England, 69
Diversification, of Chesapeake, 88
Diversity, ethnic and social: in Lower South, 50–51; in Middle Colonies, 48–50, 138–41
Doctors: in New England, 69
Dominica: as new colony in 1763, 159
Dublin, Ire., 114, 115, 117, 119, 121–22; site of Parliament House and Trinity College library, 122
Dunn, Richard S., 44, 52
Durham, Eng., 110
Dutch: as settlers in Middle Colonies, 48–49
Dutch Reformed church: in Middle Colonies, 49